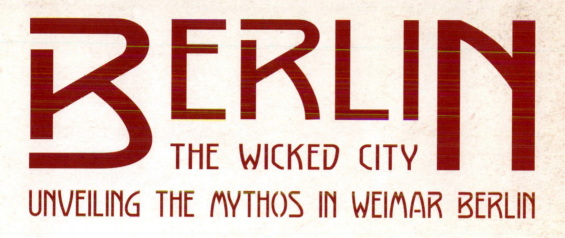

BERLIN
THE WICKED CITY
UNVEILING THE MYTHOS IN WEIMAR BERLIN

DAVID LARKINS
WITH MIKE MASON AND LYNNE HARDY

CHAOSIUM INC.

CREDITS

Authors
David Larkins with Lynne Hardy and Mike Mason

Editing and Development
Lynne Hardy and Mike Mason

Cover Art
Loïc Muzy

Interior Art
Sam Beck, Kristina Carroll, Caleb Cleveland, Emanuele Desiati, Trevor Henderson, Chris Huth, Pat Loboyko, Michelle Lockamy, Magdalena Mieszczak, Löic Muzy, Odessa Sawyer, and Dimitar Stoyanov

Cartography
Matt Ryan and Vandel J. Arden

Handouts
Matt Ryan

Art Direction
Lynne Hardy with Mike Mason and Nicholas Nacario

Layout
Nicholas Nacario

Copy Editing
Dave Gross and Matt Click

Call of Cthulhu Line Editor
Mike Mason

Special Thanks
Special thanks to Alex Drusts and the Esoteric Order of Roleplayers and Friends (Desiree Valdez, Jennifer Pearson, David Schimpff, Sage Morris-Greene, Alexander Marcus, Jade McLellan, Scott White, and Aidan Kallas) for their invaluable feedback and playtesting assistance. Thanks to Jeff Richard for his contributions, and also to Sam Riordan for sensitivity reading.

Clear Credit

All Berber and Droste poems excerpted from Dances of Vice, Horror, & Ecstasy, edited and translated by Merrill Cole (Newcastle upon Tyne: Side Real Press, 2012). Used with permission. Cagliostro quote excerpted from Voluptuous Panic by Mel Gordon (Los Angeles: Feral House, 2000). Netley Lucas quote excerpted from Ladies of the Underworld (New York: J.H. Sears & Co., 1927). All Joseph Hergesheimer quotes excerpted from Berlin (New York: Alfred A. Knopf, 1932). Original text of the Tucholsky quote ("Die menschliche Dummheit ist international") excerpted from Kurt Tucholsky: Gesammelte Werke in zehn Bänden. Band 9 (Reinbek bei Hamburg: Rowohlt Verlag, 1975). Gerald Biss quote excerpted from The Door of the Unreal (New York: G. P. Putnam's Sons, 1920). Rathenau quote excerpted from In Days to Come, translated by Eden and Cedar Paul (New York: Alfred A. Knopf, 1921). Scripture quotations marked (LEB) excerpted from the Lexham English Bible; copyright 2012 Logos Bible Software. Lexham is a registered trademark of Logos Bible Software. The "Descent of the Goddess Ishtar Into the Lower World" was translated by Morris Jastrow, excerpted from The Civilization of Babylonia and Assyria (Philadelphia: J. B. Lippincott Company, 1915). Original German Horst Wessel quote excerpted from Ralf Georg Reuth's Goebbels (Munich: Piper, 1990); translated by Jeff Richard/Claudia Loroff. Peter Levenda quote from Unholy Alliance: A History of Nazi Involvement with the Occult (London: Bloomsbury, 2002). Used with permission. For the limited edition version of this book the Brandenburg Gate Icon made by Freepik from www.flaticon.com

Rules for heroin, morphine, opium, and cannabis are adapted from "Narcotics in the Decade" by David Conyers and Richard Watts, appearing in Secrets of San Francisco by Cody Goodfellow, et al. Rules for alcohol use and abuse adapted from Pulp Cthulhu by Mike Mason, et al. Cat-things were first mentioned in the Arkham Gazette, issue 3, in an article entitled "Rat-Things and Worse Horrors" by Chris Huth with Bret Kramer.

Public domain images from Wikimedia Commons. Bertolt Brecht (Bundesarchiv, Bild 183-W0409-300/Kolbe, Jörg/CC BY-SA 3.0 DE); Claire Waldoff (Bundesarchiv, Bild 183-R07878/CC-BY-SA 3.0); Kurt Weill (Bundesarchiv, Bild 146-2005-0119/CC-BY-SA 3.0).

Find more Chaosium Inc. products at www.chaosium.com

Chaosium Publication 23161   Printed in China

TABLE OF CONTENTS

MATURE CONTENT WARNING

The "Wickedest City on Earth" did not earn its reputation lightly. Although we have endeavored to engage with this place and time in a non-exploitative manner, it remains to be said that much of the material in this book deals with mature themes—primarily, drugs, racism, and sex. The latter, in particular, in terms of sex magic, prostitution, sexual murder, and all manner of sexual practices is, at least, touched on, if not outright highlighted. Keepers are advised to adjust their presentation of this subject matter in accordance with their own and their group's comfort levels.

INTRODUCTION

WELCOME TO BERLIN!

Stepping off the train at Anhalter Station, you are plunged into a cacophony of sounds reverberating from the soaring, cathedral-like roof, crisscrossed with iron girders. All around you swirl fellow travelers from across Europe and around the world. Nearby, a legless veteran of the Great War, propped against the back of a ticket booth, shakes his cap at passersby, jingling the few coins within. His entreaties are ignored.

Dressed in a heavy frock coat and wearing an impressively ostentatious shako helmet, a policeman approaches.

"Auto, Droschke, oder Gepäck?" he asks. He is inquiring which mode of conveyance you require. You ask for a cab, and he hands you a metal ticket with a stamped number. Hefting your luggage, you walk out of the station, clutching your coat collar tight against the cold wind blowing in through the arches of the vast foyer with its ever-swinging doors.

The vista outside is even more bustling than the station within. The streets, still wet with the day's earlier rain, gleam like glass in the darkness of the night, reflecting the neon and electric lights that adorn the gray buildings ringing the square. Cars compete for space with horse-drawn carriages and double-decker omnibuses. Trains and trams rattle by on elevated platforms. Everywhere pedestrian traffic swarms: men and women, young and old. A newspaper vendor seated on a one-legged stool with several different papers hung around his neck shouts the day's latest headlines: the value of the *Reichsmark* continues to fall and there is talk of an economic collapse.

You spot the cab with the number matching yours. Hurrying over, you hand the ticket to the cabbie and slide into the back. You give him the address of your ultimate destination: the Hundegustav, a cabaret of ill repute in north Berlin. Your contact there, a dissolute man known only as "The Anti-Franz," has tracked down a fascinating old book he thinks might interest you.

"THE WICKEDEST CITY ON EARTH"

With the conclusion of the Great War in November 1918, the city of Berlin undergoes a transformation. After suffering from paroxysms of rebellion led by extremists from both ends of the political spectrum, the city rapidly gains a reputation for licentiousness. It is the place where anything—*anything*—may be had for the right price. It is both a city of sin and a city of *Betrieb* (a word variously translated as "business" or "bustle"). Its streets overflow with prostitutes, disabled veterans, destitute immigrants, and political agitators, all rubbing shoulders with buttoned-down businessmen, working girls, scholars, and artists.

The city also develops a reputation for danger. In just the first three years of the new republic's existence, the gutters run with the blood of dozens of political assassinations. Street violence is not uncommon, as Communists and *völkisch* Nationalists clash with each other and with the police. An overall "moral indifference to violence" develops among the populace.

But the true danger lies with the city's nightlife. Long into the evenings, Berlin's world-famous cabarets offer seemingly unlimited amounts of music, dance, and titillating entertainment, a stark contrast to the lowering gray buildings that run on for endless miles along the sprawling city's byways.

Into this bubbling stew, *Berlin: The Wicked City* introduces the uncanny elements of the Cthulhu Mythos. The city is a hotbed of occult organizations, strange cults, and half-whispered lore. Berlin's population has swollen by a factor of 400 percent over the previous 50 years, and with all these new arrivals come unspeakable secrets and strange new gods. Amid the wicked air of the world's capital of sin, what it means to be human is questioned. And as the city hurtles toward its inevitable dark destiny, the oppressive atmosphere intrudes more and more, pushing the sanity of investigators to its breaking point.

Opposite: The Wickedest City on Earth

WHAT'S INSIDE?

Chapter 1: The City, presents an overview of 1920s Berlin as it would be experienced by visitors and residents of the time. Guidelines are provided for creating investigators for a Berlin-centric campaign, as well as advice for bringing in existing player characters. Investigator organizations are provided to help bind the group together, while Experience Packages are designed to add new dimensions to investigators. A brief look at the city's history, as well as its topology, identifies key areas, streets, and squares that best reflect the character of Berlin. Details are provided on travel, communications, housing, crime and punishment, drug use, the city's underworld, and its high culture.

Chapter 2: Uncovering Berlin presents a range of locations of interest for investigators, from libraries and museums to cafés and nightclubs. Due to the city's sheer size, we eschew a block-by-block description, instead highlighting a few locations of likely investigator interest and filling in the blanks with a simple system for generating details of the urban landscape on the fly. Berlin's predilection for hedonism centers on the city's relationship with prostitution, food and drink, and cabaret. As who you know is often more important than what you know, guidelines are provided for a range of investigator contacts. Finally, the chapter concludes with a series of tables covering neighborhood details and street encounters, providing the Keeper with inspiration for cabarets and clubs, architectural details, and businesses. With the tools provided in this chapter, the Keeper should both glean an understanding of what makes Berlin unique and gain the tools to bring the city to life at the gaming table.

Chapter 3: Oh! You Pretty Things presents notable historical personalities to provide color and insight into the city. Whether Marlene Dietrich or Joseph Goebbels, short biographies highlight the time certain individuals lived or worked in Berlin, providing possible inspiration for encounters and scenarios.

Chapter 4: Strange Berlin considers how the Cthulhu Mythos festers in the dark corners and shadows of the city. Presented here are a range of scenario seed ideas for the Keeper to develop in between the three scenarios presented, setting up the potential for a decade-spanning campaign of horror.

Brandenburg Gate

Chapters 5 to **7** consist of three scenarios spanning the history of Berlin between the end of the Great War and the rise of Adolf Hitler and the Nazi Party. Many of the colorful details of Berlin and its inhabitants appear within the events outlined in the scenarios, which may be run as stand-alone episodes or linked together to form a mini-campaign. There is a presumption of continuity between the scenarios—that at least some of the investigators survive from one to the next. Keepers wishing to run one of the scenarios as a one-off may, of course, tinker with the madness and deadliness inherent in each—the tools are there to do so. But be warned: the scenarios are already calibrated to imperil investigators' physical and mental health and push them to their absolute limits.

The Devil Eats Flies is set in the summer of 1922, as Germany teeters on the brink of economic ruin and political chaos. The ghost of a madman stalks the city, turning its citizenry against itself and manifesting the monstrous forces inside us all. In order to stop the demonic spirit and save a Russian princess in exile, the investigators must strike a bargain with other sinister forces and ask who else they are prepared to see die to save the city.

The second scenario, **Dances of Vice, Horror, & Ecstasy**, takes place primarily in 1928 with a short prelude set in 1926. These are the city's golden years, when things have become superficially stable and prosperous again. A bungling sorcerer, a debauched dancer, and a strange cult of gnostic Saturn-worshippers threaten to put all of that to an end and turn Berlin into a veritable pit of madness and depravity.

In **Schreckfilm**, the final scenario of the trio, it is the winter of 1932, and Berlin is racing toward its grim future. The investigators come face to face with a shadowy cabal of the city's movers and shakers who are determined to turn the city's world-famous film industry toward ill ends. Trapped in a labyrinth of their own making and hounded relentlessly by dark forces beyond their ken, the investigators must confront the fundamental question of what is real and what is merely illusion, deciding whether survival is worth the price of becoming someone else entirely.

Concluding the book is a selection of inspirational media, including books, film, or television for those wishing to delve even deeper into the mysteries, history, and geography of Berlin.

Kaiser Wilhelm Monument

THE CITY

The history and environs of Berlin, its institutions and people. Getting around and getting into (or out of) trouble. The role of expatriates, political parties, and occult societies. Famous faces seen in shadowed cabarets.

"A disgusting city, this Berlin, a place where no one believes in anything."

—Cagliostro, 1775

LIVING IN THE CITY: INVESTIGATORS IN BERLIN

"And now we come to the most lurid Underworld of all cities—that of post-war Berlin. Ever since the declaration of peace, Berlin found its outlet in the wildest dissipation imaginable. The German is gross in his immorality, he likes his Halb-Welt or underworld pleasures to be devoid of any Kultur or refinement, he enjoys obscenity in a form which even the Parisian would not tolerate."

—Netley Lucas, *Ladies of the Underworld* (1927)

Berlin offers amazing scope for Mythos investigations. It is a teeming, chaotic city where, it is said, if you know where to look and are willing to pay the price, you can have anything imaginable. Even for native Berliners, it is simultaneously familiar and alien.

The investigators, in the course of a single evening, may move between a political rally of anarchists and radical Communists to an upper-crust cocktail party at one of the city's many upscale hotels, to the backstage labyrinth of an all-nude dance revue to a sleazy underground club where vice detectives rub shoulders with pimps and prostitutes—and still call that a normal night on the town! Add in the Mythos and the supernatural, and things get even weirder.

It is highly recommended that the investigators belong to a formal or informal organization or group (see **Investigator Organizations**, page 16, and **Cultivating Contacts**, page 60). Not only is this appropriate to a city where it seems that everyone belongs to some sort of club, group, or political party, but such bonds of mutual interest and support provide some small measure of stability in a city that embodies chaos and change.

EXPATS AND IMMIGRANTS

The city's singular reputation draws visitors from around the world, despite a world-weary contemporary's question, "Who goes to Berlin voluntarily?" Indeed, in 1927 the city itself adopts the slogan (with a sly wink), "Everyone Once in Berlin!"

The economic and cultural dislocations caused by the Great War mean Berlin quickly establishes a reputation as an outsider's paradise, drawing sex tourists, dissipated aesthetes, and queer folk like moths to a flame. It is not unusual to encounter in a single cabaret men and women of all colors, from around the world, all mixing together, united by the heady alchemy of the non-stop party atmosphere of the city's nightlife—for reference, the most common tourist groups by nationality are the Swedes, Dutch, French, British, Turkish, and Japanese.

Those who come to Berlin in search of work usually do so with no illusion of glamor or good times, seeing it as both heaven and hell on Earth. Yet for many—journalists and writers, musicians, the ambitious and talented, Germans and foreigners alike—Berlin, much like New York City for Americans, is where you inevitably end up, where you either make it big or are ground up in the city's uncaring gears.

Germany's capital city also attracts those who have already been through the ringer. In the aftermath of the Great War, the streets teem with destitute veterans and other displaced victims of the great collapse that followed the Armistice. Such concerns are exacerbated by the inflation years of 1922–23, which destroy savings accounts and cast many formerly comfortable bourgeoisie into poverty—Christopher Isherwood's famous "bankrupt middle class."

Finally, Eastern European immigrants looking for new opportunities are a much-noted (and often scorned) feature of the city. These new arrivals, debarking at the Silesian Station in the lower-class neighborhood of Friedrichshain,

Opposite: The Brandenburg Gate

have little to look forward to. Most immediately go off the grid, forgoing registration with the police, as required of all new arrivals to the city. Their poverty, lack of language skills and urban savvy, and unregistered status means they are vulnerable to exploitation and victimization. Countless hard-luck cases come to Berlin hoping to make good, but few ever make it out again.

GERMAN PRONUNCIATION MADE EASY

German pronunciation can sometimes seem intimidating to non-native speakers. Presented here is a quick-and-dirty guide to assist new arrivals at the *Fremdenverkehrsbüro* (tourist information office).

The good news is that German pronunciation is extremely regular. When confronted with a compound word (such as that given in the previous paragraph), sound it out one syllable at a time, putting the stress on the final syllable. This won't always be precisely correct, but close enough! The German alphabet is functionally the same as English, with only a few modifications.

Vowels are pronounced "ah" (a), "eh" (e), "ee" (i), "oh" (o), and "oo" (u). The letter v is usually pronounced with a soft "eff" sound. The letter w is pronounced like the English v. The letter j is soft, pronounced like the English y. The letter r is pronounced farther back in the throat, more like the French r than the English. The letter s should be pronounced with a slight "sh" sound. An h after a vowel indicates a lengthened vowel sound.

The modifications to the alphabet are in the form of umlaut verbs: ä, ö, and ü. Each of these should be pronounced with some variation of the "ee" sound. Thus, "ay" (ä), "er" (ö), and "ew" (ü). The simplest way to do this is to purse the lips and pronounce the vowel—the form of your mouth will lend the vowel an approximately correct sound.

German writing features a unique character called an es-tset, rendered as ß. This symbol is used when two s letters appear together in a word and should be read as such. Thus, instead of writing Strasse (street), one would write Straße.

German plurals are generally formed by adding "e" or "en" to the end of the word.

A final note: German nouns are always capitalized, whether or not they are proper nouns.

Languages

As a world capital, Berlin is home to many languages. German is, of course, the common tongue, though the trademark *Berliner Schnauze* ("Berlin snout") is readily distinguished from the more formal High German of classroom instruction—the difference is not quite enough to merit its own skill, however.

After the 1917 Bolshevik Revolution, Berlin is inundated with Russian émigrés and refugees; the district of Charlottenburg is laughingly referred to as "Charlottengrad" for its number of Russian residents, and some skill with Russian will get you far in certain neighborhoods.

Despite the physical distance, Berlin has a long and complex history with French émigrés going all the way back to the Huguenots of the 17th century, and it is not unusual to hear French spoken among upper-class Berliners, as well as still retaining its status as the literal *lingua franca* of continental Europe. Quickly moving up to replace French is English, and this is especially so in Berlin, whose residents have taken quite a shine to Americans and their culture.

Other languages are spoken more commonly and exclusively among immigrant communities. Although one is unlikely to need Yiddish when dealing with the average Berliner, it could come in handy when walking the streets of the Scheuenviertel and Schöneberg, two districts with large Jewish populations. Likewise, Polish allows one to communicate with the great number of immigrants from the east.

NATIVES

"The city of Berlin, I recognized, had a definite color of its own; it had, plainly, become a world metropolis… now Berlin had acquired an authentic entity. It resided in the young, and was composed, mostly, of a direct recognition, a faintly bitter but undisturbed acceptance, of all, all, the realities of existence. It was an attitude nowhere, that I could see, irradiated by hope. The customary optimism, the romantic confidence, of youth, were absent in Berlin… So much, the bearing of the young showed, had failed them, turning out false or hypocritical or insubstantial, that they had concluded all the celebrated reassurances and rewards were lies."

—Joseph Hergesheimer, *Berlin*

Berliners have long been notorious for their idiosyncratic qualities. The dichotomy of being both an industrial arsenal and center of culture during the 18th and 19th centuries left an indelible mark on the city's character. In the 1920s, at a time when one out of five Londoners and one out of three New Yorkers attend church every Sunday, barely one in twenty Berliners do the same.

GENERATING GERMAN NAMES

1D10	Male Names	Female names	Surnames A*	Surnames B*
1	Alexander	Anita	Baum	Mainz
2	Arthur	Brigitte	Becker	Mann
3	Conrad	Cäcilie	Berend	Muller
4	Erich	Charlotte	Borngräber	Neher
5	Franz	Dinah	Busch	Neumann
6	Fritz	Elisabeth	Desmond	Oswald
7	Georg	Elsa	Eisler	Puttkamer
8	Hans	Elsie	Frick	Raeder
9	Hermann	Gerda	Gessmann	Reiter
10	Hubert	Gertrude	Grimm	Schäffer

Key:

*Roll on the Surname column of your choice or roll once on each and create a hyphenated name. Remember, "von" names always come first.

GENERATING GERMAN NAMES II

1D10	Male Names	Female names	Surnames A*	Surnames B*
1	Joachim	Gilda	Grünbaum	Schnitzler
2	Karl	Leonie	Herzl	Thiem
3	Klaus	Lene	Hildenbrandt	von Feytag
4	Kuno	Lotte	Kahan	von Loringhoven
5	Max	Lucie	Knobloch	von Meyernick
6	Moritz	Maria	Koch	von Nathusius
7	Otto	Marlene	Krauss	von Schrenck
8	Paul	Martha	Langer	Walden
9	Werner	Olga	Lanz	Walter
10	Wilhelm	Rita	Levy	Wolpe

Key:

*Roll on the Surname column of your choice or roll once on each and create a hyphenated name. Remember, "von" names always come first.

Example: a roll of "1" on column A and "5" on column B results in the hyphenated "von Meyernick-Grünbaum."

The Berliner attitude is not unlike the stereotypical American: disdainful of the pretenses of authority, slightly cynical and crude, and playfully anti-authoritarian. The sharp wit of Berliners is legendary; they are said to possess a *Berliner Schnauze,* a term that signifies not only their accent, but also the fact that the city's inhabitants are always ready with a barbed comment or a bit of gallows humor.

To other German-speakers, the Berlin accent is distinctive—a sort of side-of-the-mouth drawl that places an emphasis on short, sharp sounds, yet turns the hard "g" into a soft "j," contracts compound words to near-unrecognizable briefness (viz. "Kurfürstendamm" to "Ku'damm"), and readily adapts foreign terms and customs, particularly Anglo-Americanisms.

Beginning in the mid-1920s, Berlin is positively swept up by a mania for all things American: slapstick comedies, boxing matches, Ziegfeld Follies dancers, crossword puzzles, and the beautification regimens of Hollywood stars.

How Did You Spend the War?

For Germany, the Great War was a catastrophe on an apocalyptic scale. Over two million German men, most in the flower of youth, marched off to war never to return. Another 4.2 million returned home as casualties of war,

suffering long-term chronic physical ailments. The number of veterans also grappling with the psychological effects of the war is beyond counting.

Meanwhile, the British blockade and other disruptions caused by the conflict led to an estimated half-a-million civilian casualties from malnutrition and disease. Whole swathes of the German middle class were effectively wiped out by incipient poverty that led families to sell off treasured heirlooms and ancestral houses just to put food on the table. Eventually, when the material assets ran out, many German women turned to selling the only thing they had left: their bodies. The Great War fundamentally changed the solid roots of Wilhelmian society, breaking down many social barriers but also leaving average Germans scratching their head, wondering what had happened to the world they grew up in.

Due to the all-pervasive nature of the war, German-born investigators, men and women alike, need to decide how they spent the war years, for the conflict touched everyone's life. For German men of military age (those born in the 1880s and 1890s), there is a 40% chance that they served under arms in some capacity, although this needn't necessarily mean service in the trenches of the Western Front. For one thing, there was the sweeping war on the Eastern Front from 1914–17, encompassing territories from the Baltic to the Balkans.

Tourists visiting the city

BRINGING EXISTING CHARACTERS TO BERLIN

As one of the great cities of its age—only London and New York outrank it in terms of population—Berlin is a natural destination for existing investigators. Some suggestions based on occupational type follow.

Professors and Academics: one of Berlin's few nicknames is "Athens on the Spree," reflecting the city's long tradition as a center for culture and learning. Professors (particularly those with a background in the sciences) may come to Berlin for a sabbatical at Frederick William University or to study at the Kaiser Wilhelm Institute for Physics under its director Albert Einstein. Those with a background in the humanities may wish to delve the extensive archives of the Prussian State Library or plumb the collection of one of the city's many museums (**Berlin's Libraries and Museums**, page 45).

The stately Pergamon Museum is under construction over the course of the 1920s, finally opening in 1930. An archaeologist or antiquarian could easily justify a trip to Berlin to consult on an artifact housed in that museum or in one of the several other institutions on **Museum Island** (page 46).

Lastly, there is the **Institute of Sexology** (page 50). Any academic with an interest in the burgeoning field of human sexuality might make it a point to visit the Institute and meet its eccentric founder, **Dr. Hirschfeld** (page 77). A sabbatical to study at the Institute makes for an excellent line item on such a professor's curriculum vitae.

Antiquarians and Collectors: investigators with an interest in antiques and artifacts may be drawn to Berlin thanks to its reputation as a freewheeling city where anything may be had for the right price. The shady storefronts and back-alley cabarets see a brisk business in all manner of illicit and black-market items, and there is no reason to think these couldn't include long-lost or heretofore-unknown relics and *objets d'art*, proscribed tomes, strange fetishes, and much more besides. Perhaps there is a book or other artifact long sought after by the investigator? After coming up empty elsewhere, Berlin may finally offer it for the taking.

Cops and Robbers: Berlin, a city of vice, attracts attention from those who would enforce the law—and those who would break it. While such concerns fall under the aegis of the Criminal Police and the *Ringvereine* (ring clubs) of the city (**Beinls and Bulls**, page 37), there is still room in the Naked City for a few more stories of foreign criminals and

of the detectives hot on their trails. What better place to disappear, after all, than in the swirling morass of Berlin?

Famous consulting detectives may be invited to provide their expertise on a case. Private investigators may follow a mark to Alexanderplatz and beyond. There is also the classic canard of cozy mysteries: the professional investigator travels to Berlin for a little R&R, only to be swept up in a new mystery soon after arriving.

Although Berlin is a generation away from earning its Cold War cloak-and-dagger reputation, it is, thanks to its status as capital of a nation on the losing end of the Great War, still a site for intrigue and dubious dealings among representatives of His Majesty's Secret Service and other comparable agencies. For example, in 1921, British and Russian agents tracked Talaat Pasha, former Ottoman official and architect of the Armenian Genocide, to a residence in Berlin. They informed a member of the Armenian Revolutionary Federation, and days later Pasha lay in the gutter outside his Berlin flat, a bullet in his brain. Investigator agents from external government spy agencies or revolutionary groups may find themselves called to Berlin for similarly grim wetwork.

Dilettantes and Artists: for investigators of this stripe, a trip to Berlin is not just justifiable but almost mandatory! If ever there was a city for the dissipated dilettante and the rootless entertainer, Berlin is it. Indeed, the city's reputation is built on the back of "Bright Young Things" flocking to Berlin's neon-lit squares and streets, looking to join the non-stop party.

For entertainers and artists, Berlin offers a pulsating scene that welcomes them with open arms, at least at first. The city is a hub of Expressionistic art, and, through the Berlin Secession, an early adopter of the Dada "anti-art" movement (a forerunner of Surrealism). Singers, musicians, dancers, and actors may expect to find steady employment in any one of the city's innumerable clubs, cabarets, and revues, though lasting fame will elude almost all of them. Even established performers from Britain or the States may come to Berlin to work with such noted directors as Fritz Lang, F. W. Murnau, or G. W. Pabst (as did real-life cinema star Louise Brooks in 1929).

Tourists: finally, it should be noted that Berlin is one of the top tourist destinations in the world during the 1920s. With few exceptions, nearly any investigator may justify their presence in the city simply by virtue of being part of a package tour.

Albin Grau, the creative impresario behind 1922's classic *Schreckfilm* (horror movie) *Nosferatu* (dir. F. W. Murnau), got the idea to do a vampire movie while serving on the Eastern Front, where he met a Serbian farmer who claimed his father actually was one! Germany also fought abroad to protect its colonial holdings, particularly in East Africa, and characters may have served in the equatorial tropics or in the Far East.

Alternatively, there is service at sea, either as part of a ship's crew (many of whom were instrumental in leading the uprisings that forced the Kaiser's abdication in 1918), or in the clanging, claustrophobic chaos onboard a U-boat.

Or perhaps the war was spent in the air? Tales of modern-day knights aboard their colorful wood-and-canvas "steeds," twisting and turning in aerial dogfights high above the trenches and battlefields of the war, captured the imagination of the public and made national heroes of aces such as the Richthofen brothers, Ernst Udet, Werner Voss, Oswald Boelcke, and Hermann Göring. Life expectancy was

INVESTIGATOR OCCUPATIONS AND EXPERIENCE PACKAGES

The following occupations from Chapter Four of the *Investigator Handbook* are particularly well-suited for evoking the special flavor of campaigns centering on Berlin: Actor, Artist, Author, Bartender, Book Dealer, Criminal (particularly Conman, Fence, Forger, Street Punk, and Thug), Cult Leader, Dilettante, Driver (Taxi Driver), Elected Official, Entertainer, Foreign Correspondent, Journalist, Musician, Occultist, Parapsychologist, Photographer (and Photojournalist), Police Detective/Officer, Prostitute, Psychiatrist, Union Activist, and Zealot.

Any of the Experience Packages provided on pages 61–62 of the *Investigator Handbook* are also perfectly suitable for Berliner investigators. Provided here are three more that draw upon specific aspects of this particular time and place.

Street Fighter Experience Package

Ever since the end of the Great War and the subsequent collapse of the Reich, it has been obvious that the battle for Germany's future will be fought not just in the voting booths but also on the streets. Whether representing left-wing, centrist, or right-wing politics, you are a seasoned instigator and bravo, always ready to throw fists and rocks in defense of your cause—a cause that you ardently believe holds the key to the country's salvation.

- Choose a starting age of 35 or younger.
- Deduct 1D10 from SAN.
- Add an Injury/Scar to the investigator's backstory.
- Add 60 bonus skill points, divided among any of the following skills: Dodge, Drive Auto, Fast Talk, Fighting (Brawl), First Aid, Intimidate, Law, Mechanical Repair, Psychology, Stealth, Throw.
- Note on the investigator sheet: immune to Sanity losses resulting from witnessing violence against another human being or viewing a corpse.

Underclass Experience Package

You are a member of Berlin's seething underclass. You are not a professional criminal, but you have been known to turn to crime when times get rough and have a few connections among the organized criminal syndicates in the city. You may be a cabaret singer, a prostitute, a down-on-their-luck theatrical impresario, a disabled veteran, an immigrant from Eastern Europe or farther abroad, an orphan, or some combination of the preceding. Whatever you are, you have learned how to get by in this gray, unforgiving city.

- Deduct 1D10 from SAN.
- Credit Rating may not be above 20%.
- Add one of the following to the investigator's backstory: an Injury/Scar, a Phobia/Mania, or an Encounter with a Strange Entity associated with their experiences on the mean streets and in the darkened alleys of the city.
- Add 70 bonus skill points, divided among any of the following skills: Appraise, an appropriate Art/Craft (Acting, Dancing, Singing, Musical Instrument, Writing, and so on), Charm, Disguise, Fast Talk, Intimidate, Language (Other), Listen, Locksmith, Persuade, Sleight of Hand, Stealth.
- Note on the investigator sheet: immune to Sanity losses resulting from witnessing violence against another human being.

generally measured in days, but glory awaited those who took to the air, unlike the poor *Landsers* in the trenches.

Also, keep in mind that military service does not necessarily imply front-line duty. It takes a great number of rear-echelon service personnel to power a modern army, from field surgeons to quartermasters to entertainment and morale-boosting operations such as theater troupes and orchestras. Where an investigator served in the Great War and saw combat, be sure to give them the **War Experience Package** (*Investigator Handbook*, page 61).

For those who didn't serve, and for female investigators, it's a good idea to give some thought to how the war impacted their personal lives. Did they lose a loved one in the war? Did they lose their livelihood or fortune? Germany suffers territorial losses due to the Treaty of Versailles—were the investigators forced to pick up stakes from Alsace or Western Prussia and move to Berlin with only what they could carry on their backs?

What of the Turnip Winter (1916–17) and the subsequent starving years, when the British blockade finally brought the specter of famine to the once-prosperous nation? What did the characters do to survive? What did they have to give up? Did they participate in the food riots that swept Germany during the latter half of the war and into the immediate post-war years? By answering these tough questions, players may create more well-rounded investigators while connecting with the trauma that continues to haunt every German gaily drinking and dancing the night away in the clubs of Berlin.

INVESTIGATOR OCCUPATIONS AND EXPERIENCE PACKAGES (CONTINUED)

Former Corpsstudent

You attended a German university in your youth and were a member of a Corps, a type of student fraternity. Corps, made up of fellows from the same home region, are based around the twin pillars of German Idealism and the Mensur (fencing). The former is expressed in the beliefs of the *Corpsstudenten*, who espouse an apolitical and tolerant philosophy. Membership is open to all men, as long as they can prove their character. This is accomplished, at least in part, through the latter ritual (Mensur), a highly formalized type of fencing in which the two participants stand a yard apart and whip razor-sharp sword blades at each other's faces. Participants wear special goggles for the eyes and nose, and armored padding for the throat, chest, and arm, but the face and scalp are completely exposed. This, combined with the special sword's flexible, whipping blade and high-guard position, leads to bloody wounds around the head—which is precisely the point! The Mensur is not a test of dueling puissance but rather a test of bravery and manliness. To dodge or even flinch from a blow is to lose the match. The scars earned from the duels are seen as a badge of honor and a testament to the bearer's bravery.

Perhaps most importantly, the bonds forged between members of the Corps last a lifetime. Long after university, members may be counted upon to support each other, provide favors, and come to one another's aid when needed.

- Must be male.
- Deduct 3D10 from APP.
- Credit Rating may not be less than 60% after applying bonus skill points (see below).
- Add the following to the investigator's backstory: one prominent Injury/Scar to the face or head for every 10 points of APP lost.
- Add 50 bonus skill points, divided among any of the following skills: Credit Rating, Fighting (Sword), Intimidate.
- At the Keeper's discretion, you may apply a bonus die to any opposed social skill roll (Charm, Fast Talk, Intimidate, Persuade) when dealing with someone who would be impressed by your dueling scars—generally anyone with old-fashioned or Nationalistic tendencies. Conversely, gain a penalty die when dealing with someone who might be horrified or put-off by such facial scarring.
- You start the game with one contact automatically. Choose the field of the contact's expertise: Politics, Empirical Science, Social Science, or Fine Arts. Also, going forward, any roll to establish another contact in the same field is made with a bonus die, with success indicating that you have reconnected with an old chum from your days in the Corps.

INVESTIGATOR ORGANIZATIONS

Berlin is rife with clubs, organizations, and informal *bünde* (associations or leagues), providing ample opportunity for creating investigator organizations. Some sample organizations are provided here; see also **Cultivating Contacts** (page 60) for more examples of various organizations active within the city.

The Independent Order of Owls

One of innumerable esoteric societies operating in Germany, the Independent Order of Owls is certainly one of the stranger examples. Originally founded in the United States, it boasts a limited roster of expatriate members, as well as a handful of native Berliners. The Order was founded in the 1890s in St. Louis, Missouri, by a group of Master Masons. It is unknown whether the original association (called the "Supreme Nest of the World") still exists. For all intents and purposes, the Owls of Berlin are an independent group.

The Owls of Berlin now take their moniker quite seriously: from their eyrie at the Red Eagle Hotel they watch the night, always on the lookout for occult vermin.

Concept: occult vigilantes.

Origin: founded as part of a wave of animal-themed societies that cropped up in the Anglophone world around the turn of the century (Elks, Moose, and so on), the Owls never took themselves too seriously until they started uncovering some strange goings-on among other the secret societies operating in Berlin. Currently, the Order is focused on what they believe to be an underground network of Satanists that runs beneath the staid façade of Berlin's upper class. They have yet to encounter any overt Mythos elements in their investigations, but it is just a matter of time until they do.

Organization: despite their deadly serious mission, some traces of the group's light-hearted origins remain—the lodge-house is referred to as the "Nest" and the head of the Order is called the "Sapient Screecher." Apart from this, the Order also retains other, cosmetic touches typical of other quasi-Masonic fraternal orders: there is a secret handshake, a semi-serious initiation ritual for new members, and so forth. Currently the group is exclusively male, but a determined woman (particularly one with some level of occult expertise) could probably talk her way in.

Resources: the Order maintains its "Nest" on the top floor of the Hotel Roter Adler (Red Eagle Hotel), a grand old building located at Schützenstraße 6 in the heart of the Friedrichstadt. An extensive suite provides accommodation and sleeping quarters for members. A small but growing library of occult and esoteric reference material (books and pamphlets) is housed at the Adler as well. The space is rented monthly, paid for out of membership fees of $10/year.

Suggested investigator occupations: Alienist, Antiquarian, Big Game Hunter, Dilettante, Explorer, Gentleman/Lady, Librarian, Occultist, Parapsychologist.

Hilde-Film

A small, struggling film production company, this group has recently stumbled across something straight out of one of its own movies. The company got its start in 1922 when noted young actress Hilde Schön used her earnings to buy equipment and rent space in one of the hangars at Berlin's Tempelhof Airfield. Hilde believed in promoting actor equity and bringing the philosophies of New Objectivity to the big screen. She pays fair wages to her crew and acting troupe, who repay her with undying loyalty and a willingness to go without until the next influx of cash.

Concept: ghost-hunting movie crew.

Origin: in the midst of editing the company's latest film (*The Infernal Power*), it became obvious that something strange had been captured on film. The shot in question was just a bit of footage of traffic around the City Palace to use as an establishing shot, but the editor's keen eyes picked out what could only be described as a ghostly apparition floating along the ramparts of the palace! At this point, Hilde and her trusty crew are debating what to do with the footage, possibly to use it as the basis of a ghost film or else go looking for more ghosts in the city and capture them on celluloid. Either way, the whole troupe is electrified with the knowledge that they have in hand evidence of something beyond our material world, and they wish to find out more.

Organization: a small film company, with Fräulein Schön at the top as executive producer and boss. As with all such small outfits, everyone is expected to do double- or triple-duty on set. No *prima donnas* here!

Resources: razor-thin. The company has produced three films to date, and while all have managed to turn a profit, none have been big hits. The crew has had to work without pay more than once. While there is a very small office in central Berlin, the rented hangar at Tempelhof serves as a convenient place to hide away from prying eyes, if necessary.

Suggested investigator occupations: Accountant, Actor, Artist, Author, Designer, Lawyer, Mechanic (and other skilled trades, such as carpenter, electrician, film editor, and so on), Photographer (specializing in motion-picture cameras), Secretary, Stuntman.

Landsberger Tenants' Association

Nestled between Alexanderplatz and the Volkspark Friedrichshain is the smaller, less well-known Landsberger Platz. Once the site of an east-facing gate in the city walls, it is now a pleasant little square with a pair of fountains and some modest statuary.

Overlooking the square from across the intersection of Friedenstraße and Landsberger Allee is an old tenement building, home to several hundred souls. Although many of the tenement residents come and go, remaining mostly faceless and unknown, there is a small core of long-time residents who banded together during the starvation years of 1917–18 (or, depending on the time-frame of the campaign, the inflation years of 1922–23, or after the Crash of 1929) as a sort of mutual-aid group. This group, the Landsberger Tenants' Association, has maintained close ties ever since, presenting a unified front whenever matters of rent or building maintenance become too onerous. In the manner of all *Mietskaserne* (housing blocks, see page 37) in the city, several even room with each other.

The mix of members in this group reflects the city's diverse population: there are old Hausfraus, weary taxi drivers, cabaret singers, Line-Boy prostitutes, Russian immigrants fleeing the Bolsheviks, committed Communists, natives of the former German colony in Africa, and so on. In spite of their vast differences in background and belief systems, they mostly manage to get along with each other or at least stay out of each other's way.

Concept: mutual-protection society.

Origin: matters recently took a more serious turn, above and beyond mere issues of rent hikes and leaky pipes, when one of the Association members unearthed a strange artifact in a sub-cellar beneath the building. This part of Berlin has been inhabited since the 13th century, but this particular artifact looks even older. Carved from soapstone, it is a grotesque manikin reminiscent of a mandrake root in shape and size. Periodically, it perspires a milky-white liquid in noticeable quantities. The Association realizes it has something uncanny and possibly valuable in its possession but lacks the knowledge or expertise to know quite what it is. They only know that the building now seems to be under surveillance by shadowy men in dark coats, their hats pulled down low over their eyes. Currently, they are debating whether to take it to a museum or the University for identification.

Organization: a regular motley crew of poor and working-class tenants, held together by the mutual bonds of affection that can only be forged by adversity; the Association has no formal leaders or structure.

Resources: nothing monetary. Plenty, if measured in emotional support and some shared bread and coffee on a cold day.

Suggested investigator occupations: Artist, Author, Bartender, Boxer, Butler/Valet/Maid, Craftsperson, Criminal (Conman, Gun Moll, Fence, Forger, Smuggler, Street Punk), Driver, Entertainer, Gambler, Gangster, Journalist, Laborer, Musician, Private Investigator, Prostitute, Salesperson, Secretary, Shopkeeper, Tribe Member, Union Activist, Waitress/Waiter.

The Apache Pathfinders

Beginning in the Berlin suburb of Stieglitz in 1896, a new youth movement swept across Germany at the turn of the century: the *Wandervogel* (Wandering Bird). Reminiscent of the contemporaneous Scouting movement in Britain and America, Wandervogel groups espoused a certain back-to-nature Romantic idealism, denigrating the corrupting influence of the urban lifestyle in favor of extended hiking and camping trips, singing traditional folk ballads, and eschewing the consumption of meat and alcohol.

Sadly, many involved in the first wave of the Wandervogel movement matured just in time to march off to fight and die in the Great War. In the wake of the war, a new movement arose that attempted to syncretize the philosophies of Wandervogel with the German Scout movement. The result is the *Bündische Jugend* (the free youth movement).

Bündische Jugend groups make use of the trappings of scouting groups (uniforms, pennants, badges, and so forth) but retain the radical Romantic idealism of the Wandervogel movement. They reject political stances at a time when nearly everyone else is intensely involved in politics, lead a "clean" life free of alcohol and cigarettes, and continue to reject consumerist, urban lifestyles.

One of several such Bündische Jugend groups in Berlin styles itself the Apache Pathfinders (a typical name; this particular strain of Romanticism embraces the growing German fascination with the American West). Open to boys and girls between the ages of 15–21, they organize nature hikes in the Grunewald and beyond, and boating trips on the Havel. They also engage in volunteer work in the city, helping to clear litter from city parks. It was during one such outing that the little group was forced to grow up quickly.

Concept: youth in over their heads.

Origin: it happened in the Tiergarten, of all places, not some far-off woods out of a Grimm fairy tale, but right in the middle of the city. It was a beautiful, late-spring day. The Apaches, on one of their litter-collecting missions, were spread out among the sun-dappled groves of trees and shrubbery when they heard one of their own give an inhuman cry. Running, they found poor Karl-Heinz cowering beneath a bush, his uniform torn and disheveled, and his mind broken.

Through repeat visits to Karl-Heinz, now an inmate at Dalldorf, the Apaches have started to put together an understanding of what transpired that day. Of the strange, shambling creature that set upon him in the middle of the park, its unwholesome caresses, and of the egg Karl-Heinz insists is growing inside his abdomen even now. No one is allowed to bring so much as a penknife into Karl-Heinz's cell lest he try to slit his own belly open again.

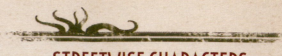

STREETWISE CHARACTERS

Life in Berlin is tough and it takes a certain "savvy" just to make it from day to day for much of the population. Characters from the lower classes and poor immigrants who have been living in the city for a while soon learn to make the most of the skills they acquire on the mean streets if they are to survive.

Such streetwise investigators should look to Navigate, Spot Hidden, Listen, and social skills, as well as making use of Know rolls and their suggested contacts to figure out where the best underground dives are located, which charities and garbage bins to scrounge food and drink from, and to get a sense of what's going on down at the street level. Have the police been raiding lately? Is trouble brewing with the Reds or the Nazis? Have folks been disappearing in the Friedrichshain again? And so on.

Forging and developing ongoing relationships with the contacts they need to get by makes for excellent roleplaying opportunities, which can then be backed up with the aforementioned skill rolls to keep the plot moving, as required. Suggested contacts can be found for occupations under their description in the *Investigator Handbook*.

Organization: the Pathfinders are organized into three troops—one in Reinickendorf, one in Kreuzberg, and one in Pankow. Each troop is led by its most senior member (generally 20 or 21 years of age) and further organized into "squads" of 10.

Resources: every member pays a small fee to belong to the Pathfinders, which provides a modest fund for miscellaneous expenses. In addition, members are expected to have their own tent and camping gear. Troop meetings generally take place at the house of the troop leader. For all its posturing, the group is largely made up of children of solidly bourgeois background, and parents can generally be counted on to provide a little extra money, if asked politely.

Suggested investigator occupations: as this is a youth organization, most investigators should take the Student occupation; however, older members could certainly justify a degree of specialization. Those who are most committed to the back-to-nature ethos of the group may be Outdoorsman/ Outdoorswomen, while those who enjoy accompanying the march with guitar and song might take Entertainer. See the *Investigator Handbook*, page 45, for guidelines on age and playing younger investigators.

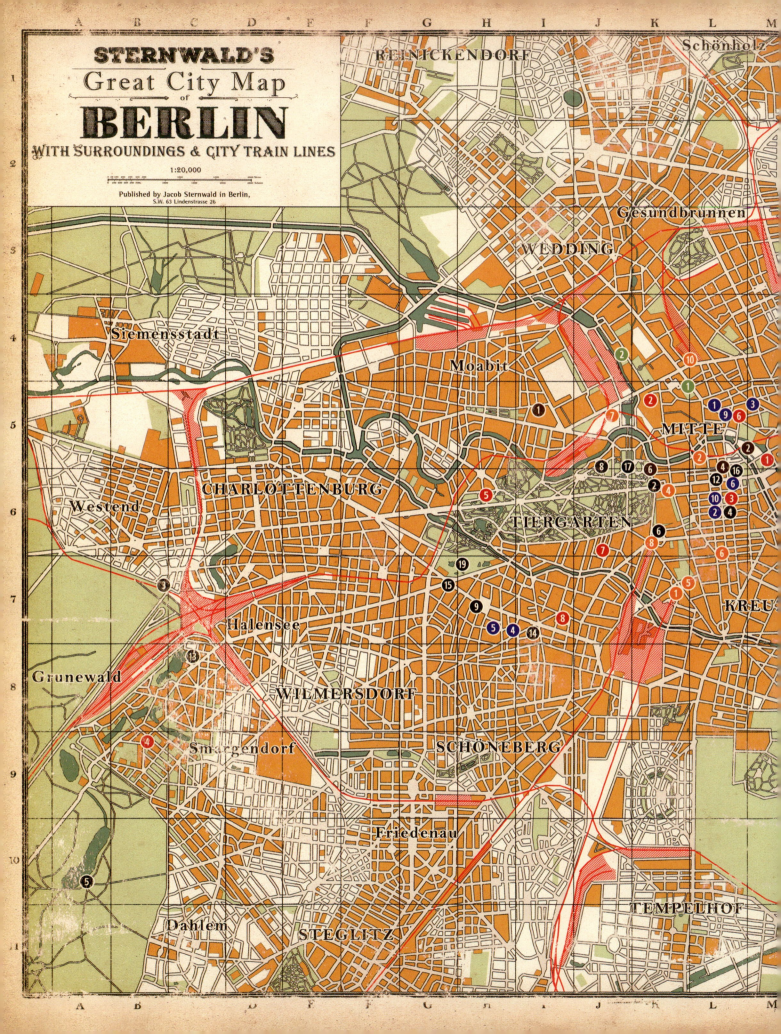

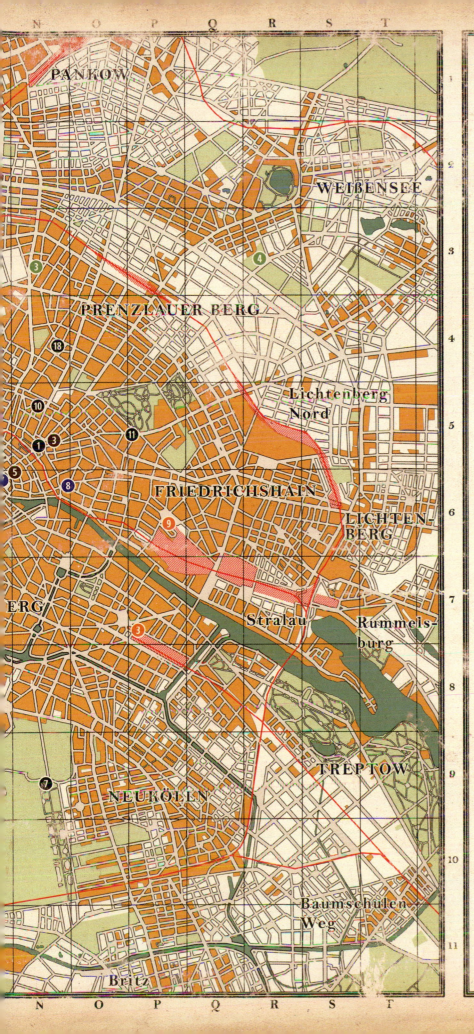

Location Index

Points of Interest

Cemeteries

Churches and Hospitals

Clubs and Cafes

Government Buildings

Hotels and Stations

Lith., Druck, Verlag u. Eigentum: Sternwald-Verlag G.m.b.H., Berlin SW 68, Lindenstr. 13

BERLIN'S HISTORY: A BRIEF OVERVIEW

Much of what makes Berlin unique in the Jazz Age becomes apparent through the scenarios presented later in this book. Here, we are concerned with the more prosaic side of the city. This distinction does not, of course, make such information any less valuable. Quite the contrary, *liebchen*!

Histories of Berlin are legion both in print and online, and we shall not linger long on the topic. Presented here is a potted history, suitable to provide to players as a basic primer on the city and how it came to be.

Situated on marshy, heavily wooded plains along the banks of the River Spree, the site that would one day grow to be the mighty metropolis of Berlin was first settled sometime in the 12th century, likely during the reign of Albert the Bear, first Margrave of Brandenburg. By the following century, Berlin was a recognized settlement. The year 1237 is the official date of Berlin's founding. Perhaps because of Albert's nickname, or (perhaps) because the first syllable in the city's name is a homonym with the animal (*Bär*), Berlin has taken the bear as its symbol since these earliest times.

Albert the Bear's line died out in 1320. After a series of interim rulers, in 1415 the Hohenzollern family, under Frederick I, took the reins of the Brandenburg Margraviate and held them for the next 500 years. The ascension of the Hohenzollerns also marked the beginning of Berlin's rise. The center of power in the Margraviate shifted from Brandenburg to Berlin when Frederick I took residence there. His son and successor, "Irontooth," built a royal palace in the town, suppressing a so-called "Indignation" of the populace in the process—even in medieval times, Berliners could not abide pompous authority.

Increasingly, Berlin came into its own as a political power. As Electors of the Holy Roman Empire, the Margraves wielded great influence. Berlin withdrew from the Hanseatic League in 1451. Protestantism came to Berlin in the 1530s, and many church lands and possessions were seized, the money used to pay for the construction of the grand avenue called the Kurfürstendamm (Prince-Elector Way).

To offset massive population loss from the Thirty Years' War, the "Great Elector" Frederick William began to encourage immigration in the 1640s, particularly from displaced French Huguenots, who eventually came to constitute a significant minority population. At the dawn of the 18th century, upward of one in three Berliners were French. Another of Berlin's great avenues, Unter den Linden, was laid down by Frederick William as well, its six rows of titular linden trees making it an instantly recognizable landmark of the city. Around this time, the Margraviate of Brandenburg, which had been in a personal union with the Duchy of Prussia for nearly a century, combined the two titles and became the Kingdom of Prussia. Despite the name, the state's centers of power and population remained firmly in the state of Brandenburg and Berlin, which absorbed several neighboring towns, pushing its population to over 100,000 by mid-century.

The most famous Prussian ruler, Frederick II (called "the Great" in his own lifetime and forever after) ascended to the throne in 1740. He continued the traditions of the first Prussian king, pushing a political agenda that combined military might with cultural and artistic refinement. Frederick's father was a model Enlightened Monarch, and under his direction universal education was introduced, and the great hospital, the Charité, opened its doors. It was probably around this time that Berlin earned one of its few enduring nicknames, "Athens on the Spree," so-called for its status as a great center of learning and culture. Despite this reputation, the city turned almost all its economic attention to supporting a powerful standing army and producing munitions to drive its war machine.

Frederick the Great made good use of all he inherited and established Prussia as the premiere German state in Europe, a reputation it maintained into the 19th century and all the way up to the birth of the German Empire. Frederick continued promoting policies favorable to immigration, allowed for an uncensored press and free speech, reformed the legal system, and opened government posts to non-aristocrats, who were allowed to rise to positions based on merit and not birth. At the same time, he took his father's already formidable army and expanded it even further. Fully four-fifths of the country's budget went to the military; a huge percentage of Prussia's men served in the army at any given time. All of this led the French intellectual Mirabeau to quip famously, "Prussia is not a state in possession of an army, but an army in possession of a state." Be that as it may, the Prussian army successfully defended the state's scattered holdings, gradually linking them together through a series of wars, the most notable being the Seven Years' War (1756–1763). Shamefully, Frederick, who for all his Enlightenment ideals was both a hard-bitten political realist and no friend of the Poles, also happily participated in the First Partition of Poland, gobbling up a large chunk of northern Poland and linking his western and eastern holdings.

Frederick reigned for 46 years and cast a long, looming shadow over subsequent German history. His legacy was revered by generations of German nationalists; the Nazi party all but worshiped him and even felt they were channeling his will in their rise to power. His reign was a watershed moment not just for Berlin and the Prussian state, but also for all of Europe.

The fate of Prussia took another dramatic turn in 1861 with the appointment of Otto von Bismarck as Minister President under King Wilhelm I. Perhaps the greatest diplomat of his age, Bismarck adroitly grew Prussia's power within the greater German sphere, slowly creating a unified German state with a series of treaties, alliances, and short, decisive wars with Denmark (1864), Austria (1866), and France (1870–1871). With the conclusion of the latter war, the German Empire was proclaimed, with Bismarck as its Chancellor and Wilhelm I as its Emperor. The "Second Reich"—the first being the Holy Roman Empire, which had dissolved during the Napoleonic Wars—was to last for 47 years.

Bismarck was forced out in 1890 by the new Emperor, Wilhelm II. The carefully constructed web of alliances Bismarck had spent 30 years building up to ensure Germany's security was unraveled by Wilhelm over the following two decades. The result was the Great War, lasting four years, three months, and two weeks, ending on November 11th, 1918. In addition to causing over six million German casualties, it ended a dynasty that had ruled for five centuries and sent Germany's economy into a tailspin. Berlin's citizens suffered greatly in the latter years of the war, with millions in the city and the surrounding countryside enduring privation and hunger.

On November 9th, 1918, Chancellor Prince Max von Baden declared Kaiser Wilhelm II's abdication in Berlin. Communist leader Karl Liebknecht immediately proclaimed the "Free Socialist Republic of Germany" at the City Palace, while the centrist social democrat Philipp Scheidemann prematurely pronounced the formation of the "Free German Republic" at the Reichstag.

Berlin, still Germany's capital, was rocked in the months following by street battles, mass marches, and attempted revolutions, first from the left (the Spartacist Revolt of January 1919) and then the right (the Kapp Putsch of March 1920). The assassination of Karl Liebknecht and his associate Rosa Luxemburg in January 1919 at the hands of right-wing *Freikorps* militia shocked the nation but merely signaled the beginning of three years of hundreds of political assassinations across the country. From the turmoil of these post-war years arose the shaky and uncertain Weimar Republic, so-called because the constitution was drafted in the town of Weimar, far from the turmoil of Berlin. This is the volatile situation in which Germany finds itself in the 1920s. It is telling that the German people cannot even agree on what to call their new state; some still call it the "German Reich," others favor the "German Peoples' State," while still others opt for the "German Republic." The phrase "Weimar Republic" is not coined until 1929 by Adolf Hitler, and does not achieve widespread currency until after the Republic's demise in 1933.

As if in defiance of the shattered world that surrounds it, Berlin expands in 1920, formally incorporating seven towns, 59 villages, and 27 estates. The towns of Charlottenburg, Neukölln, Spandau, and Wilmersdorf, among others, become official suburbs of Berlin, which now sprawls over 341 square miles and claims four million souls. After 500 years, Berlin is making its debut as a world city, a great sprawling metropolis to rival London or New York. With this physical transformation comes a massive shift in public and private morality that soon earns the city the nickname of "Sin Capital of the World" and the reputation as, "the prime breeding ground for evil," in the words of the *Chicago Tribune*.

Such transformation did not arise *ex nihilo*. Rather, it is the direct result of the shattering consequences of the Great War. A disaster on nearly every level for Germany, the war ruined the economy, toppled the monarchy, killed millions, and instilled its citizenry with a deep-seated distrust of the formerly invincible "Men of Iron" who had guided Germany's fate for centuries.

For the Germans who lived through the war far from the front, the last years of the conflict were marked by privation. Corruption became widespread as resources became scarcer, and ancient bonds of service and trust broke apart. Priests and officials became embroiled in get-rich-quick schemes or strange sexual scandals. The middle class, for the first time ever, acquainted itself with the realities of petty crime and black marketeering. Unplanned pregnancies were no longer the stuff of backyard gossips but instead all too common across all classes. Day-to-day survival replaced the more abstract concepts of virtue and patriotism in many minds. The psychic scars caused by these upheavals are still livid.

Berlin's openness with sex is also a result of the traumas of the war. At the front, the German soldier was issued a book of coupons, redeemable at local brothels, in an effort to somehow corral and regulate lust. The coupons determined the class of prostitute available to the soldier, as well as when he could go, how long he could stay, and which services were available, all calculated with punctilious Prussian efficiency taking in an array of variables, such as rank, class, and length of time on the front lines. The rear-area staging grounds (*Etappe*) were notorious for catering to the raunchy needs of the senior officer class, who indulged in nightly debauches with the local escorts, downing magnums of champagne amid luxurious surroundings—not unlike the scenes in many a Berlin cabaret in the decade to come.

Meanwhile, on the home front during the last, desperate months of the war, as family heirlooms and other valuables were sold off, many a Hausfrau and "straw-widow" (war bride) turned to selling her body to put food on the table. In Berlin, the city streets were flooded with desperate teens from the countryside and, eventually, from the bourgeois suburbs, peddling their flesh. This turn to the sex trade was the death knell of middle-class German respectability.

TOPOLOGY OF THE CITY

With the Greater Berlin Act of 1920, the city absorbs a number of its neighboring communities and, in so doing, becomes a sprawling metropolis covering an area four times larger than Paris. The city is officially divided into 20 boroughs. For the purposes of this book, the core of the city is divided up into "zones" based on local character and regional resources. Each of these zones is ideal for developing scenarios or simply providing local color as the investigators move about the city. Every zone description concludes with a list of features and encounters that Keepers may draw upon to communicate the character of the area.

A CITY OF SQUARES

Before getting into a discussion of the city's zones, a brief word on the overall layout of the city. Due to its fitful development, as well as its lateness in emerging as a world capital, Berlin benefits from a degree of urban planning and layout not often found in old European cities. Its main boulevards are, for the most part, straight and broad. Even the side streets tend to be spacious outside of the Alt-Berlin core, particularly more so as one moves west. Indeed, a Londoner is apt to understand Berlin's layout right away: an old city center perched upon the banks of a mighty river, with the poorer districts to the east and the newer, more upscale neighborhoods stretching off to the west, grouped around a large and rambling public park.

The real key to understanding Berlin, and navigating its environs, is to recognize the significance of the *Platz* (city square). A Platz may range in size, from a small plot of land scarcely large enough to accommodate a couple of statues and a fountain, all the way up to a massive pavilion swarming with automobile and train traffic surrounded by (or even containing) monumental civic and commercial structures.

Unter den Linden

Arguably Berlin's most well-known avenue, the boulevard called Unter den Linden (Under the Lime Trees) traverses the cultural heart of the city. The street's unusual name is derived from the now four rows of linden trees that run along much of the avenue's length. The first trees were planted in 1647 by the order of the Great Elector, back when the path linked the royal palace complex with the western hunting grounds beyond the city walls in what is today the Tiergarten. Nowadays, the street provides access to both vehicular traffic and pedestrians (along a central mall in the latter case).

Like the old Hohenzollerns, the boulevard's glory days are behind it. In the words of travel writer Joseph Hergesheimer,

it resembles "a discarded shell inhabited by parasites, empty of dignity… that belonged to the past, the world before the most recent war…" Yet, it is still a popular draw for tourists who wish to see all the classic sights of Germany's capital. Many stay at the Hotel Adlon, located within a short walk of the Brandenburg Gate. The hotel itself is a mini-palace with all the amenities one might wish for and a parade of famous and infamous guests passing through its gilded lobby on a nightly basis.

All in all, the Linden proper only runs about a mile (less than 1.6 km), starting at the world-famous Brandenburg Gate at the entrance to the **Tiergarten** (page 27), it proceeds east to the Spree River. There, it turns into Kaiser-Wilhelm-Straße and continues into Alt-Berlin, the ancient city center. But first the street must cross a wide island in the river, site of the former city of Cölln. The northern half of this island is the zone known as **Museum Island** (page 46). Also, to the north of the street, are the *Lustgarten* (Pleasure Garden) and *Berliner Dom* (Berlin Cathedral).

The Lustgarten was once a parade ground; Prussian kings would watch their troops march past from the balcony of the **City Palace** (page 46). Nowadays, the Enlightenment-era formal garden, framed by the eminent structures of the Cathedral and the **Old Museum** (page 47), and with its broad lawns and geometrically arranged promenades, serves as a public park and site for rabble-rousing political rallies—in its largest such gathering, the park overflows with 500,000 left-wing protesters in August 1921.

Although there has been a major church structure on the site of the Berlin Cathedral since 1451, the current building was completed in 1905. A massive dome rising to over 380 feet (more than 115 m) dominates the Renaissance/Baroque-revival basilica, an unusually ornate church for a Protestant faith.

Looking back down the Linden from Museum Island, we see the imposing Staatsoper (State Opera), the neoclassical temple dome of St. Hedwig's Cathedral, the Prussian State Library (**Berlin's Libraries and Museums**, page 45), and the campus of Frederick William University (also simply called the University of Berlin). It is here that the famous rows of linden trees begin.

Proceeding up the stately boulevard, we see the Brandenburg Gate dominating the end of the street. Long ago, this was the location of the city gates; in 1791, with the completion of this neoclassical monument, Berlin first earned its nickname of "Athens on the Spree." A statue of Eirene, goddess of peace, surmounts the gate, which separates through traffic into five paths amid its rows of Doric columns.

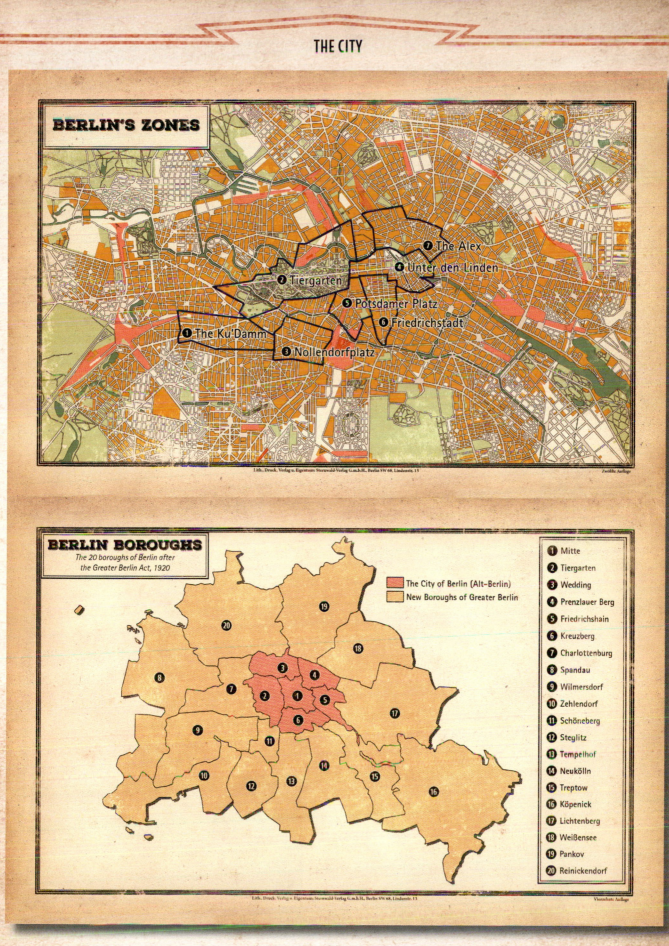

BERLIN'S ZONES

1 The Ku'Damm
2 Tiergarten
3 Nollendorfplatz
4 Unter den Linden
5 Potsdamer Platz
6 Friedrichstadt
7 The Alex

Lith., Druck, Verlag u. Eigentum Sternwald-Verlag G.m.b.H., Berlin SW 68, Lindenstr. 13 — Zwölfte Auflage

BERLIN BOROUGHS

The 20 boroughs of Berlin after the Greater Berlin Act, 1920

The City of Berlin (Alt-Berlin)
New Boroughs of Greater Berlin

1 Mitte
2 Tiergarten
3 Wedding
4 Prenzlauer Berg
5 Friedrichshain
6 Kreuzberg
7 Charlottenburg
8 Spandau
9 Wilmersdorf
10 Zehlendorf
11 Schöneberg
12 Steglitz
13 Tempelhof
14 Neukölln
15 Treptow
16 Köpenick
17 Lichtenberg
18 Weißensee
19 Pankov
20 Reinickendorf

Lith., Druck, Verlag u. Eigentum Sternwald-Verlag G.m.b.H., Berlin SW 68, Lindenstr. 13 — Vierzehnte Auflage

Berlin zones and boroughs map

Beyond the Gate, the Linden turns into Charlottenburger Chaussee and runs on through the Tiergarten.

To the north of the Linden at its western end sits the Reichstag, seat of the national parliament, and the towering *Siegessäule* (Victory Column), called *Goldelse* ("Golden Lizzy") by the locals for the shining bronze sculpture of the goddess of victory that surmounts the 200 foot (61 m) high column. The monument commemorates Prussian victories over the Danes, Austrians, and French in the 1860s and 70s, and is ringed along its entire height with captured cannon barrels from those countries.

From the area of the Gate, one may access two large public squares: Pariser Platz (where may be found the American and French embassies, as well as the grand Adlon) and the Platz der Republik (formerly the Königsplatz), where may be found the Victory Column.

On the other side of Museum Island, the north bank of the Spree constitutes Old Berlin, the original site of the city. Here may be found the towered *Rotes Rathaus* (Red City Hall), the densely populated area around the *Marienkirche* (St. Mary's Church), the Berlin Exchange, the Neues Stadthaus (a new city administration building), and the pocket district of the Nikolaiviertel. The latter is a preserved section of medieval Berlin centered on the 13th century Romanesque basilica of St. Nicholas' Church. Claustrophobic alleyways and shadowed streets wind their way out from the church to the surrounding city. Yet here may also be found some of Berlin's finest residences: the Rococo splendor of the Ephraim-Palais (said to comprise "Berlin's finest corner") and the red sandstone riverside expanse of the *Kurfürstenhaus* (Prince-Elector's House), whence Elector John Sigismund of Brandenburg fled and subsequently died of fright after seeing a White Lady haunting the halls of the City Palace in 1619.

UNTER DEN LINDEN

Site	Name/Details
House of Worship	Berlin Cathedral
Site of Interest, Mundane	Prussian State Library
Site of Interest, Unusual	The eponymous trees
Chief Contact	Doorman at the Hotel Adlon
Gang or Organization	*Immertreu* (Always Faithful)
Nightlife	The Hotel Adlon
Ongoing Problem	Public drunkenness
Prostitution	Fohses, Demi-Castors

The Victory Column

The Tiergarten

Literally "Animal Garden," this region (currently covering 630 acres/255 hectares) was once a hunting preserve for the Kings of Prussia and populated with bounding deer. Nowadays, a different sort of animal, the "Grasshopper," may be found here, peddling her fleshy wares (**Prostitution**, page 53).

The largest public park in the city, the remoter parts are dimly lit and dangerous after dark, but the Siegesallee (Victory Avenue) is a popular spot for promenades. This broad boulevard is adorned with 32 marble statues of kings, margraves, and electors from the history of Prussia and Brandenburg stretching all the way back to Albert the Bear. Behind each statue is a semi-circular marble bench flanked by busts of two of that ruler's advisors.

The park also features a large zoo, the Zoologischer Garten, opened nearly a century ago as the first of its kind in Germany. Over 13,000 animals dwell here, including lions, elephants, and tigers; many are kept in architecturally distinctive animal houses: the main gate is constructed in a Japanese style, the Antelope House is Moorish in fashion, while the Ostrich House recalls ancient Egypt. Fronting on Kurfürstendamm but accessible from the zoo is the city's aquarium, opened in 1913, housing both saltwater and freshwater fish, crocodiles, amphibians of many varieties, and even an "insectarium" on the top floor. Also to be found on a secluded and quiet street within the park is the Institut für Sexualwissenschaft, the **Institute of Sexology** (page 50).

The northern edge of the Tiergarten proper is formed by the winding banks of the Spree, but the district encompasses land to the north of the river as well. For the purposes of this book, the "zone" of the Tiergarten runs along Alt-Moabit and includes the *Kleiner* (Little) Tiergarten and the nearby Criminal Court complex: two massive, stern buildings completed in the late 19th century that serve as a central clearing house for all criminal cases from all levels of Berlin law. Large prison complexes on the property hold male and female defendants awaiting trial, while a labyrinth of offices provides judges and lawyers with cramped working spaces to prepare and review cases. The air quality in these echoing halls and chambers is so bad that lawyers have been known to pass smelling salts to witnesses to keep them alert during testimony.

Walking farther east to the termination of the Alt-Moabit and crossing the Alsen Bridge over Humboldt Harbor one arrives at Berlin's greatest hospital, the Charité. Founded in 1709 by Frederick I to function as a quarantine house for victims of the plague, it has functioned as a teaching hospital associated with Frederick William University since 1810.

TIERGARTEN

Site	Name/Details
House of Worship	Kaiser-Frederick-Memorial Church
Site of Interest, Mundane	Zoological Gardens
Site of Interest, Unusual	Dr. Hirschfeld's Institute of Sexology
Chief Contact	Criminal Court Judge
Gang or Organization	*Libelle* (Dragonfly)
Nightlife	Picnics and evening strolls
Ongoing Problem	Muggers in the park
Prostitution	Line-Boys, Grasshoppers

The Zoological Gardens

Alexanderplatz

One of the city's great public squares, the Alexanderplatz ("the Alex") is located in Berlin's *Mitte* (middle) district. The ten blocks encircling the Alex are home to over 320 whorehouses, or at least places to meet up for a quick tryst ("Hour Hotels" and "Transient-Quarters"). Among the most luxurious of the "proper" brothels is one catering exclusively to heterosexual women. Many back-alley businesses in this area do double-duty, as with an ice cream parlor on the Mehnerstraße that gives new meaning to the term "soda jerk" after 10:00 pm.

The most desperate prostitutes walk around the Alex, and in it may be found the most disreputable dives. Yet, it is also a beating heart, constantly alive with vehicular and pedestrian traffic, the Stadtbahn roaring by overhead. Those in search of the most forbidden pleasures and experiences are advised to start here.

As if placed here as a guardian over the square's shifty inhabitants, the *Polizeipräsidium* (Police Headquarters) looks down over the square with its grand neo-Baroque, glass-domed tower. Inside the Headquarters, in a small annex on the ground floor, is a Museum of Crime, open to the public,

in which may be found several small exhibition halls. Each hall contains tables and glass cabinets full of displays of evidence used in successful criminal prosecution: kitchen knives, bits of rope, poisoned nutmegs, old jars, tattered clothing, and so on. There are also copious photographs of criminals, their victims, and crime scenes; examples of criminal identification technology (fingerprints, photos of earlobes); and dusty gewgaws of the forensic science trade (test tubes and assorted laboratory apparatus).

Emphasizing the working-class nature of this area, just off the square sits Karl-Liebknecht-Haus, a five-story former factory that now serves as the headquarters of the Communist Party of Germany. The nerve center of Berlin's powerful Red population, the purpose of this building is unmistakable: it is festooned with massive letters proclaiming various Communist slogans, as well as a large portrait of Vladimir Lenin.

The Alex also encompasses the surrounding neighborhoods of north Berlin. Like the Alexanderplatz itself, these are, as a general rule, the low-rent, seedier mirror images to the glitzier neighborhoods of the **Friedrichstadt** (page 29) or the **Ku'damm** (page 30). Some of the city's roughest underground dives may be found among these streets, nestled in between rambling tenements overflowing with *Ostlanders* (Poles, Roma, and Jews from the east). Indeed, Oranienburger Straße has formed the core of Berlin's Jewish population since the 18th century, when Frederick William I allowed Jewish settlement in this quarter of the city known as the *Scheunenviertel* (Barn Quarter). Here stands the incomparably grand New Synagogue (completed 1866), with its glazed bricks and Moorish-style domes. The interior, lit by innumerable delicate stained-glass windows, seats 3,000 and, in addition to the usual religious functions, hosts musical concerts, including one in 1930 with Albert Einstein on violin!

Oranienburger Straße brings the scuzzy charms of the Alex right up against the gay nightlife of Friedrichstadt, and nowhere is this more obvious than at the Friedrichstraßenpassage. Prior to the Great War, this five-story mall with entrances on both Oranienburger Straße and Friedrichstraße was a consumerist mecca. After the war, the businesses inside failed and the owners abandoned the property, leaving it to stand for a decade as an empty shell inhabited only by prostitutes and drug dealers. In 1928, it is taken over and refurbished by the electrical giant AEG and turned into a massive showroom for new technology, called the Haus der Technik.

THE ALEX

Site	Name/Details
House of Worship	The New Synagogue
Site of Interest, Mundane	Clärchens Ballhaus
Site of Interest, Unusual	The Blue Stocking (page 54)
Chief Contact	Police Inspector
Gang or Organization	*Norddeutscher Ring* (North German Ring)
Nightlife	Stork's Nest Cabaret (page 66)
Ongoing Problem	Sexual slavery
Prostitution	Grasshoppers, Chontes

Nestled in between the Friedrichstraßenpassage and the Weidendammer Bridge over the Spree is the *Großes Schauspielhaus* (Great Playhouse), the city's most singular performance space. Originally a market hall, then a circus, in 1919 the building is converted into a performance space and playhouse. The stage extends out in to the circular auditorium under a massive dome ringed with stalactite-esque ornaments in a truly breathtaking example of Expressionist architecture. Lights set into the rows between the "stalactites" create night-sky effects by sending constellation patterns across the cavernous dome's interior. The lobby and other areas of the building are lit by a variety of colored bulbs inside recessed and organically shaped pillars. Backstage, cast and crew enjoy their own fine accommodations: a barber, spacious dressing areas, and even a bar.

Finally, amid the general squalor and desperation of the Alex may still be found the occasional jewel of culture. *Clärchens Ballhaus* (Clara's Ballroom) on Auguststraße offers the incongruous pleasure of rough-handed workmen and tough ex-cons taking their wives and molls out for an evening of fine dancing in a large mirrored ballroom—to be followed by a few rounds of bowling in the ballroom's basement.

The Friedrichstadt

Berlin's downtown district stands in stark contrast to the Alexanderplatz. Bisected by the Friedrichstraße, the city's main north-south artery, are luxury hotels, government buildings (the Prussian parliament meets here), churches, museums, business high-rises (chiefly financial and publishing houses), many upscale theaters such as the Konzerthaus, and indoor shopping arcades like the Kaisergalerie. Many of these are centered on the Gendarmenmarkt, the original cultural center of Berlin; Friedrichstraße has sometimes been called "Berlin's Champs-Élysées."

Yet the Friedrichstadt's glory days are behind it. The chief destination for shopping and entertainment prior to the War, it has since lost that crown to the Ku'damm. Now its square-mile area is increasingly home to gay bars, strip clubs, massage parlors, and greasy spoons, as well as the sleazy Linden Passage, an arcade 300 yards (274 m) long. Like the Friedrichstraßenpassage, it was once an upscale shopping and entertainment emporium that nowadays mostly serves as a place for Doll-Boys (young male teenage prostitutes) to strut their stuff. No other spot in Berlin more aptly illustrates the fallen fortunes of the city than this Wilhelmine monument

An illegal transaction in "The Alex"

THE FRIEDRICHSTADT

Site	Name/Details
House of Worship	French Cathedral
Site of Interest, Mundane	Kerkau-Palast
Site of Interest, Unusual	Anatomical Wonder Cabinet
Chief Contact	Well-off Pimp/Theatrical Agent
Gang or Organization	*Reichsverein ehemaliger Strafgefangener* (Rich Ex-Convicts' Club)
Nightlife	The Chat Noir
Ongoing Problem	Pickpockets and beggars
Prostitution	Doll-Boys

to Neo-Baroque excess and splendor now serving as a pick-up joint for underage prostitutes.

These two sides of the Friedrichstadt operate independently of each other. When the sun comes up, the area is flooded with businessmen and civil servants in hat and tie, going about their daily business; however, after the commuter hordes leave at 5:00 pm, the bars open and the real fun begins, lasting until around 3:00 in the morning. In addition to a profusion of clubs and bars, the swarming hordes of tourists and party-goers might spend some time at the Kerkau-Palast, a massive hall containing 48 pool tables—as well as rooms for chess-playing—founded by the carom billiards champion Hugo Kerkau, or indulge in a bit of titillation at the Anatomical Wonder Cabinet, an all-nude show dedicated to "documenting female beauty—no children allowed!"

The Ku'damm

The city's neon-lit midway for high-end shopping and expensive nightclubs, the Kurfürstendamm is almost universally referred to as "the Ku'damm." Running through the western boroughs of Charlottenburg and Wilmersdorf, the Ku'damm also boasts some of the finest examples of Berlin nightlife: cabarets featuring cross-dressing performers, cafés catering to lesbian clientele, bars in the American style, and pleasure palaces. The Ku'damm is where most of the semi-professional "Half-Silk" prostitutes come after they knock off their day shifts, and where Boot-Girls stand outside expensive boutiques, offering their own version of merchandise.

Heading east along the boulevard at the Auguste-Viktoria-Platz, the Ku'damm turns into Tauentzienstraße, hunting grounds of the infamously stylish "T-Girls"—mother-daughter prostitute teams that are always on the cutting edge of fashion and ready with a quick quip for journalists (or investigators) looking for the latest street gossip. The Auguste-Viktoria-Platz is also the site of three famous Berlin institutions: the Romanisches Café, the Kaiser Wilhelm Memorial Church, and the Heaven and Hell Club (**Romanisches Forum**, page 49).

Anchoring Tauentzienstraße at its eastern end is the formidable Kaufhaus des Westens (colloquially and affectionately called the "KaDeWe"), one of Berlin's great department stores. Opened in 1907, the sprawling site covers 260,000 square feet (more than 24,150 square meters) spread over five stories. So popular is the store that it single-handedly transforms Tauentzienstraße from a quiet residential street to a bustling commercial extension of the Ku'damm. In 1929, the store is enlarged even more. Within, customers may shop for everything from luxury Paris fashions and exotic foods to everyday items. The store provides a bridal registry, tailor,

hairdressing, hotel and home delivery, money changing, and even buggy and car rentals. The top-floor food court is one of the most popular destinations for casual dining in the city.

The Ku'damm's destination status is strictly a post-war phenomenon. Long a quiet suburban avenue, it is only after the Great War that the Ku'damm supplants Friedrichstraße as the city's premier hotspot; this does not sit well with traditionalists and reactionaries, many of whom see the Ku'damm as emblematic of Berlin's fallen status. The region's large Jewish population only adds fuel to the fire of anti-Semitic Nationalists (Organisation Consul in the early-1920s, Bund Wiking in the mid-1920s, and the National Socialists in the late-1920s and early-1930s) who link Berlin's moral degradation with imagined Jewish conspiracies. As a result, the street and its neighborhoods are subject to increasing civil unrest and turmoil, culminating in 1932 with mass attacks on Jewish-owned businesses and worshippers leaving synagogues on the night of Rosh Hashanah.

THE KU-DAMM

Site	Name/Details
House of Worship	Kaiser-Wilhelm-Memorial Church
Site of Interest, Mundane	KaDeWe
Site of Interest, Unusual	Romanisches Café
Chief Contact	Mother & Daughter T-Girl Team
Gang or Organization	Organisation Consul/Bund Wiking/National Socialists
Nightlife	Heaven and Hell Club
Ongoing Problem	Agitation and street battles started by right-wing groups
Prostitution	Half-Silks, Boot-Girls

Potsdamer Platz

Located in the geographic heart of the city, at the intersection of five major thoroughfares, this is perhaps the city's most iconic single locale—the Piccadilly Circus or Times Square of Berlin, if you will. The traffic is nonstop; the Platz is said to be one of the first places in the world where traffic lights were installed. In its very center stands an instantly recognizable control tower where a solitary policeman manually switches the lights, monitoring traffic from on high.

Potsdamer Platz and the adjacent Leipziger Platz are homes to shopping venues, restaurants, hotels, and cafés. Just west of the square may be found a number of former foreign embassies (the so-called "Millionaire's Quarter"); many now converted into multi-unit rentals. In the early part of the 1920s, the most prominent hotel in the area is the Hotel Fürstenhof, situated directly on the Platz, with its neo-Baroque, proto-Art Nouveau architecture.

The massive Wertheim department store towers over the plaza, offering thousands of square feet of consumerist bliss and, with its own bank, theatre, restaurants, laundry, and gardens, is practically a city unto itself.

POTSDAMER PLATZ

Site	Name/Details
House of Worship	St. Matthew Church
Site of Interest, Mundane	Hotel Excelsior (from the mid-1920s)
Site of Interest, Unusual	Traffic Light Tower (from 1924)
Chief Contact	Foreign Ambassador
Gang or Organization	*Freie Vereinigung* (Free Association)
Nightlife	Haus Potsdam/Vaterland
Ongoing Problem	The busiest intersection in Europe
Prostitution	Half-Silks, Pharmacies

The Haus Potsdam (after 1928, the **Haus Vaterland**, page 48) is the greatest pleasure palace in the city, encompassing a massive cinema, grand café (the largest in the world), and a number of restaurants, each themed around a particular cuisine of the world. The locale's slogan is *"die Welt in einem Haus"* ("the world in one house").

Unlike other major city centers, Potsdamer Platz is relatively free of evident vice. The upper-class neighborhoods around the site would never permit it, at least not overtly. Yet, it is said, many are the seemingly innocuous residences and storefronts that are in actuality covers for high-end brothels and scandalous underage prostitution rings (the so-called "Pharmacies", see **Prostitution: Medicine**, page 54).

The busiest train station in the city is the Potsdamer Bahnhof, its façade fronting directly onto the square. The main station plus its two wings services both long-haul trains from Paris, Strasbourg, and other points west, as well as the suburban Ringbahn and the Wannsee lines that take Berliners out to the lush woods and sparkling lakes of the western Havelland.

A half-mile (800 m) south of Potsdamer Platz proper sits the great brick-and-glass monument to industry known as Anhalter Bahnhof; the "Gateway to the South," this is one of Berlin's five principle train stations and is the largest and grandest station not just in Berlin, but in all of Germany. Completed in 1880, the 100-foot-high (30.5 m) steel and glass roof encompasses six station platforms that accommodate up to 40,000 travelers per day aboard trains that arrive and depart every five minutes. The station's lines service Munich, Frankfurt-am-Main, Dresden, Vienna, Rome, Athens, and other southerly destinations.

After 1929, travelers arriving via the Anhalter station may take a 300 foot (90 m) long underground tunnel (complete with its own shops) connecting to the Hotel Excelsior, the latest crown jewel of Berlin's high-end hotels. Expanded over the 1920s from a failing 200-room facility, by 1930 the Excelsior sprawls over 81,000 square feet (more than 7,525 square meters) and 600 rooms, nine restaurants, and a library, making it the largest hotel in Europe at the time. The hotel maintains its own bakery and butcher shop, and its newsstand stocks 200 daily papers from Europe, the Americas, and elsewhere.

Nollendorfplatz

This working-class area, which includes the adjacent neighborhoods of Nollendorfplatz and Wilmersdorf, is located to the south of Berlin's sparkling west end. It is also a hub of Berlin's gay and lesbian community and home to Erwin Piscator's Communist theater, the Neues Schauspielhaus, which seats 1,200 people; on the upper floor is the Mozartsalle, now a major cinema hosting film premieres.

The Schubert-Saal, a "neighborhood" theater, is the site of frequent gay and lesbian balls, as well as "Bad-Boy Balls" and "beach parties" put on by the *Damenklub Altes Geld* (Old-Money Ladies' Club). This area abounds with lesbian and gay *Dielen* (bars) and clubs. In 1928, the famous drag club Eldorado opens a second location just off Nollendorfplatz proper. Here, is the neighborhood of Christopher Isherwood, W. H. Auden, Jean Ross, and many other expatriate writers and bohemians. This proletarian stronghold is also a major distribution point for the city's cocaine trade and a locus of various sadomasochistic clubs and brothels catering to clients of both sexes.

The run-down apartments in this district are blackened and soot-stained, and a constant smog hangs over the area due to the proliferation of coal fires burning in stoves and heaters. The once-grand buildings are falling into ruin, victims of economic collapse. Stucco and plaster peel off and fall like snowflakes to the ground below. In the words of Sir Stephen Spencer, "A peculiar and all-pervading smell of hopeless decay comes out of the interiors of these grandiose houses, now converted into pretentious slums."

NOLLENDORFPLATZ

Site	Name/Details
House of Worship	Twelve Apostles Church
Site of Interest, Mundane	The Neues Schauspielhaus
Site of Interest, Unusual	The Eldorado Clubs
Chief Contact	Communist Party Organizer
Gang or Organization	Berliner Ring
Nightlife	The Pyramid Women's Club (see **Claire Waldoff**, page 86)
Ongoing Problem	Urban decay
Prostitution	Race Horses

Schöneberg

Located to the south of Nollendorfplatz, Schöneberg has transformed over the last 30 years from an almost provincial village to one of city's classiest, most upscale districts. Home to a large number of Bavarians, the district is also sometimes called the Bavarian Quarter. But it is the district's Jewish population who are chiefly responsible for its transformation. Starting in the late 19th century, the textile manufacturer Salomon Haberland and his son Georg began buying up properties in the village of Schöneberg and building large, country-style houses with an eye toward creating a desirable commuter suburb for well-off Berliners. The plan worked better than they might have hoped, and by the dawn of the Great War, the town was populated with sprawling 10-room estates, all decked out in full Wilhelmine splendor.

The district's centerpiece is Viktoria-Luise Platz (called "Vicki" by the locals). Less than a mile south of the Ku'damm, with its fountains and border colonnades, it feels like a different world entirely. Here may be found some of Schöneberg's finest mansions, as well as a variety of restaurants and cafés catering to locals and visitors alike.

The area around Bayerischer Platz, meanwhile is home to many artists and intellectuals, including psychoanalyst Erich Fromm and film writer/director Billy Wilder. The district's most well-known resident, however, is unquestionably the physicist Albert Einstein, who maintains a residence at Haberlandstraße 5 from 1911 to 1933.

"Vicki"

The Grunewald

Six miles (9.6 km) southwest of the bustling city center, the 7,500-acre (3,035-hectare) Grunewald forest stands in stark and bucolic contrast to the nonstop urban mania of Berlin. A mixture of coniferous forest and glacial lakes, the Grunewald is also dotted with the so-called "mansion colonies" of the city's industrialists and political movers and shakers. Foreign Minister Walther Rathenau, famously, is assassinated in 1922 while driving from his Grunewald mansion to the Reichstag. But the Grunewald isn't an exclusive retreat for the super-rich; although the countryside around Berlin is replete with lush forests and cool lakes, the Grunewald remains the favorite destination for Berliners of all classes to escape for an afternoon or weekend of recreation and relaxation.

There are eight lakes within the Grunewald proper, and the Wannsee, a lake-like bight of the mighty River Havel, with its famous artificial beach, is only a short distance from the woods. Berliners flock to these lakes in the hot months for cooling dips in the water or stately jaunts aboard boats and small yachts. On the banks of one of these lakes, the Halensee, at the very terminus of the Ku'damm, sits Luna Park, a massive, rambling amusement park deliberately modeled on New York's Coney Island. The largest amusement park in Europe, complete with restaurants, theaters, cabarets, and beer halls, as well as a large water slide, a swimming pool with an artificial wave machine, a mountain railway, and a shaking staircase with a skirt-lifting fan at the end. Shuttered during the Great War, the park re-opens in 1918 as a shadow of its former glorious self; a creaking, dilapidated remnant of past glory—Luna Park is featured in **Schreckfilm**, page 208.

Other attractions in the forest include the all-brick Kaiser Wilhelm Tower (180 feet/50 m tall), situated on top of the Karlsberg and offering spectacular views of the surrounding countryside, along with the Grunewald Casino, a restaurant and gaming parlor. Also of note is the building that gave the region its name: the Grunewald Hunting Lodge. The oldest Prussian palace in Berlin (built in 1543), it passed to state ownership in 1918 after 350 years of use by the Hohenzollern nobility. There are currently plans under consideration to turn the building into an art gallery. Who's to say what strange ghosts haunt its ancient halls?

On the topic of ghosts, there is one section of the Grunewald shunned by the usual crowd of happy tourists: the so-called **Suicides' Cemetery** (page 67). It is an unhappy phenomenon of nature that suicides throwing themselves into the Havel and tributary waterways wash up along the same stretch of riverbank here, well outside the city. For more details on their nearby burial site, see **Berlin's Cemeteries** (page 67).

Suicides' Cemetery

THE GRUNEWALD

Site	Name/Details
House of Worship	Grunewaldkirche
Site of Interest, Mundane	The Funkturm
Site of Interest, Unusual	Suicides' Cemetery
Chief Contact	Rich Industrialist
Gang or Organization	Wild-Boys
Nightlife	Luna Park
Ongoing Problem	Suicides in the Havel River
Prostitution	Grasshoppers

VERWALTUNGSBEZIRKE OF BERLIN

Berlin comprises 20 administrative boroughs (*Verwaltungsbezirke*) grouped according to their former administrative status prior to the 1920 unification.

Players creating investigators living in Berlin may simply choose where their characters reside or leave it up to a random roll. For truly random results, roll 1D20 on the **Berlin Boroughs** table. For results distributed more in accordance with population density, roll 1D100. Keepers may, of course, also use this table to determine the borough of origin of minor NPCs.

BERLIN BOROUGHS

1D20	1D100	Borough
1	01–09	Friedrichshain
2	10–19	Kreuzberg
3	20–27	Mitte
4	28–35	Prenzlauer Berg
5	36–42	Tiergarten
6	43–51	Wedding
7	52–60	Charlottenburg
8	61	Köpenick
9	62–66	Lichtenberg
10	67–74	Neukölln
11	75–80	Schöneberg
12	81–83	Spandau
13	84–87	Wilmersdorf
14	88–89	Pankow
15	90–91	Reinickendorf
16	92–95	Steglitz
17	96–97	Tempelhof
18	98	Treptow
19	99	Weißensee
20	00	Zehlendorf

FEATURES OF BERLIN

This section focuses on different aspects of Berlin, including the weather, transportation, communications, and housing.

WEATHER AND CLIMATE

The fact that Berlin was built on a swamp never escapes the mention of those who condemn it as a breeding-ground of immorality and evil. The city possesses its own distinctive, alkaline air ("*Berliner Luft*"), said to stimulate and degrade the central nervous system—leading to an unleashing of long-repressed passions, or so claim the moralists.

Berlin boasts a temperate maritime climate. Winter temperatures hover around the freezing point in general, while summers are mild and not terribly humid. Spring remains chilly until May, and the fall sets in quickly after harvest time. Rainfall is moderate (around 1–2 inches/2.5–5 cm per month) but steady; gray skies and precipitation are encountered year-round, though summer months can be quite sunny and pleasant. Snowfall usually starts in December and lasts through February, but almost never in great heaping amounts—just enough to lend the city a storybook air and rime the windows with frost.

What this amounts to (for the Keeper) is license to drape the city in whatever sort of weather best fits the scenario's atmosphere. Chill winds and fog? Pouring rain? Eerily quiet snowfall? For much of the year, some—or all—of these meteorological phenomena are perfectly acceptable. As the world-weary reporter Joseph Roth famously observed, "Berlin is freezing even when it's 60 degrees"—granted he was talking more about the coldness and callousness he saw around him, but there's no reason this shouldn't be reflected in the literal climate of the scenario as well.

GETTING AROUND

Despite the city's sprawling size, it is relatively easy to get around in Berlin. Two urban rail networks, electric tramlines, and a large fleets of cabs and busses serve the city. Getting to the city is best accomplished by rail, but airplanes and automobiles are also an option.

There are daily flights from London's Croydon airfield to Berlin's Staaken Aerodrome. The flights are not direct, stopping over in Rotterdam, Amsterdam, Bremen, or Hamburg. Other flights, from Paris or Rome for example, may arrive at Tempelhof Airfield.

Berlin has five great terminal railway stations: Anhalter, Potsdam, Lehrte, Stettiner, and Görlitzer. These stations serve travelers arriving from the southwest, the west, the northwest, the northeast, and the south, respectively. The

Stadtbahn stations of Charlottenburg, Friedrichstraße, Alexanderplatz, Silesian, and Zoo also serve cross-country trains. The Stadtbahn (it will not earn its moniker of "S-Bahn" until 1930) comprises two steam-locomotive metro rail lines: the Stadtbahn itself, which runs over 8 miles (13 km) of track around the north side of the city, and the Ringbahn, which connects the northern suburbs with the southern districts over 24 miles (39 km) of tracks. Trains run nearly 24 hours a day (from 4:30 am to 1:00 am), with cars arriving every 2–5 minutes (for the Stadtbahn) or 6–15 minutes (for the Ringbahn). Rarified passengers may purchase second-class tickets (in contrast to the general third-class ticket), but even the second-class cars are packed at rush hour.

The U-bahn (short for *Untergrundbahn*, or underground railway) is an electric metro rail line. Despite its name, some sections travel on elevated platforms or through railway cuttings. There are seven lines in all, each providing access to the city center. Trains running between Alexanderplatz and Wittenburgplatz (at the terminal point of Tauentzienstraße in the Ku'damm) run every 5 minutes; wait times on other lines and at other stations are more typically 10–20 minutes. Like the Stadtbahn, tickets may be purchased in second- or third-class. The U-Bahn is extremely popular, and cars are nearly always crowded; during rush hour and on holidays, they are crammed full.

The city is crisscrossed with electric tramway routes (the Straßenbahn): 103 in all, with the last cars departing Mitte at 1:45 am. Fares and services are extremely variable. The tramlines serve mostly the central city districts, but there are three lines running out to the suburbs of Spandau, Köpenick, and the southwest districts.

Where trams or urban rail won't suffice, a bus or cab is almost always close at hand. Buses are double-decker designs of the type familiar to any Londoner. In the evenings, horse-drawn buses are available to ferry theatergoers back to their home districts. Cabs proliferate and may be hailed from the curbside or called for (at an extra charge). Police only guarantee passengers' safety within a radius defined by Pankow in the north, Friedrichsfelde in the east, Britz and Friedenau in the south, and Grunewald in the west. Beyond this radius, cab drivers are also free to charge whatever fares they like.

One of Berlin's more unusual features is the Cyclonette Cab, a three-wheeled, open-air vehicle, offering a less costly alternative to an automobile cab (around 25% cheaper), for the obvious tradeoff of a less salubrious ride. What's more, they cannot accommodate any luggage beyond a valise and seat, at most, two passengers.

Getting around town in style!

MEDIA AND COMMUNICATION

Berlin, being a world capital, boasts every form of media and communication available, from the telegraph to radio, and from the cinema to newspapers. It is in this last regard that Berlin is particularly notable. This is a golden age of journalism in Germany, and Berlin is the unquestioned giant for those who wish to work in the industry. The city boasts a staggering 60 daily newspapers, along with 630 weekly or monthly periodicals. Newspapers (*Zeitungen*) are far and away the most common form of mass-media communication in Berlin, outstripping even radio, and many a Berliner may be seen walking with a paper tucked under an arm or reading in cafés or on trams.

AVIATION

Tempelhof Airport

One of the first airports in Berlin, Tempelhof is designated an airport in 1923, with its first route being between Berlin and Munich. By 1925, routes include Moscow, Peking (taking over a month to arrive!), and Zürich. Transatlantic flights begin in 1928. Tempelhof also services flights between London and Berlin. The airport's name stems from the site on which it was built, which was formerly land owned by the Knights Templar in medieval Berlin.

Johannisthal Airfield

Situated southeast of central Berlin, Johannisthal was Germany's first commercial airfield, opening in 1909. From 1910, the site was the home of several well-known aviation companies, like Fokker Aeroplanbau, Albatros Werke AG, and Luft-Verkehrs-Gesellschaft AG. The first airship hangar was erected in April 1910, with a second following in 1911. With the opening of Tempelhof Airport in 1923, the use of the airfield diminishes.

Berlin-Staaken Aerodrome

An airfield on the west side of Berlin, Berlin-Staaken is situated close to what was a Zeppelin construction plant, now, one of the large hangars is rented out as a sound stage for epic-scale film projects. The site is a hub for for people traveling across the Atlantic by airship, as well as those heading to London.

Popular papers include the conservative *Berliner Lokal-Anzeiger*, the centrist *Voßische Zeitung* (founded in 1722, it is Berlin's oldest periodical), the Socialist *Vorwärts*, the Communist *Rote Fahne*, and the nationalistic and anti-Semitic *Deutsche Zeitung*. English-language papers are also widely available at stalls and kiosks. The *Chicago Tribune* maintains an office and reading room at the Hotel Adlon, while the *Chicago Daily News* has an office on Unter den Linden. The *Manchester Guardian* has offices in Berlin, on Potsdamer Straße. Lastly, a locally produced paper called *The Daily Berlin American* prints stories of local interest in English.

Berlin's innumerable post offices are divided into nine districts, each office designated with a letter (for the district) and number. *Poste Restante* (general delivery) letters and parcels may be picked up at Office C2 on Heiligegeist Straße in Alt-Berlin, just a short walk from Marienkirche. Letters may be delivered to any office, but parcels may be sent only to the larger distribution centers. Airmail letters may be dispatched from the red letterbox at the Hotel Bristol on Unter den Linden.

Post offices, regardless of size, are open from 8:00 am to 7:00 pm Monday through Saturday, but just from 8:00 am to 9:45 am on Sundays and holidays. Nearly all offices also offer telegraph, telephone, and pneumatic mail services for a nominal fee. Telegraphs may be sent via one of 113 branch offices attached to post offices (or sometimes found on their own), which are open 24 hours a day.

Public telephone booths can be found in post offices, some government and public buildings, and the larger city squares (Alexanderplatz, Wilhelmplatz). Local calls are charged in increments of three minutes. Trunk calls (long-distance calls booked in advance) may be made from one of 63 post offices.

The whole city of Berlin is connected by a spider's web of 250 miles (402 km) of underground pneumatic tubes. Called the Rohrpost, this system enables letters, cards, telegrams, and small parcels to be sent from any of 90 offices around the city to their intended recipient within two hours of sending. Post offices offering this service have a red lamp hanging outside the door.

HOUSING

Some three-quarters of Berlin's buildings are relatively modern, the results of the construction boom in the 19th century. Travelers from other parts of Europe, particularly Londoners and Parisians, have been known to criticize Berlin for its drab, uniform architectural style, citing a sort of gray sameness on street after street. The predominant architectural styles are a mix of Neo-Baroque and Italian Renaissance Revival, but more and more Modernist buildings are appearing, particularly in the city's peripheries. Residential buildings nearly always boast balconies and terraces that inevitably sport potted flowers and plants in the warmer months.

The city's avenues are broad; even in the old parts of town there are very few dank, winding alleys of the sort you might encounter in Paris or London. In the busiest parts of the city, traffic (human, animal, and motorized) is near constant regardless of the time of day or night and is often overwhelming.

New arrivals in the city may seek accommodation at a variety of hotels and hostels. The best hotels in Berlin, located in or near Unter den Linden, Potsdamer Platz, and the Zoological Garden, boast central heating, electric light fixtures, private baths, and elevators, as well as their own bar-and-grill restaurants. Breakfasts are included in the fee, and guests are expected to eat their morning meal there.

In the city, there are a dozen hospices ("especially recommended for ladies traveling alone," according to Baedeker); some provide meals in addition to lodging. There are also *hôtels garni*, equivalent to the English "bed and breakfasts," some of which also serve hot or cold lunches and suppers. *Pensionate* (boarding houses) are available for those with more long-term plans for staying in the city.

Mietskaserne

Beginning around 1860 and lasting until the Great War, Berlin underwent an ambitious construction boom that left the city nearly unrecognizable. Many of the buildings that went up in the new Reich's capital were housing blocks called *Mietskaserne* (tenements). These massive housing blocks take up every available square inch of real estate on their lots, cramming in as many tenants as possible. Collectively, they squat in a large ring around the old city, comprising their own district of sorts: the Wilhemine Ring. Universally five stories high, with stucco-fronted facades that come right up to the sidewalk, the tenement blocks famously boast interconnected corridors of tiny courtyards, each a mere 300 square feet (28 square meters) in area: the legal minimum to allow fire truck access.

Floor plans and amenities serve considerations of space first, while tenants' comfort comes second. The flats facing the street are the most luxurious, with wooden molding, fine parquet floors, and other thoughtful architectural touches, not to mention plenty of natural light from the windows. Most flats in a *Mietskaserne*, however, are best described as resembling a shoebox: a long rectangle with bedrooms at the front and back, and a common area and kitchen in the middle. The farther back one goes in the tenement block, the grimmer and smaller the flats become, with some lacking windows entirely. Overall, only about one in seven have their own toilet and bath, while two-thirds cannot claim any bathroom facilities at all, relying instead on water closets installed at the staircase landings.

Population in a *Mietskaserne* skews toward the working class, with middle-class residents taking the street-side flats. Many flats are sub-let, housing "shifts" of tenants who occupy the flat at different times of the day and night. Nearly one in five tenants, the so-called "sleepers-in," are too poor to afford even this, and instead rent bed space by the hour. Tenancy in these blocks can reach as high as 2,000 people, necessitating their own beat cops to patrol the premises.

One final note for Anglophone investigators: it is standard practice in Germany (even to this day) not to number apartments; mail is delivered by surname, not apartment number.

BEINLS AND BULLS: CRIME AND PUNISHMENT

Much like America in the 1930s, Jazz Age Germans are fascinated with crime, criminals, and gangsterism. The financial and political turmoil of the post-war years has proven ripe for the rise of criminality. Berlin is, for the first time, a world city and a major metropolis, and its residents are just waking up to the fact that with such status comes a certain anonymity that emboldens thieves and murderers. Berlin's citizens track daily newspaper reports of crime with a certain fascinated avidity; after all, *anyone* could be the next victim. There is a widespread sense that security is a rapidly disappearing memory and that the rule of law is disintegrating.

UNDERGROUND BERLIN

The pneumatic tubes of the Rohrpost run through hundreds of miles of service tunnels. The U-Bahn traverses more than 70 miles (113 km) of subterranean tubes. Five thousand miles (8,050 km) of sewer tunnels crisscross the entirety of the city. There are even numerous private tunnels, like that connecting the Anhalter Bahnhof and Excelsior Hotel, to say nothing of "unofficial" connections between ancient cellars and basements. For those who know how to navigate this system, they can travel great distances beneath the city streets, safe from the prying eyes of those above ground.

Just as the city is coming into its own, so too is Berlin's criminal underclass. After all, someone has to manage all the sex and drugs flowing through the city. These managers operate behind the open lie that they are members of "professional sports clubs," "entertainment clubs," or "benevolent societies" (all categorized under the umbrella term *Ringvereine*, or "ring clubs," so-called for the rings or other such badges worn by members). These clubs present every indication of being organized for the benefit of sport enthusiasts or like-minded brethren, and they even have membership dues, statutes and rules, and weekly meetings. Behind the deception of mutual aid societies, of course, are sophisticated criminal syndicates.

As seen in Fritz Lang's 1931 film *M*, the *Ringvereine* exist as much to collar and neutralize the dangerous and psychopathic criminal elements—the loose cannons of the underworld—as they do to facilitate criminal activity. Indeed, though membership in the *Ringvereine* is usually restricted to ex-convicts, the clubs generally maintain prohibitions against admitting anyone convicted of manslaughter, murder, rape, or child molestation. Use of firearms when operating on *Ringverein* business is prohibited, as is violence against police. The *Ringvereine* even go so far as to cultivate a certain "gentleman thief" image and are known to develop personal relationships with favored police detectives in a sort of cat-and-mouse game.

In spite of the work of the *Ringvereine*, most crime in Berlin is perpetrated by small-time crooks: muggers, burglars, bank robbers, or political operatives looking to destabilize their rivals or stir up support for their own cause. Violence ebbs and flows, but it always seems to escalate. A great sense of powerlessness grips a disoriented and resentful citizenry.

Counteracting such rampant lawlessness is the city's formidable police force, the Berlin Criminal Police (or Kripo). Employing about 15,000 personnel to cover all of Berlin's 4,000,000 inhabitants, law-enforcement in the city places an emphasis on highly trained and motivated officers holding back the teeming, lawless hordes. New recruits (usually drafted from the countryside rather than the city) spend a full year in training and then serve 3–4 years in riot control units (the Sicherheitspolizei or Sipo). Only then may they serve on regular precinct beats.

Overall, the Criminal Police are seen as reactionary monarchists, particularly as regards the higher-ranking officers. They oppose the democratic reforms of the Republic and skew right-wing and authoritarian. Despite their discomfort with the democratic regime and left-wing and centrist parties, the police hold themselves to a high professional standard; outside

of suppressing street protests, committing violence against a suspect is frowned upon, and "roughing up" a suspect is grounds for internal investigation and censure. Officers "on the take" are at risk of being turned in by their fellows. There is, nonetheless, the classic code of silence that dictates officers attempt to solve their problems internally. There is also a tremendous sense of frustration and persecution running through the police force. Governmental shortages make for aging equipment and fewer opportunities for advancement. The press is a constant thorn in the side of the police, with many papers waging a never-ending war of words against the face of statist authoritarianism.

The ratio of police to civilians is higher than in many other major cities, particularly American metropolises, and out-of-town visitors often remark on the ubiquitous presence of police around town. Nevertheless, thanks to the accruing stresses outlined above, after 1925 the police are increasingly incapable of maintaining public order in the face of spiraling political violence and agitation from both the left and right.

A final word about the "Bulls" of the Criminal Police: the vice officers, charged with investigating violations regarding the drug trade, prostitution, and other illicit activities. The Bulls are the exception to the stereotypical Berlin police officer; they know that the best way to find out what's going on among the dregs of society is to mix with the rabble. The fashionable "T-Girl" prostitutes of Tauentzienstraße maintain a friendly, joking relationship with the Bulls, providing them with information in exchange for leaving them alone to ply their trade. Many an underground cabaret counts a handful of Bulls among its regular clientele. In short, the Bull makes an ideal player-investigator.

GUN LAWS

The 1920s mark the first time in German history that guns are heavily regulated. The level of such regulation changes over the course of the decade and is worth examining in some detail. Like most European countries, the German states maintained a tradition stretching back to the Early Modern Period of regulating the ownership and carrying of weapons. After the formation of the German Empire, laws were passed that added special circumstances to any crime committed with a gun. The end of the Great War necessitated a complete rethinking of German firearms and weapons laws. For one thing, millions of soldiers returned from the front with their rifles and side arms; the country was suddenly awash in gray-market weaponry, including serious ordnance like machineguns and submachine guns. Secondly, the Treaty of Versailles specifically called for the disarmament of the German government, a prospect that did not mesh well with a nation suddenly swarming with armed paramilitary groups.

Accordingly, the 1919 Regulations on Weapons Ownership and the 1920 Law on the Disarmament of the People outlaw all privately owned firearms and ammunition, as well as calling for all guns to be handed over to the government. Special permits are issued for hunting guns, but otherwise possession of a firearm or ammunition, or even aiding and abetting a gun owner are subject to extreme penalties. The punishment for a convicted gun owner is five years in prison and a fine of 100,000 marks. Despite these harsh provisions, the laws do little to curb the now-underground trade in guns, as evidenced by the revolutionary activity and political assassinations of the early 1920s, nearly all of which are undertaken with firearms.

In light of the laws' failure, a new ordinance is passed in 1928; the Law on Firearms and Ammunition significantly relaxes the ban on private gun ownership, but, as a trade-off, requires extensive licensing. Gun owners must possess separate licenses to own a gun, to carry a gun, to sell a gun, and so forth. Furthermore, prospective gun owners must prove their trustworthiness and need for a firearm before being issued a license.

Armed Investigators

In game terms, prior to 1928 all guns (save for 16- and 20-gauge shotguns) are banned. To own even a fowling piece requires a suitable occupation. Outsiders attempting to bring firearms into the country will have them confiscated upon arrival and returned when they leave.

Paradoxically, thanks to the underground gun market, it's quite possible for German investigators to start play heavily armed. (Foreign Minister Walther Rathenau's assassination is carried out in 1922 using a sub-machine gun and a hand grenade!) The Keeper may allow players to pick and choose as they like, but players are well-advised that although they can lay their hands on some serious firepower, the penalties for being caught bearing unlicensed arms are severe, so discretion must be exercised.

After 1928, handguns and rifles are considered legal with the right permits. Acquiring these permits is as simple as succeeding with a **Credit Rating** roll, though the Keeper may rule that anyone with a particularly low score (less than 40%) is not eligible at all due to lack of "trustworthiness."

THE PENAL SYSTEM

The Republic, never on the firmest footing and always under attack, vacillates wildly between brutal authoritarian measures and genuine attempts at reform and rehabilitation. Over the course of the decade, the Kripo take their cues more and more from the Sipo units, adopting a "kick in the door" philosophy that prizes collaring suspects over diligent investigation.

Once in the penal system, the outlook can be grim, particularly for a suspect identified as having left-wing political leanings. The judiciary, like the police, are reactionary and anti-democratic, and almost universally hand down much harsher sentences for Communist and Socialist suspects, while often letting off members of far-right parties with a slap on the wrist, much to the howling indignation of Red journalists, pamphleteers, and activists. The prisons are a hotbed of revolutionary resentment, with frequent clashes between the inmates and prison staff. Such clashes are invariably met with the harshest of crackdowns for even the most minor violations; it is not unheard-of for prisoners to be seriously injured or even killed during these disturbances. There are also systemic issues at play, such as inadequate food, overcrowding in cells, and poor hygiene.

The philosophy of prison reform divides inmates up into "reformables" and "incorrigibles." Those in the former category are apt to receive better treatment and even rehabilitation. Those in the latter category are simply locked away to rot.

Police in Berlin

DRUGS

"My father warned me about men and booze, but he never mentioned a word about women and cocaine."

—Tallulah Bankhead

Aside from sex, drugs and mind-altering substances are the Berliner's favorite vice. Cocaine is omnipresent, but also widely enjoyed are opiates (heroin, morphine, and opium) and cannabis. Alcohol reigns supreme as intoxicant of choice in this Prohibition-free country.

Investigators driven to indefinite insanity may turn to the pernicious and dubious escape offered by such substances; others may indulge in an attempt to infiltrate a crowd of debased dilettante cultists, the better to further their ultimate investigatory aims. Presented here are overview rules for drug use and addiction. These are optional and should only be introduced with the Keeper's permission.

Cocaine

Duration: 1D3x10 minutes per dose.

Effects: one bonus die to **Fast Talk**, **Listen**, and **Spot Hidden** rolls, and to **CON** rolls to avoid exhaustion. Ignore the requirement to make a CON roll to stay conscious when suffering a major wound. Immune to the knock-out blow maneuver (*Call of Cthulhu Rulebook*, page 125), and can only be rendered unconscious when reduced to zero hit points.

Side effects: one penalty die to all skills requiring mental concentration. Lose 0/1D3 Sanity points per additional dose beyond the first if taken within an hour of one another—it is possible to suffer indefinite insanity if too much of the drug is taken too quickly. Characters already indefinitely insane suffer a bout of madness if they lose any Sanity from taking the drug. Make a **Luck** roll for every dose after the first; a failure results in the loss of 1D4 hit points. Coming down off the high imposes a penalty die to all **CON** and **POW** rolls (and certain skill rolls as determined by the Keeper) for 1D6 hours (plus one hour for each additional dose taken).

Addiction: an investigator is addicted after 1D4 uses, needing to take the drug once per day. If more than 24 hours pass without a dose, all characteristic and skill rolls suffer a penalty die. To kick the habit, the investigator must stay off cocaine for 1D4+3 weeks, requiring a successful Hard **POW** roll every week if the investigator is still able to (theoretically) procure the drug.

Cthulhu Mythos: not applicable.

Heroin

Duration: 1D3+1 hours.

Effects: a bonus die is applied to all **Sanity** rolls. Insanity effects that would normally be suffered by an investigator are negated for the duration. Ignore requirement to make a **CON** roll to remain conscious when suffering a major wound. Immune to the knock-out blow maneuver (*Call of Cthulhu Rulebook*, page 125), and can be rendered unconscious only when reduced to zero hit points.

Side effects: nausea, constipation, and immobility for 1D3 hours. The investigator must attempt a **Luck** roll (or the person administering the drug makes a **Medicine** roll) each time heroin is injected; failure results in the loss of 2D6 hit points, while a fumble results in the same damage plus the permanent loss of 1D3–1 multiplied by 5 points of both CON and POW.

Addiction: an investigator is addicted after 1D3 uses, needing to take the drug once per day; failure to do so results in agitation, with all skills (except Cthulhu Mythos) suffering two penalty dice. If able to stay off heroin for 1D3+3 weeks, requiring a successful Extreme **POW** roll per week to do so, the penalty dice are removed.

Cthulhu Mythos: a successful **Cthulhu Mythos** skill indicates an investigator receives otherworldly visions, costing 1/1D8 Sanity points each time heroin is taken. Such visions may prove beneficial to the current scenario, at the Keeper's option.

DRUGS - CONTINUED

Morphine

Duration: 1D3+3 hours.

Effects: a bonus die is applied to all Sanity rolls. Insanity effects that would normally be suffered by an investigator are negated for the duration. In addition, an investigator ignores all pain-related CON rolls (a major wound, for example).

Side effects: nausea, constipation, and immobility for 1D3 hours. The investigator must attempt a Luck roll (or the person administering the drug makes a Medicine roll) each time morphine is injected; failure results in the loss of 1D6 hit points, while a fumble results in the same 1D6 hit point loss plus the permanent loss of 1D3–1 multiplied by 5 points of CON.

Addiction: an investigator is addicted after 1D6 uses, needing to take the drug once per day; failure to do so results in agitation, with all skills (except Cthulhu Mythos) suffering one penalty die. If able to stay off morphine for 1D3+3 weeks, requiring a successful Extreme POW roll per week to do so, the penalty die is removed.

Cthulhu Mythos: a successful Cthulhu Mythos skill indicates an investigator receives otherworldly visions, costing 1/1D6 Sanity points each time heroin is taken. Such visions may prove beneficial to the current scenario, at the Keeper's option.

Opium

Duration: 1D3+1 hours.

Effects: a bonus die is applied to all **Sanity** rolls. Insanity effects that would normally be suffered by an investigator are negated for the duration. In addition, an investigator ignores all pain-related CON rolls (a major wound, for example).

Side effects: nausea, constipation, and immobility for 1D2 hours. Each time opium is smoked an investigator should attempt a **Luck** roll, with failure resulting in the loss of 1D2 hit points.

Addiction: an investigator is addicted after 1D6 uses, needing to take the drug once per day; failure to do so results in agitation. All skill rolls are made at an increased difficulty (Regular success now requires a Hard success, and so on) or suffer a penalty die. If able to stay off opium for 1D3+3 weeks, requiring a Hard **POW** roll per week to do so, the modifier/penalty to skill rolls is removed.

Cthulhu Mythos: a successful **Cthulhu Mythos** skill indicates an investigator receives otherworldly visions, costing 0/1D3 Sanity points each time heroin is taken. Such visions may prove beneficial to the current scenario, at the Keeper's option.

Cannabis

Duration: 1D8 hours.

Effects: gain one bonus die when making a **CON** roll to resist pain (major wound, for example).

Side effects: one penalty die applied to skills involving physical agility or communication.

Addiction: while it is not possible to become addicted to cannabis, long-time users find their memory affected. Make a **Luck** roll each year for ongoing, regular use; with failure, for the following year, the character receives 1D6 points (rather than 1D10) for all improvement checks during Investigator Development Phases.

Cthulhu Mythos: not applicable.

DRUGS - CONTINUED

Alcohol

The rules presented here assume the investigator is "drinking to forget," partying, or attempting to get "blackout drunk." Moderate social drinking never imposes a mechanical bonus or penalty, whereas trying to keep up with Anita Berber or Klaus Mann for an evening should impose some penalty! Alcohol is measured by consumption level in "shots" (one shot of hard liquor or one pint of beer). Consult the **Alcohol Effects** table to find the level of consumption and its concomitant duration and effects.

Effects: in addition to the physical impairment effects listed on the **Alcohol Effects** table, investigators who consume a moderate or higher level of alcohol also become immune to Sanity losses to a limited degree (see note on table).

Addiction: drinking to high consumption levels more than 1D6 times in a week results in addiction if a **CON** roll is failed. If addicted, the character must have an alcoholic drink at least once per waking hour of the day; failure to do so results

in one penalty die being applied to all skills (or difficulty increased by one step) for every hour without a drink, up to a maximum of two penalty dice/two difficulty steps. Such penalty modifiers are erased as soon as the character takes a drink; however, at that point, the investigator must succeed at a **POW** roll or go on a bender, drinking as much alcohol as quickly as possible.

Addicted characters suffering from deprivation must make a **POW** roll to avoid drinking any kind of alcohol in their vicinity, including dangerous varieties (such as lighter fluid or rubbing alcohol).

Going three days without a drink eliminates such penalties; however, once addicted, even a single episode of drunkenness reactivates the addiction. Furthermore, if the character was addicted for more than three months, there is a 35% chance that withdrawal symptoms include delirium tremens, which completely incapacitates the character for 1D6 days and requires a successful **CON** roll to avoid lengthy hospitalization (a fumbled CON roll may result in death at the Keeper's discretion).

A black market alcohol sale

ALCOHOL EFFECTS

Consumption Level	Example	Duration	Physical Impairment	Sanity Effect
Low	1–4 shots	1 hour	No impairment	None
Moderate	5–8 shots	3 hours	Make a **CON** roll: if failed, all skill and characteristic roll difficulties are increased by one level for 3 hours.	Temporarily immune to Sanity losses of up to 2 points*.
High	9–14 shots	4 hours	Make a **CON** roll: if failed, all skill and characteristic roll difficulties are increased by one level for 4 hours.	Temporarily immune to Sanity losses of up to 4 points*.
Excessive	15+ shots	6+ hours	Make a **CON** roll: if failed, all skill and characteristic roll difficulties are increased by one level for 6 hours. In addition, all rolls in this period suffer one penalty die.	Temporarily immune to Sanity losses of up to 6 points*.

* If the Sanity loss is equal to or lower than the amount negated by alcohol, the loss is ignored entirely. If Sanity loss is higher than the amount negated, the Keeper secretly records the amount. After the duration expires, call for a **Luck** roll: if failed, the investigator recalls the Sanity-shaking event and suffers the full loss immediately. If the roll is successful, the event is only hazily recalled, and the Sanity loss is halved.

For example, Paul is highly drunk and encounters a creature provoking a total of 6 Sanity loss. Being inebriated, Paul negates 4 points of the loss, and records the loss of 2 Sanity points only. On sobering up, Paul fails a Luck roll, meaning he now recalls some of the experience and suffers the immediate loss of 4 further Sanity points (equal to the 4 points negated by alcohol).

UNCOVERING BERLIN

"The time would be easy to know, for then mankind would have become as the Great Old Ones; free and wild and beyond good and evil, with laws and morals thrown aside and all men shouting and killing and reveling in joy. Then the liberated Old Ones would teach them new ways to shout and kill and revel and enjoy themselves, and all the earth would flame with a holocaust of ecstasy and freedom."

—*H.P. Lovecraft, The Call of Cthulhu*

The intention of this section is not to provide an exhaustive catalog of keyed locations, but rather to highlight some of the city's more notable places, selected to present a cross-section of everything Berlin offers investigators. Several tables are presented later in this section (**On the Town**, page 56) as an aid for Keepers to flesh out unexplored parts of the city, should the investigators wander off the main avenues. Other locations and districts are detailed in the scenarios provided in this book.

BERLIN'S LIBRARIES AND MUSEUMS

Berlin boasts a number of research collections. This section contains selected libraries and museums to be discovered in the city.

Ethnological Museum: located near Potsdamer Station on Königgrätzer Straße, this massive, cramped complex collects relics and artifacts from around the world on a scale to rival the famous British Museum in London. The glass-covered courtyard and open-air vestibule alone boast a massive Japanese sculpture of the Buddha, a Polynesian outrigger, a 33-foot-high (10 m) plaster cast of the eastern entrance to the Sanchi stupa in India, a chariot from southern India, a cast of a monolithic pre-Incan gateway from Tiahuanaco in Bolivia, totem poles from Pacific Northwest Indian tribes, a chieftain's throne from Cameroon, and casts of altar-slabs from Palenque. Within the museum's three floors of galleries are found rooms devoted to ancient civilizations from every inhabited part of the globe. Particularly of note is the "Oceania" gallery, which houses the greatest collection of Polynesian artifacts in Europe.

Hohenzollern Museum: the former Château of Monbijou, its park-like grounds situated on the north bank of the Spree across from the Kaiser-Friedrich-Museum on Museum Island, is now the Hohenzollern Museum devoted to the history of Brandenburg's (and later Germany's) now-defunct ruling dynasty.

Märkisches Museum: in Alt-Berlin, the Märkisches Museum is situated on Märkischerplatz, just south of where the Spree splits to flow around Museum Island. An architectural mishmash of Romanesque, Gothic, and Renaissance styles, the museum was founded in 1874 and houses artifacts from the history of the Mark of Brandenburg, as well as Berlin itself, stretching from the pre-historic to the modern.

Museum of German National Costumes and Domestic Industries: near to the Märkisches Museum, this museum is crowded with life-size mannequins wearing historical and ethnic outfits from all classes and regions of Germany.

Museum of Industrial Art: of a somewhat esoteric note, the library at the Museum of Industrial Art (Dr. Jessen, director), is adjacent to the Ethnological Museum and open to the public from 9 am to 9 pm. It contains the "Library of Costumes" (30,000 plates and 12,000 volumes) from the collection of Baron Lipperheide, as well as 135,000 other graphic plates and engravings. The museum hosts frequent lectures.

Museum of Natural History: located on Invaliden Straße, across from the Charité, the Museum of Natural History is actually three museums in one: the Geological and Paleontological, the Mineralogical and Petroglyphical, and the Zoological Institutes. Each has a ground floor open for public exhibitions and two further floors reserved for academic study.

Opposite: A cabaret in Berlin

Oceanographical Museum: a block north of Unter den Linden on Dorotheen Straße, the Oceanographical Museum features a history of German nautical engineering going back to the medieval merchantmen of the Hanseatic League, as well as examples of naval firepower and uniforms over the ages.

Prussian State Library: while there are only a handful of public libraries in Berlin, this paucity is largely compensated for by the sheer size of the State Library (F. Milkau, director). Situated on the Unter den Linden and completed in 1914, the building encompasses the Academy of Science (founded in 1700 by Leibniz), a massive domed reading room accommodating up to 400 readers at a time beneath its 125-foot (38 m) ceiling, and the University Library (open only to students, it contains 678,00 volumes). The State Library's main collection dates to 1661, when it was endowed by the Great Elector. The collection was later increased under Frederick the Great and now contains some 1,777,000 volumes and 64,000 manuscripts, as well as 250,000 works of music.

The collection includes illuminated manuscripts dating as far back as the 5th century CE and even some Late-Roman manuscripts bound in carved ivory. The library also holds Martin Luther's original *95 Theses*, the handwritten draft of "Deutschland Deutschland Über Alles," Gutenberg's 42-line Bible, the sole extant copy of the late-15th century printing of the Wormius translation of the *Necronomicon*, the rare 17th-century *Cronike von Nath* (written and published in Berlin by the alchemist Rudolf Yergler), Vogel's 19th-century treatise on German and European cults (*Von denen Verdammten*), and the first Bible printed in the German language (ca. 1465).

LOST LITERATURE

The Prussian State Library is notable for one other feature: it was bombed and destroyed between 1941–45, and the collection disbursed around Germany. Many books and manuscripts ended up in the hands of Polish, Russian, American, and British "collectors," and it is estimated that 700,000 volumes were destroyed or lost for good. In other words, although the destruction and redistribution happens beyond the timeframe presented in this book, this is as good a place as any to deposit any "volumes of forgotten lore" that won't survive the Second World War or could otherwise go missing.

From 9 am to 9 pm, the reading room is open to the public, but books must be requested from the librarians, who fetch the requested volumes from the closed stacks and hand them off at a kiosk at the foot of the library's grand staircase. This is first and foremost a research library, and academic credentials (or an appropriate social skill or **Credit Rating** roll) are required to access research materials. The rarer and more valuable the requested item, the more difficult it will be to obtain, even to look at.

Note: the Prussian State Library is featured in **Schreckfilm**, page 219.

Museum Island

As the Spree winds its way through central Berlin, it splits to form a large island, site of the former city of Cölln. Across from the island on the northern banks lies Old Berlin, while to the south Unter den Linden stretches out toward the Brandenburg Gate. The northern third of the island, demarcated by the east-west progress of Kaiser-Wilhelm-Straße in the south and by the river on all other sides, is referred to as "Museum Island."

Here are gathered many of Berlin's greatest cultural sites. The Berlin Cathedral, the City Palace and its massive monument to Wilhelm I, the Lustgarten, and the island's namesake: a cluster of grand museums and galleries.

Town Library: this is the city's other major *bibliothek* (Dr. A. Buchholtz, director). Located on the upper floors of the former Royal Stables on Museum Island, the library holds 225,000 volumes, including a 40,000-volume collection of German political works and books on Berlin history. Other specialties of the collection include literature and pamphlets from the 1848 revolutions, books on proverbs, and literature from the 1918 revolution. The library, open to the public from 9 am to 9 pm, has its own reading room and lends books to members.

Palace Museum: on the southern side of Kaiser-Wilhelm-Straße, anchoring the eastern end of the Linden in counterpart to the Brandenburg Gate, squats the *Stadtschloß* (City Palace). The former royal palace (and before that, a castle erected in 1451)—once the winter residence of Prussian kings and, later, German emperors—is now a museum. The Palace Museum chiefly houses paintings, sculpture, and "industrial art" from the 18th and 19th centuries, but also boasts tapestries and metalwork from the Renaissance and Middle Ages.

National Kaiser Wilhelm Monument: standing on the west side of the Palace Museum, erected in 1897, this monument is dedicated to Germany's first emperor, Wilhelm I (1797–1888). This Neo-Baroque monolith is the largest piece of sculptural art in the country, with an overall height of nearly 70 feet (almost 21 m), the monument is dominated by the 30-foot (9 m) equestrian statue of the Kaiser, flanked by the four Goddesses of Victory. The red granite steps leading up to the pedestal feature monumental statues of War and Peace personified, reposing on the stairs. At each corner stands a lion, which has led Berliners, in their usual fashion, to waggishly dub the whole monument "the Kaiser in the lion's den." The monument, due to its central location, size, and layout (bordering the Lustgarten, **Unter den Linden**, page 24), is often the site of civic events, political rallies, and clandestine rendezvous.

Altes Museum: moving north on the island, one encounters the first proper museum. The Altes Museum ("Old Museum"), completed in 1830, is the second-oldest museum in all of Germany. A massive and masterful example of neoclassical architecture, the museum looks like an outsized Grecian temple. Passing through the Ionic colonnade, visitors find within a collection devoted mostly to Greco-Roman art, sculpture, pottery, metalwork, and glasswork, spanning from the Archaic Greek period to the Late Roman Empire. The exception is the entrance vestibule, which features statues of noted German artists and collectors; the walls of the vestibule are decorated with rapidly deteriorating frescoes depicting the rise of Mankind from primordial Chaos.

Neues Museum: crossing Kaiser-Wilhelm-Straße, the wayfarer arrives at the Neues Museum ("New Museum"). Despite its name, construction on the museum started only a decade after the Old Museum's opening; however, due to difficulties caused by the soft ground and the disruption of the March Revolution of 1848, the museum did not open to the public until 1855. From the outset, the New Museum has functioned as a sort of spillover collection for the Altes Museum, a connection emphasized by the pedestrian overpass connecting the two buildings across Kaiser-Wilhelm-Straße. The New Museum is best known for its extensive collection of Ancient Egyptian artifacts—most famously the iconic, painted limestone bust of Nefertiti (not on public display until 1924). The ground floor's centerpiece is a colonnaded courtyard made to look like an Egyptian temple. Among the collection are an obelisk from the reign of Ramesses the Great, a model of a royal tomb from the 28th century BCE, a mummy from the 21st century BCE (the oldest well-preserved specimen in the world), an "unrolled" mummy from the New Empire period, pre-dynastic mummies (sewn up in leather bags), and numberless artifacts, coffins, furniture, everyday objects, and treasures spanning 3,000 years of Egyptian history, from before the 1st Dynasty to the twilight years of Roman domination. The second floor of the New Museum hosts the "Cabinet of Engravings"—a massive collection of 300,000 engravings, woodcuts, and lithographs—illuminated books and manuscripts from the 11th–16th centuries, and an extensive collection of artist's sketches from before 1800 along with photographs and drawings of famous paintings. Artists represented in the collection include Dürer, Rembrandt, Botticelli, and various Italian and Dutch masters. Portfolios of engravings may be examined by appointment Tuesday through Saturday, between 10 am and 3 pm.

The eastern colonnade hosts the most important of the statues awaiting placement at the Pergamon Museum, pending its completion.

National Gallery: situated to the east of the Neues Museum, the National Gallery presents an edifice of Doric columns constructed in red sandstone. A massive equestrian statue of Frederick William IV sits at the top of the grand staircase entry, and a frieze by Otto Geyer depicts German history ascending the interior staircase. The paintings contained with the temple-like gallery's three floors comprise the entirety of 19th-century German fine art traditions, from Romanticism to Idealism to Naturalism and the Berlin Secession.

North of the National Gallery is a large construction area, where buildings that will eventually house the **Pergamon Altar** and the **Western Asiatic Museum** are under construction. Beyond this, a Stadtbahn line crosses the island.

Kaiser-Friedrich-Museum: at the very northern tip of Museum Island, the Kaiser-Friedrich-Museum was completed in 1903. The museum's collection focuses on Medieval and Renaissance sculpture and painting. The first floor contains sculptures from early Christian, Byzantine, and Gothic sources, as well as works of art from North Africa and Persia (both Coptic Christian and Moslem, including several early Christian sarcophagi). Also featured are casts of Italian and German sculptures, Italian altarpieces, and ancient coins. More coins (350,000, to be precise) may be found in the Museum's basement in its "Coin Cabinet." The upper floor contains paintings from Italian, Dutch, and German masters: van Eyck, van der Weyden, Holbein, Cranach the Elder, Rubens, Giotto, Fra Angelico, Titian, Caravaggio in abundance, Dürer, Altdorfer, 14th-century German masters, Donatello, Verrocchio, Botticelli, Raphael, Michelangelo—the rooms go on and on, and contain many more paintings from the 17th–18th centuries as well.

OTHER PLACES OF INTEREST

HAUS VATERLAND

Utterly dominating the Potsdamer Platz is the Baroque-Modernist temple of consumerist pleasure, the "Department Store of Restaurants," Haus Vaterland. The building is instantly recognizable, thanks to its great illuminated domed tower, standing like a vaguely phallic beacon in the Berlin night.

For the entrance fee of one mark, visitors may pass through the gates (under a lit-up sign declaring "Every Nation Under One Roof!") and roam through five stories of the grand pleasure palace, choosing from among 12 restaurants or the variety show in the Palm Tree Ballroom (which costs an additional three marks to enter).

Vaterland's restaurants boast a culinary tour of the world, from the Bavarian *Biergarten* of Löwenbräu (complete with buxom, rosy-cheeked serving girls and roaming yodelers), to the Viennese café of Grinzing, to the kitschy Americana of the Wild-West-Bar (where the servers wear ten-gallon hats and carry their order-pads in holsters while serving up cocktails to the strains of jazz music led by Somali-German drummer Willi Mac Allan).

Other cuisines on offer in the various themed restaurants include Turkish (a sidewalk café), Spanish (a wine cellar), Japanese (a tea house), North German (the seaport at Bremen), Italian (a Milanese bistro), Hungarian (a peasant town), and Prussian (an old-fashioned Berlin beer hall)—perhaps not quite as "global" as the advertisements make out, but impressive nonetheless.

At the Rhineland Wine Terrace, an artificial river flows around the perimeter of the room, past a mural depicting the picturesque castle ruins of the Rhine River Valley. Once every hour, "the Storm on the Rhine" briefly interrupts diners as inky-black storm clouds darken the room, flashes of thunder and lightning provide an exhilarating show, and rain drenches the scenic enclosure. This is all dispelled by a "sunburst" provided by a bank of electric lights, creating a rainbow effect over the "river" to universal applause and appreciation by the patrons.

Haus Vaterland keeps its doors open until 3 am and accommodates up to 6,000 diners at a time, plus those who

Haus Vaterland at night

have turned up to take in one of the Palm Tree's 50 cabaret shows amid its eponymous, Edenic silver palm fronds, featuring the famous Vaterland-Girls and *Jazzmeister* Bill Bartholomew and his orchestra.

Haus Vaterland is actually the second pleasure palace to occupy the sprawling site; originally opened in 1912 as Haus Potsdam, and remaining as such until 1927, the site was originally given over to a mix of office and retail space. The lower floors featured a large, 1,200-seat cinema (the Lichtspieltheater im Piccadillyhaus) and the massive Café Piccadilly, which seated 2,500 diners at a time. When the site re-opens as Haus Vaterland in 1928, the theater, now called the Kammerlichtspiele im Haus Vaterland, is expanded to seat 1,415 patrons.

In both incarnations, the Haus is a popular place to cruise for prostitutes. Half-Silks roam the sprawling site in the evenings, hoping to add a special kind of dessert to the dining experience.

British travel author Sydney Clark writes of Haus Vaterland in 1934, "I can think of no better way to top off a Berlin night… than an hour or two or three in Haus Vaterland. The place is certainly not 'high hat,' nor is it low hat, but it is of the very essence of Berlin."

ROMANISCHES FORUM

Where Kurfürstendamm and Tauentzienstraße meet is a square formally called Auguste-Viktoria-Platz but more commonly known as Romanisches Forum. No better visual juxtaposition for Berlin's casually irreverent attitude toward piety and tradition exists than here. Facing each other across this bustling, neon-lit square are the stately edifice of the Kaiser-Wilhelm-Memorial Church and the shamelessly exploitive Heaven and Hell Club. But the site that lends the plaza its informal name is a coffee house and bar, the Romanisches Café.

The "Romanesque Café" is located on the ground floor of the Romanisches Haus, a four-story Italianate structure with two square bell towers. Since the closing of Café des Westens in 1915, the Romanisches has become *the* place to see and be seen by the city's leading lights in the artistic and intellectual communities. Here may be found renowned writers and critics, acclaimed artists and theatrical impresarios, cinema directors and movie stars, and award-winning journalists. In addition, those just starting out a career in these fields can be found here, hoping to get some face-time with such influential personages as frequent the café. (**The Devil Eats Flies**, page 97, begins in the Romanisches Café.)

The Heaven and Hell Club broadcasts its titillating attractions across the square with illuminated signs and posters promising an evening of risqué fun. This heavily themed cabaret attracts the top-drawer of Berlin's nightlife:

old-money playboys mingle with ambitious young politicians, all arriving with statuesque beauties on their arms. Arriving patrons are confronted by two doormen: one dressed as Saint Peter, the other as a stereotypical Satan, complete with mustache and pitchfork. In choosing your doorman you choose the theme of your dinner for the evening, though both "heaven" and "hell" offer equally fine views of the main stage, called the Cabaret Montmartre.

Those who go to Heaven enter a space illuminated with diffused blue light and are seated at votive-lit tables amid angelic statuary. Bowls of "holy water" sit at every place setting alongside illuminated menus scribed on parchment scrolls. On the walls hang old prints of sermons and scripture. Potted palm trees provide some privacy between tables. Seraphic waiters flit about, their faces powdered white, wire halos balanced between gauzy wings. The sound of a church organ floats through the din of conversation and clinking silverware.

To enter Hell is to pass into a red-lit room, glowing phosphorescent against plaster walls made to look like a chthonic chamber. The waiters here, predictably, are costumed to look like devilish imps, and they have the attitude to match. "This *bockwurst* will seal your intestines for 20 years!" cackles one as he delivers the meal to the table.

The revues at the Heaven and Hell are always elaborate and bawdy. Usually built around a suitably salacious theme by French choreographer Madeleine Nervi, sample revues include "The Naked Frenchwoman: Her Life Mirrored in Art," "Beautiful Body Unveiled," and "25 Scenes from the Life of the Marquis de Sade." Up to 50 dancers, some—or most—completely naked, may be on stage at once, and only rare customers leave Heaven and Hell feeling like they didn't get their money's worth.

In contrast to the intelligentsia at the Romanisches Café and the hedonistic pleasures to be found at the Heaven and Hell Club stands the Kaiser-Wilhelm-Memorial Church, dominating the square. Initiated by Kaiser Wilhelm II in 1891, it was completed in 1895 and dedicated to the first German Emperor, Wilhelm I. With its 370-foot (113 m) Neo-Romanesque spire, it is a major city landmark. Seating up to 2,000 parishioners, it is dedicated to the German Evangelical Church Confederation, a federated alliance of 22 German Protestant churches. The fact that such a holy site is hemmed in by movie palaces and ribald cabarets is a constant source of consternation to right-wing agitators; Joseph Goebbels gives a radio address in 1928 condemning the situation.

Immediately inside the church is a floor mosaic depicting the Archangel Michael fighting a dragon. Mosaics proliferate throughout the building, covering nearly 30,000 square feet (2,800 square meters) of surface area. The subject matter of these mosaics (as well as statuary and stained glass) is both secular and spiritual: one sees depictions of emperors and electors, and of Hohenzollern princes and princesses, alongside more familiar Biblical subject matter: the life of John the Baptist, Saints Peter and Paul, Moses and the prophets, archangels and church fathers. Great stained-glass rose windows pierce the north, west, and south walls.

With the opening of the Ufa-Palast am Zoo in 1919, the Forum also becomes a major center of cinematographical entertainment. No fewer than four major movie houses encircle the square: the Ufa-Palast am Zoo, Capitol (opened in 1925), Gloria-Palast (opened in 1925 on the second and third floors of the Romanischen Hauses, across the square from the Romanisches Café), and *Marmorhaus* ("Marble House," so-called for its five-story marble façade). There are ancillary theaters for live entertainment, as well as a variety of small cafés, bars, and restaurants, all combining to turn the Romanisches Forum at night into a bewildering panoply of blinking lights, roaring traffic, and drunken revelry. Comparisons to New York City's Broadway district would not far miss the mark.

INSTITUTE OF SEXOLOGY

Located in a quiet, leafy corner of the Tiergarten (at Beethovenstraße 3), the rambling *Institut für Sexualwissenschaft* (Institute of Sexology) spreads out over two former estates, encompassing three buildings in total. Among the institute's 65 rooms may be found lecture halls, outpatient clinics, laboratories, X-ray rooms, office space, living and domestic quarters, and, most famously, the Museum of Sexology.

Opening in 1919, the Institute is the product of one man's vision: **Dr. Magnus Hirschfeld** (page 77) created the non-profit foundation as one of the first such centers in the world. Here, Hirschfeld and his staff treat sexually transmitted diseases, provide education on contraception and disease-prevention, conduct research into human sexuality, offer marital counseling and pediatric care, conduct clandestine abortions, perform surgeries to cure impotency and frigidity, as well as "sexual correction" operations, and advocate for women's emancipation and abortion rights (abortion is outlawed in all cases prior to 1926, when a law

Romanische Haus

LGBTQI INVESTIGATORS

For many queer folk living in the city, Berlin is far more than a destination for sex tourism. Between the end of the Great War and the rise of Nazism, Berlin becomes Europe's—and the *world's*—most welcoming capital for lesbian, gay, bisexual, transgender, questioning, intersex, and other queer people, supplanting Paris' long-held status as a destination for queer culture.

A Berlin police commissioner estimates the city's gay male population at 100,000 in 1922; by 1930, the estimate is revised up to 350,000. That same year, Dr. Hirschfeld puts the city's lesbian population at 400,000, though it should be noted his definition of "lesbian" would encompass many women who might today identify as bisexual. All in a city whose total population is roughly 4 million. And, as noted elsewhere, Hirschfeld is one of the first academics to seriously examine transgender identities and coined the (now outdated) term "transvestite." Berlin in the 1920s boasts around a dozen bars specifically catering to the cross-dressing community, the most famous being the Eldorado.

This is all to say, having an LGBTQI investigator in the group is not only possible but probable. Certainly, such investigators will encounter much less resistance and discrimination in Berlin than they will in any other city of the period. However, despite the city's large queer population, there remain legal instruments of repression, which are used from time to time when it suits those in power to do so. Paragraph 175 of the Prussian Penal Code forbids male-male sex acts, while Paragraph 168 forbids "cross-dressing" in public. Police occasionally raid drag clubs and cross-dressing bars, and arrest patrons for cross-dressing on a public thoroughfare. Paragraph 175 is condemned by Hirschfeld and his allies as nothing more than an instrument for blackmail, as indeed it often is. One of the slang terms for gay men, particularly activists attempting to legalize gay sex, is "One-Seven-Fivers."

Notably, lesbianism is completely ignored by the law. This blind spot around female sexuality, heterosexual and queer alike, is common in most cultures where female sexuality is minimized or blatantly ignored due to sexist values, and is well-exploited by Berlin's large lesbian population.

While many people in Berlin welcome and enjoy its progressive stance of inclusion, there are those with extreme beliefs at both ends of the spectrum. For example, the "Militant Homosexuals.," led by magazine editor Adolf Brand, extols males homosexuality as the apex of the social order; the "ideal man" to Brand's followers is young, muscular, Aryan, and "manly" gay. Next in Brand's "order" come heterosexual men, again ranked by appearance and race, with blond-haired, blue-eyed Nordic types at the top. Following these categories of straight men are women of all types, who are barely tolerated for their ability to propagate the species. At the very bottom are "effeminate" gay men and cross-dressers, whom the Militant Homosexualists blame for giving the gay community a bad name and marking out gay men for mockery. The rejection of the feminine and the effeminate is, in this case, a mirror of larger trends within extreme right-wing Nationalist groups that prize "masculinity" and "maleness" above all else. Notably, the Sturmabteilung—Hitler's "Brown Shirts"—counts the openly gay Ernst Röhm and Edmund Heines among its leadership and is said to have a large percentage of gay men among its ranks.

At the other end of the spectrum are the "Third-Sexers," who are championed by Hirschfeld and his disciples. This philosophy sees "men with female souls" and "women with male sexual dispositions"as another naturally occurring facet of evolution. They coin the term "Third Sex" to describe those who are "neither full man nor full woman." Despite the misguided language of the movement, the Third-Sexers advocate for full protection under the law of all consensual sexual activity—an extremely radical position for the times.

is passed allowing the procedure in cases of danger to the mother), and advancement of gay and transgender rights. A small legal team provides *pro bono* work toward these ends. Lectures by leading sexologists are regularly given and are always open to the public at no charge. It is rumored that most of the Institute's operating costs are covered by Hirschfeld's considerable inheritance.

This is the first institute of its kind in the world, and the studies conducted within its walls represent the first concerted effort to understand human sexuality from a rational, scientific standpoint. Because the discipline is in its infancy, Dr. Hirschfeld and his assistants maintain extraordinarily open minds when it comes to what they deem

LGBTQI INVESTIGATORS (CONTINUED)

The Militant Homosexualists and Third-Sexers approximately align with the political philosophies of, respectively, Nationalism and Socialism. As is the case with regular politics, of course, the large majority of Berlin's lesbian and gay community occupy a vast middle ground, called the Libertarians. To this group, sexual orientation and identity is not a matter for political organizing or lofty theorizing—they simply want to meet like-minded people and do so through social ties rather than at clubs or rallies. Despite the city's massive queer population, there is in fact very little intermingling on either a social or political basis. Rather, different cliques tend to maintain their own social circles. There is one exception to this: straight or gay, Homosexualist, or otherwise, the one segment of Berlin's queer population consistently placed on the bottom rung are cross-dressers (who may or may not identify as transgender people). Some visitors to the Eldorado come simply to gawp at the drag queens on display—a highly visible yet non-threatening manifestation of the tumultuous Berlin nightlife. Such derision is more than a little ironic considering the fact that the beautiful androgyne—the drag queen, the cabaret chanteuse in tux and top hat—all are shorthand visual symbols for Berlin (even in their own era) and continue to be so in modern times. This rejection and repression, sometimes even from within the queer community, causes the transgender and cross-dressing communities to come together as a small but hardcore group dedicated to resisting legal and social prejudice from all sides.

"rational." They consider not simply anatomy and biology, but also cultural and folk medicine, psychology, religion, fine art, criminology, phrenology, and hypnotism. Issues of eugenics are explored and considered. Biochemistry and endocrinology are included among the disciplinary studies. Hirschfeld goes out of his way to hire so-called "transitional" employees to help with meal preparation, organization of archives and records, and other mundane tasks.

The Institute conducts more than 1,800 consultations a year (with poorer patients being treated for free) and hosts visits from 1,100 doctors every year. Hirschfeld is perennially interested in cross-dressing and gender dysphoria, and much of the counseling that takes place at the Institute is oriented toward those that Hirschfeld categorizes as "sexual intermediaries"—despite the fervent opposition to the Institute from Nationalist and conservative Catholic organizations, Hirschfeld even counsels a number of Nazi cross-dressers.

Patients coming in for a consultation are asked to fill out a rigorous "psycho-biological questionnaire" that covers everything from, "During sex, have you ever fantasized you are with another partner?" (Question #104) to, "Do any of your siblings exhibit any aspects of the opposite sex?" (Question #17), "Are you left-handed?" (Question #61) and "Can you whistle?" (Question #44). Ultimately, the questionnaire is circulated among 18,000 Berliners.

The Museum of Sexology draws 20,000 visitors every year—both locals and foreign tourists come to peer at the museum's unparalleled collection of erotic and sexual artifacts from across the spectrum of human history. Famous visitors include George Gershwin, Douglas Fairbanks, André Gide, Sergei Eisenstein, and Anita Loos.

In the museum may be found ancient sex toys, Sanskrit sex manuals, supposed chastity belts, steam-driven vibrators, torture devices from a local S&M brothel—there is even a collection of women's undergarments found on the corpses of German officers killed in the line of duty during the Great War. Far more disturbing is the museum's collection of sadistic drawings and primitive sculptures taken from the cells of men convicted of *Lustmord* (sexual murders) prior to their executions.

Adjacent to the museum space is the Institute's library, which contains Europe's largest collection of sexual, erotic, and pornographic literature. Like most other aspects of the Institute, the library is open to the public.

The Institute also provides living accommodations at a reasonable monthly rate; among those who stay at one time or another are Christopher Isherwood, Anita Berber, Communist activist Willi Münzenberg, and the post-operative transsexuals Dörchen Richter and Lili Elbe.

PROSTITUTION

Berlin has no official "red light district;" prostitutes, male and female, number in the tens of thousands (perhaps even exceeding 100,000). These two factors combine to ensure that the city is nearly overrun with sex workers, no matter where you go. They may be found on every major street corner, in clubs, at cafés, and in hotel lobbies.

Because Prussian law prohibits verbal solicitation, Berlin prostitutes resort to other means (dress, gestures, key phrases) when advertising their services. And with so many working professionals in the city, these services can be quite specialized indeed. Here follows a short selection of the many categories of working girls and guys in Berlin. Numbers in parentheses give a rough idea of commonality.

Age of Consent: in Germany, the age of consent is 14, although the involvement of a full adult (over 21 years) with a person under 16 years of age carries the assumption of exploitation and the adult may face prosecution. In comparison, the age of consent in the UK and most of Australia is 16 years old, while in the U.S. it varies between 16 and 18 (dependent on the state).

Boot-Girl: dressed in fur coats and thigh-high patent leather boots, these are street-walking **Dominas** (following). The color of their boots indicates specialty: black for cropping, lacquered gold for physical torture, poisonous green for psychological torture, and so on. Other colors include brown, cobalt blue, brick red, and scarlet. (350)

Chonte: a Jewish prostitute, often Polish-born, working out of Chonte-Harbors (brothels). (Numbers unknown)

Demi-Castor: a high-class version of the **Half-Silk** (following), this is a woman from a wealthy family who allegedly uses prostitution as a form of thrill-seeking and to supplement her allowance. Tend to work out of exclusive, secretive brothels. (500)

Doll-Boys: penniless teenage and pre-pubescent hustlers (ages range from 9–14), these "street rats" often trade their sexual favors for food, cigarettes, and a warm place to sleep. The Linden Passage in Friedrichstadt is their preferred congregating place. (2,000–3,000)

Domina: powerfully built woman clad in leather, specializing in whipping and humiliation. Often working out of lesbian clubs that allow male clientele and heterosexual couples, or else in "Body Culture" clubs. (1,500)

Fohse: independent sex worker who advertises in the papers as manicurists or massage therapists, as advertising for sexual services is banned. (2,500)

Grasshopper: a streetwalker too poor to afford a room who conducts business in secluded outdoor areas. Also called Fresh-Air Girls. (600)

Gravels: a woman with missing limbs, a hunchback, or other serious physical abnormalities. Popular with veterans who lost limbs of their own in the Great War. (600)

Half-Silk: an office girl, secretary, shopkeeper, or similar "working girl" who uses prostitution to supplement her income. Also called Five-O-Clock Girls. (40,000–55,000)

Kontroll-Girl: a licensed prostitute; grouped into one of three classes and subject to periodic checks for venereal disease by police physicians. Such workers signal their status by opening conversations with, "So, sweetheart?" Also called Bone-Shakers, Line-Girls, and Joy-Girls. (Authorities issue 8,750 Control Books in 1930)

Line-Boys: far and away Berlin's most prolific male prostitutes. Known to travel in small packs, they cruise for clients in hotel lobbies, at bars around the Alex, and in the leafy promenades of the Tiergarten. Ages range from 15–19. (20,000–25,000)

THE BLUE STOCKING

Traveling on Oranienburger Straße through the slum of the Scheunenviertel, the massive shopping arcade of the Friedrichstraßenpassage rises up out of the night, towering five stories high. Opposite the arcade's façade is the modest side street of Linienstraße. Turning onto that street, a short walk leads behind the redbrick St. Johannes Evangelical Church. Here, among the row houses, may be found a non-descript door with a fading piece of text painted on the lintel: "LINIEN-CELLAR." At the door, seated on an old wooden block, is not so much a man as a well-aged side of beef named Karl. This is the entrance to the infamous Blue Stocking, opened in 1923 during the height of the inflation crisis.

Karl takes his job seriously, and just getting past his squinty-eyed evaluation may be considered a small endorsement of one's street credibility. Investigators with a Credit Rating of 65% or greater must be vouchsafed by an established patron to get in the door.

The Blue Stocking is typical of many of Berlin's underground dives and is presented here as a template for Keepers who wish to develop their own locations, as well as for use in its own right.

With a clicking signal from Karl, the heavy door swings open. A short flight of stairs takes patrons down into a sparse interior, dimly lit in icy blue hues. Visitors may take a seat

PROSTITUTION (CONTINUED)

Medicine: a child prostitute of age 12–16. Their pimps pose as physicians operating "pharmacies" around Potsdamer Platz, and clients indicate their preference by bringing in a "prescription" indicating "length of illness" (desired age) and "color of pill" (desired hair color). (No more than 100)

Münzi: a pregnant woman who waits under streetlights on the Müntzstraße in the Alex. Their sessions are quite expensive, as they cater to an upper-class clientele. (Never more than a couple of dozen)

Nutte: a boyish, coquettishly dressed teenage girl, working out of her family's house and disguises her prostitution as dating. Often go on double dates with another Nutte. (25,000–30,000)

Race Horse: a masochistic prostitute who works out of an "Institute for Foreign Language Instruction"—in actuality, a brothel with "classrooms" outfitted with torture and bondage furniture. Due to the risk to the worker, clients are rigorously screened prior to their first visit. (200)

T-Girl: the "T" is short for Tauentzienstraße, the street where these brash, frank, fashionable streetwalkers most often ply their trade (sometimes in mother-daughter pairs). The press corps, regardless of political stripe, has a close working relationship with the T-Girls, as do many Bulls of the Criminal Police. (2,500)

Table-Lady: at Berlin's fanciest nightclubs, clients may pay "table-money" for an evening of stimulating conversation, scandalous gossip, delicious *hors d'oeuvres*, and fine champagne in the company of a lady in the employ of the club. The evening ends with an erotic backroom encounter. Table-Ladies are hired and groomed to conform to one of several ethnic stereotypes: Demonic German, Exotic Eurasian, Gypsy-Girl, Nordic, or Spanish Aristocrat. Their numbers decline precipitously after the 1929 global economic crisis. (500 prior to the Crash)

Telephone-Girl: child prostitute, aged 12–17. Ordered by telephone and conveyed to the client by limousine, they go by the names of movie stars (Lya de Putti, Dolly Haas, Marlene Dietrich, Lilian Harvey), whom they are made up to resemble. Their rates are astronomical, in part because they play the part of virgins. (3,000)

Wild-Boys: inhabiting the peripheries of the city, the Wild-Boys are gangs of homeless male youth (ages 12–18) leading a Peter-Pan-like existence. Will trade sexual favors for food and lodging. (2,000–2,500).

at one of the venue's 15 bare-topped tables or prop up the bar and have a chat with the "Boost," an old gossip everyone simply calls Uncle Hans. The venue is usually quiet until around 1 am, when things finally begin heating up and the Blue Stocking earns its nightly reputation as the "Hub of Berlin's Lowlife." Clientele may on any given night might include prostitutes, limbless **Gravels** (page 53) with their disabled veteran companions, washed-up boxers, *Kokain* addicts, smugglers, pickpockets, wealthy jewel thieves and safecrackers, as well as flashy pimps. In short, it is Berlin's very own wretched hive of scum and villainy, and in a city like Berlin, that's saying quite a lot!

Such entertainment as exists is provided by an indifferent zither-player in the corner. On most nights, Blue Stocking regular (and rumored disgraced former member of the Komische Oper) Singer-Franz closes out the festivities with a rousing suite of obscenely comic ditties, his "backup dancers" usually being the rival topless *Beinls*, Bootjob-Else and Cold Ente. Other colorful regulars at the Blue Stocking include Snot-Faced Adolf and Hedwig with a Cold Hand. As may be divined from these names, members of the Berlin underworld often sport rather colorful nicknames.

Uncle Hans makes an ideal contact for lower-class investigators. He is a font of information on the comings and goings of Berlin's underworld, and happy to share what he knows with trustworthy friends and associates.

WISEGUY TONGUE

Berlin has its own "thieves cant," called *chocum-loschen*, or "wiseguy tongue." The *patois* is a cosmopolitan combination of Yiddish, Low German, Romany, and underworld slang. Presented here are some colorful examples of the argot.

Alphonse: pimp, also called Hackers, Ludwigs, Oilers, and Quick-Businessmen.

Beinl: prostitute, a corrupted version of the Romany word for "daughter," also called Brides, Lauras, Violins, and Wall-Sliders, among much else.

Boost: the proprietor of any cabaret, bar, or club that serves as a front for a criminal organization.

Bull: police detective; specifically, a member of the vice squad.

Children's Car: police wagon.

Exchange: brothel, other names include Chonte-Harbors, Slut Huts, or Traffic Houses.

Gontiff: thief.

"H": heroin; pronounced in the American fashion: "aitch."

Hour-Hotel: primarily found in the Alex, a hotel that rents rooms by the hour for the purposes of clandestine meetings.

Kaschemenn: criminal dive.

Kietz: the street life, or the criminal life.

Kupplerin: procuress.

Nachtlokal: after hours erotic cabaret.

Nose: a criminal who informs on his friends.

Polenta: police.

Schlepper: street boys hired to lead customers to Chonte-Harbors and *Nachtlokals*.

Screen: cat burglar.

Snow: cocaine, also called Cement, Cocoa, or Koks.

Sohre: "hot" (stolen) goods.

Spanner: street lookout or club bouncer.

Stocking-money: traditionally, pimps and procuresses allowed prostitutes to keep the entirety of their first payment of the night, which was tucked into the top of a stocking.

Suitor: a prostitute's client, also called Fleas.

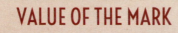

VALUE OF THE MARK

Year	Marks to Pound (£)	Marks to Dollar ($)
Pre-War	20.4	4.2
1920 (Feb.)	340	100.5
1920 (Apr.)	240	60.5
1920 (Jun.)	160	40.25
1920 (Oct.)	240	70.45
1921 (Jan.)	215–262	57–74
1921 (Jun.)	245–280	63–75
1921 (Oct.)	463–712	124–180
1922 (Jan.)	790–862	186–201
1922 (Feb.)	873–1,009	204–227
1922 (Mar.)	1,022–1,485	230–338
1922 (Jul.)	1,770–2,975	402–670
1922 (Aug.)	2,860–8,850	644–1,975
1922 (Oct.)	7,925–20,350	1,815–4,500
1922 (Dec.)	31,000–39,000	6,750–8,470
1923 (Jan.)	32,000–225,000	6,890–48,390
1923 (Jun.)	265,000–900,000	57,000–193,500
1923 (Aug.)	4.5mil–52mil	900,000–11.4mil
1923 (Oct.)	1bil–8bil	250mil–1.7bil
1923 (Dec.)	15bil–25bil	3.43bil–5.72bil
1924 (Jan.)	19bil	4.47bil
1925	20	4.22
1926	20.3	4.18
1927	20.4	4.2
1928	20.45	4.21
1929	20.4	4.2
1930	20.4	4.2
1931 (Jan.)	20.4	4.2
1931 (Oct.)	17	4.36
1932	14.25	4.24

Note: during the 1920s, £1.00 is roughly equivalent to $5.00

ON THE TOWN

"All Berlin, it appeared, the poor and the comparative rich, was dancing or drinking, lingering on the terraces of the cafés along the Kurfürstendamm, on expensive or modest roof gardens, sitting in wine restaurants and gardens, in the Zoo, or streaming through the amusements of Luna Park, resolutely ignoring all oppressive reality."

—Joseph Hergesheimer, *Berlin*

Berlin nightlife is unlike anything found elsewhere in Europe or America. Bars have a formal closing time of 3 am, and many establishments don't even get busy until the small hours of the morning. One of the great attractions of Berlin throughout the Weimar period is the cheapness of its charms. The economic dislocation caused by the Great War, compounded by ruinous war reparations imposed by the Western Allies and the German government's need to keep printing money to pay said reparations, means the value of the once-mighty German mark plummets in the years after the war. This reaches unsustainable proportions after the assassination of Walther Rathenau in the summer of 1922. The year 1923 is remembered as an *annus horribilis* that wipes out savings and investments at a stroke and decimates the middle class—see the nearby table charting the **Value of the Mark** for a breakdown.

But Germany's woe is the tourist's boon, and Berlin draws flocks of foreigners eager to spend money at outrageous exchange rates—anyone with even a few pounds sterling or gold dollars is suddenly a prince! The Inflation Crisis ends when Germany goes back on the gold standard in 1924 and the value of the mark returns to pre-war levels, but Berlin's reputation as a tourist mecca is by now cemented.

FOOD AND DRINK

As a cosmopolitan city of immigrants, Berlin cuisine differs from traditional German in some ways. The Huguenots brought with them cauliflower, white asparagus (*Spargel*), and peas to supplement the basic diet of beets and cabbage that was the typical Berliner fare of old; *Spargel* remains a great favorite. Frederick the Great was instrumental in encouraging Berliners to develop a love for the cucumber and potato, both New World vegetables, due to their affordability, which suited his Prussian sensibilities. The potato went on to become a central ingredient in Berliner (and, indeed, German) dishes; the cucumber wound up pickled in salt, known forever more as the pickled gherkin.

Potatoes are used to create such classic Berliner recipes as the *Senfeier*: hard-boiled eggs served on mashed potatoes and covered in a mustard sauce. The *Eisbein* is another classically simple dish, consisting of a steamed or boiled pork knuckle served with potatoes and sauerkraut. The *Hoppel Poppel* is a lunch or supper dish consisting of leftover meat and potatoes fried up with eggs and onions. And, of course, there is the simple joy of fried potato pancakes, or *Kartoffelpuffer*.

Although one may find plenty of pork dishes, including *Schweinsfilet mit Parmesan* ("pork cutlets with parmesan cheese"), veal is perhaps the preferred meat of the Berliner, at least when dining out. A typical menu of the day features nine pork dishes and *26* veal varieties. Noodle dishes are second only to veal in popularity.

Among side dishes, pea soup reigns supreme as a first-course dish. But nothing beats the *Pfannkuchen*, known as a "Berliner" to everyone except, well, Berliners. This is a type of doughnut filled with jam or marmalade and topped with icing or powdered sugar. A classic holiday treat, these also serve as quick afternoon pick-me-ups for the harried, hurried residents of the city.

Berlin is a restaurateur's dream. With more than 20,000 establishments in the city, there is one restaurant for every 280 residents. By way of comparison, New York City at this time boasts one restaurant for every 433 residents. Restaurants are broadly divided into "wine" and "beer" establishments. The best of the former are often located in hotels such as the Kaiserhof or Central, but there are large establishments operating in their own right, such as Kempinski & Co.

A Berlin market stall

and the Rheingold. Wine restaurants are always upper-class establishments, where mixed dining may be enjoyed and music provided in the evenings after the theaters close. Beer restaurants may also be upscale, particularly the lovely "beer gardens" (often situated with scenic views of the river), which open at dawn and remain so well into the night. Beer restaurants serve Bavarian, Bohemian, and local brews; smoking is usually permitted, and the overall feel of a beer restaurant is usually a bit rougher than that of a wine restaurant. Nevertheless, most are suitable for female diners.

Some restaurants also specialize in serving liqueurs or Spanish and Portuguese wines. The favorite wine-based drink of many a Berliner, however, is a curious mixture called *Bowle*. Particularly favored in the summertime, *Bowle* is made from equal parts champagne (or Sekt) and white Rhinish wines. To this mix are added strawberries and lemon zest marinated in sugar or brandy. In May, the *Maibowle* also features sprigs of fresh-cut herbs.

As one might expect, there are a variety of foreign cuisine restaurants in Berlin. Russian restaurants are especially common in the wake of the Revolution and are centered in Charlottenburg. Also of note is The Biltmore, a restaurant specializing in "American cuisine."

Cafés in Berlin are in the typical European terrace-style, with tables set out adjacent to the sidewalk, sometimes separated from it by a small fence and sometimes not. The Ku'damm is the heart of the city's café life, with the majority of Berlin's establishments strung out along that stately avenue, a reflection of the west side's more cosmopolitan orientation. Popular gathering spots for artists and intellectuals, most café menus offer a variety of coffees, including coffee and brandy, as well as teacakes and appetizers. Like the rest of the city, cafés remain open long into the night.

Bars, or *Dielen* (singular *Diele*), are places for social mixing, unlike the traditional American saloon. *Dielen* more closely resemble hotel lounges, with their sophisticated lighting and requisite musician tickling the ivory of a grand piano in the corner. Ladies and gentlemen sit and converse at tables or atop the high stools of the bar, drinking beer or strange cocktails (the Ohio is a particular favorite) and eating caviar. An American observer writes of the bar at the Eden, "The men, German, English, from South America and France, were meticulous in their attentions: hands were kissed, engagements made, drinks purchased, with a complete urbanity. No one there, it appeared, was ever drunk… the girls, gay like birds of paradise on the high stools that were their perches, drank slowly…"

Like cabarets, *Dielen* tend to cater to select clientele. Some *Dielen* serve only private members, an exclusive privilege. Altogether, there are 400 licensed *Dielen* in Berlin by 1932. By 1930, there are 85 *Dielen* in the city exclusively serving

The El Dorado

may buy a drink for "Big Dick" and his buddies "the Anti-Franz" and "Insect Paul," be entertained by the bar's greatest raconteur (the mononymous "Shithead"), or chat with local prostitutes "All-Tits," "Cocaine-Betty" (or her rival "Cognac-Betty"), and "Bottom-Girl Ede."

Yet even the *Kaschemmen* do not scrape the bottom of Berlin's proverbial barrel of illicit nightlife. For that, one must visit the *Nachtlokal* (literally "night pub," this may be roughly translated as "private nightclub"). Most common in the Friedrichstadt (and never numbering more than a few dozen across the whole of the city), the *Nachtlokal* is typically located in a residential flat a few blocks off the main boulevard. Young sharps called *Schleppers* are sent out to scout for likely suckers, offering inducements of illicitly erotic floorshows to couples and groups or female companionship to solitary males. The *Schlepper*, having gotten his hooks in, then leads the catch back through a maze of side streets and back alleys before landing them at the door of the *Lokal*.

Typical *Nachtlokal* shows are a mix of overpriced Sekt champagne and awkward nude dances in the Isadora Duncan mode, perhaps with a bit of lap dancing thrown in for particularly generous patrons. *Nachtlokals* are universally derided by all but the most naïve as hopelessly kitschy and déclassé, the domain of sad old men drinking bubbly from shoes of giddy whores; they grow increasingly rare as the decade wears on.

Cabarets are, of course, the iconic entertainment venue of Berlin. Originally appearing in Paris in the 1880s as the *cabaret artistique*, the first cabaret in Berlin opened in 1901.

In Berlin, the word is often spelled *Kabarett* (pronounced with a hard "T" sound) to differentiate it from the French-influenced model. When spelled this way, the tone of the entertainment may be relied upon to be overtly political and satirical in nature, with a world-weary ironic detachment used as a mask for commenting on controversial contemporary topics. This style evolved during the Wilhelmian years as a way to get around strict censorship laws banning any form of public criticism of the government. When spelled (and pronounced) in the French manner, the entertainment is bound to be much lighter in tone, with an emphasis on song-and-dance routines, comedy, and amateur theatrics.

Whether spelled in the German or French fashion, the final distinguishing feature of the cabaret is its intimate setting. Stages are small and the audience is seated close, usually at tables. Performers sometimes leave the stage to move among the audience, and, even when they don't, there is an expectation of engagement between performer and viewer that would be discouraged in a more formal theatrical environment. Further adding to the ambience, cabarets are often set up in converted cellars or small neighborhood theaters, giving many the feeling of a somewhat more sophisticated *Diele*.

Berlin's lesbian community. Just in the Friedrichstadt, there are 38 *Dielen* catering to same-sex male couples, with a city-wide total of between 65 and 80. The *Diele* is one of the primary social outlets for gay Berlin natives, with many serving as little more than pick-up bars. Others are attractively themed (the "Lion Club" is decorated to look like a Wild West saloon) or feature some sort of salacious draw (the "Dé Dé" is well known for its nude "hermaphrodite," who coolly sits upon an elevated chair, smoking a cigarette, for patrons to gawp at). Other gay *Diele* dress their beefy waiters (called "Cubs") in sailor uniforms.

Not all *Dielen* are classy lounges or gay pick-up bars, of course. The scummy, shadowy neighborhoods around the Alex conceal upwards of 70 underworld *Dielen*, mostly converted cellars, packed with hopeless drunks and thugs drinking, fighting, gambling, and gossiping. Constituting "darkest Berlin," inevitably there's a travel agency that offers tours of these criminal dives. In addition to criminals and tourists, these underground *Dielen* (also called *Kaschemmen*) are a favorite haunt of off-duty vice cops and reporters, both keeping an ear open for the latest juicy bits of street stories from the colorful clientele. And colorful they are, at least in name. The Hundegustav is so-called because its proprietor, Gustav, once worked as a dogcatcher; he is said to still enjoy a flank of broiled dog flesh on special occasions. Here, one

The Tanz-Kabarett

INVESTIGATOR-OWNED CLUBS

An investigator-owned *Diele* or *Lokal* makes for an excellent base of operations or even the basis for a full-blown investigator organization. The constant circulation of patrons also presents a way to introduce scenario hooks and interesting non-player characters.

The club may be owned by one or more investigators—encourage the investigator-owners to get creative with their club: come up with an interesting name, describe the desired clientele, outline what sort of entertainment is on offer, and so on.

Keepers should gauge the club's location and success by the average **Credit Rating** of the owners, while setting a minimum for ownership (40% is reasonable). A club with a Credit Rating of 40%–60% is struggling, while one with a rating of 61%–75% is doing well, with anything higher than being positively booming.

Clever gimmicks (like having a trained bear tending bar, serving novelty drinks, or booking famous acts for the stage shows) should be worth a certain boost to the club's effective Credit Rating but should also commensurately reduce the owners' spending level. Likewise, an investigator's available assets should be considered in terms of where to locate the club. Something on the Friedrichstraße or Ku'damm is going to be much pricier than a dive off Oranienburger Straße or in the Friedrichshain.

Starting in 1923, the titillating pleasures of the naked dancers of the *Nachtlokals* and erotic cabarets are commercialized and put on big stages in the form of massive theatrical revues. Patterned on the Ziegfeld Follies of America and similar routines in Paris, the Berlin revues take things, predictably, to ever-greater extremes, parading endless numbers of bare-breasted dancers across the stages of shows with names like *What the World Has Not Seen*, *Berlin Without a Blouse*, *Strictly Prohibited*, *From Bed to Bed*, and *Everyone Naked!*. These shows often feature upwards of 50 different acts, moving from sex farces to torch songs to precisely choreographed naked kick-lines of Tiller-Girls.

Shifting public tastes and the Great Crash of 1929 effectively put an end to the glory days of the massive stage revue, whose costs grow exponentially each year as various producers attempt to outdo one another. In many ways, the revue comes to symbolize the brief interlude of Berlin's Golden Age, between the twin economic crises of 1924 and 1929 and the crushing influence of authoritarian regimes.

On a final, more mundane note, Berlin is the birthplace of the original fast food dining establishment, the "*automatisches* restaurant," or automat. The first automat opened in 1897 on Leipzigerstraße, and they remain a common sight throughout the city. The interior of an automat looks like a typical mid-level dining establishment, with tiled floors and Formica-topped tables. An attendant in a glass booth at the front changes paper money for coins, the first indication that something is different here. The key difference of the automat lies in the walls: row upon row of small, glass-fronted compartments about the size of post office boxes, each with a dish of freshly prepared food inside: soups, sandwiches, hot dishes, and desserts are all on offer. Drop in a coin or two next to the box with the food you want, turn the knob, and remove the dish from within. Cooks behind the wall make sure the boxes stay stocked with freshly prepared choices. Automats are popular destinations for busy clerks and office workers, blue-collar stiffs, and underemployed creatives. With their lack of wait staff and pretensions of *haute-cuisine*, they become bizarrely democratic establishments where Berliners from practically every walk of life come together to eat cheap comfort food.

CULTIVATING CONTACTS

As with all great cities, in Berlin, it is often not a question of *what* you know, but of *who* you know. With the right phone call or Rohrpost card, doors (both literal and figurative) formerly closed to the investigators may suddenly open.

See the section on **Contacts** in the *Call of Cthulhu Rulebook* (page 97), as well as the Suggested Contacts for the occupations listed on pages 14–15 and **Skills and Contacts** (page 219) in the *Investigator Handbook* for more details on how contacts work in the game.

Presented here are additional ideas for contacts based on Berlin's particular socio-political mélange. Think of these as supplementary to the contacts presented in the *Investigator Handbook* and as a way of adding a *Berlinerisch* flavor to characters.

PARTY MEMBERSHIP

One of the most effective ways to establish contacts and network within the city is through joining a political party, club, or organization. Around 40 political parties are represented in the Reichstag, not counting the many fringe or splinter parties that are unable to win even one seat, nor does it count trade unions, political unions, or paramilitary groups. In short, there are a bewildering number of political groups operating in Berlin—more than enough to accommodate any political philosophy one cares to name.

Prior to 1930, the most common parties are the left-wing *Kommunistische Partei Deutschlands* (Communist Party of Germany) and the *Sozialdemokratische Partei Deutschlands* (Social Democratic Party of Germany)—usually simply referred to as the KPD and SDP, respectively—the center-left *Deutsche Demokratische Partei* (German Democratic Party), the socially conservative *Deutsche Zentrumspartei* (German Center Party), and the center-right *Deutsche Volkspartei* (German People's Party). After the September 1930 elections, the NSDAP (Nazi) Party begins making significant gains in the Reichstag but remains hugely unpopular in the capital itself—not for nothing did Joseph Goebbels call Berlin "the reddest city west of Moscow." Political party contacts could range anywhere from a lowly factory worker all the way up to a standing member of the Reichstag, depending on the investigator's background.

For investigators looking for contacts of a more martial bent, each of the three political groups (left, center, and right) boast several paramilitary organizations. These grow out of the tumultuous days following the Great War, when political marches and rallies are in danger of violent disruption from opposition forces. These paramilitary groups are formed under the auspice of providing "protection"

for their own side's rallies, but many quickly take a more proactive approach and begin targeting "enemy" gatherings, using a combination of intimidation and open violence. Street battles are a frequent result.

On the left, the *Roter Frontkämpferbund* (Alliance of Red Front Fighters) represent the KPD and number some 130,000 members at their height. Their actions against right-wing parties and the Berlin police grow increasingly violent over the decade, culminating in their ban in 1929, an action that only serves to drive their members underground.

The Red Front Fighters most often clash with the infamous Brownshirts of the NSDAP's Sturmabteilung (SA), but there are other, less extreme right-wing paramilitary groups active in Berlin as well. Most notable is the *Jungdeutscher Orden* (Young German Order). Inspired by the Teutonic Knights, the order is nationalistic but rejects the philosophies of Hitler and his cronies, aligning themselves instead with the German Democratic Party. Inspired by the ideals of the pre-war Wandervogel movement (**Apache Pathfinders**, page 18), they grow to become the largest paramilitary group in Germany by 1933 (when they are banned by the Nazi Party), boasting a total membership roster of some 300,000.

Even the centrists have their own paramilitary groups. The most well-known is the *Reichsbanner Schwarz-Rot-Gold* (Black-Red-Gold Banner of the Reich). An alliance of factions from the GDP, the Center Party, and the SDP, this group stands against extremism and subversion from *both* the right and left, and uses its organizational muscle to promote respect for the new Republic.

Regardless of their political affiliation, a paramilitary contact represents a potentially powerful resource for investigators. A street fighter and possibly even a military veteran, the contact will know all sorts of things about the black market, the illegal weapons trade, and so forth. Furthermore, contacts can provide access to more of their kind; investigators who are able to demonstrate a clear and present threat against the contact's ideologies may well find themselves with a group of hardened combat veterans at their backs when setting out to confront the Mythos!

OCCULT SOCIETIES

Almost as profligate as political organizations are secret societies devoted to the study of occult matters. The most well-known occult society in Berlin is the Ordo Templi Orientis (OTO). Founded by the Austrian Karl Kellner in 1895, the OTO doesn't begin its rise to prominence until Theodor Reuss takes over as head of the Order in 1905. A blend of Masonic and other esoteric rites, membership in the OTO is divided up into lodges, its members advancing through degrees of initiation. Under Reuss, the OTO spreads beyond Austria and Germany, opening lodges in France, Britain, the United States, Switzerland, and other European countries.

In 1912, Reuss meets the British occultist and sorcerer Aleister Crowley, and the two quickly form a mutual understanding resulting in Reuss putting Crowley in charge of all OTO lodges in Britain and Ireland. Crowley's influence within the order continues to grow, and in 1922 he takes over as its head in the wake of Reuss' suffering a stroke. Crowley subsequently introduces the rituals and rites of his own religious system, Thelema, into those of the OTO, causing a major splintering of the group in Germany. Although Crowley's name becomes intimately associated with the OTO, there are many German sects that maintain a "pure" version of the group's rituals, while others forge unique paths.

One such splinter group is the *Fraternitas Saturni* ("Brotherhood of Saturn"), founded by the occultist Gregor A. Gregorius (**Dances of Vice, Horror, and Ecstasy**, page 147). The Brotherhood, in taking the sex-magic rituals of the OTO and Crowley's Thelema and blending them with Freemasonry, devil-worship, and alchemy, produces something that could only come out of Weimar Berlin.

Countless more societies exist, from the remnants of the Theosophical Society to its offshoot, the increasingly secular Anthroposophical Society; the Orion-Bund to the United Old Order of the Druids; the Hermetic Brotherhood of Light to the New Gnostic Church; the General Pansophical School to the Pansophical Society; from the Order of the Grail to the Order of the Knights of the Holy Grail. Yet even these esoteric orders are relatively well known when compared to those that are spoken of only in whispers.

Once such example, cloaked in shadow, is the so-called Vril Society. Founded in 1925, the Society's mission is to expound on and master the mysterious energy source known as vril, first described in the 1871 novel *The Coming Race* by English author Edward Bulwer-Lytton. Despite the concept's clearly fictional origins, many prominent European Theosophists maintain that the Rosicrucian Bulwer-Lytton had simply channeled a long-suppressed truth in the form of a made-up narrative, and, thus, take vril seriously. The membership roster of the Vril Society is highly exclusive and consists of wealthy German occultists, all of them of a Nationalistic bent. Rumors swirl that the founder of the society is General Karl Haushofer, said to be a student of the famous transcendental mystic George Gurdjieff and close associate of the high-ranking Nazi official (and occultist) Rudolf Hess. Through Hess, Haushofer's ideas on *Lebensraum* ("living space") prove hugely influential on Adolf Hitler and the development of

Nazi Party ideology. The members of the Vril Society are even rumored to form the inner sanctum of the NSDAP's "occult wing," the Thule Society.

Contacts within an occult society have obvious utility for investigations: a contact may have personal knowledge of rituals or lore relevant to uncovering the Mythos nature of a mystery, or they may be able to provide access to various tomes and other hidden information. What's more, membership in these societies tends to be those with the time and money to devote to such seeming fripperies—an occult society member is bound to be well-connected!

CRIMINAL ORGANIZATIONS

The *Ringvereine* and other criminal groups in Berlin are discussed in greater detail in the **Beinls and Bulls** section (page 37). Here, we merely consider the pervasiveness of such groups and the utility of contacts associated with them.

There are two types of *Ringverein*: the official groups, formed to run underworld clubs and bars, and the unofficial organizations, who merely borrow the name and concept but go their own way. The official *Ringvereine* are called "the Great Ring," "the Free Band," and "the Free Union." Of the unofficial groups, police estimate there are no fewer than 85 operating in the city at any given time. Membership estimates vary wildly, from as few as 1,000 to as many as "the overwhelming majority of all criminals in Berlin." Keepers may decide for themselves just how much the *Ringvereine* constitute an "empire of crime" within Berlin society—see Fritz Lang's various *Dr. Mabuse* movies for ideas.

The smaller, unofficial clubs often adopt names invoking a sporting club or else a sort of middle-class sentimentality: "the Always-True," "the Echoes of Home," and "the Hand-in-Hand." Beneath such maudlin epithets are groups of hardened ex-cons who run protection rackets, facilitate burglaries and robberies, and help get their brothers out of legal hot water.

A criminal contact belonging to one of these rings could do the same for investigators who, doubtless through no fault of their own, find themselves on the wrong side of the law. *Ringverein* members will happily bear false witness to police in order to bolster an alibi, or post bail to get a friendly asset out of jail. Naturally, favors will be expected in return. And, of course, if it is indeed true that every doorman, shoe-shine boy, vendor, and prostitute is in the employ of the *Ringvereine*, a well-placed contact in such a group could function not unlike Holmes' Baker Street Irregulars, providing on-the-ground feedback and information, tracking the movement of individuals, and reporting back with the latest word from the streets.

NEIGHBORHOOD DETAILS AND STREET ENCOUNTERS

Although the scenarios presented in this book provide plenty of interesting locales for the investigators to visit and interact with, a certain level of player-driven exploration of the city is both expected and to be welcomed. Whether it's establishing the details of their local neighborhood or canvassing the back streets of an unfamiliar section of town while chasing down an errant clue, the investigators will want to know what's around them, and the Keeper should be prepared to answer such questions.

If the investigators decide to forget their troubles for the evening, consult the table of **Random Cabarets and Clubs** (page 63), which provides names and thumbnail sketches of various venues around town. Turning onto a random street, a few rolls on the **Architectural Details** and **Random Business** tables (pages 67 and 68, respectively) provide a quick and easy way to give the area a bit of its own flavor.

The Keeper should not be too concerned with consistency. One of the central themes of a Berlin-based campaign is chaos and mutability. Don't worry about using the same name for a business located in a wholly different neighborhood. Indeed, use the duplication to play up a sense of unease and coming loose from one's moorings. (*"Wait, I thought S. Schropp was in the Ku'damm?" "No, no. We've been at this location for 30 years!"*)

The architecture of Berlin in the 1920s is an interesting clash between the fin-de-siècle excesses of the Wilhelmian construction boom and boldly provocative modernist designs. Although Berlin still boasts some neighborhoods with architectural styles dating back to the Renaissance and Early Modern eras (particularly in the Nikolaiviertel of the Old City), the majority of its buildings date from the 19th century. Great buildings of cultural importance tend to fall under the usual Neo-classical umbrella, while many other buildings—both official and residential—display an Italian Renaissance revival look, with towering edifices of Romanesque arches and colorful brickwork.

The building boom that followed the birth of the German Empire brought in Neo-Baroque styles, with a love of colonnades and decorative excess and domes on top of everything, from atriums to cupolas. The wake of the Great War brings an interest in a totally new style: Modernism. Like so many other things in post-war Germany, this soon becomes a political topic, with right-wing traditionalists decrying the brutal simplicity of Modernist architecture, while left-wing socialists hail it as the look of a communal future.

The first Modernist housing estate (Garden City Falkenberg) is built during the war, southeast of the city in the small district of Bohnsdorf (the "Paintbox Estate," so-called for the brightly painted stucco that fronts every house), but the great Modernist building boom doesn't get going until the mid- to late-1920s, with estates going up around the city's periphery, from Wedding to Reinickendorf to Charlottenburg. These estates are built as part of a government housing plan, in keeping with a provision in the Weimar constitution that declares that every German has a right to, "a humane dwelling place." A special rental tax pays for the construction projects.

Left: The Babylon Theater
Right: The Kaiser-Friedrich-Museum

RANDOM CABARETS AND CLUBS

1D20	Name (Original Location)	Atmosphere	Clientele	Décor	Entertainment	Unusual
1	Alexander-Palast (The Alex)	Upscale	Quaint, conservative gay couples in top hats and tails	Massive American-style ballroom	A stage for cabaret performances; a large orchestra provides music for dancing	Monthly "Transvestite Balls;" weekly "Lesbian Nights"
2	Auluka-Lounge (Nollendorfplatz)	Weird and loud	Chic lesbians, Japanese and Chinese tourists with their *Nutte* escorts, and male voyeurs	"Japanese Cherry Blossom"—paper lanterns, overhanging cherry branches, red sofas	Dance music performed by a former Russian prince	The female *maitre d'* wears a short skirt and a blue sport coat, open to reveal her breasts
3	Cabaret of the Spider (Unter den Linden)	Wacky	Mature, middle-class gay men	A large mural depicting a spider and her web	Floor shows on Saturdays and Sundays: a male twin song & dance team, Liselott from the Mikado, and so on	No cover charge, but women and straight men are not admitted
4	Café Braun (The Alex)	"American"	Bohemian	Standard dance club	Dancing and live music; "love porticos" out back	Wait staff hired on resemblance to world leaders, serve appropriate cuisine to "their" nationality; band wears masks of famous celebrities
5	Café Dorian Gray (Potsdamer Platz)	Uneasily hot	Lesbian couples, cross-dressing couples on Wednesdays; "gentlemen" are allowed, but must pay double the cover	Artistic café serving high-quality Viennese cuisine	Live tango music; a violinist who plays table-to-table and won't leave until tipped	Theme nights like "Three Days in the Wild West" or "Rhineland Wine-Growers' Holiday;" gay and lesbian clientele tend to dress in leather blouses or sailor uniforms

RANDOM CABARETS AND CLUBS - CONTINUED

1D20	Name (Original Location)	Atmosphere	Clientele	Décor	Entertainment	Unusual
6	Cosy Corner (Kreuzberg)	Hard-drinking	Working-class, rough trade in lederhosen, British writers, and poets	A leather curtain grants entrance to a dim, homely interior festooned with photos of boxers and cyclists	Drinking and card games	The lavatory has no partitions between toilets
7	Eldorado (Nollendorfplatz)	Glamorous, ostentatious, and titillating	Cross-dressers, transgender people, high society, high-class prostitutes, and foreign tourists lured by hotel ads	Large banner outside reads: "Here it is right!" Oriental interior	An orchestra in unisex clothing playing haunting French and Argentinian tunes; midnight drag revue in six acts; the beautiful cross-dressing showgirl, Muguette	One of Berlin's most (in)famous clubs, many come here simply to gawp; the American-style bar features a disturbing assortment of S&M photos mounted above the all-female staffs' heads
8	Hundegustav Bar (The Alex)	Mischievous and friendly	Beinls and bulls freely mixing, gangsters, and tourists	Coal cellar	A guitarist, banjoist, and piano player try (and fail) to play the Charleston	"Dog-Gustav," the owner, reputed to have a taste for dog flesh
9	Kakadu Bar (The Ku'damm)	Exclusive	Artists and foreigners	Mock Tahitian; "longest bar in the city"	Vegetarian restaurant; five-act cabaret; cocktail bar	A caged parrot over every table; tapping the glass signals the bird to literally call for the bill!
10	Karls-Lounge (Tiergarten)	Crowded, depressed, oddly smoke-free	Line-Boys and waiters both dressed in sailor uniforms, coke dealers, and male bisexual university students	Jeweled walls and lampshades; massive bar and dusty liquor cabinet; porcelain tchotchkes	A pianist and fiddler provide music for dancing couples	No alcohol is served here— only Hungarian pastries and lemonade; drugs are openly traded and used at tables

RANDOM CABARETS AND CLUBS - CONTINUED

1D20	Name (Original Location)	Atmosphere	Clientele	Décor	Entertainment	Unusual
11	Mali & Ingel (The Ku'damm)	Very selective and always packed	Exclusively, defiantly lesbian; artists, intellectuals, stars of stage and film; men admitted only by invitation, and then ignored	Permanent sign outside: "Closed for Private Party;" inside is small and stylish, with comfortable chairs and a red traffic light over the dance floor	Male pianist plays hot jazz and tear-jerking love songs; Mali & Ingel, the owners, are vivacious and refined (if promiscuous) hosts	Front desk manned by two *Bubi* (butch) attendants in thick makeup, each fondling a giggling femme on their lap
12	Mikado Bar (Friedrichstadt)	Comically aggressive	Drag queens and curious tourists	Tacky Oriental	A full "Transvestite Revue" on weekends; "the Baroness" on piano playing tango duets	Drag divas going table to table, demanding dances from straight men
13	Monte-Casino (Kreuzberg)	Unorthodox	Bourgeois couples, British and Dutch tourists, gay men, transgender people, and cross-dressers	Run-down bar with elevated stage	Amateurish drag show featuring malnourished adolescent Line-Boys; emceed by a teenager called "Pretty Adolf"	Number-one tourist destination in the city for those interested in Berlin's "gay nightlife"
14	Rio Rita Bar (The Ku'damm)	Chic and intimate	Playboys, diplomats, and industrialists	Warm and simple: cream and gold panels plus murals	Tangos from 9 pm; exotic-looking "table ladies"	Well-known supplier of high-grade cocaine and opium
15	Silhouette (The Ku'damm)	Calm and smoky	Film stars like Berber, Veidt, and Dietrich, male and female impersonators, and "butch" lesbians	Long narrow room lit by red Japanese paper lanterns; twin bars facing each other and manned by youths in white shirts	Dancing on a red carpet to the tunes of a dapper orchestra; drag queens singing rhapsodies	A dozen partitioned, recessed booths on second-floor balcony provide plenty of privacy

RANDOM CABARETS AND CLUBS - CONTINUED

1D20	Name (Original Location)	Atmosphere	Clientele	Décor	Entertainment	Unusual
16	Sing-Sing (The Alex)	Rough and bizarre	Gangsters, pimps, Kontroll-Girls, and ex-cons	Based on the dining hall at Plötzensee Prison—bars on the windows, waiters in striped convict uniforms, electric chair	Open from 1 am–6 am; each night a customer is selected to be "executed" in the electric chair and is expected to put on a good performance	Food is served in tins and is of prison-kitchen quality; anyone without a year's hard time in the pen is suspect
17	Stork's Nest Cabaret (The Alex)	Sordid dive	Working-class, students, and criminals	Well-worn; photos of performers displayed outside	Classic cabaret stage show (said to be the inspiration for the movie *The Blue Angel*)	Customers send up beer steins to performers; may purchase seats on stage
18	Toppkeller (Nollendorfplatz)	Dangerous and sexy	"Bohemian" lesbians, Dominas and masochistic straight men, curious couples, tourists, and famous entertainers	Beer-hall tables and dim lights; paper herons hang from the ceiling; erotic murals in the back	"Prettiest Female Calves" competition; a four-piece brass band provides music for line dances; at midnight, the Black Mass dance is led by a statuesque woman in a black sombrero	Despite being a lesbian club, a prime pick-up place for heterosexual prostitutes; straight men lured here by flyers advertising titillating contests
19	Weiße Maus (Friedrichstadt)	Wicked	Gentlemen lechers, lesbian groupies, and intellectuals	Classy cabaret with a curtained stage	Close-up naked dances performed after midnight; Anita Berber's favorite venue	Audience members don black half-masks
20	Zauberflöte (Friedrichstadt)	Wild, aggressive, and fun	Gay men and lesbians on separate floors	Two massive dance halls: "the American Dance Palace" and "the Florida Dance Hall"	Each dance hall accommodates up to 1,500 dancers; live orchestra playing jazz and German folk tunes	Gay and lesbian floors strictly segregated; lesbian floor holds "Silver Spider" costume ball on New Year's, names "Princess of the Moon"

ARCHITECTURAL DETAILS

1D10	Exterior	Interior
1	Gables	Paper lanterns
2	Oriels	Mural/wallpaper of geometric patterns
3	Elaborate scrollwork	Modernist steel & glass furniture
4	Baroque statuary	Mongolian tapestries
5	Domed turret	Persian rugs
6	Neon signage	Peeling wallpaper
7	Large plate-glass windows	Expressionist paintings
8	Peeling stucco	Checkered linoleum floors
9	Rococo spires	Orientalist statuary
10	Neo-Classical colonnades	Water-stained ceiling

BERLIN'S CEMETERIES

As befits a great European capital, Berlin boasts a host of eerie cemeteries. Particularly startling to foreigners is finding tags on certain headstones reading *"stelle abgelaufen"* ("time's up"). These tags are placed on graves due to be dug up and reused, as gravesites in Germany are leased for a fee; in Berlin, leases generally run for 20 years. Descendants or benefactors may renew leases, and some wills even set aside funds for extended gravesite leases. But once "time is up," if no one comes forward to renew the lease, the headstone is taken away and a new body is laid in the grave. Graves of famous persons are leased through government dispensation and thus tend to be more permanent than mere civilian graves.

Dorotheenstadt: founded in the late 18th century, this cemetery lies just north of Oranienburger Tor and its neighboring plot, the French Cemetery, which dates from the same period and was intended for descendants of French Huguenots. Due to its proximity to Berlin University, Dorotheenstadt hosts the graves of many prominent intellectuals and academics, including the philosophers Solger, Fichte, and Hegel. The cemetery is noted for its many elaborate tombs and headstones, carved and cast alike.

Friedhof Grunewald-Forst: out on the periphery of the city is the "Greenwood Forest Cemetery." As the name implies, this cemetery is set among the pines and spruces of the Grunewald, the River Havel flowing by not far away. It's this river that gives the cemetery its grim origins. Due to quirks in the river's flow, many suicides who drown themselves in the Havel and its tributary, the Spree, wash up here, and it is here, in an overgrown and rural district of the city, that the bodies are quickly buried in unhallowed graves with only a simple wooden cross to mark the burial. Because of this, the cemetery is usually called by a different name: "the Suicides' Cemetery." During the Great War, many Russian prisoners of war were also buried here. Now, with hard times returned to Germany, suicides are on the rise again and many more bodies are washing up from the Havel within hailing distance of the Grunewald.

RANDOM BUSINESSES

1D10	Bookshop	Café	Restaurant	Boarding House	Theatre
1	Amelang	Bauer	Ratskeller	Barbe	Deutsches Opernhaus
2	Gsellius	Victoria-Café	Gourmania	Bavaria	Komsiche Oper
3	Akademische	Kaiser-Café	Atelier	Bismarck	Komödien-Haus
4	Nikolaische	Palast-Café	Peltzer's	Fortuna	Küntzler-Theater
5	Speyer & Peters	Café Austria	Kempinski & Co.	Gretsel-Behr	Lessing
6	S. Schropp	Café Woerz (billiards)	The Jockey	Korfu	Metropol
7	Eisenschmidt	Englisches Café	Rheingold	Ludwig	Opera House
8	Martin Breslauer	Luisen-Café	Höhn's Oyster Saloon	Stinde-Cranz	Schiller
9	Paul Graupe	Café Josty (terrace)	The Continental Bodega Company (Spanish)	Von Lützow	Volksbühne
10	Inveha* (occult bookshop)	Konditorei	Kämmerer (Vegetarian)	Von Saucken	Des Westens

*See **Dances of Vice, Horror, and Ecstasy**, page 175, for details on Inveha.

Invalidenfriedhof: the Invalid's Cemetery, located north of the **Charité** (page @@), is one of the city's oldest. Many of the Prussian generals of the Wars of Liberation against Napoleon (1813–1815) are buried here, as are Schlieffen and Moltke. In 1925, the remains of Manfred "the Red Baron" von Richthofen are reburied here, transferred from their original resting place in France.

Pappelallee: a uniquely Berliner cemetery, located in the northern district of Pankow. Proving that there's a place for people of all persuasions in the city, this graveyard, opened in 1848, is reserved for atheists. Above the entrance gate is an inscription: *"Schafft hier das Leben gut und schön, kein Jenseits ist, kein Aufersteh'n"* (Enjoy life while you can; there is no afterlife, no resurrection).

Weißensee: Berlin's most prominent Jewish cemetery; at 100 acres (40 hectares), it is the second-largest Jewish cemetery in all of Europe. Tens of thousands of graves cover the plot, with the most elaborate tombs and mausoleums, many constructed in an exuberant Art Nouveau style, ringing the outer perimeter.

OH! YOU PRETTY THINGS

The draw of Berlin lies in its vibrant character, provided in part by the wild array of natives and expats mixing together amidst the fading Wilhelmine and emerging Modernist splendor. Presented here are selected biographies for some of the city's more notable residents: artists, dilettantes, and politicians, among others. Keepers should feel free to utilize some of them to add local color to explorations of the city, or as point of interest when designing scenarios.

Some of these characters are lifelong residents of Berlin, or they may simply use the city as a home base for their travels, while others merely pass through, leaving an indelible mark in the process. When available, the years of their residency in Berlin are indicated next to their names. In a similar vein, the personages presented are focused primarily on their time in Berlin and their significance to the city during the Weimar period. Details on their lives before and after this time interval may be readily found elsewhere.

One final note: other notable residents of the city (Aleister Crowley, Anita Berber, and others) appear in the scenarios contained elsewhere in this volume and are not repeated here.

Bertolt Brecht (1924–33)

I, Bertolt Brecht, come from the black forests.
My mother carried me into the cities
When I was in her belly. And the chill of the forests
Will be in me till my dying day.

The asphalt city is my home. Furnished
From the outset with every sacramental prerequisite:
With newspapers. And tobacco. And brandy.
Distrustful and idle and contented to the end.

—Bertolt Brecht, *Of Poor B.B.*

One of the most important and transformative figures in 20th-century theatre, Bertolt Brecht is born in Bavaria in 1898. After a brief stint in the military at the tail end of the Great War, Brecht embarks upon a literary career. His first play, *Baal*, is produced in 1923 and causes a scandal on its opening night, inaugurating a pattern that follows much of Brecht's later works. Brecht relocates to Berlin in 1924, initially working as a dramaturg but continuing to write plays and poetry and, in collaboration with other theatrical producers like **Erwin Piscator** (page 80), refines his vision of

what comes to be called "Epic Theatre." By 1927, he has also become a committed Marxist with Bolshevik sympathies, and his intense political views are reflected not just in his writing but also in his productions.

Epic Theatre is confrontational, aiming to reinforce the artificiality of the theatrical experience as a way of reminding the audience of the artificiality of their own realities. In Brecht's hands, it is also a propagandistic tool, communicating his views on social justice, the class system, religion, and Marxism. Brecht's *Threepenny Opera*, with music by **Kurt Weill** (page 87), premieres in 1928 and quickly becomes the greatest theatrical hit in Weimar Germany. Over the next five years, it is translated into 18 languages and performed more than 10,000 times across Europe.

Much like his plays, Brecht the man is confrontational, provocative, and chaotic. He is an inveterate womanizer and an apologist for Bolshevik excess. In short, he is a colorful character sure to liven up any party or social gathering, though not always for the better.

Lya de Putti (1920–26)

Born in present-day Slovakia to a Hungarian family in what was then the Austro-Hungarian Empire, the dancer and actress Lya de Putti comes to Berlin after divorcing her magistrate husband and leaving her two daughters behind, setting off in search of a more adventurous life.

Once in Berlin, she dances in music hall revues, including those at the famous Wintergarten. She begins appearing in movies in 1921 and, by 1922, her smoldering looks, heavily lidded eyes, and short, black bobbed hair have caught the imagination of the public, leading her to a career of being typecast as a vamp.

De Putti reaches the height of her popularity in 1925 when she appears in the film *Varieté* (dir. E. A. Dupont) with Emil Jannings. This leads to an invitation from Hollywood, and she sails for America in February 1926.

During her residence in Berlin, de Putti is a frequent sight at nightclubs and parties in the Friedrichstadt and Ku'damm. She is also a popular subject for Telephone-Girl prostitutes to model their appearances.

Marlene Dietrich (1901–30)

"I am, thank God, a Berliner."

—Marlene Dietrich

Born in the Schöneberg district at the end of 1901, Dietrich grows up in Berlin with dreams of becoming a concert violinist. A wrist injury ends these ambitions, and she instead begins finding work in 1922 as a chorus girl in various **Max Reinhardt** (page 81) productions, despite being rejected from his drama academy.

Lya de Putti

Marlene Dietrich

Over the course of the 1920s, Dietrich works steadily in film and theater, gradually moving up into increasingly important roles as the decade wears on. She makes her first big splash in the revue *Es Liege in der Luft* (It's in the Air), where she sings a duet with Margo Lion (*Wenn die beste Freundin*) that becomes an instant anthem for Berlin's lesbian community. However, it is the role of cabaret singer Lola Lola in Josef von Sternberg's *The Blue Angel* (1930) that catapults her to stardom. The advance publicity surrounding the movie is enough to secure her a ticket to Hollywood before the movie is even released. Dietrich attends *The Blue Angel*'s Berlin premiere, takes her bows at the end of the film, then boards a train to start her journey to America.

Dietrich marries assistant director Rudolf Sieber in 1923 and she gives birth to her only child, a daughter named Maria, the following year. Although Dietrich remains married her whole life, she is famously promiscuous, carrying on affairs with a cavalcade of men and women well into her 70s.

For many, Dietrich embodies the earthy, sensual, transgressive qualities of Weimar Berlin. She is a fashion icon who mixes male and female dress, and who doesn't blink in the face of crossing gender lines. During her time in Berlin, she trains with Turkish prizefighter Sabri Mahir, one of only a handful of women to join his boxing studio. Although her Berlin years come prior to her international stardom, she is a fixture of the city's nightlife and the German film industry prior to her departure for American shores.

Otto Dix, George Grosz, and Käthe Kollwitz

Berlin in the 1920s is a vibrant hub for art. The first half of the decade is dominated by the continuing influence of the German Expressionist movement (most visible in the worlds of dance and film), but around 1925 a new movement that had hitherto been bubbling under the surface bursts forth. Called *Neue Sachlichkeit*, the term is most often translated into English as "New Objectivity" but may also be rendered as "New Matter-of-Factness" or "New Dispassion." Like Expressionism, this new movement is represented across a wide field of the arts, from architecture to literature to film, but it is the pieces produced by a small school of fine artists that most clearly define the look, both of New Objectivity and of Weimar Berlin. Otto Dix and Georg Grosz, both Berlin residents, are the most famous artists to arise from the New Objectivity movement.

When the Great War breaks out, Otto Dix (1891–1961) enthusiastically enlists. His patriotic zeal does not last long as he witnesses horror after horror on the battlefields of the Western and Eastern Fronts. He survives the war and is awarded the Iron Cross, Second Class. His experiences haunt him for the rest of his life. In 1924, he produces a portfolio of 50 etchings entitled *Der Krieg* (The War)

depicting the brutality of modern warfare, this following a series of etchings and paintings depicting *lustmord* (sexual murder) in 1922. His style then evolves to one of tempera paint and oil glazes in the style of the Old Masters but used to depict the bizarre realities of post-war Berlin; his portraits of Sylvia von Harden and Anita Berber are startlingly grotesque, while his 1928 triptych *Metropolis* perfectly sums up the city's non-stop party in the face of grim realities of the past and worry about the future. Despite being branded a "degenerate artist" by the Nazis, Dix remains in Germany and survives the Second World War.

George Grosz (1893–1961) also serves during the Great War but does not see combat, being hospitalized for a sinusitis infection in 1915. In 1919, he participates in the Spartacist uprising, which marks the high point of his direct involvement in radical politics. Over time he grows disillusioned with Communism, though he retains his left-wing political sensibilities even after leaving the party. His caricatures and oil paintings from this period portray a Berlin of mutilated war veterans, prostitutes, debased capitalists, and wild parties—in short, much of what we associate with Weimar Berlin today. His early 1920s work is heavily influenced by the Dada movement and depicts grotesque humans and robotic automatons. Grosz departs Berlin just before Hitler becomes Chancellor, moving to the United States, for which he has long harbored a fascination.

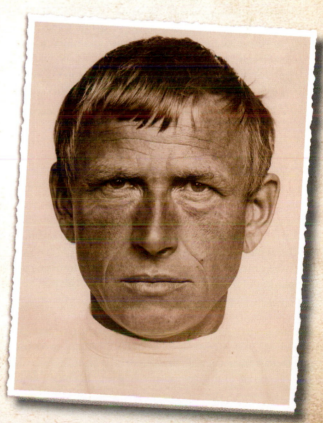

Otto Dix

EXPRESSIONISM

This artistic movement originated in Germany before the Great War and encompassed painting, theater, film, dance, music, and literature. Essentially a Modernist movement, Expressionism aimed to present the world from a subjective viewpoint, distorting the natural to evoke a specific mood, theme, or idea in reaction to the dehumanizing effects of mass industrialization and the move from rural to urban life. One could say Expressionism rejected the ideology of realism. Expressionistic art tends to be intense, non-naturalistic, and emotional. Such pieces were envisioned as coming from "within" the artist and not as a depiction of the world around them. Thus, the art produced often revolved around social criticism and alienation.

Although not formally associated with the New Objectivity movement, and being of an older generation than either Dix or Grosz, the post-war woodcuts of Käthe Kollwitz (1867–1945) derive from the same impulse to strip away all sentimentality and portray only the brutal, naked truth. Her cycle of "War" woodcuts (1921–23) and her 1924 posters *Germany's Children Starving*, *Bread*, and *Never Again War* show the human toll of loss and suffering, and the dark side of war and its aftermath in such unflinching terms that she is put on the Gestapo's watch list in the 1930s. Fortunately, her worldwide fame prevents any further action, and she continues to reside in Berlin until 1943.

Friedrich Ebert (1905–25)

The first President of the German Republic, Ebert is often a leader without any allies. Although he is the leader of the Social Democratic Party (SPD) and an avowed socialist, his centrist policies anger other leftist leaders—both the Independent Social Democrats and the German Communist Party form as splinter groups of the SPD in reaction to Ebert's policy decisions during the Great War.

Ebert tries desperately to salvage the monarchy during the final days of the war, but, once he accepts the inevitability of that institution's demise, he devotes his energies full-time to building a democratic republic.

In January 1919, Ebert is elected president. Over the next two years, he spends much of his time quelling violent uprisings from the right and the left. It is his decision to enlist the aid of the nationalistic Freikorps in putting down

the 1919 Spartacist uprising, an action that earns him the undying enmity of the Communists and other radical left-wing parties. Even political moderates criticize this decision, as it leaves an unfortunate stain on Weimar-era politics that is never quite washed away. As the diplomat Count Kessler writes, "The paradox of a republican-social-democratic government allowing itself and the capitalists' safes to be defended by hired unemployed and royalist officers, is simply too insane." Right-wing groups, meanwhile, put Ebert up as a representative of the "November criminals" who, in their view, sold out Germany's military by agreeing to an armistice and later signing the ruinous Treaty of Versailles.

Under constant attack from the right and left, Ebert's health quickly begins to deteriorate. After a judge rules that Ebert technically committed treason when supporting a workers' strike during the Great War, Ebert's health takes a turn for the worse, and he dies while still in office in 1925.

Albert Einstein (1914–32)

Albert Einstein, one of the world's foremost scientific minds, is brought to Berlin in 1914 from his home in Zurich, Switzerland, attracted by offers from Max Planck and Walther Nernst. Once in the city, he is given membership of the Prussian Academy of Sciences and a non-teaching professorship at the University of Berlin. He sets up a home office at his flat in Schöneberg

and completes his work on his General Theory of Relativity, winning the Nobel Prize for Physics in 1921.

Over the next two decades, Einstein maintains his primary residence in Berlin. His work on relativity has made him a scientific superstar. From this point on, he focuses much of his attention on unsuccessfully disproving quantum theory, but he also engages in research on wormholes, gravitational waves, superconductivity, and a unified field theory, none of which bear fruit.

A great music lover, he frequently attends concerts when in the city and is even known to sit in on performances with his violin. He also performs chamber music with Max Planck and his son in private.

An ardent Zionist, Einstein is well aware of the rising tide of anti-Semitism in Germany. He visits the United States several times between 1930–32, and is traveling in California when the Nazis seize power in January 1933. Knowing he can never return, Einstein settles permanently in America. The Nazi regime confiscates all the belongings in his Berlin residence and puts a price on his head.

As a world-famous scientist, Einstein is often abroad for months at a time, although he is frequently to be found in Berlin during the summer months. Investigators wishing to meet him have their best chances to do so in attending lectures and functions at the University, or at orchestral music performances.

Ruth Fischer (1919–33)

An ultra-leftist gadfly for proletarian revolution, Austrian-born Ruth Fischer arrives in Berlin in 1919. By 1921, she is appointed chair of the KPD (German Communist Party) in Berlin. Fischer's politics are described by her opponents as "infantile radicalism." She refuses to kowtow to Lenin when she meets him on a trip to Moscow, and she rails against the KPD's policies as overly timid and ineffectual. *Time* magazine calls her "a bundle of sex appeal and intellectual fire." Her star is rising.

With the ascension of Stalin in the Soviet Union, Fischer is summoned to Moscow in 1925, where she becomes a virtual prisoner at her room at the Hotel Lux. After 10 months, she feigns a nervous breakdown and returns to Berlin but, thanks to Stalin's influence, is expelled from the KPD in August 1926.

Fischer is also a member of the Reichstag from 1924–28, representing the more radical, Trotskyite wing of German Communism. By this point, *Time* magazine, feeling much less generous, describes her presence in parliamentary meetings thusly: "She's a sneerer and a snarler. She sits on the far left of the house, interrupting Stresemann, Ludendorff, and Tirpitz with cries of Phooey. She is fat... and addresses the house with a vaudevillian shimmy that is unique."

After 1928, Fischer's political power in Berlin is minimal. She flees the country in 1933 ahead of Hitler's seizure of power. Later in life, she becomes an avowed anti-Stalinist and anti-Communist, testifying against her brother and other associates at House Unamerican Activities Committee meetings.

In short, Fischer is a captivating, contradictory, passionate individual who inspires great devotion or passionate opposition, with little middle ground. She makes an ideal contact for leftist investigators; prior to 1928, she wields considerable political influence as well.

Joseph Goebbels (1926–45)

"What the man showed of oratorical and organisational talent, is unique. There was nothing he could not rise up to. The party members were attached to him with great love. The S.A. would have allowed themselves to get torn into shreds for him. Goebbels, that was like Hitler himself. Goebbels, that was just our Goebbels."

—Horst Wessel

The arrival of the "Marat of Red Berlin, a nightmare and goblin of history" in 1926 marks a dark day in the city's history. A committed Nazi and master of propaganda, Goebbels transforms the party in Berlin; previously a marginalized, fractious group, it quickly becomes a machine for promoting National Socialist interests and the Führer myth.

Joseph Goebbels

Joseph Goebbels is born into a strict Catholic family in 1897. A childhood case of polio leaves him with a deformed foot, a physical malady that keeps him out of the Great War but also forms the core of his spiteful inferiority complex.

An opportunist first and foremost, Goebbels, after joining the NSDAP in 1922, accomplishes a remarkable pivot in 1926, going from co-authoring a pamphlet calling for the expulsion of "petty-bourgeois" Hitler from the party earlier in the year, to being named district leader of Berlin-Brandenburg by Hitler before the year is out.

A frustrated poet and author, Goebbels turns his creative energies toward organizing, myth-making, and rabble-rousing. He founds and runs a paper, *Der Angriff* (*The Attack*), designs posters, stages parades, and deploys his Stormtroopers at politically opportune moments to instigate street battles, stir up trouble in beer halls, and perpetrate drive-by shootings, all the better to sow chaos and disorder—which, of course, only the deific Hitler, acting as brave shield-bearer against the agents of collapse, can tame.

Goebbels openly talks about destroying the system from within. Upon becoming a Reichstag member in 1928, he is quoted as saying "We are entering the Reichstag, in order that we may arm ourselves with the weapons of democracy from its arsenal. We shall become Reichstag deputies in order that the Weimar ideology should itself help us to destroy it."

Despite his best efforts, the popularity of the Nazi Party in Berlin remains low. But with the global economic collapse of 1929, things turn around as desperate voters begin looking for a savior, leading to his appointment as Reich Propaganda Leader of the NSDAP. Over the next three years, Goebbels helps steer the party first to greater representation in the Reichstag and then a total takeover of the government in January 1933. In May of that year, Goebbels organizes one of the most infamous acts of Nazi propaganda, the mass burning in Berlin of books deemed to be "un-German" in spirit. This includes Communist and Marxist works, pacifist literature, Jewish literature, "degenerate art" books, writings by liberal Weimar politicians and thinkers, such as Walther Rathenau, and much of **Dr. Hirschfeld's** (page 77) library on human sexuality.

Goebbels is utterly cynical and amoral. He is deeply hateful toward himself and turns this hate against the human race, and Jewish people in particular. He is one of the most virulently anti-Semitic members of the Nazi leadership and openly expresses his feelings without reservation.

Valeska Gert (1892–1933)

Valeska Gert is born to a Berlin Jewish family in 1892 and from an early age expresses an interest in dance. She trains with Maria Moissi and is a contemporary student to Anita Berber when the latter is just starting out.

Much like Berber, Gert is interested in revolutionary dance; her routines often verge into the realm of performance art, though that term has not yet been coined. A famous example is her piece "Pause," in which she takes the stage in between film showings at cinemas and simply stands still for the duration of the piece. She creates dances that replicate boxing matches, traffic accidents, and orgasms.

She also designs her own dance costumes and street fashion to be as transgressive as possible. Her anarchic style is very much in keeping with the Dada philosophy, and she is a fixture at Berlin cabarets and dance halls. In addition, she works as an artist's model and acts in several films, most prominently in G. W. Pabst's *Diary of a Lost Girl* (1929).

She is fearless in her artistic expression, and a great lover of life. Unlike Berber, she does not burn out, instead fading to obscurity after being forced to leave the country by Nazi prohibition on her dancing.

Max Hermann-Neiße (1917–33)

A writer and journalist, Hermann-Neiße and his wife, Helene "Leni" Gebek, are fixtures on the Berlin cabaret scene for the entirety of their 16-year residence in the city. Out of a professed deep and abiding love for the art form, Hermann-Neiße spends much of his time writing about how post-war cabaret in Berlin has fallen from its lofty Wilhelmian heights, going for cheap sensation and empty-headed entertainment in place of what was once a vehicle for smart, in-depth social critique. The following passage from 1925 is typical of his rantings: "A decisively independent, purposefully intellectual and fighting cabaret no longer exists, only amusement locales on approximately the same level, each of which has its own method of acceding to the wishes of the public."

Hermann-Neiße is an early and enthusiastic supporter of the transgressive dancer Anita Berber and, later, the lyricist Friedrich Holländer, who, in his estimation, are the only figures in cabaret maintaining the form's old emphasis on parodic deconstruction of Berlin society.

Dr. Magnus Hirschfeld (1896–1933)

A controversial and polarizing figure, Dr. Hirschfeld is called "the Einstein of Sex" by his admirers and openly disparaged by his detractors, chief among them the Nazi Party. Hirschfeld is both gay and Jewish, making him a double target for right-wing reactionaries. The fact that he openly discusses sex and vigorously advocates for legal recognition for gay men ensures his stature among certain groups. To many, he is a hero, opening up his **Institute of Sexology** (page 50) as a font of research and medical treatment for people from all spectrums of human sexuality.

Max Hermann-Neiße

Dr. Magnus Hirschfeld

Hirschfeld is active in Berlin's queer community, and considered as something of a father figure. He is a frequent target of harassment from **Joseph Goebbels** (page 76) and his Stormtroopers. Hirschfeld is on a worldwide speaking tour when the Nazis seize power and never returns to Berlin after 1933. He dies in Nice, France just two years later.

Christopher Isherwood (1929–33)

It is through the writings of British author Christopher Isherwood that the Anglophone world has developed its impressions of Weimar Berlin. In addition to his *Berlin Stories*, a play (*I Am a Camera*), the musical *Cabaret*, and the film of the same name are all based on his works and the characters he developed therein.

As much as Isherwood attempts in his writings to maintain a sense of narrative remove (his famous line, "I am a camera with its shutter open, quite passive, recording, not thinking," opens the first of his Berlin books, *Goodbye to Berlin*), he is very much a part of the city, particularly its gay scene.

Invited to visit Berlin at the age of 25 by his old chum and sometime lover, the poet W. H. Auden, Isherwood sets his mind on taking up residence in the city after witnessing its open attitude toward queer people. Auden and mutual friend Stephen Spender drift in and out of Berlin, but Isherwood remains for four years, departing when he sees the winds of history shifting.

Christopher Isherwood

After taking a room at Dr. Hirschfeld's Institute of Sexology, Isherwood eventually moves to a room in Nollendorfplatz, where he writes much of what becomes his *Berlin Stories*. He also meets a flat mate, **Jean Ross** (page 81), who informs the characterization of his most famous creation, Sally Bowles.

Isherwood's favorite haunt during his time in Berlin is the Cosy Corner, a den of Line-Boys, rough trade, and expatriates like Isherwood. He also spends time at the New Eldorado, situated not far from his Nollendorfplatz residence. Investigators moving around Berlin in the late 1920s and early 1930s may well catch a glimpse of a handsome young British man absorbing the scenes around him, silently cataloging all he sees for later consignment to the page.

Fritz Lang and Thea von Harbou (1920–33)

One of the great visionary auteurs of silent cinema, Fritz Lang is born in Vienna in 1890 to a Jewish mother and Catholic father. After serving in the Austro-Hungarian army during the Great War (over the course of which he is hospitalized three times and eventually attains the rank of Lieutenant), he is hired by Berlin film studio Ufa to write screenplays. It doesn't take long for him to start directing as well.

Lang marries Thea von Harbou in 1922, inaugurating a decade of productive collaboration. Harbou, born in 1888 to a wealthy Bavarian family, comes to Berlin in 1917 with her husband, the actor Rudolf Klein-Rogge, and immediately makes an impact as a screenwriter. She and Lang meet and fall in love while collaborating on a project for Ufa. Following the death of Lang's first wife (under mysterious circumstances) and Harbou's divorce from Klein-Rogge, they are free to wed.

Lang and Harbou are collaborators on every film he produces for the remainder of the decade. From the crime thriller *Dr. Mabuse: the Gambler* (1922) to the five-hour epic *Die Niebelungen* (1924) to the ground-breaking sci-fi spectacular *Metropolis* (1927) and, finally, to Lang's first "talkie" feature, *M* (1931), he and Harbou produce one classic after another.

For most movies, Harbou also writes a novelization of her script and serves on set in a variety of roles, even peeling potatoes and preparing food for the crew. Lang, for his part, is the model of the classic dictatorial director, pacing the film lot with a monocle clenched over one eye, shouting commands and maintaining an iron grip on production, arranging the actors in his shots like delicate pieces of a visual puzzle. It is even rumored that he throws Peter Lorre down a flight of stairs prior to shooting the final scene in *M*, in which Lorre's character has been severely beaten—all the better to give the actor a properly bloody appearance.

Lang's films tend to dwell on themes of individual will being crushed under the uncaring boot-heel of corrupt institutions. This, along with his Jewish heritage, puts him at odds with the new Nazi regime, and he flees Germany for Paris (and ultimately Hollywood) in 1933.

Harbou, an open admirer of Hitler, remains behind, eventually joining the Nazi Party and making films for the state-run movie industry. She and Lang are divorced the year he leaves.

During the golden years of their marriage, Lang and Harbou are two of Berlin's most luminous stars. Their home in Berlin is a virtual museum of exotic artifacts collected from Asia and the Pacific Islands, and their films and books often make them the toast of the town. Encountered in person, Lang is difficult if he doesn't get his way, while Harbou is quietly self-effacing but possesses a sharp intelligence and genuine passion about Nationalist politics.

Vladimir Nabokov (1922–37)

Just one man amid the sea of 300,000 Russian émigrés that pour into Berlin in the years after the Bolshevik Revolution, during his 15-year residence in the city Vladimir Nabokov is not yet the towering literary giant he one day becomes, though over the course of this time he begins to earn that reputation.

Fritz Lang and Thea von Harbou

He comes to Berlin shortly after graduating Cambridge University to join his family, who've been living in the city since 1920. Tragedy strikes not soon after, when Nabokov's father (also named Vladimir) is gunned down while successfully preventing the assassination of the liberal politician Pavel Milyukov. Nabokov's remaining family leaves the city after this, but Vladimir stays. While he never fully integrates with the German community, picking up only a bit of the language and remaining within the large Russian expatriate population on the west side of the city, Berlin touches him deeply and informs his writing for the rest of his career.

With his keen observer's eye, he notes small details that others miss. In particular, he describes the state of affairs among the émigré community—once comfortable bourgeois and aristocratic folk (like himself), now forced to live an uncertain lifestyle in a foreign land, "urban vagabond[s] with an early evening thirst," as he puts it in his 1925 work *The Fight*. Despite being tri-lingual, speaking French and English as well as Russian, during this time he writes almost exclusively in the latter tongue under the pen name "Sirin."

Although his prolific writing output is well received among the Russian community, it still is not enough to pay the bills, and Nabokov devotes much of his time to language tutoring, as well as teaching tennis and boxing and appearing as a film extra. In 1921, at a masquerade ball, he meets a woman wearing a "black mask with a wolf's profile"—this is Vera Slonim, a Russian Jew and soon to be Nabokov's wife.

Although Vladimir loves his peculiar life in Berlin, he is eventually forced to give it up. His own family's left-wing political history combined with his Jewish wife makes life increasingly tenuous under the Nazi regime, and he and Vera (along with their three-year-old son Dmitri) leave everything behind to start anew in France.

Lola Niedlich

The star of the Stork's Nest evening cabaret shows, with her cascading blonde coiffure, bedroom eyes, and smoky voice, the chair-straddling Lola Niedlich ("Lola Cute") is the prototypical underground chanteuse. Much as the Stork's Nest is the model for the eponymous Blue Angel cabaret in the movie of the same name, Niedlich is the model for Dietrich's Lola Lola. An inveterate self-promoter, Niedlich is known to circulate among the Stork's Nest patrons in between her numbers, peddling racy photo-postcards of herself in a variety of scintillating poses. She bills herself as "the Prize-Winning Torch-Singer, Three Times Engaged at Marienbad" and does indeed fly from the nest for periodic touring engagements around Germany and Austria.

Asta Nielsen (1910–36)

The Danish-born Nielsen is one of the first international movie stars of the young cinema industry. Her rise to fame in the years leading up to the Great War is facilitated by her revolutionary acting technique, which replaces the previously vaudevillian theatrics of film acting with a raw and immediate naturalism. This technique goes a long way toward legitimizing film in the eyes of cultural critics, who previously dismissed short-form nickelodeons as the lowest of low culture.

Her naturalistic style includes a certain overt and captivating sexuality, leading her films to be heavily censored in the Anglophone world. On the Continent, however, she is a superstar, referred to simply as *Die Asta* (The Asta). She commands a truly remarkable annual salary of $80,000 a year and forms her own distribution and production company, Asta Films, at Berlin's Tempelhof field, helping to launch the Berlin film industry.

The arguable peak of her career comes in 1921, when she plays the gender-flipped lead role in an adaptation of *Hamlet*, playing the Danish "prince" as a woman in disguise. Die Asta retires from film at the dawn of the talkies; although Adolf Hitler personally begs her to return to the silver screen and make propaganda films in the 1930s, she declines, fleeing the Nazi regime for her home country in 1936.

Erwin Piscator (1922–31)

Like many of his contemporaries in the arts, theatrical producer/director Erwin Piscator's life is irrevocably shaped by his time serving in the Great War. As with **Otto Dix** (page 73), Piscator's experiences as a front-line infantryman on the Western Front imbue him with a deep hatred of warfare and war profiteers. Piscator is also heavily radicalized, forming one of the first post-war soldiers' soviets mere hours after the Armistice.

When the revolutionary ardor dies down, Piscator returns to his pre-war theatrical training, coming to Berlin in 1922 to form a theatre company at the *Volksbühne* (People's Theatre) on Alte Jakobstraße in the Friedrichstadt.

From 1924–27, Piscator produces and directs plays with a political message. He begins developing production techniques that will come to be called "Epic Theatre" when they are expanded and refined by his colleague, **Bertolt Brecht** (page 71). Piscator's productions are intentionally confrontational and radical in their staging, making use of film and still photograph projections, mechanical devices, and unusual audio effects to both draw in an atypical working-class crowd and confront it with his message. When Piscator is tapped to put on a production of the classic *Sturm und Drang* play *The Robbers* at the prestigious Preußisches Staatstheater, he nearly causes a riot with his unconventional

Asta Nielsen

Erwin Piscator

production and the heavy changes he makes to the script, casting the tale of two antagonistic aristocrats into a struggle between the ruling class and the working class. After that debacle, Piscator opens his own playhouse at the Theater am Nollendorfplatz. Here, he continues producing his own version of politically charged epic theatre, penning a 1929 explication of his theory entitled, appropriately, *The Political Theatre*.

Piscator travels to Moscow in 1931 to produce movies; while this is meant to just be a temporary move, with the rise of the Nazis in 1933, he has no choice but to stay in Moscow. Like his colleague Brecht, Piscator is deadly serious about his art and his politics, seeing the two as inseparably intertwined.

Max Reinhardt (1894–1933)

A towering giant of German theatre, the name of Max Reinhardt is one surely to be invoked in any conversation involving actors and performers, for he wields the ability to make or break careers almost at will. Born on the fringes of the Austro-Hungarian Empire to a Jewish family, Reinhardt first comes to Berlin in 1894 as an actor in the company of Otto Brahm. Chafing under the demands of his Naturalist director, Reinhardt decides to forge his own path.

In 1901, he founds the *Schall und Rauch* (Sound and Smoke) *Kabarett* with two partners, the first of its kind in Berlin. The productions are a mixture of song, dance, and

political satire, and they set the template for the city's world-famous cabaret scene over the ensuing three decades. At the same time, Reinhardt revolutionizes the role of the theater director. Previously seen as being more of an organizer and administrator, Reinhardt creates the template of the director as creative *auteur*. In his first three years, he directs 42 plays, culminating with a joyous production of *A Midsummer Night's Dream* that is rapturously received and turns Reinhardt into an overnight success and millionaire.

With his funds, he purchases the Deutsches Theater in 1906 for one million marks. For the next quarter-century, Reinhardt maintains his position as the city's premier theatrical producer. In 1920, he co-founds the Salzburg Festival with Richard Strauss and Hugo von Hofmannsthal.

During the Weimar era, Reinhardt effectively commutes between Berlin, Vienna, and Salzburg, residing for part of the year at an Austrian castle in semi-retirement; however, he has left an indelible mark on Berlin and continues to exert an influence on the entertainment industry there.

In addition to the Deutsches Theater, Reinhardt opens several others, large and small. Immediately adjacent to the Deutsches Theater, for example, is a converted tavern that Reinhardt calls the *Kammerspiel* (Chamber Play), a venue for staging smaller, more intimate productions. At the other end of the spectrum is his spectacular monument to Expressionist architecture, the Großes Schauspielhaus (**Alexanderplatz**, page 28).

Reinhardt's influence is also felt in the effect he has on German cinema. In addition to founding and operating his own production company, many German directors are influenced by his theatrical productions and their striking combinations of costume, lighting, staging, and scenic backdrops, and among his disciples may be counted **Fritz Lang** (page 78), F. W. Murnau, Ernst Lubitsch, and Otto Preminger.

By the 1920s, Reinhardt's name is much more likely to be encountered than the man himself. He is a character moving around in the shadows of Berlin's entertainment complexes. An actual meeting with him should be a moment of great portent and trepidation for any investigator involved in theater or film.

Jean Ross (1931–33)

Born in Alexandria, Egypt to British parents, Jean Ross comes to Berlin in 1931 at the age of 20 to find what the city holds. A bright student—too bright for the boarding schools and finishing schools her parents send her to—she discovers early on a love of the written word.

In Berlin, she makes ends meet with cabaret performances and fashion modeling; she is possessed of a striking sense of style, often favoring blousy trousers, berets or fedoras,

Max Reinhardt

and a silver-tipped cane. Her true passion lies with the Communist cause, and she writes extensively for various Red publications.

She meets and befriends her neighbor, a fellow British expat by the name of **Christopher Isherwood** (page 78), a few months after her arrival in the city. Her sparkling personality and sense of style greatly informs his fictional invention of the cabaret singer Sally Bowles. Ross is not terribly flattered by the character, who is far less political or witty than Ross.

In 1933, after nearly dying from a botched abortion while on holiday in England, Ross opts not to return to Berlin when Hitler seizes power.

Joseph Roth (1920–25)

Perhaps the most popular and well-read journalist in Germany in the 1920s, Joseph Roth's heyday in Berlin lasts only about four years but leaves us with a vibrant portrait of the city from the point of view of one of the most trenchant minds of his day.

Like so many others, Roth comes to Berlin from lands far afield. Born to a Jewish family in Galicia on the Austro-Hungarian frontier, Roth serves some time in the Great War before turning his attention to journalism, writing for left-wing papers in Vienna and earning the nickname "Red Roth" in the process.

Joseph Roth

He comes to Berlin in 1920 and writes for several papers, filing observational pieces as well as news reports. The former are later collected in a book, *What I Saw*, which presents a fragmentary portrait of Berlin's social and political life before, during, and after the Great Inflation.

Roth begins writing for the internationally renowned *Frankfurter Zeitung* in 1923, and by 1925 has left Berlin for good. He returns from time to time over the ensuing years, but his career shifts to writing about international affairs and writing fiction. The acerbic wit characterizing Roth's writing is a mask for a deeply pessimistic personality. The stresses and upheavals afflicting Europe in the 1930s eventually prove too much; he collapses and dies at the age of 45 while living in exile in France.

Encountered during his time in Berlin (or later, during one of his periodic visits prior to 1933), Roth is the prototypical reporter, always keenly observing with notebook in hand. His cynicism and cold observations are a perfect match for the typical Berliner but also take a toll on him personally. He abandons Communism (for the most part) after a 1926 visit to the Soviet Union opens his eyes to the tyrannies of Bolshevism, and increasingly comes to rely on the comforts of alcohol to fill the increasing void in his life.

Annemarie Schwarzenbach (1930–33)

Though a resident for only three years (a period punctuated by repeated trips abroad), writer, photographer, and dilettante Annemarie Schwarzenbach in many ways embodies the libertine spirit and transgressive nature of Berlin in a way few others do.

Born into a well off, German-speaking Zurich household in 1908, Schwarzenbach shows both a prodigal intelligence and an interest in androgyny, traits her parents encourage. For the remainder of her too-brief life, she wears her hair and clothes in a boyish mode—the look enraptures both male and female admirers, though Annemarie limits her romantic affairs almost exclusively to women. One of her deepest relationships forms in 1930 when she meets Erika, daughter of the famous novelist Thomas Mann. Much to Schwarzenbach's chagrin, the relationship is mostly one-sided, and Erika ultimately leaves her for another woman (though the two remain friends).

Through Erika, though, Schwarzenbach makes the acquaintance of another child of Mann, Klaus. She moves to his Westend residence in Berlin, and the two are soon availing themselves of every vice the city has to offer: drinks, drugs, fast cars, and faster women. In 1932 and 1933 she travels with Klaus to Scandinavia, Italy, and France, as well as taking a tour of the Pyrenees in 1933 with photographer Marianne Feilchenfeldt-Breslauer, though a scheduled driving tour of Persia is sadly put on hold when one of the participants, artist Ricki Hallgarten, shoots himself on the eve before their departure.

Schwarzenbach finances her wild lifestyle and travels across Europe with journalistic and fictive writing, as well as photography, building a reputation as a multi-talented creative force. One of her many admirers, Marianne Breslauer, later writes of Schwarzenbach, "She was neither a man nor a woman but an angel, an archangel."

Encountered during her heyday in Berlin, Schwarzenbach is the prototypical dissipated dilettante-cum-genius. She lives dangerously and expects those around her to keep up. Her drugs of choice are hard liquor and morphine, and she is never in bed before dawn.

Kurt Tucholsky (1899–1924)

"Human stupidity is international."

—Kurt Tucholsky

A native of the city, Tucholsky spends some childhood years abroad in Poland before returning to Berlin. With the exception of three years spent serving on the Eastern Front in the Great War, he spends the next quarter-century of his life in the city he loves, trying, in the words of one admirer, to stop catastrophes with his typewriter.

Annemarie Schwarzenbach

Tucholsky's writing output is truly awe-inspiring. Working primarily as a journalist and satirist, he produces so much material that he is obliged to adopt four pennames—Ignaz Wrobel, Theobald Tiger, Peter Panter, and Kaspar Hauser—simply to avoid his name showing up under every single by-line in the papers *Ulk* (Prank) and *Die Weltbühne*. At the latter paper, he forms a close working relationship with Carl von Ossietzky.

But Tucholsky is not simply a reporter. He is also a poet and lyricist, penning some of the most acidic and hilarious cabaret songs of his age—his most popular tune is *Die Rote Melodie* (The Red Melody), an anti-war anthem written specifically for the famous cabaret singer Rosa Valetti. His ultimate cause is the health and success of the Republic (he is a committed member of the SPD, although often its most vocal critic also), and he sees as much danger in radical leftism as in right-wing Nationalism.

He lives and breathes the politics of the day, condemning the spate of assassinations and lynchings that ravage Germany in the five years following the Armistice, and the tacit support given by the ultra-conservative judiciary, which he summarizes as, "The German political murder of the past four years is schematically and tightly organized. Everything is certain from the outset: incentives from anonymous financial backers, the deed (always from behind), sloppy investigation, lazy excuses, a few phrases, pitiful skiving, lenient punishments, suspension of sentences, privileges—'Carry on!' That is not bad justice. That is not poor justice. That is not justice at all. Even the Balkans and South America will refuse to be compared with this Germany."

His writing is marked by a satirical cynicism; it is he and not Stalin who first coins the phrase, "The death of one man: that is a catastrophe. One hundred thousand deaths: that is a statistic!" He often speaks at public events, particularly SPD rallies and at lectures given by the German League for Human Rights.

A committed pacifist, Tucholsky writes his most controversial article in 1931, when reminiscing on the Great War, "For four years, there were whole square miles of land where murder was obligatory, while it was strictly forbidden half an hour away. Did I say: murder? Of course murder. Soldiers are murderers."

He also assists Ossietzky in investigative reporting uncovering the Republic's secret re-armament program in violation of the Treaty of Versailles, work that confronts him and Ossietzky with treason charges.

By the time Tucholsky writes these controversial articles, he is long gone from Germany, decamping first to Paris in the spring of 1924, then to Sweden in 1929. These changes are the result of a restless spirit looking for new outlets, but they also accompany significant changes in

Tucholsky's personal life, each being marked by a divorce and a new love.

Encountered, Tucholsky is utterly charming in a completely unexpected way. Despite his short stature, pudgy build, and hangdog expression, he makes friends easily and woos women with aplomb. Women in particular are Tucholsky's great non-political obsession, and they in turn fall hard for him, leaving behind their husbands and children to accompany him on his wild adventures. Female investigators of above-average APP will certainly find themselves objects of his dangerous charms.

Like his fellow journalist and social observer **Joseph Roth** (page 82), Tucholsky dies far too young in exile. His friend Ossietzky does not make it out of Germany before the Nazis come for him in 1933 (he dies a slow and agonizing death in a concentration camp); Tucholsky never forgives himself for not traveling back to Germany to defend his friend, though under no illusions that he would have escaped the same fate. Tucholsky, long a savage foe of the Nazi Party, is declared a "degenerate artist" and has his German citizenship revoked once Hitler is in power—his books are among those burned by **Joseph Goebbels** (page 76) in Berlin in 1933.

Kurt Tucholsky

Francis Turville-Petre (1928–31)

The British archaeologist Francis Turville-Petre, in addition to playing a crucial role in bringing W.H. Auden and **Christopher Isherwood** (page 78) out to the city, is a fascinating character in his own right.

Turville-Petre is born in 1901 to a wealthy Catholic family in Leicestershire, England. He attends Exeter College, Oxford, taking a Diploma in Physical Anthropology in 1924. The following year, while digging near the Sea of Galilee in Mandatory Palestine, Turville-Petre makes a remarkable find: the skull of an ancient hominid, the first ever discovered in Western Asia. The skull is later identified as that of an *H. heidelbergensis* man and is dubbed Galilee Man. All of this would come as a surprise to Isherwood and his literary associates. After Francis (whom his friends call "Fronny") moves to Berlin, he completely shifts his career focus. An openly gay man, Fronny takes up residence at the **Institute of Sexology** (page 50), giving lectures and joining the Scientific Humanitarian Committee, where he lobbies tirelessly for legalization of homosexuality and tolerance of queer people. As a rule, he does not share his archaeological past with his friends.

Fronny makes the most of his time in Berlin, shocking his friend Isherwood with his promiscuity. In 1931, Fronny leaves the city for life on a private Greek island (Agios Nikolaos), surrounded by strapping Greek youths. Isherwood later parodies Fronny's time on the island in his 1962 novel *Down There on a Visit*, in which Turville-Petre is re-cast as a mad Greek king. Fronny ultimately moves on to Egypt, where he dies under mysterious circumstances at the age of 40 in 1941.

Conrad Veidt (1893–1933)

Berlin-born Conrad Veidt is one of Germany's greatest actors during its Golden Age of silent cinema. Veidt gets his start in the acting trade while recuperating from jaundice and pneumonia while serving on the Eastern Front during the Great War. There, the army grants him leave to perform for troops serving on the front lines in the Baltics.

After being discharged from the army for medical reasons, Veidt returns to Berlin and makes a name for himself treading the boards in **Max Reinhardt's** (page 81) Deutsches Theater. "God save him from the cinema!" a theatre critic declares, but Veidt, like so many others, follows the money to the silver screen.

He first makes his mark playing the lead in the 1919 picture *Different from the Others* (dir. Oswald). Co-written by **Dr. Hirschfeld** (page 77), it is the first movie in history to explicitly portray queer characters and does so in a compassionate way. The following year, Veidt's popularity explodes when he plays Cesare, a sleepwalking murderer, in the Expressionist-horror classic *The Cabinet of Dr. Caligari* (Wiene, 1920).

Veidt also stars in a string of pictures with the fiery dancer Anita Berber, including the horror anthology *Eerie Tales* (Oswald, 1919), and becomes a fixture of Berlin nightlife—some wags even claim that Veidt works the streets as a cross-dressing prostitute, though these are never more than scurrilous rumors. Becoming something of a genre pioneer, Veidt stars in three other highly influential and well-received horror/thriller pictures, *Waxworks* (Leni and Berinski, 1924), *The Hands of Dr. Orlac* (Wiene, 1924), and *The Student of Prague* (Galeen, 1926).

Ultimately, Veidt makes 119 films. While most of these are shot in Berlin, he does, rather uniquely, enjoy a two-part Hollywood career. The first comes when John Barrymore sees Veidt's performance in *Waxworks* and insists on bringing him out to Hollywood to co-star in Barrymore's historical epic *The Beloved Rogue* (Crosland, 1927). Although initially planning to just shoot the one movie and return to Germany, Veidt is warmly welcomed by the German filmmaker émigré community in Los Angeles and stays on for two more years, starring in several more pictures, the most notable being 1928's *The Man Who Laughs* (dir. Leni)—Veidt's chilling makeup depicting a man with a permanent smile carved into his face eventually inspires the creation of comic book villain The Joker.

With the advent of talkies, the thickly accented Veidt is obliged to return to Berlin. By this point, Hitler and his Nazis are beginning their ascent to power, and Veidt uses his celebrity to criticize them as much, and as publicly, as possible. Matters become even more personal for Veidt when he marries his third wife, Ilona "Lily" Prager, a German Jew.

In 1933, when laws are passed requiring all members of the movie industry to fill out "racial questionnaires," Veidt marks his "race" down as *Jude* despite having been born and raised Lutheran. This act of defiance spells the end of Veidt's acting career in Germany, and soon he, Lily, and their daughter flee to Britain.

Veidt's previous two wives were the cabaret performer Augusta "Gussy" Holl (the marriage lasted from 1918–22) and the dilettante Felizitas Radke (1923–29).

During the silent era, there are few male actors in Europe who can match Veidt for popularity. He is quietly devoted to socially progressive causes and believes in using his fame and fortune as capital to advance his beliefs. During the Second World War, he donates his life savings and nearly all of his earnings to helping the British war effort. For many, Veidt will be remembered for appearing in *The Thief of Bagdad* (dir. Powell, Berger, Whelan, 1940) and playing the role of Major Strasser in *Casablanca* (dir. Curtiz, 1942).

Investigators encountering him during his time in Berlin will find an intensely passionate individual who, nonetheless, understands the importance of having a bit of fun from time to time.

Paul von Hindenburg (1925–33)

Second President of the Republic, and one of the chief architects of its demise, Paul von Hindenburg is a former general in the Imperial German military and one of Germany's greatest war heroes. An archconservative in the old mold of tough-as-boot-leather Prussian military nobility and a committed monarchist, Hindenburg seems an odd choice for leader of a constitutional republic. Certainly, he thinks as much himself, but, upon the death of **Friedrich Ebert** (page 74) in 1925, Hindenburg is convinced by friends and advisors that he must come out of retirement and lead the country.

After the war, Hindenburg was one of the chief architects of the "stab in the back" theory (that Germany had been on the verge of winning the war but was sold out by self-serving politicians and Communists), and he deeply dislikes the Weimar constitution and its government. Nevertheless, he takes his oath to uphold the constitution seriously, at least at first.

He is deeply influenced by a coterie of unofficial advisors (including his son Oskar), called the Kamarilla, who push him toward a "soft coup" within the government. By invoking a

Conrad Veidt

triad of articles in the Weimar constitution, Hindenburg and his Kamarilla attempt to form a "presidential government" that can govern by decree rather than through the consent of the Reichstag. Hindenburg sees this as a transitional step on the way toward establishing an "anti-Marxist, anti-parliamentarian" dictatorship and, eventually, restoring the Hohenzollern monarchy. Thus, through such maneuverings, is the fate of the Republic sealed.

Hindenburg's goal of a presidential government begins to be realized in 1930, just as his term is set to expire. The old general, who often complains in private of the stresses of his office and his lack of understanding of the deeper complexities of national politics and policy, must once again be convinced to run. This time, the threat is from the right, as Hitler and his National Socialists see their star rising in the uncertainty following the global economic collapse of 1929. Hindenburg dislikes the Nazis and positively loathes Hitler (whom he hardly ever mentions by name but rather as, "that Austrian corporal"); due to Hindenburg's continuing popularity among the German public, he is seen as the best hope for defeating Hitler's run for the presidency.

Taciturn to the point of cowardice (a lifelong personality trait) and in ailing health, the 83-year-old Hindenburg allows others to campaign for him and wins the election with a slight majority. Despite Hindenburg's determination to stymie his rival, within three years, the Republic lies at

Hitler's feet. The following year, Hindenburg dies and Hitler merges the office of President with Chancellor, declaring himself Führer.

When encountered, Hindenburg appears like a grumpy old bear of a man surrounded by advisors and sycophants. After his career-making victory at Tannenberg in 1914, his overinflated sense of ego never suffers a deflation—he truly believes he is Germany's savior and last hope. Those who cater to these beliefs, or to his old-fashioned sense of propriety (such as his close confidant Franz von Papen, who personally swears a feudal oath of fealty to Hindenburg) earn his respect and support. He loathes Marxists of all stripes and wages a near-personal war against the Social Democrats.

Claire Waldoff (1906–35)

The queen of Berlin's cabaret scene, the stocky, red-haired Waldoff makes a name for herself with her matter-of-fact, street-smart performance that eschews the usual wink-and-grin style of the cabaret in favor of overt mockery and provocation. Her delivery is an unforgettable gravelly drawl, *sprechgesang* (sing-spoken) in a distinctive Berlin street patois. Indeed, Waldoff so comes across as the ultimate Berliner that it may come as a surprise that she is a girl of the provinces, arriving in Berlin only at the age of 22. She quickly falls in love with the city and makes it her own.

Her rise to fame as a performer comes relatively quickly, with a three-song set at the Roland von Berlin cabaret in 1907. Throughout her career, and despite amassing an eventual repertoire of 300 pieces, Waldoff maintains a strict performance schedule of three songs and no encores, allowing her to perform at multiple venues each night and always deliver something a little different each time, keeping her appearances fresh and exciting. After a brief residence at the Roland, she moves on to the Chat Noir on Friedrichstraße and the Linden-Cabaret on Unter den Linden, though she performs all over the city during her three-decade career.

Openly lesbian, Waldoff is just as well known for her sartorial style, most usually sporting men's suits and ties both as part of her daywear and in performances. She and her lifelong companion, Olga "Olly" von Roeder, host a popular gay and lesbian salon at the Pyramid Women's Club near Nollendorfplatz; despite its designation, these salons are open to all—men and women, gay, bisexual, straight, or otherwise—as long as they are able to contribute meaningfully to the conversation.

With the rise of the Nazis and the closing of Berlin's cabarets, Waldoff finds her main source of income cut off and sees many of her Jewish and gay friends fleeing the country. She eventually departs her beloved Berlin as well, riding out the war with Olly in the Bavarian Alps.

Claire Waldoff

Kurt Weill (1920–33)

Born in 1900, by his 25th birthday Kurt Weill is well on his way to establishing his reputation as the greatest German composer of this generation. Weill is born to a Jewish family in the town of Dessau. The son of a cantor, he develops an interest in music at an early age and begins learning piano and writing music at the age of 12.

After a musical education, Weill moves to Berlin in September 1920 to study with the Italian composer Ferruccio Busoni at the Prussian Academy of Arts. While still a student of Busoni, Weill joins the Novembergruppe, an association of left-wing artists. In 1924, he meets the dancer and *Diseuse* (cabaret singer) Lotte Lenya. They marry two years later and form a collaborative and creative partnership that lasts off and on until Weill's death in 1950. Supporting himself by playing piano in beer halls, Weill begins writing music across a variety of genres: from concert pieces to vocal works to musical theatre pieces. It is with the latter that he finds his greatest success and lasting fame.

Weill's music is Modernist in its use of a variety of styles (including American dance music) as well as its "provocative ambiguity," in the words of one critic. Beginning in 1927, Weill inaugurates a short-lived but highly productive phase of collaborations with the playwright **Bertolt Brecht** (page 71). Weill's modernist sensibilities and political leanings prove a perfect fit with Brecht's "Epic Theatre" agenda, and his most well-known works and songs emerge out of these collaborations.

The most successful of these collaborations, *Die Dreigroschenoper* (*The Threepenny Opera*), premieres in Berlin in 1928. It is a takedown of capitalism masquerading as a portrait of the Victorian London underworld. "The Ballad of Mack the Knife" quickly becomes a standard as the "play with music" instantly secures its status as a classic of modern stage.

In 1930, Brecht and Weill score another hit with *Aufstieg und Fall der Stadt Mahagonny* (*Rise and Fall of the City of Mahagonny*), an even more pointed critique of capitalism set in a strange town on the American frontier. "The Alabama Song," with its disturbing paean to hedonistic pleasures, instantly captures the teetering good-time zeitgeist of the Weimar era and also becomes a standard. Indeed, *Mahagonny* may be read as a critique as much of the hypocritical Republic as of capitalism in general.

Ultimately, Brecht's unapologetic Communism becomes too much for Weill to bear and he and Brecht part ways. Their productions earn considerable condemnation from the Nazi Party, which organizes protests and attempts to disrupt performances. With the cementing of Nazi power in Germany in 1933, Weill flees the country, going on to a successful career in America.

Kurt Weill

MYTHOS BERLIN

The scenarios in the latter part of this book present examples of the presence of the Mythos in Berlin; however, a city does not earn its reputation as the "Wickedest Place on Earth" and not also attract the perfidious, pervasive influence of the Mythos, and Keepers may rest assured that it may be found nearly anywhere one cares to look.

Sorcerers studying suppressed tomes at the Prussian State Library worship Yog-Sothoth and Azathoth, calling upon these unknowable Old Ones for keys to transcendent power. Some wish it for themselves, others to advance their political causes, but all represent an existential threat to every citizen of Berlin. Meanwhile, the cultists of the Fraternitas Saturni enact mirror-magic rituals to contact Tsathoggua and his spawn on far-distant Saturn, while Shub-Niggurath exalts in the hedonistic abandon and rampant fornication of the Friedrichstadt and Ku'damm. Initiated priestess-prostitutes make obeisance to the Black Goat of the Woods with a Thousand Young, asking for her protection from the polenta, oilers, and fleas (police, pimps, and johns, respectively) that present constant on-the-job hazards.

Drugs and sex and general debasement, meanwhile, draw other cults and worshippers here, as well as other horrors beyond human ken, lurking just on the other side of human consciousness, feeding lies and temptations to the desperate and the depraved, and finding many an unwitting worshipper—and vessel.

Lastly, Nyarlathotep, that great tempter of mankind, walks unnoticed among the throngs in the Alex, or whispers to worshippers among the bracken and brambles of the Grunewald and Tiergarten. Whether a nightclub artiste, emcee, or a knowledgeable gent or lady, the Crawling Chaos and those who serve him can certainly be found in the smoke-filled, hazy, corridors of Berlin.

BERLIN'S CULTS

Nyarlathotep's Emcee

Rumors are swirling through Berlin's shadiest cabarets and *Nachtlokals* of a strange emcee who appears unannounced in the midst of wild parties and turns the evening into something truly unforgettable. Calling herself Nefertiti, she does indeed bear a striking resemblance to the famous bust housed at the Neues Museum, albeit with a rather androgynous figure. Regardless, Nefertiti tends to appear only in the most obscure and exclusive clubs, and only once the party is fully underway.

Once Nefertiti starts leading the ceremonies, things tend to take uncanny turns. Servers start pouring glasses of strangely colored cocktails instead of champagne; unscheduled acts appear on stage—comedians who veer from exuberant comedy to nihilistic rapture, launching into extended monologues about the joke of life and the farce of existence; singers who perform popular standards in Aramaic or who just seem to dart about screaming into the audience's faces; stage magicians who make people disappear and *not* return; and naked revues that are far more unsettling than titillating for reasons no one can quite put their finger on.

Simply attending a party hosted by Nefertiti is likely to provoke a **Sanity** roll (1/1D3 loss or more, depending on the acts witnessed). Those who fail succumb to the madness of an evening's revels, falling into temporary or indefinite insanity, becoming obsessed with Nefertiti, being able to think of little else than finding the next event where she'll be hosting and seeking to gain her favor. When not in her presence, those affected sink into a lethargic malaise that can be offset only through the use of stimulating drugs or the promise of seeing Nefertiti soon.

The strange emcee knows her biggest fans well and rewards them with personal attention at her shows and free drugs

Opposite: Mythos of Berlin

(usually cocaine) at highly exclusive and private after-show parties held in secret places. Nefertiti seems particularly delighted whenever she manages to hook an influential or well-respected member of the community, going out of her way to offer such people "a little something extra" as she calls it—what this phrase means is anyone's guess, but some suspect it may involve some form of initiation or membership to a clandestine group with Nefertiti at its head. It seems Nefertiti is well informed about her audience, as she knows just what to say to have everyone hanging on her words. Whatever her patron's desire, she seems able to supply it, encouraging and preying on humanity's worst impulses, be they desire, greed, lust, or hate.

Y'golonac

In the heart of Alt-Berlin, amid the medieval byways of Nikolaiviertel and within sight of the twin spires of St. Nicholas' Church, there sits a congenial café called the Kirchenklause. Open from 11 am to midnight, the Kirchenklause serves up several varieties of beer (Bavarian, Pilsen, and local Weisse-Bier) alongside hearty plates of sauerkraut and pig knuckles. The restaurant is closed on Sundays, holidays, and, without exception, on the first day of every month.

The locals who regularly frequent the Kirchenklause may all be distinguished by their outsized physiques; men and women alike are universally of ample proportion. Their eyes shine brightly, their cheeks perpetually flushed, their brows dappled with sweat, as if they have just finished polishing off an especially hearty meal—as most likely they have.

The proprietor of the café, one Gustaf Roth, is even more corpulent than his most loyal customers. Old pictures of Roth from before the Great War show a slim and muscular man, hardly recognizable as the man who now serves the beer and meat at the Kirchenklause. Indeed, Roth is much changed, as it was during the Turnip Winter of 1916–1917 when he first encountered the unwholesome entity called Y'golonac and, quite literally, took the god into himself.

Shortly afterward, Kirchenklause opened up. Roth attracted a loyal following of customers who were similarly dedicated to the many pleasures offered by the Defiler. In monthly rituals, they gather in the ancient brick cellar of the café, where they worship the god as it manifests through Roth's body and offer a living sacrifice (usually taken from the teeming, unregistered immigrant masses around Alexanderplatz) to be consumed by their lord. Then the feast of depravity begins.

Seemingly, the cult holds no particular ambitions outside of feeding its insatiable hungers, but as those appetites continue to grow, the number of missing persons in Berlin grows as well.

Die Schwarze Ziege

Among the wild youth of Berlin, there is one gang that takes their strange lifestyle seriously indeed. Calling themselves "Lost Boys," they self-consciously adopt the costumes and personae of the characters from the English-language Peter Pan tales written by J. M. Barrie.

Somewhere along the way, influenced by a battered and abridged translation of Frazer's *The Golden Bough* stolen from a bookshop, they began to actually worship Pan as a god, little suspecting they were actually communing with an avatar of Shub-Niggurath, the Black Goat of a Thousand Young.

Deep in the Grunewald is an ancient glade where the Lost Boys make their home; those who sleep in the glade under a cloudless sky during the new moon are transported to "somewhere else," where they meet the Great God Pan in its aspect as a handsome, goat-hoofed youth, and listen to its hypnotic piping.

Although the gang is eccentric even by Wild Boy standards, it is relatively harmless—for now. Unfortunately, in their latest venture to Pan's domain, the Lost Boys' god imparted knowledge of the spell Summon Dark Young (see *Call of Cthulhu Rulebook*, page 263) to the gang's leader, Nibs. While Nibs has yet to try the spell out, he knows that it promises him great power and the ability to visit retribution upon his enemies. It is only a matter of time before the Lost Boys acquire the required sacrifice and unleash a horror in the Grunewald.

Kosmische Ballette

Inspired by the "Triadic Ballets" of Oskar Schlemmer, a dance troupe recently began rehearsals in an abandoned warehouse near the Havel in the district of Spandau. Like the Triadic Ballets, these so-called "Cosmic Ballets" are highly structured—ritualistic, even—and feature a cavalcade of strange and unsettling costumes representing a variety of odd concepts: the Render of Veils, the Hydra, the Unclean, Illimitable Androgynous Desire, Darkness, the Nameless Mist, the Flautist, and the Unbegotten Source.

The costumed dancers move to the strains of wild piping performed by a small flute orchestra of musicians who are always found dressed in hooded black robes that concealing all but the outsized bone flutes they play with waxen, flabby fingers that seem to move about the instruments in distinctly unnatural ways. The music they perform does not seem to conform to any Earthly scales (costing 1/1D4 Sanity points to hear).

In fact, the "orchestra" consists of five human musicians who have been driven utterly insane by contact with the company's chief composer and choreographer: a Servitor of the Outer Gods (see *Call of Cthulhu Rulebook*, page 304), summoned by the company's former director (now a catatonic patient of Dalldorf asylum) in a desperate attempt to gain new creative insights. Needless to say, he got far more than he bargained for.

The company's 13 human members (seven men and six women) are fervent in their desire to bring what they call "clear vision" to the stage. For now at least, no theater in Berlin is willing to grant this, as every producer and promoter who attends a rehearsal has left feeling somewhat unsettled, if not outright reduced to tears or visceral anger.

The company's chief composer, who resides out of sight in the warehouse, is growing bored with this latest distraction, and thinks more and more of returning to its place at Azathoth's side. The company is desperate to prevent this, for they cannot imagine a life now without the servitor as their visionary leader, and they are attempting any number of schemes to ensure their master remains with them. As a result, they are likely to take matters a step too far, resorting to blackmail, bribery, and even murder to find a suitable venue so that their visionary ballet can be performed in public.

SCENARIO SEEDS

Die Weiße Frau (The White Lady)

Location: Unter den Linden.

Discovery: the White Lady of the City Palace has returned! Not seen in over a century, the ghost of a lady dressed in white is once again roaming the halls of the Stadtschloß, ancient residence of Prussian kings and now a museum (**Museum Island**, page 46).

Research: looking up the history of the White Lady reveals a multitude of sightings between 1625–1790. Who the White Lady is and why her visitations stopped are unknown. Three sightings have been reported in the last month, two by members of the Palace Museum staff and one by a member of the public—a cameraman with the small production company, Hilde-film (**Investigator Organizations**, page 16), who has the footage on celluloid.

Keeper Notes: the White Lady is none other than Countess Kunigunda of Orlamünde (d. 1382), who fell in love with Albrecht the Beautiful and murdered her two children with a sewing needle because she believed they stood in the way of winning his hand. (He told her that "two pairs of eyes" prevented him from marrying her; he actually meant his own parents.) Exactly why the Countess has chosen this precise moment in history to reappear is for the Keeper to decide. Use this seed to develop a connection to Berlin's medieval past, as a note of quiet pathos in the middle of a bustling metropolis, or as a good old-fashioned ghost hunt.

A Pox on Your House

Location: the Tiergarten.

Discovery: patients admitted to the Charité (**The Tiergarten**, page 27) are suffering from a strange malady unknown to modern medicine. The whole of the hospital is suffused by a charnel smell that even the most powerful disinfectants cannot overcome.

Research: a cursory investigation of the history of the Charité notes that it was originally a quarantine house, and the grounds upon which it sits are filled with the remains of plague victims. Further research correlates the symptoms of the current pandemic to the 1709 plague that prompted the Charité's construction.

Keeper Notes: this may be a case of ghostly infection carried out by the spirits of the restless dead buried beneath the hospital. Exhumation and reburial of the unhallowed dead may be in order. Alternately, a crazed doctor on the hospital staff may have unleashed a Mythos force, whose presence amplifies or imparts disease, as part of a misguided research project. The entity spreads its malign influence through a long-dormant disease, now brought back to life. How do the investigators combat something that can't even be seen, particularly after they begin to feel the symptoms of the pox themselves?

Der Ring

Location: the Alex.

Discovery: something positively unwholesome is being served up at the automat located in the lobby of the Babylon Cinema on Kaiser-Wilhelm-Straße: suspicions of what exactly is in the bratwurst are aroused when a gold ring is found inside the sausage. For maximum effect, this discovery should come at the expense of a poor investigator biting into the meat and discovering the ring with their teeth! (1/1D4 Sanity loss.)

Research: finding out details about the automat's owners and operators is surprisingly difficult. The establishment rents space from the cinema but is owned by a mysterious consortium that has ties to the local criminal syndicate, the *Norddeutscher* ("North German") Ring. Indeed, the ring the investigators found in the sausage is that typically worn by members of the Norddeutscher Gang.

Keeper Notes: the Norddeutschers are working in concert with a community of Mythos-aware tcho-tcho, who are supplying the gangsters with a new type of lotus-based drug. Unfortunately, the tcho-tcho, as is their wont, are spreading their debased corruption through the ranks of the gang, which now finds itself engaging in previously unthinkable criminal activities, such as the butchering and sale of human meat. There is a significant minority of gangsters in the Ring who disapprove of this new direction and who could make useful, if unlikely, allies for the investigators in their fight against the tcho-thco menace.

The Liao Solution

Location: Nollendorfplatz

Discovery: the latest craze among the heroin and opium addicts around Nollendorfplatz is the Solution of Liao, a black powder that can be smoked or melted and injected, rendering users insensate with visions of the past. Some users report seeing Christ on the cross at Calvary, others prehistoric hunter-gatherers, while some even claim to have seen civilizations that do not appear in the historical records, races of strange serpent people, herds of mammoths or dinosaurs, or simply great stretches of protoplasmic goo under methane-yellow skies. Whether connected or not, several gruesome, yet oddly bloodless, murders have been discovered in Nollendorfplatz.

Research: repeated doses of Solution of Liao (also called Plutonian Drug, see *Call of Cthulhu Rulebook*, page 273), exposes the user to the hounds of Tindalos, who latch on and follow the traveler back to the present day. Use of the drug is spreading beyond its point of origin, as a small cabal of historians and anthropologists has taken to using it during their bimonthly salons. Perhaps an investigator's friend is one of the users, either near Nollendorfplatz or among the halls of academia?

Keeper Notes: to halt the spread of the drug and prevent further incursions of the hounds of Tindalos, the investigators must locate the mysterious source of the drug's manufacture. Could this be an opportunistic chemist or alchemist who found a recipe in the *Book of Eibon*, a foreign sorcerer trying to fund research, or even the enigmatic Nefertiti (**Nyarlathotep's Emcee**, page 89)?

False Idols

Location: the Ku'damm

Discovery: Fritz Lang and Thea von Harbou (page 78) have recently brought home the latest acquisition for their museum-like apartment at Hohenzollerndamm 52: a strange idol from the South Seas. Now, odd-looking men haunt their doorstep at all hours, and they have already suffered a break-in, thwarted only by Fritz's unexpected arrival home. They are fairly certain the idol has a part to play in this and would very much like the investigators to discovery who wants the idol so badly and why.

Research: the idol is a classic example of the sort produced by the Cthulhu cult, though without a successful **Cthulhu Mythos** roll this should be a difficult detail to turn up. Shadowing or kidnapping one of the pathetic specimens who have been harassing the Lang-Harbou residence reveals them to be foreigners, recently arrived from far-distant ports, summoned by strange dreams to this city and address.

Keeper Notes: develop this seed as a classic confrontation with the Cthulhu cult and its foul, monstrous members, albeit one that takes place unexpectedly far from the cult's usual centers of power. Alternatively, play this as a bit of bait and switch for a change of pace, or to fool seasoned players: the "cultists" are members of a degenerate family of antiques collectors who were outbid at the auction where Lang and Harbou acquired the idol, and they simply want to steal it for themselves. Their talk of strange dreams and cults is merely an attempt to seem mysterious and intimidating so that they may be left alone.

Either way, Fritz and Thea pose as much of an impediment to the investigation as a help. They are a tempestuous couple: Lang is an ill-tempered control freak, and Harbou harbors Nazi sympathies. They may be brilliant creatives, but they are exasperating as human beings.

Dunkler Schatten

Location: Pfaueninsel

Discovery: those taking an evening walk around Pfaueninsel (Peacock Island), an island on the River Havel in southwest Berlin, have been terrorized by a dark figure, said to have red burning eyes, haunting the island. Despite a police search, no trace of the dark figure can be found. The newspapers are calling the man the *Dunkler Schatten* ("Dark Shadow").

Research: in times past, an alchemist called Johann Kunckel had a secret laboratory beneath Pfaueninsel, where he conducted experiments with black magic. Kunckel was born around 1630, later becoming an apothecary to the dukes of Lauenburg and to Johann Georg II. Later, he was the director of a laboratory in Brandenberg and was ennobled by Charles XI the King of Sweden. His work included the discovery of the process to create phosphorus, the creation of artificial rubies (red glass), and observations on putrefaction and fermentation.

Keeper Notes: Kunckel's mind and spirit have woken and taken possession of the body of a wandering tramp. Unfortunately, the possession causes the host body to quickly deteriorate, with the flesh dying rapidly and putrefying. Kunckel has reopened his secret laboratory to find a means to prevent host body decay, but he needs test subjects (and new host bodies). Combing both alchemical and Mythos magic, the undead Kunckel is likely to leave a trail of woe in his wake.

When One Door Closes

Location: anywhere there is a blank wall large enough.

Discovery: a grandiose-looking doorway has appeared in a city backstreet. It definitely wasn't there before, and it may well look out of place in its current location. The imposing rectangular doorframe is constructed of dark brown bricks set with numerous terracotta plaques depicting people and foliage. The double doors appear to be made of some sort of hammered metal, although this may just be a decorative overlay on a wooden base. Each door contains four panels, all with a central medallion containing the portraits of serious-looking men who stare at each other from their side of the door. Only the right-hand door has a handle.

Research: those who are familiar with Berlin's classical architecture recognize the doorway as being virtually identical to those found on the Bauakademie, the higher education building academy designed by renowned city planner and architect Karl Friedrich Schinkel, and located close to the Stadtschloß (**Museum Island**, page 46).

Keeper Notes: there are (at least) two potential options as to where the wandering door leads—either back to the Bauakademie or to a strange realm that forms part of Berlin's Dreamlands. Should the door open on the Bauakademie, those stepping through it find themselves exiting a rather unassuming looking cupboard door into the Staadtliche Bildstelle's photographic archive, housed in the academy's basement and home to more than 20,000 glass photographic negative plates that largely depict historic buildings. For reasons unknown (but potentially caused either by a member of staff's sorcerous experimentation or the institute's unwitting acquisition of a powerful artifact), the doorway appears on the side of the building whose negative was last viewed using a particular magic lantern, currently housed in the adjacent archive viewing room. The portal effectively acts as an unusual Gate that could lead to any of the buildings depicted in the institute's vast archive, which covers not only Berlin and Germany but also other architecturally important buildings worldwide. Could someone at the institute be using the Gate to commit bizarre crimes, appearing and disappearing at will right across the city? Or is there some other purpose to the user's wanderings? Could a collector have heard of the magic lantern and want it for nefarious purposes? And what might happen if the magic lantern is pressed into service by the wider academy when the one in the main lecture theater is accidentally damaged?

Alternatively, the doorway opens into a sylvan realm inspired by Germany's many "back-to-nature" proponents and dreamed into being by Berlin's disillusioned residents as a result of their ever-increasing longing for a romanticized past that never was. The forest is home to many small settlements, including two that closely resemble the fishing villages that eventually grew into the modern city. But, being the Dreamlands, not everything is as it at first appears. The realm may lead to other parts of the Dreamlands, and hence to further exploration, or it may be a self-contained world, populated by re-envisioned Germanic myths and legends. Should the Keeper choose to use this option, some clue as to what is hidden behind the door could be hinted at in its plaques and motifs—not only do the larger tiles now depict activities such as hunting, farming, and fishing, but the foliage is twisted, the angel tiles on the lintel are warped and bestial, and there are hints of Mythos creatures incorporated into the decorative designs surrounding the portrait medallions.

I Think, Therefore I Am
Location: Romanisches Forum

Discovery: a young and outspoken artist is gaining a reputation within artistic circles for his pronouncements about creating a god in man's image. The artist says his great work is near completion, and then it shall stride through Berlin as a living god.

Research: the artist's "Manifesto of Deity" (as he calls it) mentions certain phrases, such as "neb-lon Yog-Sothoth," "k'luu muuni Azastari," and "Ia! Dak-Nyarlat," which may ring alarm bells with investigators. Two months ago, a copy of *Rituale von toten Fleisch* (*Rituals of Dead Flesh*), said to be an unauthorized translation of parts of the French edition of the *Cultes des Goules*, was stolen from the restricted collection of the Prussian State Library. Those who read the witness reports for the robbery may realize the thief has some physical similarity to the outspoken artist.

Keeper Notes: the artist is indeed building a god; using the strange words within *Rituale von toten Fleisch*, he has crafted new rituals that he incants over his hideous creation—a bizarre collection of metal, wood, animal parts, and human flesh, all sculpted into a nightmarish caricature of what he thinks a god should be. With clawed hands, a head constructed from a bear's skull from which metal spikes protrude, covered in loose human flesh, and standing more than 8 feet (2.4 m) tall, his creation will be infused with living energy siphoned through ritual from Yog-Sothoth itself! What horror will be unleashed if the investigator cannot find a way to stop it?

Precious Bodily Fluids
Location: Prenzlauer Berg

Discovery: strange organic matter has been found in Berlin's water supply, with some who have unwittingly consumed pieces complaining of feeling unwell.

Research: a small cell of anti-Bolshevik anarcho-communists has unearthed a strange metal capsule, seemingly long buried in the ground below the Wasserturm in Prenzlauer Berg (northeast of Alexanderplatz). The capsule's contents are believed to be toxic and it is said that the group is preparing to release the toxin into the city's water unless their demands for political change are met. Some think the group will go ahead and poison Berlin's water whether or not their demands are met, as the resultant mass panic will instigate a proletarian revolution. In addition, late at night, residents near the Wasserturm have reported hearing a strange piping voice reciting fragments of passages from Marx and Kropotkin.

Keeper Notes: the capsule, engraved around its surface with strange and unintelligible characters, contained an immature shoggoth. Having released the creature, the communists have been studying and feeding it—on a steady supply of compost and the occasional dead body fished from the river, and also metaphorically with communist and anarchist political doctrine. For unknown reasons, parts of the shoggoth have begun to flake off into the water supply, infecting those who drink it with shoggoth protoplasm (in time, such individuals will be consumed from within and transform into new shoggoths).

This odd hook may be enough to involve the investigators, or else the sad transformation of one of their friends or contacts into a monstrous shoggoth may lead them to the Wasserturm. Although these communists aren't terribly bright and are blinded by their ideology, they make up for their deficiencies in sheer zealotry. One possible twist is to make the creature a shoggoth lord (*Call of Cthulhu Rulebook*, page 307) that infects the members of the communist cell, thereby creating "extensions" of itself; thus, one shoggoth lord with multiple bodies across the city, all mentally conjoined and working in unison—but to what purpose?

In the Family Way
Location: Grunewald

Discovery: the Lost Boys' worship of Shub-Niggurath (**Die Schwarze Ziege**, page 90) is having more unintended consequences. In their latest visit to meet with Pan, the youth's dark god commanded them to find it a mate. The Lost Boys are now scouring Berlin in search of a suitable "Wendy" to bring back, which does not bode well for a fairy-tale ending, as the experience of spending a night with Pan leaves the unfortunate partner a raving lunatic.

Research: Pan's motive is to start a brood of offspring within the city, a legion of beautiful children (any child fathered by Pan is born with APP 95), all utterly faithful to their Great God and eager to do its will on Earth.

Keeper Notes: either set this scenario before the Lost Boys enact their plan, giving investigators a chance to save poor "Wendy" (whomever that may end up being) or—for a much grimmer twist—place this scenario some years into Pan's dark "marriage," creating a series of cascading moral dilemmas for the investigators. What they do with the insane "Wendy" and her family of eerily beautiful offspring? Do these "children of the damned" remain living and cavorting among the trees of the Grunewald or is Pan's plan more insidious, with the children given up for adoption and now living in the homes of Berlin's great and good?

The Temple's Secret
Location: Potsdammer Platz

Discovery: thanks to beer cellars, U-bahn lines, the Rohrpost system, sewers, ancient tunnels, and other chambers, there is a lot going on beneath Berlin. Many of these subterranean spaces are clustered around Potsdamer Platz, including the Anhalter Bahnhof Ringbahn platforms and the massive tunnel/shopping concourse that runs from the Bahnhof to the Hotel Excelsior—this tunnel is excavated in 1929 at a cost of 1.2 million Reichsmarks. At more than 80 yards/meters long and some 10 feet (3 m) wide and 10 feet (3 m) high, the tunnel requires a truly epic amount of earth moving. Construction is halted halfway through, however, when workmen come upon an ancient subterranean ruin directly in their path.

Research: archaeologists brought in to study the cyclopean structure estimate it belongs to the Neolithic era, although further scrutiny leads the team to believe the structure may be so old as to predate humanity, a development they are at pains to keep out of the papers. The investigators are called in as consultants in the hope they can shed some light on the strange carvings in the structure's rock menhirs or make sense of the strange gold jewelry found scattered about the site that appears not to have been made for human limbs.

Keeper Notes: the exact nature of the temple is left to the Keeper. Perhaps it was (and still remains) a locus for some Mythos entity, currently biding its time until the most opportune moment to rise presents itself. Perhaps it is an ancient temple of the serpent people, now long vanished, who left behind dire and mind-shattering spells for summoning their god Yig in the rock carvings, waiting only for a hapless investigator to decipher and intone. Or perhaps the rocks really are Neolithic remnants, but all the underground activity attracts a nearby colony of ghouls from the U-Bahn tunnels.

THE DEVIL EATS FLIES

Blood and murder in a crumbling, post-apocalyptic world. Amid hyperinflation and political unrest, a body-hopping cannibal spirit stalks the street, committing terrible acts of lustmord; a madwoman claims to be the heiress to a toppled throne; and a shadowy Russo-German alliance enacts its sinister scheme to sacrifice Germany's greatest politician at the altar of their pagan gods.

KEEPER SUMMARY

"[T]he horrors of war and the worse horrors of Bolshevism have taught us that nothing is too ghoulish to be true."

—Gerald Biss, *The Door of the Unreal*

The scenario begins—after a bit of street violence—with the investigators being drawn into a mystery regarding the possible murder in Berlin of the Grand Duchess Anastasia Romanov at the hands of the notorious serial killer and cannibal Carl Großmann, who has just hanged himself in his cell while undergoing trial for murder. A winding trail of clues leads from the murderer's old neighborhood to an eerie garden shed and an insane asylum on the edge of town, then to the estate of an aging baron, where the purported princess is found, semi-coherent and covered with deep bite marks.

As the mystery unfolds, the investigators learn more about their secretive employers, which only serves to complicate matters further. Initially representing themselves as agents of the Romanov family, they turn out to be far more sinister in nature: a strange cabal of extremist German nationalists on the one hand, and Russian monarchists claiming descent from the Knights Hospitaller on the other. Worse, the employers are connected with the infamous assassination squad Organisation Consul, which is in the process of planning a sacrificial ritual of shocking proportions.

AUTHOR NOTE

The theme of this scenario is *lustmord*. It is set up as a sort of Lang-esque noir procedural in which multiple factions bump up against each other and the investigators don't know who to trust. The violence serves as a metaphor for Germany's violent reassertion of its national spirit after the "emasculating" defeat of the Great War—anxious masculinity abounds. In Stephen King's *Danse Macabre* analysis of horror, the primary category featured in this scenario is the Gross-out, which he defines as, "When the lights go out and something green and slimy splatters against your arm."

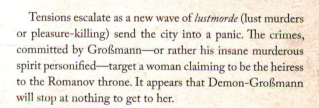

Tensions escalate as a new wave of *lustmorde* (lust murders or pleasure-killing) send the city into a panic. The crimes, committed by Großmann—or rather his insane murderous spirit personified—target a woman claiming to be the heiress to the Romanov throne. It appears that Demon-Großmann will stop at nothing to get to her.

HISTORICAL FOOTNOTE

The majority of the characters in this scenario (Großmann, Shabelsky-Bork, Killinger, Rathenau, Berber and Droste, "Anna Tchaikovsky," and so on) were real people living in Berlin at this time. Likewise, many of the events herein occurred, and the organizations described existed to some extent. Dates have been fudged here and there for dramatic license, but otherwise we have attempted to remain faithful to the historical facts.

Opposite: Carl Großmann murders again

We have, when given a choice by the elisions of the historical record, erred on the side of the macabre, the sensational, and the conspiratorial when it better serves the scenario. Großmann, for instance, only ever admitted to the killing of three women, and rumors of his selling human meat on the streets were never proven.

BACKGROUND

"In the days to come, people will find it difficult to understand that the will of a dead man could bind the living…"

—Walther Rathenau, *In Days to Come*

It is Wednesday, June 21, 1922. The Great War ended three years, seven months, and six days ago, but its memory still dominates nearly every aspect of life in Berlin.

In the city proper, the most violent of the political paroxysms died down after the failed Kapp Putsch of 1920, in which thousands of armed veterans—members of the so-called *Freikorps* (Free Corps)—descended on the city and occupied government buildings in an attempt to set up a right-wing, ultra-Nationalist government that would stand in defiance of the ruinous Treaty of Versailles. Political tensions still run hot, with frequent clashes—both verbal and physical—between left- and right-wing factions.

The city swarms with émigrés from the east, from *Ostlander* Orthodox Jews to monarchist Russian exiles, all of whom crowd together in their own ethnic neighborhoods, further increasing the sense of urban isolation and dislocation.

The recent failure of international reparations conferences has seen the value of the German mark plummet; indeed, it is now trading at 1,000 to the US dollar, down from 320 marks to the dollar just a month prior. Two months ago, Foreign Minister Walther Rathenau, scion of the industrial giant AEG and widely acknowledged visionary, provided a ray of hope for many Germans. In negotiating the Treaty of Rapallo, he ensured that Germany would owe nothing in the way of reparations to the newly formed Soviet Union, inheritor of Imperial Russia. In return, Germany formally recognized the Bolshevist government, the first country to do so. This move shocked both the Western Allies and the anti-communist and monarchist factions within Germany. More than a few people now worry that Rathenau has opened the door to a Bolshevist takeover of the country and wonder where the Minister's loyalties truly lie—suspicions exacerbated by the Minister's Jewish heritage and industrialist pedigree.

Apart from worries of political upheaval and economic collapse, over the past month further signs of impending disaster have appeared to those sensitive enough to feel them. Artists across the city find their dreams haunted by visions of butchered women, savagely killed in the act of lovemaking: so-called *lustmord*. Some, such as the artist Otto Dix, have attempted to exorcise these terrifying visions through their paintings. Others drown themselves in the fleeting relief of booze, drugs, and Berlin nightlife.

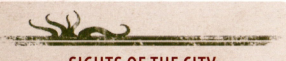

SIGHTS OF THE CITY

The Great Inflation has begun. None can anticipate the extent of the downturn, but the warning signs are clear. As the investigators move around Berlin, pepper your descriptions of the city with indicators of the storm to come.

- Boarded-up shops.
- Black marketeers peddling pornographic postcards, drugs, matches, and foreign currency.
- Blackboards in clubs and outside banks showing the hourly value of the mark measured against dollars and pounds sterling. Every time the investigators catch sight of such a board, the value has changed, and always for the worse.
- Policemen patrolling in groups, rifles slung over shoulders, on the lookout for civil disturbance and looting; however, mostly they appear blithely unconcerned with criminal activity.
- A beggar—a legless veteran of the Great War—openly competing for attention against the shouts of a barker harking the "Guaranteed naked women" to be found inside the Anatomical Wonder Cabinet.

INTRODUCING THE INVESTIGATORS

The investigators may find themselves wrapped up in this scenario in one of three ways. Of course, it is quite possible that one or more of these opportunities may apply to some members of the party and not others. At the very least, one investigator should have a compelling reason to become involved, giving the other investigators enough motivation to go along for the ride due to mutual affiliation.

- The most obvious and direct point of entry into the investigation is to be hired by Shabelsky-Bork in his guise as an agent of the Romanovs. "Prince Constantinovich" approaches one of the investigators for this purpose; see **The Case of the Wayward Princess** (page 109) for a list of possible occupational hooks.

- Journalists and writers will, of course, be fascinated by the case and the opportunity to get in on the scoop of the century. Their interest may be piqued by the appearance of **Anna in the Paper** (page 126) or **The Murders** (page 127), having already read about the death of Großmann (**Handout: Devil 1**, page 107).

- An investigator's political or social connections may also provide ample motivation to pursue the case. Communists, for example, would score a major political and propagandistic victory if they could disprove the "Grand Duchess'" claims, while monarchists and counterrevolutionaries would seek the opposite outcome.

INVOLVING INVESTIGATOR ORGANIZATIONS

Following are suggestions for investigators who are all members of one of the groups outlined in the **Investigator Organizations** section (page 16).

The Independent Order of Owls: as an association of occult detectives, the Owls fit this investigation perfectly. Shabelsky-Bork and his allies do not want to tip their own esoteric hand and so play down that aspect of the Owls. Prince Constantinovich's message is delivered directly to the Owls' headquarters at the Hotel Roter Adler, addressed to the Order rather than to any specific person. If asked why the Prince wishes the Order to investigate the Sasnovski matter, the prince replies that he has heard of the Owls' capabilities when it comes to discreet inquiries.

Hilde-Film: Shabelsky-Bork contacts the filmmakers at Hilde-Film with the promise of exclusive rights to make a movie about the investigation; he drops strong hints that Sasnovski is indeed the Grand Duchess, which should be enough to pique the interest of a struggling studio in need of a big hit.

Landsberger Tenants' Association: Großmann's old hunting grounds are only a few blocks southeast of the Landsberger estates; many in the Association recall that one of their own, a young maid named Lucie, disappeared shortly after taking a housecleaning job at Großmann's apartment. Shabelsky-Bork initially contacts just one of the members of the Association (the one most fit for undertaking an investigation, as detailed under **The Case of the Wayward Princess**; page 109), but the prospect of uncovering the truth behind one of Großmann's other murders opens up the possibility of finding out what happened to Lucie as well, which should be enough to get the other tenants on the case too.

The Apache Pathfinders: a group of investigators belonging to the Pathfinders is one invoking the boy/girl detective genre, and a certain level of suspension of disbelief in keeping with that genre's conventions is necessary in such campaigns. Nevertheless, a credible case could be made for Shabelsky-Bork looking to employ a group known for their self-reliance and capable skill-sets; the relative youth of the Pathfinders would also be an asset for the master manipulator, who would see them as an ultimately disposable cat's paw. As with the Owls, Shabelsky-Bork addresses his request for aid to the group in general, rather than to any one individual. Keepers are advised that additional wrinkles may be introduced into the scenario based on the political or social backgrounds of the Pathfinders' parents.

DRAMATIS PERSONAE

Key non-player characters are described in this section, along with their motivations and agendas during the scenario. Note that profiles for each can be found in the **Characters and Monsters** section beginning on page 138.

Carl Großmann, *58, deceased serial killer*

Despite being dead, Carl Großmann plays a central role in this scenario. Completely insane, he stalked the poorest districts of the city, always on the lookout for ways to indulge his insatiable hunger for flesh and hedonistic pleasures. It is his rumored murder of a woman who may have been an incognito Anastasia Romanov that instigates the scenario.

Großmann's death is the final act in a "game" he has been playing for the past five years. His suicide enacts a magical ritual that disperses his spirit across the city, potentially possessing every person who ever ate the human flesh he peddled on the black market—and that turns out to be quite a few people.

- **Description:** Großmann was in life beady-eyed and of ill aspect, with a ferocious temper and a foul mouth. He was capable of charm when trying to get his way, but mostly he relied on proffering money and food to the desperate or naïve to fulfill his perverted desires. Demon-Großmann's porcine, bloodshot eyes manifest in those he "possesses" after his death.

- **Traits:** the Demon-Großmann is every bit as sadistically and lustily insane as its mortal predecessor. Its chief preoccupation is to murder every woman who escaped its clutches during life; at the top of its list is "Sasnovski"—also known as **Anna Tchaikovsky** (following).

- **Roleplaying hooks:** people possessed by Großmann's spirit exhibit the same wild swings in personality that he displayed in life. They will use a combination of sweet words and extreme violence to meet their ends, often lurking in plain sight until the moment to strike presents itself. See **The Demon-Großmann**, page 140, in the **Characters and Monsters** section for more information.

Anna Tchaikovsky, *26, Romanov pretender*

The attempted murder of the woman currently calling herself Anna Tchaikovsky is the instigating incident of this scenario, though she does not know it. After being attacked by Großmann in 1920, she attempted suicide by hurling herself off a bridge over the Landwehr Canal. Pulled from the water an insane amnesiac, she was admitted to an asylum as "Miss Unknown." She has recently gained her freedom under the watchful eye of **Baron Kleist** (page 103), who wishes to use her claims of being Russian royalty to his own ends. Little does the Baron know that he is calling down a world of trouble upon his stately residence, as Anna becomes a target of Großmann once again, albeit in a manner none could have predicted.

Carl Großmann

Anna Tchaikovsky

- **Description:** Anna remains attractive despite the many trials of her young life. Petite in build, she wears her long, strawberry-blonde hair tied up in a bun. Her almond-shaped eyes are a piercing blue and possess a mischievous twinkle. She has a distinctive face, with high cheekbones, a long and well-sculpted nose, and rounded lips. She has many scars on her shoulders, neck, arms, hands, and feet.
- **Traits:** in contrast to her delicate physical appearance, Anna is possessed of a combative, even sour, personality. She reacts with extreme offense to anyone who confronts her about her supposed past, and she is given to taking to her room in seclusion after such incidents. She is also extremely sensitive about her scars and does not easily consent to discussing them.
- **Roleplaying hooks:** Anna has coyly claimed to be one of the Romanov princesses for nearly a year now, but she remains inscrutable. At Baron Kleist's apartment, she meets exiled Russian monarchists, some of whom openly scoff at her claims, while others swear she is in fact Anastasia. Her very existence is the hook that brings the investigators into the scenario.

Pyotr Shabelsky-Bork,
29, cold-blooded conspirator

In his guise as Prince Gabriel Constantinovich, Pyotr Shabelsky-Bork hires the investigators to look into the rumors regarding a murder of great concern to the Romanov dynasty and those who would see it restored.

In reality, Shabelsky-Bork is a member of the Sovereign Order of St. John, a secretive fraternity of Russian Hospitaller Knights. A fanatical monarchist, he gunned down the political activist Vladimir Nabokov (father of the novelist of the same name) on March 28 of this year, and he avoided a lengthy prison sentence only through a general amnesty levied just a couple of weeks later. He is in Berlin thanks to the efforts of a counterrevolutionary conspiracy calling itself Aufbau Vereinigung, which also pulls the strings of Organisation Consul.

- **Description:** a former cavalry officer, Shabelsky-Bork is of medium height and military bearing. His face is somewhat cadaverous, with an aquiline nose, hollow cheeks, and sunken eyes. He keeps his hair shorn close to his scalp and is always clean-shaven. He sports a monocle most of the time. In his disguise as Prince Constantinovich, he wears his old cavalry officer's uniform to add an extra sense of gravitas.
- **Traits:** he is an expert at setting those around him at ease. The true heart of his personality is all poisonous hate; he

THE MANY FACES OF ANNA

"Anna Tchaikovsky" is just one of many aliases adopted by the woman claiming to be the Grand Duchess Anastasia. Her many pseudonyms are an inherent part of her character, and the Keeper should be familiar with the following short list to avoid later confusion (at least on their part!):

- **Franziska Schanzkowska:** birth name and alias used when traveling incognito.
- **Sasnovski:** the semi-literate Großmann's spelling of Schanzkowska.
- **Fräulein Unbekannt:** literally "Miss Unknown," the name under which Schanzkowska is admitted to Dalldorf Asylum.
- **Anna Tchaikovsky:** the first alias adopted after her release from Dalldorf. "Anna" is a sly nod to her supposed true identity, while Tchaikovsky is supposedly her married name, taken from the Soviet soldier who rescued her from execution.

Assuming she survives the scenario, Anna later adopts a variety of other false names, most famously Anna Anderson, but also going by Anastasia Tchaikovsky and Anastasia Manahan.

Take her many identities as the most outward symbol of Anna's unpredictable personality; some level of confusion among the investigators is an inevitable outcome of trying to pin down this singular character.

is an active promoter of *The Protocols of the Elders of Zion* as a true document revealing the Jewish conspiracy to control the world, and he behaves accordingly. As Prince Constantinovich, Shabelsky-Bork affects a friendly, regal air. If confronted with evidence that he is not who he claims, he remains calm and refutes the accusations to the best of his ability—at first. He hides his scorn of Jewish investigators only with great difficulty

- **Roleplaying hooks:** keen to promote his cause and inveigle himself into the Baron's inner circle, and he is more than happy to use the investigators for as long as it remains expedient to do so.

Manfred Freiherr von Killinger,
36, assassin on a mission

As the leader of Organisation Consul, the appropriately named Killinger is in charge of planning assassinations and heading up the group's system of *vehme* (vigilante) courts, which arrest "traitors" and "November criminals" and pass death sentences in illegal, underground proceedings. Since Consul's formation two years ago, Killinger has, directly or indirectly, been a part of more than 350 political killings across Germany. He has come to Berlin to oversee the group's greatest planned assassination: that of Walther Rathenau, Minister of Finance, and to enact a magical ritual that uses Rathenau as a blood sacrifice.

- **Description:** a pudgy man of middling height and appearance, Killinger is always smartly dressed (whether in the Consul's paramilitary uniform or his own civilian garb). He wears a broom-handle mustache and carefully coiffed hair. His button eyes only reflect back the observer and reveal nothing of the man inside.
- **Traits:** Killinger is fond of his leather riding crop and carries it wherever he goes. He is not shy about using to it lash his "inferiors" (particularly any underlings he considers insubordinate, as well as his nightly prostitutes).

- **Roleplaying hooks:** despite his strutting martinet exterior, Killinger prefers to have others do the dirty work whenever possible. He doesn't hesitate to use extreme violence to restore order, however.

Police Inspector Krieg, *54, hardboiled cop*

The chief detective on the Großmann case, Inspector Krieg is perhaps the best link to the deceased murderer's motivations and personality.

- **Description:** Krieg's dark hair is shot through with white and gray thanks to the daily stresses of his work. His baggy eyes, though bloodshot, are keen and always observant. Wears a shabby suit.
- **Traits:** a chain smoker, Krieg reeks of tobacco smoke even when he doesn't have a cigarette dangling from his chapped lips.
- **Roleplaying hooks:** Krieg is a busy man and keeps his conversations brief; however, if presented with new evidence of a past crime or with the potential of more murders, he will take as much time as necessary to ascertain the validity of the claims.

Pyotr Shabelsky-Bork

Manfred Freiherr von Killinger

Baron Arthur von Kleist,
67, scheming monarchist

A Baltic German and former Chief of Police for Russian Poland, Kleist remains a committed counterrevolutionary, much more devoted to the Russian monarchist cause than to Germany's. He takes in Anna Tchaikovsky after her release from the asylum but immediately begins to manipulate her claims to royalty for his own ends, believing that if he can help confirm her lineage and restore the Romanov dynasty, he will be richly rewarded.

- **Description:** a pencil-thin man with pince-nez glasses and an old-fashioned manner of dress. He has a livid dueling scar running along his left cheek. His hair is thin and snowy white, and he sports an impressive goatee and waxed mustache, also white.
- **Traits:** the baron uses his pocket watch as a social weapon, pointedly checking it if he feels that an interaction is going on too long or leading nowhere.
- **Roleplaying hooks:** normally officious, Kleist turns instantly sycophantic in the presence of Russian nobility or anyone else he thinks may be of assistance in his rise to fame and power.

Anita Berber, 23, Berlin's naked goddess

Currently one of the city's most famous (and infamous) personalities. Star of stage and screen, she is mostly known for her transgressive and transformative dances, and for her wild and unpredictable persona.

- **Description:** Berber commands attention wherever she goes. Her flaming red hair is cut short in a fashionable bob, and she is never seen in public without copious makeup: drawn-on eyebrows, plenty of kohl around the eyes, cherry red lips, and white face powder. Her body is thin and lithe, almost androgynous, and she dresses to accentuate this look.
- **Traits:** Berber is a rock star ahead of her time. She is loud and brash, coked-up, professionally outrageous, and increasingly disconnected from reality.
- **Roleplaying hooks:** when dealing with the investigators, she responds positively to anyone who presents an unusual or striking appearance or personality, or who offers her drugs (particularly cocaine). Investigators are advised to mind her violent mood swings and profane outbursts. She does not shy away from physical attacks, often at the slightest provocations.

Anita Berber

DREAM VISIONS

At the outset of the scenario, the Keeper should determine whether any of the investigators in the group are artistically sensitive. This may include professional artists, of course, but also those with traits like "dreamer" or "hedonist." If in doubt, ask any investigators with POW 65 or above to make a **POW** roll; success means they are affected. Such investigators, like many other sensitive souls in the city, are plagued by disturbing images in their dreams. Each morning of the investigation, affected investigators must make an **INT** roll to remember their disturbing dreams. Those who succeed receive one of the following visions (and the associated Sanity loss) in the following order:

1. **First-person vision:** entering a crowded nightclub (the Red Mill Cabaret, though investigators won't know this unless they've been there before). The air is filled with cigarette smoke, the atmosphere lively. A prostitute approaches, smiling and cooing. The dreamer looks around and spots a pretty Slavic girl in simple garb. Chasing off the prostitute, the dreamer heads over to talk to the girl.

Keeper note: once the dreaming investigators meet Anna Tchaikovsky, they recognize her as the girl from this dream. Dreamers loses 0/1 Sanity point for the Red Mill Cabaret vision and 1/1D3 Sanity points for seeing Anna Tchaikovsky; if the investigators have yet to visit the café or meet Anna (or both), defer the Sanity loss until those events transpire.

2. **First-person vision:** a sexual liaison with a prostitute in an apartment (Großmann's). The image quickly dissolves to the dreamer lying naked in bed while the woman stands in a dormer window, also naked, smoking. The dreamer's body is not their own; it is a middle-aged man's, underweight, flabby, and venous.

Keeper note: the dreamer loses 0/1 Sanity point. If the investigator has visited Großmann's apartment and recognizes their surroundings, they lose one further point of Sanity; otherwise, the point is lost once the apartment is visited.

TIMELINE

Wednesday, June 21: Großmann commits suicide. Investigators hired to look into Großmann/"Sasnovski" case.

Thursday, June 22: first reports of violent murders across the city (**The Murders**, page 127). In the evening, Baron von Kleist puts out the word about his "special guest" (**Anna in the Paper**, page 126). Anna Tchaikovsky is attacked this evening (**The First Attack**, page 124).

Friday, June 23: the *lustmorde* increase. Anna Tchaikovsky runs away to hide in the Berlin Zoo. Manfred von Killinger offers his Devil's bargain.

Saturday, June 24: Walther Rathenau is assassinated.

3. **First-person vision:** a different prostitute lies bound and gagged on the bed in the same apartment (Großmann's), sweaty and unconscious; the dreamer looks down to see their gore-covered hand—it is the investigator's own hand, not Großmann's! The bed sheets partially covering the woman are soaked with blood.

Keeper note: the dreamer loses 1/1D3 Sanity points.

4. **First-person vision:** a bloody butcher's block in a kitchen (Großmann's). The linoleum is slick with blood, and there are cuts of bloody meat stacked up on the tile countertop. Clearly visible among the piles of meat are a human hand and woman's head. The head has a different face from those seen in previous dreams.

Keeper note: the dreamer loses 1/1D4 Sanity points.

5. **First-person vision:** the investigator rides in the back of an open-topped car. Their body, again, is not their own, but it is a different body from the other dreams: a man in a fine suit. The car's uniformed driver is slowing down to cross a set of railroad tracks. At this moment, another car pulls up alongside. A man the investigator recognizes as Kern (from the **Incident at Romanisches Square** confrontation, page 106) leans out of the car's passenger window, holding an MP 18 submachine gun, and opens fire. The dreamer feels the bullets ripping into their body, tearing open their throat and smashing their spine. Then, another man in the backseat of the adjacent car tosses out a "potato masher" grenade that lands at the dreamer's feet. Moments before the grenade goes off, the investigator wakes up drenched in sweat, convinced they've been shot.

Keeper note: the dreamer loses 1D3/1D8 Sanity points.

Below: The Ku'damm map

Keeper Map

The Ku'damm Map

1. Berlin Zoo – Elephant Gate
2. Berlin Zoo – Ostrich House
3. Romanisches Café
4. Eden Hotel
5. Baron Arthur von Kleist's Apartment

⎯⎯ Subway (Underground)

╫╫╫ Elevated Railroad

▮ Subway Station

▨ Elevated Platform

Scale (in meters) 1: 1000
0   1000

Keeper Map

START: INCIDENT AT ROMANISCHES SQUARE

Keeper note: before getting into the scenario proper, ask the players to make a **Luck** roll. Note down those who failed but do not reveal the reason for the roll at this time—the results of this roll determine who may be targeted in a later scene, see **The First Attack** (page 124).

Now on with the show…

It is the lunch hour, and the investigators are gathered at the Romanisches Café on Auguste-Viktoria-Platz (**The Ku'damm,** page 30), enjoying the fine summer weather. Perhaps they have met here for luncheon, or perhaps they have coincidently found themselves in the same area for one reason or another and are seated together.

A warm breeze moves through the laughing boughs of the trees in the nearby Zoological Garden; the sidewalks are full of the usual mix of shoppers and tourists. A fashionable mother and daughter pair of T-girls (see **Prostitution**, page 53), not far from their home stomping grounds of Tauentzienstraße, relax across the street, testing the waters of the noontime crowd for potential customers. Inside the

café is the usual mix of artists and intellectuals—the Keeper should feel free to drop a couple names from **Oh! You Pretty Things** (pages 71–87) to dress up the scene.

The view across to the center of the square, hardly obscured by the bustling cars and busses whizzing through the traffic circle that rings it, is of the towering 370-foot (113 m) spire of the Kaiser-Wilhelm-Memorial-Church, a truly grand edifice even to the non-religious. Beyond the church, on the far side of the square, sits the Heaven and Hell Club, not due to open for several more hours, as well as the all-marble façade of the Marmorhaus movie palace.

Newspaper vendors make their way around the square, shouting out the day's headline: the infamous cannibal-murderer Carl Großmann has cheated justice by hanging himself in his jail cell! Anyone who was living in Berlin in 1921 recalls the sensational Großmann case, the events of which are summarized in **Handout: Devil 1**. If all of the investigators are newly arrived in the city, the article brings them up to speed—the newspaper sellers have titles available in French and English as well as German.

As the investigators sip their coffee and read their papers, the air of bohemian comfort is disturbed by the arrival of a dozen men and adolescent boys. They are smartly dressed in custom dark gray, military-style uniforms. Some bear

military medals on their breast, and a few the scars of war as well—an eye patch here, pockmarked mustard gas scars there. All wear a large pewter badge pinned to their left sleeve depicting a Viking long ship cutting across the waves with the name "Ehrhardt" beneath it. Berlin natives, or those who have been living in the city for a while, may recognize the name on the badge with a successful **Know** roll: Hermann Ehrhardt was one of the most prominent leaders of the Kapp Putsch in 1920.

Certainly, other café patrons recognize the men's badges and uniforms: hisses and jeers erupt here and there. The eldest of the uniformed men, a riding whip tucked under one arm, merely salutes courteously. Some of the youth begin singing a jaunty tune to the melody of the song "Let Us Be Glad and Cheerful"—but the happy melody belies the shocking lyrical content, which predicts the imminent return of the Kaiser and calls for violence against Chancellor Joseph Wirth and Foreign Minister Walther Rathenau. The song concludes with the sickening couplet:

"Knock off Walther Rathenau,
The God-forsaken Jewish-sow!"

As they sing, the young men move among the café patrons sitting on the terrace, powering through as if they were still on the promenade, intentionally bumping tables, sending flower vases toppling and drinks sloshing out of cups. One of the men, whose handsome features are spoiled by his undisguised sneer, stops at the table where the investigators are sitting. Reaching into his pocket, he produces a piece of chalk and draws a right-facing *hakenkreutz* (broken cross)—or, as it is better known, a swastika—directly on the table's surface, grinning the whole time in a provocative fashion.

German investigators, or expatriate investigators who have lived in Germany for more than a year, may make a **Know** roll; if successful, they recall that the Munich-based National Socialist Workers' Party uses a swastika as its symbol, while a Hard success further recalls that the NSDAP's version of the swastika faces the opposite direction to the one drawn here. Even without a roll, the *players* may reasonably assume these men are members of the Nazi Party. They are not—but they are just as bad.

Currently operating as a *Ringvereine* (**Beinls and Bulls: Crime & Punishment**, page 37) under the title of "Olympia Sports Association" (*Sportverein Olympia*), the men are actually members of an infamous and illegal terror group known as Organisation Consul. Some of their number are native to Berlin, while others have recently arrived from the group's Munich headquarters for another reason (which will become manifest later in the scenario, see **Baldur's**

Handout: Devil 1

Redaktion
Herrengasse Nr. 12, 1. Stock.

Administration
Herrengasse Nr. 12, Parterre.

B·Z am Mittag

Morgen-Ausgabe.

XXXIX. Jahrgang   Donnerstag, 22 Juni 1922   10 Pfennig

Carl Großmann found Dead in his Cell

Who among our readers will not shudder at the memory of the infamous and outrageous acts of the Beast of the Silesian Station, Carl Großmann? Arrested 10 months ago in his flat at Lange Straße 88/89, the fiend was found with the body of a murdered woman—a destitute thing, lured into the spider's lair with promises of cash and food. Instead, she met her death, but not before her screams and thrashing attracted the notice of the building's neighbors. Police found the poor creature in Großmann's kitchen, stripped naked and trussed up like a hog for butchering.

Indeed, Inspector Krieg of the Criminal Police noted extensive apparatus for meat processing and sausage-making in Großmann's apartment. The Devil-Carl claimed that this was merely owing to his career as a butcher, but persistent rumors claim otherwise. His neighbors recall that, during the starving days of 1917–18, Großmann seemed to do quite well for himself selling homemade sausages at the Silesian Station. At the time, there was much speculation as to where he procured his meat, but nowadays most shudder to contemplate the question.

Inspector Krieg found evidence in the form of blood stains sufficient for the courts to charge Großmann with two other "lust murders," and the perverted criminal, who spent 14 years in jail prior to the War on charges of illicit activities with children, went on trial four days ago. Today, the judge was expected to announce a guilty verdict in the matter of three murders committed at Großmann's hands, but the reprobate was found hanging from his bed sheet inside his jail cell this very morning.

Sacrifice, page 131), but—never ones to miss an opportunity to bait their enemies—they decided to stroll up from their recruiting station off the square to make a bit of trouble at the notoriously left-leaning Romanisches Café.

THE VÖLKISCH MOVEMENT

"In 1875, the same year that Blavatsky founded her Theosophical Society in New York, List was invoking Baldur, the Teutonic Sun God, on a hilltop outside Vienna. In Baldur's honor, he buried eight wine bottles there in the shape of the swastika and pledged himself to the worship of the Old Ones…"

—Peter Levenda, *Unholy Alliance*

The following information is widely known inside Germany and would be known to any foreigners with an **Anthropology** or **Occult** skill of 35% or higher.

There are words in every language that are difficult to translate. In German, *völkisch* is one such word. Related to the English word "folk," but signifying much more, the *völkisch* movement arose out of the great awakening of German nationalism during the 19th century, culminating in the formation of the German Empire in 1871.

Völkisch societies took off in the decade following the Empire's birth and signified the new country's desire to connect with a mythic past. Thus, *völkisch* not only stands for "folklore" but also "populism" and "nationalism." It signifies a People with a capital P. The movement spoke of a shared heritage among the German people stretching back tens of thousands of years and cast the fate of the German peoples as being one of constant struggle against outside "polluting" influences: from the Latinate countries, the Slavs, and, especially, the Jews. Indeed, the movement largely rejected Semitic religions of all types, including Christianity, which was seen as diluting the glorious pagan German past.

At its most benign, the *völkisch* movement extolled a "back to nature" ethos called *Lebensreform* (life reform) that rejected the corrupting urban lifestyle for clean country living, free of drugs, drink, and other vices, while openly admiring fine specimens of German physiques (abundantly depicted in nude portraits and photographs). At its most insidious, the *völkisch* movement provided justification for all manner of anti-Semitic and Nationalistic belief structures, as well as crackpot theories regarding race, biology, and cosmology.

Troublemakers

The older fellow with the riding whip is a man by the name of Manfred Freiherr von Killinger (**Dramatis Personae**, page 102; his profile can be found on page 138). He has recently been acquitted, against all available evidence, of masterminding the assassination of Matthias Erzberger, Minister of Finance, in 1921, and so is in particularly high spirits. He arrived in Berlin this very morning.

The young man who drew the swastika on the investigators' table is Erwin Kern, a 23-year-old law student, anti-Semite, and right-wing fanatic (see his profile in **Characters and Monsters**, page 138). Despite what the players may assume, the swastika is a symbol of his personal hero, Hermann Ehrhardt, and not a sign of Kern's anti-Semitism or affiliation to the NSDAP.

Killinger, Kern, and their cronies are attempting to provoke a reaction from the café patrons, for that is Consul's agreed-upon *modus operandi*: incite violence from the Left wherever possible, ultimately leading to a left-wing uprising which Consul can then put down in a backdoor coup of the government. Consul wishes to sow chaos at every opportunity—the faster society deteriorates, the sooner they may seize power.

The plan is working. Even if the investigators remain calm in the face of such provocation, other café patrons do not. Heated words lead to blows and overturned tables. Investigators may wisely make a run for it (along with most of the other patrons and nearby pedestrians) or join in the fray for a while—use **Erwin Kern's** profile (page 138) for other Consul members as needed. At this point, no one is armed with anything deadlier than knuckles or boot heels and all flee if a firearm or blade is produced.

Investigators who choose to make a run for it without fighting may attempt a **Spot Hidden** roll; with success, they note a pinch-faced man in a finely tailored suit standing on the other side of the square watching the tussle avidly. He quickly notices the investigator(s) looking at him and disappears into the gathering crowd.

Keeper note: the pinch-faced man is Prince Gabriel Constantinovich, who the investigators encounter in **The Case of the Wayward Princess**, page 109.

After 1D3 rounds of fisticuffs, Killinger, to keep up appearances, wades in with his whip, shouting for calm and order as police whistles sound in the distance. The confrontation ends as quickly as it began and life soon returns to normal, the café waiters glumly sweeping up shattered cups and saucers—just another day in Berlin.

The Swastika

After the altercation, an **Occult** roll, dependent on the level of success, recalls the following trivia about the symbolism of the swastika.

- **Regular success:** the swastika, a name derived from the Sanskrit for "good fortune," is at least 10,000 years old and is represented in cultures across the globe, from Europe to Asia to the New World.
- **Hard success:** as Regular, plus the investigator knows the symbol usually stands for wellbeing, fertility, fire, and the sun. The Norse called it "Thor's hammer."
- **Extreme success:** as Hard, plus, over the last few decades, the symbol has become associated with the Indo-European "Aryan" peoples and has been adopted by German followers of the *völkisch* movement (see **The *Völkisch* Movement**, page 108) as a symbol of racial purity and nationalist power.
- **Critical success:** as Extreme, plus the investigator knows the Ariosophist philosopher Guido von List declared the swastika a "hidden rune," associating it with occult power.

THE CASE OF THE WAYWARD PRINCESS

Following the incident at the café, the investigators may attempt to go about the remainder of their day as best they can. If they look into the tussle at the café or the mysterious figure watching the scene, they meet dead ends. But as the day wears on, one or more investigators receive a message from a certain "Prince Gabriel Constantinovich"—in actuality, the monarchist conspirator Pyotr Shabelsky-Bork (**Dramatis Personae**, page 101). The "Prince" specifically attempts to contact (in order): a private investigator, reporter, police officer, or detective; a medical doctor; a dilettante or other upper-class type; a Communist organizer; or an academic. If the group includes more than one of these types, he invites each one in turn. Arrangements to meet are sent via Rohrpost (**Media and Communication**, page 36), arriving at 4:30 pm. Provide the investigators with **Handout: Devil 2**.

The Eden Hotel is one of the buildings near the Auguste-Viktoria-Platz, so it may already be familiar to the investigators. A successful **Credit Rating** roll recalls that the Eden's bar is a well-known gathering place for socialites, dilettantes, artists, and writers on the city's west side. Members of the Communist party, or anyone making a successful **Know** roll, recalls that the Eden was the site where the KPD leaders Karl Liebknecht and Rosa

Handout: Devil 2

013   Telegramm

Deutsche Reichstelegraph

BERLIN : 182 +26 +10- +12 56 3

Amt Memel

PRINCE GABRIEL CONSTANTINOVICH DESIRES THE PLEASURE OF YOUR COMPANY TONIGHT AT 8:00 PM TO DISCUSS A MATTER OF EXTREME DELICACY. ROOM 415, EDEN HOTEL. KURFÜRSTENDAMM 246/247.

Luxemburg were held by Freikorps members prior to their executions in 1919.

It is nearly the summer solstice, and it is still light out when investigators arrive at the hotel for their 8 pm appointment. Crossing the elegant, high-ceilinged lobby, the sound of laughter and conversation already drifts out of the hotel's café and its "American Bar *und* Grill." Russian is spoken here nearly as much as German.

Room 415 is on the hotel's fourth (top) floor. A knock on the door summons a sallow-faced man in the livery of a chauffeur. The room is a large suite, with views looking out over the Berlin Zoo, green and golden in the late evening sun. The chauffeur, a dour fellow by the name of Fedor, quietly offers cigars to male investigators and cigarettes to the ladies. He also asks (in Russian and without much conviction) if anyone would care for a drink from the bar; if no one speaks Russian, he does not repeat the offer in German.

At this point, the Prince enters. He is in the full-dress uniform of a Tsarist Russian cavalry officer—indeed, he is just buttoning the top button on his jacket. Fedor salutes him, but the Prince waves this gesture off.

"*Good evening. I am Prince Gabriel Constantinovich, at your service. Thank you very much for answering my summons.*" He uses the language shared in common by the investigators and is equally comfortable conversing in German, French, or English, though he speaks each with a noticeable accent.

The Prince does not launch into his full speech until he is sure everyone he invited is present. He proves himself a gracious host, repeating Fedor's offer of drinks (this time in a language everyone can understand) and engaging in pleasant small talk while waiting for everyone to arrive. If asked why and how he contacted the investigators, he merely smiles slyly and says that their reputations preceded them.

Investigators who saw the pinch-faced man at Romanisches Square earlier that day recognize the Prince as the man in question. If asked about it, he shakes his head gravely. "*These are such tumultuous times, but what are we to expect when the monarchies sanctioned by God are torn down by the unwashed hordes? What is it the poet Yeats said? Ah yes: 'Things fall apart; the center cannot hold;/Mere anarchy is loosed upon the world,/The blood-dimmed tide is loosed…' Indeed.*" At which point, he takes a thoughtful drag on his cigar before changing the subject.

Handout: Devil 3

Investigators succeeding at an **Art/Craft (Literature/ Poetry)** or Hard **Language (English)** roll recall the rest of the verse of the 1919 poem: "…and everywhere/The ceremony of innocence is drowned;/The best lack all conviction, while the worst/Are full of passionate intensity…"

Once everyone is present, drinks and cigars in hand, Prince Constantinovich gets to the evening's central matter. "*I have summoned you here tonight because you possess special skills—skills that may aid me and the parties I represent in a most macabre investigation. You are all no doubt aware of the great tragedy that befell Tsar Nicholas and his family—may the saints bless them and keep them—nearly four years ago in the city of Ekaterinburg. There, Bolshevist slime gunned down the royal family. I have personally visited the site (in disguise, of course) and confirmed that the royal family was there. I have seen the bullet holes. I took photographs. Here, you see: a photograph of a marking upon the wall! And here! I found the Tsarina's journal wedged into a crack in the wall. You see the mark upon the wall and the symbol on the journal is the same: the swastika. Her good-luck symbol,*" he notes grimly. Pass the players **Handout: Devil 3**.

The Prince looks at a local Russian-language newspaper sitting on a side table. The hateful face of Carl Großmann stares out from a photograph on the front page. The Prince sighs and then seems to change the subject, as if remembering the true nature of the evening's affairs.

"*The papers reported that this Großmann recorded names of women, possibly his victims, in his journal. One such name was "Sasnovski." This name likely means nothing to you, but it means a great deal to me and other interested parties. We believe it may refer to a Polish peasant girl calling herself Franziska Schamzkovska or similar. The date in Großmann's journal is from over two years ago. Too much time may have passed to gain a real answer, yet I must try. I ask you: with the murderer now dead in his cell and the answer to our question seemingly out of reach, will you help me, to the best of your abilities, learn whether Carl Großmann did indeed murder Franziska Schamzkovska in February 1920?*"

The Prince offers to pay in pounds sterling at the rate of £3 ($15) per day, plus expenses—a most generous rate. This may (quite rightfully) raise suspicions among the investigators. If anyone asks about the Prince's generosity, he

THE PRINCE'S DECEPTION

"Prince Constantinovich" is not who he says he is. He is Pyotr Shabelsky-Bork, operative for the Sovereign Order of St. John, a group of White Russian exiles who claim descent from the original Knights Hospitaller. He is also an assassin and anti-Semite. The "parties he represents" are the SOSJ and their German allies, the counterrevolutionary conspiracy calling itself the *Aufbau Vereinigung* (Construction Union). Through Aufbau, Shabelsky-Bork maintains connections with Manfred von Killinger and Organisation Consul, whom Aufbau often uses as muscle for its wetwork.

Obviously, these are secrets Shabelsky-Bork and his associates would prefer kept under wraps, and investigators who discover the truth—or, worse, confront "the Prince" about it—put themselves in danger, at least during these early stages of the charade (although that changes after the events in the **Cassowary Enclosure**, page 130). Note that Shabelsky-Bork has Persuade 70% and Psychology 60%, requiring a Hard success from

investigators attempting a **Psychology** roll; if successful, all they can discern is that the "Prince" is being truthful to some degree but is possibly holding something back. Of course, if pressed on this matter, Shabelsky-Bork laughs off such talk and reminds the investigator concerned of the importance of the case.

Players who think to ask may roll against their investigator's **Know** to recall that a certain Prince Gabriel Constantinovich is indeed a leading figure in the Russian monarchist movement, although he usually resides in Paris; this apparent contradiction is easily explained away by the false Prince, who claims he is in Berlin "on business of great import."

Shabelsky-Bork bears a superficial resemblance to the real-life Prince. Russian investigators who possess an appropriate background (military or aristocracy) may try their **Spot Hidden** to notice the differences between him and the actual Prince, but they must succeed at Hard difficulty owing to Shabelsky-Bork's high Disguise skill.

simply indicates that solving this mystery is of the utmost importance to the parties he represents. Questions about the connection between the murder of the Romanovs and the murder of "Sasnovski" are likewise ducked.

The Prince informs the investigators that Schamzkovska was known to frequent the cafés around Andreasplatz and suggests they might start there by asking around. Sadly, he doesn't have a photo of the girl, but he provides a description: back then, she would have been around 19 years of age, petite, with strawberry blonde hair, piercing blue eyes, and attractive features. *"If she is who we think she may be, then anyone who knew her will remember her,"* he insists.

THREADS OF THE INVESTIGATION

There are two threads investigators may pursue in their inquiries: trying to find more information about Schamzkovska/Sasnovski or looking into Carl Großmann and his history of crime.

RESEARCHING SCHAMZKOVSKA/SASNOVSKI

The following clue trail presents the steps the investigators can take following this thread through the scenario.

- Following the Prince's direction to check out Andreasplatz and its surrounding neighborhoods (**The Kietz**, page 113), the investigators can learn of Großmann's **Garden Colony** "cottage" (page 121) and of the **Red Mill Cabaret** (page 114).
- Checking out the Red Mill Cabaret, the investigators can turn up a lead about a young ingénue matching Schamzkovska's description being committed to the **Dalldorf Asylum** (page 120).
- Snooping around at the Dalldorf Asylum reveals that this young woman was just recently remanded into the care of one Baron Kleist.
- Locating Kleist, investigators get a chance to interview the young lady, possibly revealing her true origins (**Meeting Anna Tchaikovsky**, page 122). If they take too long in their investigations, they are scooped by Kleist when he leaks news

of her identity to the media (**Anna in the Paper**, page 126).

- The Baron's leak alerts Demon-Großmann to the location of the woman he suspects to be "Sasnovski," and he soon undertakes a rather violent investigation of its own (**The First Attack**, page 124). If the investigators are present for the attack, they expose themselves to potential possession from the malevolent spirit.
- Whether they solve the mystery or are scooped, the investigators are paid by Constantinovich (**An Unusual Check**, page 125).

RESEARCHING GROßMANN

If following the thread concerning Großmann, the following clue trail may be used.

- **Handout: Devil 1** lists Großmann's old address (**Lange Straße 88/89**, page 117), and the investigators may think to check this out.
- While poking around the apartment, they run into one or more of Großmann's neighbors, all of whom have rather shady pasts themselves. Investigators may also learn of Großmann's shed (**The Garden Colony**, page 121).
- Großmann's old files are under the care of Inspector Krieg and **The Police** (page 119), and some important insights into the killer's methods and goals may be gleaned from them. Particularly persuasive investigators may even lay their hands on Großmann's journal, much to their peril.
- A trip out to the **Garden Colony** (page 121) reveals more about the killer's personality and may turn up a strange doll that could prove useful in the scenario's climactic scene.

Following the Threads

As investigators pursue either of these threads, violent murders break out around the city and monstrosities roam around in broad daylight (**Lustmord: The Killings Take Hold**, page 127). If the investigators have concluded their inquiry into the fate of the Schamzkovska girl by this point, they are pulled back in when she goes missing (**The Runaway**, page 129).

As the principals involved realize the true magnitude of the problem, the scenario moves to its thrilling climax (**Baldur's Sacrifice**, page 131), in which the investigators' collected knowledge about Großmann may save or doom them.

THE KIETZ

Kietz is criminal slang for the underworld lifestyle. In taking on this case, the investigators are in for an eyeful of the Kietz as they visit seedy cabarets and rundown tenements.

Although Prince Constantinovich holds his meeting late in the evening, it is by no means too late to begin the investigation right away—this is Berlin, after all! Indeed, some avenues of investigation will offer up different opportunities and information depending on the time of day they are visited.

THE FRIEDRICHSHAIN

This district of the city, running parallel to the Spree east of **The Alex** (page 28), is one of its poorest and most run-down. It is a hotbed for the KPD (German Communist Party) and criminal *Ringvereine* organizations. Indeed, the district is known to some as "Berlin's Chicago" for its combination of working-class immigrants, leftist politics, and organized crime.

Central to the district is the massive Silesian Station, which brings in daily trainloads of Poles, Russians, and Jews from the east, along with itinerant German workers hoping to find employment, desperate runaways with dreams of

stardom, and migrant day laborers. The smoke from the trains gives the surrounding buildings a sooty coating that is never fully washed away, even after the heaviest rains.

Andreasplatz

Just a block north of Großmann's apartment is a busy little square called Andreasplatz. Many of the strays and foundlings who come rolling off the Silesian Station trains wash up here, and Großmann favored this spot for picking up women. Night or day, the square is strewn with litter and pigeons; a blind veteran, missing his left arm, sits on a bench, shaking a tin cup for spare change.

Night: the square swarms with prostitutes. If it's a weeknight, the majority of the women are "Half-Silks"—*hausfraus* and office girls looking to pick up a bit of extra money (**Prostitution**, page 53). Some of the Half-Silks haven't even bothered to hang up their blue aprons! Others, particularly on a Friday or Saturday, are of a more professional bent, including Class-C Kontroll-Girls (registered prostitutes) and Chontes (Polish Jews).

Asking around about "Sasnovski" brings up nothing, but questions about Großmann elicit testimony from the handful of Kontroll-Girls and Chontes who were working the square back in 1920 and are still here. They respond well

Keeper Map

The Friedrichshain Map

1. Andreasplatz
2. Lulu's Body
3. Grossman's Apartment at Lange Straße 88/89
4. Red Mill Cabaret

Scale (in meters) 1: 500
0   500

The Friedrichshain map

to offers of money (5,000 marks or nearly any amount of foreign currency gets them to open up), as well as a **Charm** or **Fast Talk** roll.

- One Kontroll-Girl (pickup line: "*So, sweetheart?*"), a heavily made-up Class-C peroxide blonde called Lulu, remembers Großmann cruising for ladies quite often here. She went with him once, and he took her back to his place (at **Lange Straße 88/89**, page 117) and then the next morning drove her out to a "garden shed" on Landsberger Chausee (**The Garden Colony**, page 121). "*I still have the scars from that one, but he paid well,*" she says with a wry smile. "*First time I've gotten a lay in a sausage storeroom.*" She can provide directions out to the shed if asked.
- A Chonte named Zvia recalls drinking with Großmann down at the **Red Mill Cabaret** (following). "*He liked to take girls fresh off the train and get them drunk down there,*" she says.

Day: investigators visiting Andreasplatz during daylight hours are far less likely to find any real leads. At the Keeper's discretion, they'll need a successful group **Luck** roll to find either Lulu or Zvia (see above).

Red Mill Cabaret

Located two short blocks south of Großmann's apartment, the Red Mill Cabaret sits in the cellar of a former restaurant. Access is via a side door in a rubbish-strewn alleyway that smells of vomit and urine. A short flight of stairs leads to a low-ceilinged, plaster-walled basement. After 9 pm, the cramped little joint is packed with screeching whores, drunken proles, criminals, and deadbeats. The air is positively thick with cigarette smoke, reducing clear visibility to about 10 feet (3 m). A small stage area is nominally reserved for the entertainment, but performers often do their thing out among the crowd.

As the investigators enter and are led to their table by the broad-shouldered *maitre d'*, Erich, they see a sweaty and bespectacled man up on stage, seated on a rickety chair, a rather beaten-up ventriloquist's dummy on his lap. His querulous voice is drowned out by shouts from the drunken crowd: "*Get off the stage, fart-gas!*" "*You're garbage!*" "*Ya lousy bull!*" And so forth. The ventriloquist quickly exits the stage amid jeers as the club's "Armchair Orchestra" strikes up a jaunty tune.

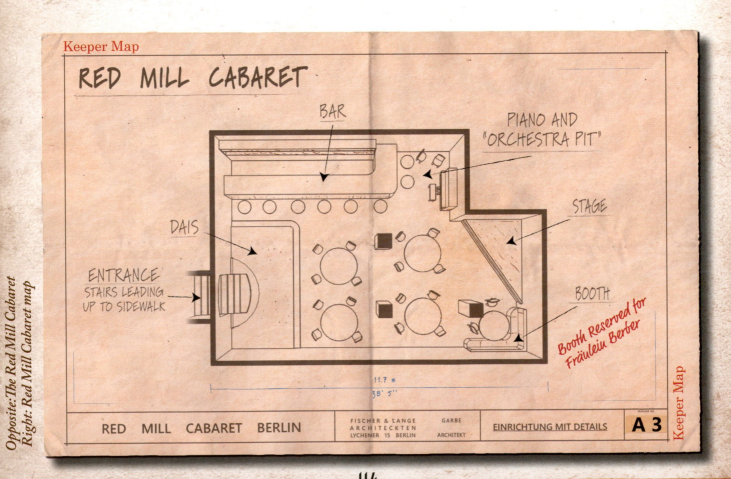

Keeper Map

RED MILL CABARET

BAR

PIANO AND "ORCHESTRA PIT"

DAIS

STAGE

ENTRANCE
STAIRS LEADING
UP TO SIDEWALK

BOOTH

Booth Reserved for Fräulein Berber

11.7 m
38' 5''

RED MILL CABARET BERLIN

FISCHER & LANGE
ARCHITECKTEN
LYCHENER 15 BERLIN

GARBE
ARCHITEKT

EINRICHTUNG MIT DETAILS

A 3

Keeper Map

Opposite: The Red Mill Cabaret
Right: Red Mill Cabaret map

Asking around about "Sasnovski" amid the rowdy, working-class crowd may prove hazardous. Investigators may use **Charm**, **Fast Talk**, **Intimidate**, or **Persuade**, but must succeed at Hard difficulty if their **Credit Rating** is above 50%, and Extreme difficulty if their **Credit Rating** is above 75%. Even Erich is apt to be surly with the well-heeled. Investigators who have had a vision of the Red Mill Cabaret in their dreams (**Dream Visions**, page 104) may make their roll with a bonus die—once they've gotten over the shock of recognizing their surroundings. Investigators offering up a bit of cash in the form of drinks on the house (cost is £1, $5, or 1,000 marks) may gain a bonus die to their roll.

A successful social skill roll turns up a couple of regulars who vaguely remember a woman matching the description and name, though one of them recalls that her surname was Schanzkowski or Schanzkowska, or something like that. She was something of a regular around the club "*She stopped coming after she chucked herself in the Landwehr and was taken off to the looney bin,*" says one of the investigators' new confidantes. However, a failed push or fumbled roll results in a challenge to fisticuffs in the alley outside (if the investigator is a man) or a hard slap across the face (if the investigator is a woman) by a particularly beefy and inebriated patron. Use the statistics for the **Red Mill Drunk** in the **Characters and Monsters** section (page 139) as required.

A Noteworthy Arrival

At this point, the orchestra is finishing its interlude and a sign is put up on stage announcing the next act: Jack the Escape-King. Nearby lurks a man carefully removing oiled chains and shackles from a trunk. His act, however, is postponed indefinitely by the surprise arrival of two strange characters: a man and woman, obviously drunk on love and cognac. The man is somewhat swarthy, a look enhanced by extensive kohl around the eyes. His hair is coiffured into elaborate curls at the cheeks and forehead. He wears a brocaded and embroidered bolero jacket with no shirt, gold bangles and rings, Turkish pants, and silver-buckled boots.

The woman's ensemble is almost simple by contrast, yet she is immediately the center of attention. Despite the evening heat, she wears a full mink coat. Around her throat and wrists are strings of glittering jewels—blood-red rubies and sparkling diamonds. Her legs are bare, but her high-heeled pumps are of crocodile leather. From her neck dangles a baby chimpanzee, looking frightened by the smoke and noise of the room. The woman's hair is cut shoulder-length and is flaming red. Her face is covered with thick makeup, as if she's just come from the stage: chalk-white skin crossed by a severe crimson slash that is her painted mouth. Her left eye flashes behind a monocle.

Any native German, as well as any foreigner who succeeds at an **Art/Craft (Dance)** or **Art/Craft (Cinema)** roll, immediately recognizes the woman as Anita Berber, a transgressive dancer, poet, and film actress. The man's identity is anybody's guess.

Certainly, some of the bar patrons recognize Anita and call out to her. She flashes a gap-toothed smile and waves. Erich is immediately at her side, bowing sycophantically. "*May I take your coat,* Fräulein?" he asks. "*Certainly,*" Berber replies.

To a chorus of gasps and whistles, she slips out of her coat to reveal her lithe, pale white, naked body, the chimp pressing itself against her flesh. Even the orchestra ceases its playing as everyone stares. Berber, in total control, moves out among the tables. Passing the investigators' table, she takes her pet and hands it off to the one with the highest **APP**, male or female, with a "*Here, hold my ape.*"

Her companion quickly heads around to the orchestra and speaks with the cellist as Berber continues to move among the tables, stopping occasionally to smile or coo at a gob-smacked patron. As the cellist strikes up Tchaikovsky's "Nocturne in D minor," Berber continuing with her naked pavane, intones a poem ("Orchids," translation by Merrill Cole):

I came into a garden
The garden was full of orchids
So full and rich
It bloomed, alive, quivering
I could not get through its sweet entanglements
I love them madly
They are for me like women and boys—
I kissed and tasted each one until the end
All died red on my lips
On my hands
On my sexlessness
That enfolds all sexes
I am pale as the moon's silver

She finishes to scattered applause. About half the room seems enraptured, the other merely confused. Anita, laughing, returns to the chimpanzee-holding investigator. "*Thanks, doll-face.*"

Berber spends the rest of the evening holding court in a large corner booth, naked as the day she was born and snorting cocaine from a special ring designed to hold bumps of the drug, having a grand old time with her new lover Sebastian Droste (he of the elaborate coif). Investigators are welcome to remain at the club and enjoy themselves, though keeping up with the pace set by Berber and Droste may prove challenging—consult the rules on **Drugs** provided on page 40 and apply them liberally if investigators attempt to do so. Any investigator, regardless of gender, with an **APP** of 75 or higher also comes under Berber's pansexually lusty gaze and is loudly invited to join in, even if trying to leave.

Berber and Droste are alight with talk of Großmann and his murders. Depending on the night of the club visit, they may also be quite talkative regarding the latest wave of *lustmorde*. Regardless, it is obvious they both find the topic of sexual murder to be perfectly titillating rather than revolting. As the night wears on, Anita confides that she and Droste are working on a new suite of dances to be called "Dances of Vice, Horror, and Ecstasy."

There is little else to be gained from Berber and Droste; however, Berber returns in a big way in the next scenario (also called **Dances of Vice, Horror, and Ecstasy**, page 147), and she will remember any investigator who makes a positive impression on her this evening.

LANGE STRASSE 88/89

As reported in the article on Großmann's suicide (**Handout: Devil 1**), the killer maintained an apartment at Lange Straße 88/89. Just two blocks west of the Silesian Station, the sound of trains coming and going is nigh constant, ceasing only in the earliest hours of the morning.

The apartments are old and cheaply built in the typical *Mietskaserne* fashion (page 37). Walking through the echoing entryway, the air smells of stale dishwater. A bank of post boxes shows a variety of names for each apartment. Although "Großmann" is not among these names, there is one box that does not have a tag. As there are no numbers on the doors of these apartments, it will take some searching to locate Großmann's apartment without guidance. A successful **Navigate** roll and a half-hour of searching do the trick. Alternatively, simply asking around soon turns up someone who was living in the tenement at the time of Großmann's arrest. Roll 1D6 and consult the list in the **Interviewing the Neighbors** section (following) to see who the investigators run into.

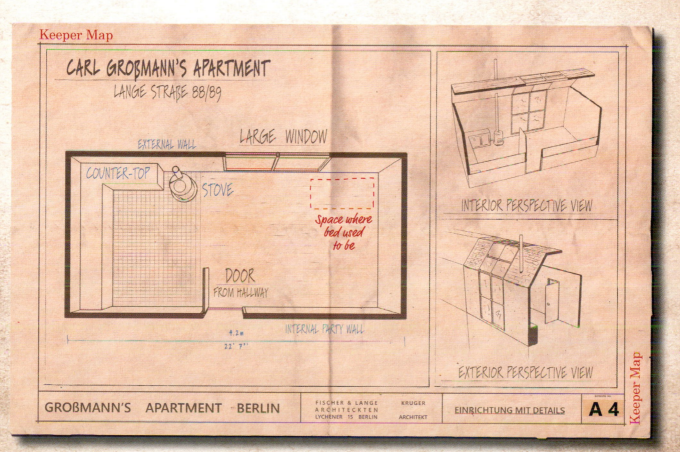

Keeper Map

CARL GROSSMANN'S APARTMENT
LANGE STRASSE 88/89

EXTERNAL WALL

LARGE WINDOW

COUNTER-TOP

STOVE

Space where bed used to be

DOOR
FROM HALLWAY

INTERNAL PARTY WALL

4.2 m
22' 7"

INTERIOR PERSPECTIVE VIEW

EXTERIOR PERSPECTIVE VIEW

GROSSMANN'S APARTMENT - BERLIN

FISCHER & LANGE ARCHITECKTEN LYCHENER 15 BERLIN | KRUGER ARCHITEKT | EINRICHTUNG MIT DETAILS | A 4

Keeper Map

Carl Großmann's Apartment map

Mannheim Itzig   **Konrad and Annie Böhm**

Frieda Klippel   **Helene Itzig**

The Neighbors

Max Hartung   **Herta Natusch**

The top-floor apartment has stood vacant since Großmann's arrest. Even with Berlin's perennial housing shortage, nobody wants to rent the apartment of a cannibalistic butcher. The door is left unlocked. A successful **Spot Hidden** roll made by the investigator opening the door notes a small hole, about an eighth of an inch (3.2 mm) in diameter, drilled through the door just above the latch.

The investigators won't find much inside. The apartment is simply a large living room cum bedroom area, with a tiled kitchen containing a wood-burning stove and tile countertop. A large dormer window stretches nearly from the floor up to the apex of the mansard roof, admitting quite a lot of light and offering a view of the courtyard area four floors below—if the investigators are here at night, they can see into many other apartment windows across the courtyard. The wallpaper is soot-stained and peeling, and there is a fair amount of soot on the floors. A successful Hard **Spot Hidden** roll locates dried blood splatter marks on the walls in several places, but an investigator must specify they are looking for such.

There is no other furniture in the apartment, nor any other clues to be had. Investigators who have suffered from **Dream Visions** (page 104) will recognize the interior of this place, perhaps even suffering a momentary visual or auditory flashback to their dream as ghostly furnishings fill the space, accompanied by stomach-turning sounds.

If the investigators haven't met her yet, their poking about now rouses the curiosity of Frau Itzig (**Interviewing the Neighbors**, following), who will come in and ask whether they are thinking of renting the apartment.

INTERVIEWING THE NEIGHBORS

Investigators may run into neighbors as they search for Großmann's apartment; they may also think to knock on some doors and talk to folk on their own initiative. Feel free to sprinkle in encounters as befits the pacing of the investigation. Hartung and the Böhms alone have worthwhile leads, so Keepers may wish to engineer an encounter with them if no one else.

Several of Großmann's neighbors still reside in the tenement. They are all poor, working-class folk who largely attempt to mind their own business. None remember a girl matching "Sasnovski's" description, but then, they tried not to look at the girls too closely—so few were ever seen again. Almost all are secretly guilt-wracked over their role in abetting Großmann's murders, for everyone in this wing of the building knew he was up to no good. They all have blood on their hands.

1. **Max Hartung** (age 47): a sweaty, rotund man with a bad comb-over, Hartung lives down the hall from Großmann's old place. He used to wait until he heard Großmann stumbling in with one or more prostitutes late in the evening, at which point he would station himself outside Großmann's door and peep through the hole Herr Itzig drilled. He claims to have never personally witnessed anything violent or depraved—this is a lie, as a successful **Psychology** roll reveals. Hartung sometimes joined Großmann for drinks at the **Red Mill Cabaret** (page 114). "*He liked to take some of his girls there,*" Hartung recalls.

2. **Frieda Klippel** (age 29): pockmarked and frumpy, Fräulein Klippel lives in the unit directly beneath Großmann's. She moved in back in the spring of 1920 and would often hear loud chopping noises very late at night coming from his unit (between 3 to 5 am, generally). She once asked him what the noises were, wondering if he was chopping wood. "*That's right, I'm chopping wood,*" she recalls him saying. The memory gives her chills.

3. **Konrad and Annie Böhm** (both aged 30): the Böhms were newlyweds back in 1920 and shared a wall with Großmann. Thus, they heard quite a lot of what went on: moans, groans, screams, and so on. They are quick to point out that the screams they heard were screams of pain (*Schmerzensschreie*), not screams for help (*Hilfeschreie*). They simply assumed Großmann had some strange sexual proclivities and left it at that. A successful **Psychology** roll indicates that they are holding something back; a successful **Intimidate** or **Fast Talk** roll is required to get Konrad to admit that he often saw Großmann leaving his apartment during the day with foul-smelling packages wrapped in butcher's paper. He once asked Großmann about the packages, and Großmann replied that he had a rabbit that had gone off. Annie remembers Großmann talking about a "garden shed" out on Landsberger Chausee where took his meat "for butchering."

4. **Herta Natusch** (age 39): a dark-complexioned woman with a nervous disposition, Herta used to be one of Großmann's neighbors but moved two floors down after she confronted him over his strange lifestyle. She recalls his exact words to her even now, "*You just shut your trap, you rotten bitch!*"

5. **Mannheim Itzig** (age 51): Großmann's across-the-hall neighbor, Mannheim's most notable feature is his protuberant, watery blue eyes. It was he who drilled the hole in Großmann's door; "*The better to keep an eye on what he was up to in there.*" Ultimately, it was Mannheim and his wife Helene who called the police. It will take a successful **Psychology** roll to figure out that the Itzigs owed Großmann quite a lot of money when they turned him in. Mannheim often drank at the Red Mill Cabaret with Großmann, despite the latter's often creepy demeanor.

6. **Helene Itzig** (age 54): a woman of ample bosom and even more ample personality, Helene is the self-appointed hall monitor for this floor. She makes it her business to know everybody else's business, including Großmann's, but Helene alone among the neighbors seems unbothered by the tardiness of her action in stopping Großmann. She takes all the credit, in fact, conveniently leaving out the detail that she essentially knew for a fact that Großmann was murdering women in his apartment for some months *before* she called the police. Helene is completely amoral, but investigators may think she had something more to do with the murders if they uncover this detail.

INQUIRIES FARTHER AFIELD

THE POLICE

Investigators may think to request the police files on the Großmann case. As mentioned in **Handout: Devil 1**, the lead detective on the case is one Inspector Krieg, who maintains an office at the Head Police Office (the *Polizeipräsidium*) on Alexanderplatz. With a successful **Law** roll, he may be chosen as one of the investigator's contacts; otherwise, a successful **Credit Rating** or **Persuade** roll secures an interview with the detective (after a wait of 1D3 hours).

Krieg recounts his arrest and investigation of Großmann, largely echoing what the investigators will have learned from the papers. He personally thinks Großmann may have killed as many as 100 people, chiefly women and children, but covered his tracks well enough that they were able to charge him only with three murders. The Inspector does reveal one detail left out of the papers. As Großmann was being led off to jail in shackles, he uttered a strange statement—one that has stuck with Krieg ever since, "*Jetzt habe ich jeden Einzigen dran.*" ("Now I have every single turn.")

If one or more of the investigators are professionally involved in law enforcement or succeed at a **Credit Rating** roll, Krieg also fetches Großmann's private journal from the evidence locker. The contents are a combination of quotidian, poorly spelled entries, sausage recipes, rules for some sort of board game he was working on, and oddly scrawled names, mixed with incomprehensible symbols and what looks like coded writing.

Krieg points out all the names, nearly 100 in all. "*Names of his victims, if you ask me. I think he had each figured out in advance. He rarely killed the first time he saw a woman. He learned about her, learned her name. Wrote it down, then went after her.*" He points to some names that have an "x" marked next to them. "*I think these are the ones that got away somehow.*" If investigators think to ask, a successful **Spot Hidden** roll locates "Sasnovski" in the book; adjacent to the name is an "x."

The Secret of the Journal

What neither Krieg nor anyone else could guess is that Großmann's journal is actually a Mythos tome (**Tomes and Spells**, page 145). It begins with an automatic-writing version of the Consume Likeness spell (*Call of Cthulhu Rulebook*, page 250), based on an incantation that came to Großmann in his dreams as he was wrapping up his prison sentence for child molestation in 1914. It further contains details of Großmann's "game" and the "strategy" he means to employ to "win" it—his transcendence through suicide into an all-powerful demon of hunger and lust via his own experiments with the spell and his developments of the ritual into something more far-reaching. These details become apparent only after a full study of the contents is completed, which takes 10 weeks—well outside the scope of this scenario.

Obtaining the Journal

As the case is now closed, Krieg is amenable to loaning the journal to the investigators, but only if one of their number works in law enforcement. Even then, a successful **Fast Talk** or **Persuade** roll is necessary. The Keeper can, at their discretion, permit other strategies to get hold of the journal through verbal sweet talk, but any such skill rolls require an Extreme success.

Großmann's Corpse

If the investigators think to ask, Krieg reveals that Großmann's body is down in cold storage in the basement morgue, adjacent to the evidence room. Krieg can show the body to the curious, if they've made a good impression or provide a compelling reason to look. What they see is a man in his mid-50s who looks at least 10 years older, spindly and rangy, with large gnarled hands and a body with lots of mileage on it. Even in death, his eyes remain hateful and pig-like.

Inspector Krieg

Assuming the investigators don't completely embarrass themselves, Inspector Krieg may remain a valuable contact as the Demon-Großmann begins its killing spree.

DALLDORF ASYLUM

Investigators asking around at the Red Mill Cabaret may get a lead to the State Insane and Idiot Asylum of Dalldorf, located in Reinickendorf on the northwest edge of the city, in the middle of a massive, park-like forest that lends the institution a distinctly rural feel despite being situated in the middle of an urban landscape. The best way to reach it is by the elevated Stadtbahn railway, getting off at Wittenau station, and walking to the grounds from there.

The asylum is open to the public between the hours of 9 am and 7 pm. A successful **Credit Rating** or **Charm**, **Fast Talk**, **Intimidate**, or **Persuade** roll is necessary to get past the front desk receptionist and talk to a staff member about patients admitted to the asylum. Even then, only a fellow psychologist or medical doctor can rightly expect access to patient records. Creative players may, of course, come up with other schemes: the receptionist is certainly open to a small bribe, while a bit of flirtation may turn a doctor's head, and so forth.

Breaking In?

Another option is to break in after hours. This is certainly a viable tactic, if perhaps a bit desperate. The asylum does not employ a dedicated security staff, and the institution is large enough that an isolated and decrepit side door can be located with little difficulty. A successful **Locksmith** roll or a shattered pane of glass (along with a successful **Stealth** roll to make sure no one hears the break-in) grants access. The medical records are in a basement office behind a locked door (requiring another successful **Locksmith** roll or breaking through the window pane in the door). A successful **Library Use** roll locates the pertinent records (see following). Each roll represents an interval of 30 minutes and requires a group **Luck** roll to avoid discovery by the night staff.

Patient Records

Whether through fair means or foul, the asylum's records don't turn up any patient admitted under the name of Schamzkovska, Sasnovski, or anything of the sort in the period under examination. There was, however, an attempted suicide admitted in February 1920—a "Fräulein Unbekannt" ("Miss Unknown") was fished out of the Landwehr Canal and brought in. A successful **Medicine** roll decodes the doctor's notes: patient suffering from amnesia and hysterics upon admittance; patient displays extensive wounding and scarring on arms, hands, legs, feet, neck, and scalp; most wounds are fresh and appear to be human bite marks.

The notes are clear on one point: her true name was never ascertained at the time of her admittance. Last year she began referring to herself as Anna Tchaikovsky, and it was under that name that she was discharged in May of this year, remanded into the custody of one Baron Arthur von Kleist. A check in local phone directories turns up the Baron at an apartment residence on Savignyplatz (**Meeting Anna Tchaikovsky**, page 122).

Keeper note: investigators with a background in law enforcement or who regularly check the social pages will recognize Kleist's name with a successful **Know** roll: a Baltic German, he served as Chief of Police for Russian Poland prior to the Revolution.

THE GARDEN COLONY

Clues gathered at Andreasplatz or Lange Straße 88/89 lead to Großmann's shed in a "garden colony" on Landsberger Chaussee. Schreber-gardens (*Schrebergärten*) are popular throughout Germany, but particularly in urban Berlin. Also called "garden colonies," these are adjacent allotments of land set aside for gardening and rural relaxation. Hundreds of acres of these gardens surround Berlin on its outer fringes.

With the directions provided by either Lulu or the Böhms, the investigators may travel out to Hellersdorf, at the eastern edge of the city. A Straßenbahn tramline runs out to the Landsberger Allee station, where the street changes its name to Landsberger Chaussee. A pleasant ten-minute walk along the tree-lined avenue then takes the investigators to Großmann's old colony.

The allotments here ring a large ornamental pond. Großmann's shed is discernable by its tumbledown appearance—it has clearly lacked care since his arrest, and (from the looks of it) even some time before that.

The shed is a small timber structure, about 10 feet (3 m) square, with a pitched roof and one window on each wall. The paint, once a pleasant blue-green, has faded and chipped to such an extent that the shed is mostly exposed natural wood, now weathered to a dreary gray, with rust running down from every nail and screw. The land around the shed is overgrown and choked with weeds, much in contrast to the carefully tended lawns and gardens of the other allotments. A gravel drive leads up to the cabin from the street and shows sign of frequent passage by heavy vehicles over the years.

The Garden Colony

The shed door is unlocked and slightly ajar. Entering, investigators find the interior to be musty and extensively cobwebbed. The floor is covered in dead leaves and the bones of small animals. Disconcertingly, rows of smoke-stained garden gnomes stare down impassively from the rafters and crossbeams—Großmann systematically stole these from neighboring plots over many years, perhaps his pettiest act of malice.

The shed is emptier even than Großmann's apartment. There is only a single, small wood-burning stove, which when opened reveals the mummified remains of a bird that flew down the chimney and couldn't get back out. Dozens of small hooks are screwed into the rafters and beams, and the walls are lined with empty storage shelves. Even now, the lingering odor of smoked sausage is just discernable.

The Gnomes

If an investigator thinks to examine one of the gnomes, allow a **Spot Hidden** roll, with success finding a handmade cloth dolly stuffed inside the hollow interior of a gnome when taken down from its rafter. Systematically looking at every single gnome nets the same find without a roll. The doll's button eyes shine strangely in the half-light of the interior. Investigators who decide to hold onto it may find the doll useful in a later phase of the scenario (**Baldur's Sacrifice**, page 131).

Johanna Pagenkopf

Regardless of what time of day or night the investigators visit, and of how stealthy they are being, Johanna Pagenkopf notes their trespass. A reedy woman in her mid-50s, Frau Pagenkopf lives at the colony year-round and makes it her business to know who comes and goes. She's happy to answer questions about Großmann, whom she despised. Here are her salient points, distributed amid much pointless gossip and speculation.

- Großmann seemed to use the shed as a place to get up to all sorts of shenanigans; he often came out here for the weekend with anywhere from 1 to 4 women at a time.
- Whenever Großmann had women at the cabin, it wouldn't be long before the sounds of violence and beatings could be heard. Pagenkopf claims (truthfully) that she offered shelter to these women sometimes, but a successful **Psychology** roll reveals that she had mixed feelings about these acts of charity because the women were clearly prostitutes.
- When Großmann was out at the cabin by himself, he always seemed to take a perennial interest in the neighbors' children. He liberally handed out sweets, chocolate, preserved meats, and even clothing. These acts of apparent charity were roundly rejected by the colonists, who warned their children to stay away from Großmann. Nothing further

ever happened, but Pagenkopf clearly thinks Großmann was up to no good.

- Pagenkopf also provides details about Großmann's business dealings. Delivery lorries from a variety of local food distributors often came out to his shed, where she would see them loading up crates of wurst and canned meat. When he wasn't using the shed as a love nest, it was clearly some sort of processing and distribution point for his black-market meat. She once asked Großmann about it, and he said that it was part of his work as a butcher, claiming that he was selling pork and beef, though he remained cagey about where he acquired the meat. He seemed to make quite a tidy profit off the sales. If asked, she recalls that his last such sale was just a week before his arrest six months ago.

Keeper note: investigators succeeding with an **INT** roll realize that many of those canned meats could very well still be in pantries across the city. The Sanity loss to realize that human meat is circulating through the Berlin food network is 0/1D4 points.

MEETING ANNA TCHAIKOVSKY

Investigators may learn of Baron Arthur von Kleist in one of two ways, either acquiring Anna Tchaikovsky's medical records from the **Dalldorf Asylum** (page 120), or seeing a notice in the paper on the evening of June 22 (**Anna in the Paper**, page 126). The language of the newspaper report may lead investigators to expect a tough time gaining admittance to the Baron's apartment and an audience with Tchaikovsky. Nothing could be further from the truth.

The apartment is located just a few blocks west of the Eden Hotel, in the heart of the Russian émigré community of Charlottenburg that Berliners cheekily call "Charlottengrad." Even by the standards of the neighborhood, however, the Baron's apartment has become a hub of Russian activity. The flat takes up an entire floor of the building, with its own private elevator granting direct access. After the news story about Anna's existence breaks (**Anna in the Paper**, page 126), and practically regardless of the time of day or night, the Baron's spacious, "tony" (expensive and stylish) living quarters are host to a chattering assemblage of White Russian exiles, monarchists, and distant Romanov relations. In the evenings, the apartment has the distinct air of a cocktail party. The first time the investigators visit, allow **Spot Hidden** rolls to see Manfred von Killinger (**Incident at Romanisches Square**, page 106) mixing with the crowd. He slips out as the investigators are introduced to the Baron.

Anna keeps to herself in her private suite. Anyone wishing to see her must go through the Baron, and his time is much occupied with the horde of visitors coming in and out at all hours. Although this would seemingly be a great bother for him, he is perfectly at ease with being the center of attention.

The Baron is more than happy to introduce the investigators to Anna *if and only if* he feels that they may be of some assistance in proving her heritage or increasing his fame, or if they have Prince Constantinovich present to provide an introduction. Without the Prince, flattery and false promises are the key to the Baron's heart. Faked credentials (**Fast Talk**) or an aristocratic disguise (**Art (Acting)** or **Disguise**) will not be scrutinized to any great degree. An investigator with a **Credit Rating** of 75% or higher gets in automatically; otherwise, if all else fails, roll against the lowest **Credit Rating** of the investigators present.

Keeper note: if the meeting takes place on the evening of June 22 or later, an attack interrupts the investigators' initial interview (**The First Attack**, page 124).

Ushered into the inner sanctum, the investigators find a well-furnished bedroom suite and a bedraggled young woman who matches the Prince's description of Anna Tchaikovsky precisely. Dressed in a nightgown and robe, her pretty face is marred by what is obviously a chronic lack of sleep and persistent anxiety. Anna's manner, too, is guarded almost to the point of paranoia. Curiously, attempts to communicate with her in Russian are met with stony silence.

"*Anna prefers not to speak in her native tongue,*" the Baron explains. "*She says it brings back painful memories.*"

Indeed, even attempting to speak to her in one of the other languages she knows (German, French, or English) is likely to be ignored. Anna is exhausted by the constant parade of visitors now swarming the Baron's apartment and is worried about "Bolshevik assassins" coming after her. Even without speaking, Anna betrays some clues about her past.

- A successful **Spot Hidden** roll notices extensive scars on her neck and hands.
- A successful **INT** roll reveals that many of these scars look like human bitemarks.
- A second **Spot Hidden** roll notes a large triangular scar on her bare right foot that appears to have been made by a bayonet.

It will take a clever and empathetic investigator to get her to open up: a **Persuade**, **Charm**, or **Psychoanalysis** roll is required to break down Anna's wall. To make such a roll, the investigator must have an "in"—a relic or other call-back

to the Romanov court; mentioning the Tsarina's personal symbol (shown to them by the Prince; **Handout: Devil 3**, page 110) is one such example. Another would be to recall that the Grand Duchess Anastasia was said to be a great animal lover, with a menagerie of pets to her name; such a recollection requires a successful **Know** roll or a personal connection to the Romanov court. Finally, investigators may think to put Anna under sedation and/or hypnosis. She will, of course, be highly resistant to this tactic, and physical force is required to administer morphine or a similar sedative (roll **Medicine** to gauge whether any further harm is done; see **Morphine**, page 41). A **Hypnosis** roll is opposed by Anna's Psychology of 45%.

Regardless of the skill employed, only one attempt (plus a pushed roll) may be made per day. If one investigator fails, another cannot make an attempt until the next day; with the exception of the pushed roll, Anna will not subject herself to repeated attempts by the same investigator. A failed push attempt results in Anna exploding into a furious tirade, kicking out all the investigators and the Baron, and locking herself in her suite. Under no circumstances will she entertain a visit from the investigators again.

A successful skill roll (**Hypnosis**, **Medicine**, **Persuade**, **Charm**, or **Psychoanalysis**) reveals the following information.

- **Regular success:** Anna recalls being pulled from the Landwehr Canal but does not remember what motivated her to jump from the bridge. If presented with the name Franziska Schamzkovska, she draws a blank.
- **Hard success:** as Regular, but Anna remembers the name Franziska Schamzkovska—she used it as an alias. Anna admits that she is indeed the Grand Duchess Anastasia. "*I tell you this in strictest confidence,*" she says with a deadly serious stare.
- **Extreme success:** as Hard, plus Anna tearfully recounts the details of her escape and life on the run: of being knocked unconscious by a grazing bullet from the Bolshevik firing squad; of waking up under the dead bodies of her family; of a soldier by the name of Alexander Tchaikovsky finding her and spiriting her away; of her falling in love with Alex, marrying him, and bearing his child, only to give it up for adoption; of Alex dying in Budapest (which she refuses to discuss further) and her subsequent flight, alone, to Berlin.
- **Critical success:** as Extreme, plus Anna's long-buried memory of Großmann's attack comes flooding back. She begins screaming, seeing the attack play out again in front of her eyes. She lashes out, screaming and babbling in Russian: "*The eyes! The eyes that see through my very soul and condemn me to Hell!*"

Keeper note: the following event—**The First Attack**—*only* occurs in front of the investigators if their interview with Tchaikovsky takes place on the evening of June 22, after her existence has been revealed in the press (**Anna in the Paper,** page 126). If the investigators reach Anna before the papers break the story, then they are not witness to Demon-Großmann's attack, which instead takes place off-screen (**What if the Investigators Move Too Quickly,** page 126).

THE FIRST ATTACK

As Anna is sharing her story (or stonewalling, as the case may be), the Baron's trusted maid, Traudl, enters the room bearing a tea service. While Anna talks, the delicate sound of tinkling china provides a most refined backdrop. If investigators state that they are watching the maid, they may attempt **Spot Hidden** rolls to note that the shadow she casts upon the wall is that of a spindly, somewhat hunched man, rather than that of a short, plump maid preparing tea, provoking a **Sanity** roll (0/1 loss).

Assuming nobody notices anything amiss, just as Anna is wrapping up her answer to the investigators' query there comes the sound of shattering china. Turning, everyone sees Traudl has dropped the teapot. She stands there, apparently unconcerned by the broken tea service, with a strange grin on her face. Her eyes look odd—small and porcine, glittering with malicious intent, and wholly inhuman. Anna screams, "*Those eyes! I have seen them before!*" Call for a **Sanity** roll for witnessing the strange transformation and Anna's reaction (1/1D2 loss).

Keeper note: Traudl has been possessed by a POW 100 spirit-fragment of the **Demon-Großmann** (**Characters and Monsters,** page 140). This is a mere reconnaissance mission on the demon's part, but it will not pass up an opportunity to cause a bit of mayhem.

In a voice not her own, Traudl growls, "*So, if it isn't Miss Sasnovski. We have unfinished business, whore.*" Snatching up a butter knife, the possessed maid lunges at Anna. Investigators may attempt a **DEX** roll to interpose themselves, if they wish. Traudl is not the most powerful physical specimen (see her profile in the **Characters and Monsters** section, page 142), so overpowering her should not be too difficult. Nor will the demon stick around if it can't get in an effective attack on Anna. Before departing, however, the spirit-fragment attempts to possess a vulnerable investigator, if there any are present. Any investigator who failed their Luck roll at

The possessed Traudl attacks Anna and the investigators

the start of the scenario is at risk (**Incident at Romanisches Square**, page 106). If more than one investigator failed, the spirit-fragment targets men ahead of women and prioritizes those with high STR scores. The spirit-fragment uses 75 of its POW in its possession attempt; this is an opposed **POW** roll. If the investigator loses, they are possessed—see **Possessed Investigators**, nearby, for more details—the spirit-fragment immediately goes dormant, not wanting to tip its hand. If it sees what seems like a sure chance to kill Anna, it will take it; otherwise, it bides its time until the finale of the scenario (**Baldur's Sacrifice**, page 131). Also, if possession does occur, make a note that from here on out the Demon-Großmann has 75 fewer points of POW to distribute among its other victims.

As soon as the spirit-fragment flees or inhabits an investigator, if still alive and conscious, Traudl collapses onto the room's fine Persian rug, sobbing. Apart from any physical injury she may have suffered in the scuffle, the experience has left her raving and drooling, her mind broken for the time being. A successful **Psychoanalysis** roll calms her down and gets her to say a few words to the effect of "*A demon took over my body!*" Beyond that, she cannot be coaxed, at least not today. Anna, for her part, casts everyone out and locks herself into her suite, where she immediately begins planning her escape from the Baron's apartment.

Investigators returning to interview Traudl later find that she has, naturally, been given the sack by the Baron. He provides her home address if asked (a tenement walkup off Oranienburger Straße). Those who seek her out may, with a successful **Charm**, **Fast Talk**, or **Persuade** roll, get a more complete description of what happened. Traudl explains how she felt an "evil presence" enter her body as she was pouring the tea. Suddenly, she was at the mercy of this presence, which used her body while she "watched" helplessly from behind her own eyes. Then, as suddenly as it came, the demon left.

Keeper note: Handout: Devil 6 concerns the attack on Anna, and should be given to the investigators on the morning of June 23, whether they witnessed the attack or not. Due to the actions of the investigators, the Keeper may need to adjust the newspaper story to align better with the events of the maid's attack.

An Unusual Check

Once the investigators have located Anna Tchaikovsky—whether through their own efforts or by getting scooped—they have every right to contact Prince Constantinovich and request payment for services rendered. If they have also wrung a confession from Anna, the Prince includes a bonus of £50!

POSSESSED INVESTIGATORS

There are several points in this scenario where unlucky investigators may put themselves in danger of possession by **The Demon-Großmann**—see his profile (page 140) for full details of how to handle such incidents. The Keeper should use this possibility to maximum effect, sowing paranoia among the group.

When a host is possessed by a dormant fragment of the Demon-Großmann, the victim should make an opposed **POW** roll once per day versus the demon's POW (as divided evenly among the number of hosts currently possessed, plus the current target), with the Keeper secretly noting the results (including mutations), but not applying them yet.

The Demon-Großmann can lie dormant within a host for as long as it likes, waiting for the right moment to strike. When an investigator is possessed, pass the player a note informing them of what has happened and telling them to await further instructions. If possible, take the player aside and explain what has happened and encourage them to add sinister touches to their roleplaying, particularly if the demon is succeeding in fully taking over their body. When the demon is ready to act, inform the player that they have temporarily lost control of their character, or, with some guidance, the Keeper may prefer to allow the player to continue roleplaying their now possessed investigator.

The check presented to the investigators, strangely, is not in the Prince's name but rather drawn from a business account: Aufbau Vereinigung (Construction Union). The investigators are most likely to note this when they go to cash the check, as the Prince hands them the payment in an envelope, and scrutinizing it in front of him would be surpassingly rude.

Curious investigators may turn up information on Aufbau Vereinigung with a visit to the Neues Stadthaus (the city's administration building) in Alt-Berlin. A successful **Library Use** roll and an hour's research uncover the public records on the so-called Construction Union—it is a private holding corporation registered to one Pyotr Shabelsky-Bork. The address given for the group is none other than Prince Constantinovich's quarters at the Eden Hotel.

WHAT IF THE INVESTIGATORS MOVE TOO QUICKLY?

It is conceivable that investigators working with great speed and diligence may find and interview Anna Tchaikovsky prior to the evening of the 22; thus, confirming her identity—this is before the Demon-Großmann becomes aware of Anna's location and comes after her through the vessel of Traudl, thus alerting the investigators to the greater danger at play.

If this is the case, Prince Constantinovich happily pays the investigators and thanks them for their services. They then read about the rise in savage murders (**Handout: Devil 5**), as well as a news item about a disturbance at Baron Kleist's apartment (**Handout: Devil 6**); however, these events alone may not be enough to motivate investigator action. Thus, Prince Constantinovich comes back into the picture when Anna goes missing on June 23, offering the investigators the double rate of £6 ($30) per day, plus expenses, if they will help him find the missing Grand Duchess—with events picking up from **The Runaway** (page 129).

ANNA IN THE PAPER

Baron Kleist, after hosting several private visitations over the last six weeks without getting the sort of support he seeks, lets slip to the media—on the afternoon of June 22—that he is hosting a woman who claims to be the Grand Duchess Anastasia Romanov. The evening editions of June 22 are abuzz with the sensational story; a sample article is presented in **Handout: Devil 4**. This is the next stage in the Baron's plan to exploit Anna for his own fame, but it is due to backfire spectacularly. This article accomplishes two things:

- If the investigators have been to **Dalldorf Asylum** (page 120) but were unsuccessful in deciphering the notes and, therefore, her name and that of her current guardian, the mention of the fall into the Landwehr Canal in 1920 is sure to be a tipoff that this may well be their "Fraulein Unbekannt/Sasnovski."
- The Demon-Großmann, having murdered several of his quarry already (see **Lustmord: the Killings Take Hold**, page 127), now knows where to look to find "Sasnovski" and begins plotting an attack on the Baron's estate.

Grand Duchess Anastasia Alive and well in Berlin?

The city's White Russian community is humming with the news that a woman claiming to be the Grand Duchess Anastasia Romanov is living here in Berlin. The woman, who calls herself Anna Tchaikovsky, was recently released from the Dalldorf Asylum and remanded into the care of Baron Arthur von Kleist, who served the Tsar honorably as Chief of Police of Russian Poland until the Revolutions of 1917 forced him to flee, like many of his compatriots, to Germany.

Miss Tchaikovsky, who is said to resemble the Grand Duchess in appearance and bearing, was admitted to Dalldorf in 1920, having lost her wits in a fall into the Landwehr Canal in February of that year. She claims that her memory is slowly returning to her, although many details remain unclear.

The Baron, who resides in a spacious third-floor apartment off Savignyplatz at Carmerstraße 11, asks that the public respect Miss Tchaikovsky's privacy at this time as he attempts to help sort out the truth of the matter.

Prince Constantinovich (Pyotr Shabelsky-Bork) sees the article and hurries to Kleist's apartment. Subsequently, investigators find him there rather than at his hotel room. The Prince is only too happy to see them, even if they have been "scooped" by the Baron's leak to the press. Indeed, the Prince would now like the investigators' help in confirming the supposed identity of Miss Tchaikovsky. She is standoffish and often contradictory. Perhaps the investigators might draw her out of her shell?

If the investigators have been to Dalldorf Asylum already, they may wish to confirm the veracity of the newspaper story before contacting the Prince.

LUSTMORD: THE KILLINGS TAKE HOLD

With his suicide, Großmann enacted the final stage of his ritual of transcendence, becoming a demon of hunger and lust. Able to possess anyone who has previously consumed his black-market human meat, he sets out on the final act of his "game"—killing all those who escaped his clutches in life. This, of course, includes Anna Tchaikovsky/Franziska Schamzkovska.

Those actively possessed by Großmann begin deteriorating and transforming into demons of mutable flesh, subject to his will. The killings begin the night of his suicide—the same night the investigators are hired to look into the case of the missing Grand Duchess.

THE POSSESSED

Thanks to his time peddling human meat, both at the Silesian Station and to unscrupulous food distributors, over the course of four years, Großmann has managed to contaminate thousands of Berliners. Anyone who has *ever* consumed human flesh from Großmann is susceptible to possession following his suicide.

Großmann's spirit can project a fragment of itself into multiple vessels at once—see **The Demon-Großmann** (page 140) for more information on how he does this and what becomes of his victims. Because Großmann sold his preserved meats and sausages to local distributors as well as through street vending, everyone is vulnerable. Investigators who failed their Luck rolls at the beginning of the session (**Incident at Romanisches Square**, page 106) have, at some point, unknowingly consumed Großmann's human meat, leaving themselves open to possession. If everyone made a successful Luck roll, a cruel Keeper may still choose one or more investigators as suitable targets, ignoring the Luck roll's results.

THE MURDERS

It doesn't take long for the Demon-Großmann to get to work. Beginning in the early morning hours of June 21, it possesses various Berliners in the Friedrichshain and stalks three of the prostitutes that, through a combination of luck and daring, managed to avoid his murderous intentions while he was still alive. Their luck has finally run out.

The late morning papers of June 22 carry news of their demise (**Handout: Devil 5**). Unless the investigators were quick off the mark and managed to speak to Lulu before the Demon-Großmann reaches her (his final victim in the early hours of June 22), then that avenue of inquiry is now closed to them (**Andreasplatz**, page 113).

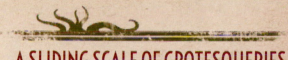

A SLIDING SCALE OF GROTESQUERIES

The real-life Carl Friedrich Wilhelm Großmann was not just a serial killer. He was a cannibal, a rapist, and a child molester. The idea of his unrestrained id unleashed upon the population of Berlin, to possess and bend them to his bloody and inhuman will, is the core element of the horror in this scenario.

That being said, the exact details of what the Großmann-controlled possessed individuals actually *do* to their victims have here been left purposely vague. Every group's definition of horror is different, particularly when it intersects with sexual violence and crimes against children.

The Keeper may evoke more than enough horror simply with descriptions of bodies torn apart and partially consumed. Although one of the recurring themes in this scenario is *lustmord*, introducing overt elements of sexual violence is left up to individual Keeper discretion, taking into account their players' (and their own) views of such matters.

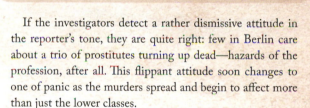

If the investigators detect a rather dismissive attitude in the reporter's tone, they are quite right: few in Berlin care about a trio of prostitutes turning up dead—hazards of the profession, after all. This flippant attitude soon changes to one of panic as the murders spread and begin to affect more than just the lower classes.

If the investigators have been to Großmann's neighborhood already (**Lange Straße 88/89**, page 117), they know that the Andreas-Gymnasium is located one block over and up the street from the killer's old apartment building, and one block east of Andreasplatz.

Interviewing the students who found the bodies reveals a trio of highly traumatized 13-year-old girls, too upset to offer much information. Getting access to Inspector Krieg or his report reveals that Lulu was indeed found up a tree, though rather spread out: limbs and organs dangling, her skull cracked open with half the brains scooped out and "probably consumed." Krieg has added a marginal note of his own: "Großmann copy-cat?" The remaining murders pan out as follows.

- The afternoon papers on June 22 carry reports of a *Scheusal* (monstrosity, beast, or ogre) seen running down Unter den Linden in broad daylight. Witness reports are conflicting, but several mention that the thing seemed to have long, birdlike talons as well as inhuman eyes. An hour later, police find a Kontroll-Girl savagely ripped apart in the Tiergarten.

Handout: Devil 5

DISTURBANCE IN CHARLOTTENBURG

Readers of this paper may recall our report of one Anna Tchaikovsky, currently in residence at the home of Baron Arthur von Kleist, Carmerstraße 11, Charlottenburg. Scandalous as it is, it is our sad duty to report that Fräulein Tchaikovsky was this past evening attacked in her residence by a servant of the Baron's household. The maid, who has subsequently been dismissed, came at Fräulein Tchaikovsky with a knife, but was fended off by friendlier hands present at the time. Fräulein Tchaikovsky is reported to be uninjured but quite rattled, as is understandable given the circumstances.

- On the night of June 22, after the attack on Anna Tchaikovsky, two more prostitutes are killed in Friedrichshain. A cyclonette driver witnesses one of the murders and is possessed by a spirit-fragment. He returns to his home in Wilmersdorf and murders his wife and two daughters in an unspeakable fashion. The tone of newspaper reports shifts from gauche to panicked.
- On the morning of June 23, rumors are flying around the cafés and public squares of more *Scheusal* sightings across the city, and of more murders—the police, they say, are covering up the true extent of the murders to prevent public panic.
- By the evening of June 23, the city is in a state of alarm. Mothers call their children home and forbid them to play on the streets and in the parks. Doors are locked and barred; windows are closed despite the summer heat. The papers are full of unsubstantiated rumors of murders from across the city.

Keeper note: in reality, the Demon-Großmann is responsible for only a handful of killings; the rest are a combination of "regular" murders blamed on the *Scheusal* and wild, unfounded rumor. Sightings of the deformed, possessed monstrosities are all too real and serve to heighten the panic even more.

See **Sample Hosts** (page 142) for examples of some of these *Scheusal*—with the exception of Schröder and Traudl. Feel free to drop one in the investigators' path as they move around the city conducting their own investigations. There will be five more Demon-Großmann murders during the night of June 23, bringing the total body count to 13.

Handout: Devil 6

DEATH STALKS BERLIN!

Police have reported three separate murders in and around the Friedrichshain neighborhood in the last 24 hours. One body, that of a woman known only to locals as "Lulu," was found by students of the Andreas-Gymnasium school (Koppenstraße 76), up among the branches of a tree. "If we didn't know better, we would say she climbed the tree to escape a wild animal, but was pursued and torn apart up there," one of the officers informed our reporter. We now must ask: is there a bear in Berlin?

Two other bodies were pulled from the Spree River. Inspector Krieg of the Criminal Police has refused to comment on the ongoing case but notes that both women were far too mangled to make a positive identification at this time. Reports of missing persons in the Friedrichshain district will be forwarded to Inspector Krieg while the case remains open, but many of the residents are unregistered immigrants and there seems little hope that these "Ladies Unknown" will be identified anytime soon.

THE RUNAWAY

Rattled by Traudl's attack and convinced it's all part of some sort of Bolshevik plot to assassinate her, Anna hatches an escape plan. At 9:30 pm on the night of Friday, June 23, as the sun sets over the city, she escapes from Baron Kleist's apartment and slips away into the hot summer night.

At first, she does not know where to go, walking along Kant Straße before turning onto Budapester Straße. Then, she spots the famous Elephant Gate of the Berlin Zoo. Using some of the spare change she managed to scrounge prior to her escape, she purchases an admission ticket and slips in.

Anna has always been a great animal lover, and she happily wanders among the various houses and pavilions before her reverie is interrupted by the announcement of the zoo's closure. Not wanting to return to the outside world, she quickly hides herself inside the Egyptian-themed Ostrich House and settles in for the night.

By 10 pm, Anna has been missed. Baron Kleist puts out a call to his Aufbau allies notifying them of the development. At 10:15 pm, the investigators receive a frantic summons from Prince Constantinovich, asking them to meet at Baron Kleist's apartment at once.

Despite the late hour, the Baron's apartment is (again) full of visitors. White Russians mingle with members of Organisation Consul, summoned here at the behest of their Aufbau masters. Investigators recognize Manfred von Killinger from their encounter with him at Romanisches Forum three days ago (if they haven't seen him since).

Prince Constantinovich emerges from a back room, the Baron at his side, and delivers the shocking news that Anna has gone missing. "*I don't need to tell you that with all these recent murders, and already an attack on the Grand Duchess, we gravely fear for her safety. I hope I can trust all of you to assist in searching for her.*"

Killinger announces that, fortunately, his contacts with the Criminal Police have yet to report any new victims matching Tchaikovsky's description. Search parties begin to form, with discussions on where to look and where she may have gone. If the investigators don't think of it, call for a **Know** roll to recall Anastasia Romanov's close connection to animals and that the Zoological Gardens are only a couple of blocks away. If none of the investigators think of this insight, Killinger (who has visited Anna on two occasions) does so instead. Regardless, Killinger organizes the zoo search party, which consists of the investigators, three of his own

Anna on the run

Consul members, and three Russians. Unfortunately, and unbeknownst to anyone, one of Killinger's men, **Sigfried Schröder** (see **Characters and Monsters**, page 142), has been possessed by the Demon-Großmann.

SEARCHING THE ZOO

The Zoological Gardens are closed, but, by the time the investigators arrive at the Elephant Gate, someone is there to unlock the gates. Clearly, Killinger has called in a favor to grant them access. "*Spread out!*" Killinger orders. The search party starts canvassing the grounds.

The zoo is dark, lit only by the moonlight and occasional street lamps. An elephant trumpets in the night, answered by the roar of a lion. The sound of traffic from the Auguste-Viktoria-Platz is completely muffled by the trees—this is a tranquil island in the middle of a bustling metropolis.

Eventually, the investigators come to the Ostrich House. It is constructed in a manner reminiscent of an ancient Egyptian temple, its entrance flanked by a mural depicting the Memnon colossi of the Theban Necropolis.

Having heard the sound of the search party, Anna has crept to the entrance of the Ostrich House, peering out through its barred gate. A successful Hard **Spot Hidden** roll

spots her amid the shadows. If the investigators fail to see her, she is spotted by Killinger, who approaches the Ostrich House from a different direction with Schröder in tow. Killinger rashly gives a shout of recognition when he sees her. Anna, startled, retreats further within.

Getting through the locked gate requires a successful **Locksmith** roll. Failing that, someone may simply shoot the lock; Schröder is happy to do so if no one else is armed or thinks to take such a course of action.

The Cassowary Enclosure

The Ostrich House contains an enclosure of cassowaries, large flightless birds from New Guinea and northern Australia, second only to the ostrich in size. Anna's footsteps can be heard receding in the direction of that enclosure.

Black of plumage and with a vibrant blue and red wattle, the cassowary stands over six feet (1.8 m) tall and weighs 180 pounds (82 kg); more worrisome is the talon—as large and sharp as a spearhead, one on each of its feet—that is easily capable of spilling a person's guts all over the ground if provoked; a successful **Science (Biology** or **Zoology)** or **Natural World** roll recalls this chilling fact.

Arriving at the jungle-like accommodations, the investigators see massive shapes moving around in the

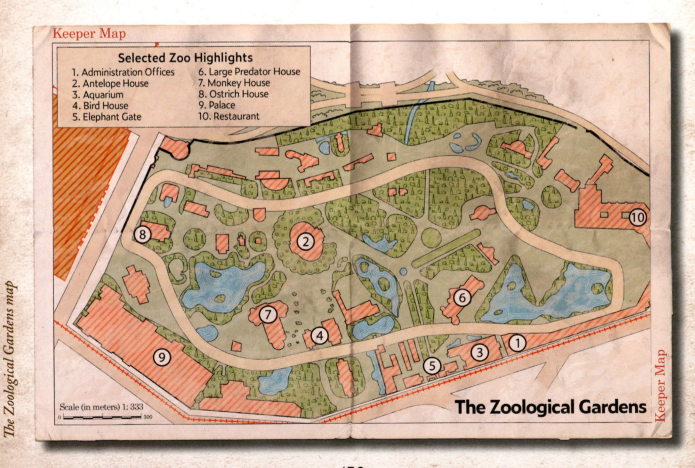

Keeper Map

Selected Zoo Highlights

1. Administration Offices
2. Antelope House
3. Aquarium
4. Bird House
5. Elephant Gate
6. Large Predator House
7. Monkey House
8. Ostrich House
9. Palace
10. Restaurant

Scale (in meters) 1:333

The Zoological Gardens

The Zoological Gardens map

Keeper Map

darkness, the animals alarmed and on guard thanks to all this nighttime commotion. Anna, in a panic, has ventured into the cassowary enclosure and is hiding among the vegetation.

This is the time for the Demon-Großmann to strike, and it will do so through its puppet Schröder. If more than one investigator is also possessed, it will use some of them as well; however, it is cunning enough to leave an ace up its sleeve, keeping at least one possessed investigator unrevealed for the time being.

As Schröder's monstrous side bursts forth (**Sigfried Schröder**, page 142), a fight erupts. Killinger, to his credit, unhesitatingly shoots to kill in the name of protecting Anna. A complicating factor is, of course, the cassowaries. Gunfire is more than sufficient to rile them up, and the Keeper should feel free to introduce one or more of the marauding birds as an additional threat, or as a *deus ex animalia* to save Anna from rampaging monsters (**Cassowary**, page 144).

Assuming all goes well, Anna is "rescued" and taken back to von Kleist's apartment. Any bloodshed is be enough to convince her to go quietly—it was never her intention for anyone else to get hurt on her account. While it is possible that Anna is killed during the encounter—with both the Prince and the Baron determined to have their revenge on the creature who caused her death, they enlist the investigators as described in the following sections—this outcome should be avoided by the Keeper if at all possible.

BALDUR'S SACRIFICE

By now, the city's clocks have chimed the eleventh hour. Back at Kleist's apartment, the mood is subdued. Anna (if still alive) retires to her suite, exhausted and inconsolable. Killinger looks thoughtful. Prince Constantinovich stands at a window, brow creased, his monocle reflecting the lights of the city. Only a few of the Baron's guests remain.

What do the investigators make of all this? By this point, the connections between their employer and a shadowy conspiracy of assassins may be clear; perhaps they've figured out even more.

If they confront the Prince or Killinger, the co-conspirators see that there is no longer any need for pretense and confess (to a certain degree) to the truth of their relationship. They will, of course, paint it in the most positive light possible, calling Aufbau Vereinigung a mutual-defense association, which has the best interests of both Germany and Russia at heart.

If Shabelsky-Bork reveals his true name, any members of the Russian émigré community or Communist party members in the group immediately recognize him as the man who gunned down Vladimir Nabokov, Sr. If ugly epithets

ensue, Shabelsky-Bork defends his actions by invoking the Sacred Order of St. John, claiming with somewhat wild eyes that he is a descendent of the *true* defenders of the Hospital and so forth.

Do harsh words lead to rash action? Allow a round or two of fisticuffs or even a single shot to be fired. If Shabelsky-Bork is injured, so much the better, though he should not die. (Not yet, at any rate.)

Quite suddenly, one and then two of the Russian courtiers begins laughing uproariously. They have both been possessed by spirit-fragments (maximum POW 100 each), and, as their laughter rises in pitch and insane fervor until it is a hideous, throat-tearing shriek, they turn on the other guests at the flat. Use the **Russian Monarchists** profile (page 140), rolling once on the **Demon Mutation Table** (page 143) for each possessed victim and apply the effects immediately as the demon manifests.

Keeper note: this chaos is exactly what the Demon-Großmann wants; during the confusion, it sends one of the possessed Russians to Anna's chambers while the other continues to cause a distraction. In the melee, ensure Shabelsky-Bork suffers a debilitating injury: he falls and sprains his ankle or is stabbed in a non-vital area. Although still cogent, he is physically compromised.

It shouldn't be too difficult for the investigators, along with Shabelsky-Bork and Killinger, to shut down this incursion by the possessed hosts, but it serves to underline how no place in the city is safe and how the demon is determined to continue pursuing poor Anna. Shabelsky-Bork makes the point explicitly clear in the aftermath of the fight if no one else does.

"*Yes, but there is one thing this demonic entity did not calculate,*" says Killinger with a wry grin. "*Tomorrow morning, as the sun rises on the solstice, my operatives are to enact a blood sacrifice. A man of light and goodness, taking the place of the ancient Teutonic sun god Baldur, will give his life for the future fortune of the Fatherland. Am I right in remembering, my good Pyotr, that Saturn's day is held to be particularly appropriate for rituals of banishment?*" Shabelsky-Bork nods. "*Then I propose we kill two flies with one strike: we enact a banishment ritual and use the magical power unlocked by Baldur's sacrifice to rid ourselves—and the rest of the city, of course—of this terrible spirit once and for all! What say you?*"

Writing the Ritual

Shabelsky-Bork is tremendously excited by this plan, for he possesses a ritual of banishment used by his order for centuries. "*It is given in the pages of* De Vermis Mysteriis, *but I believe I can remember it off by heart, if you give me a few minutes to concentrate. We will need at least three to take part. Now let me think."*

Groaning from his wound, he takes pen and paper and seats himself at a glass-topped coffee table, rubbing his brow in thought and jotting down notes. As he does so, the investigators may talk among themselves. If there is any equivocation, a secretly possessed investigator will be adamant about participating in the ritual—slip a note to the player concerned, informing them that they desire to take part.

If any of the investigators have had the dream where they are gunned down in their car, they realize that they have seen a vision of the future—and that this is how the "sacrifice" will play out. A successful **INT** roll realizes the victim is to be Walther Rathenau, Germany's Foreign Minister, a most unwilling victim! If Killinger is confronted with this fact, he nods his head sadly, *"Yes, it must be so for the ritual to have its full efficacy. Is the loss of one life too much to ask for saving the city? The country? We do not know how many more monstrous acts this demon may undertake before it is sated, after all."*

Keeper note: unfortunately, Killinger is quite mistaken in his assumption. The assassination of Walther Rathenau as a reenactment of Baldur's sacrifice will do nothing but plunge the country into chaos, initiating the *annus horribilis* of 1923 and the Great Inflation.

The Fetish

"Ah! Done!" Shabelsky-Bork has written out the ritual and now takes everyone through it (**Handout: Devil 7**). The ritual is in a language completely unfamiliar to any of the investigators— Shabelsky-Bork has written it out phonetically—and involves odd gestures, which he teaches them as quickly as possible. *"We need an object—a fetish, if you will—with a significant magical charge on it. Anything that has been invested with powerful emotion. The more dramatic, the better,"* he says. Two objects in particular are ideal for this purpose:

- **Großmann's Doll:** the doll from Großmann's garden shed (**The Garden Colony**, page 121) was one he had used many times to lure children into his private quarters. It is imbued with deep emotions of sadness, anger, fear, and indignation, and it is ideal for the ritual.
- **The Tsarina's Journal:** if the investigators don't have the doll, they might think (perhaps with a successful **INT** roll) to suggest the use of Tsarina Alexandra's journal. Shabelsky-Bork still has it in his possession (**The Case of the Wayward Princess**, page 109).

Keeper note: the investigators may have something to offer up themselves, of course, and the Keeper should use the above

items as a point of reference in judging the appropriateness of any other artifacts to the task in hand. In the unlikely event that investigators have Großmann's journal and one of the investigators is possessed, that investigator *will* vocally advocate for using it as a fetish—again, slip a note to the possessed investigator, indicating their feelings on this matter. Even non-possessed investigators may think to use it—if that is the case, then so be it, and refer to **A Very Bad Idea** (page 136) for details on what happens in such an instance.

The Location

Once the group has agreed on which fetish to use, there remains one last complication. Shabelsky-Bork explains, *"We must enact this ritual beginning precisely at midnight, under the open sky."* The Russian is in no condition to travel, and so, rather reluctantly, passes the task on to the investigators.

Baron Kleist looks at his pocket watch, *"That's only a half-hour from now!"*

Shabelsky-Bork nods, *"Ideally, we need a location that is of importance to the demon. Any ideas?"* The investigators may well have some thoughts for a location; here are some possibilities:

- **Andreasplatz:** Großmann's frequent haunt is, conveniently, located under open skies and makes an ideal spot for a ritual—if one doesn't mind a few onlookers.

The Ritual Performance

First, prepare the area. Inscribe a summoning circle using chalk, or may be traced in dust or soot on the floor. At minimum, three are required throughout the ritual. They must all stand within the circle, with the fetish sitting in the center of the inscribed space. More may participate but the number of participants must be divisible by three. Others may stand by, guarding the sacred area, ready to step in and replace those unable to continue.

i. Facing East, assume the Wand Posture. Declare: "GEH."

ii. Raise the arms at the sides. Declare: "LONDOH."

iii. Touch right shoulder with left hand. Declare: "OD MICALZO."

iv. Touch left shoulder with right hand. Declare: "OD BUSD."

v. Keeping arms crossed, bow head and declare: "GOHED."

vi. Make the Gesture Cervus: at the first point, declare "EXARP;" at the second point declare "ORO IBAH AOZPI."

vii. Turn to face North: make the Gesture, declaring "NANTA" at the first point, "MOR DIAL HCTGA" at the second.

viii. Turn to face West: make the Gesture, declaring "HCOMA" at the first point, "MPH ARSL GAIOL" at the second.

ix. Turn to face South: make the Gesture, declaring "BITOM" at the first point, and "OIP TEAA PDOCE" at the second.

Repeat these steps until the sun rises in the East.

- **Großmann's apartment:** the large window in the mansard roof can be opened up to the sky, if investigators prefer a more private location. Furthermore, far more of Großmann's psychic energy (and that of his victims) is locked up here, making for a more effective ritual.
- **Großmann's shed:** the investigators may think to conduct the ritual outside Großmann's garden shed. A car is needed to reach the site in time—a chancy option, and not the best.

Keeper note: other locations are possible, but Andreasplataz and Großmann's apartment are the two most efficacious destinations. As with the fetish, Keepers should use their best judgment as to whether a different location provides any bonuses at all.

Possible Aid

Once a location has been decided upon, the Baron offers the use of his Horch sedan, which can seat up to eight people in a pinch. The Baron, for his part, remains at the apartment to watch over Anna with Shabelsky-Bork, pistol in hand. "*I'll save the last two bullets for the Grand Duchess and myself, if it comes to that,*" he says with a grim smile.

Killinger and Shabelsky-Bork both have aid to offer the investigators, but they do so only if they didn't come to blows earlier in the scene.

- Killinger may, with a successful **Persuade** or **Fast Talk** roll, be convinced to accompany the investigators and make up an extra participant in the ritual; otherwise, he excuses himself to go make preparations for "the great sacrifice" on the morrow.
- Shabelsky-Bork has a lead "crux ansata" (an ankh) created according to instructions laid down in *De Vermis Mysteriis*. If he is well disposed toward the investigators, he gives it to the character with the highest POW, telling them to use it during the ritual—doing so grants a bonus die to the opposed POW roll at the end of **Enacting The Ritual** (following).

Right before the investigators leave, Shabelsky-Bork offers one last piece of ominous advice, "*The ritual is much more effective if blood is shed over the fetish or objects very dear to you are destroyed. Do these things at the beginning of the ritual, or once an hour on the hour.*"

ENACTING THE RITUAL

Arriving at the chosen destination with minutes to spare, the investigators should quickly go over Shabelsky-Bork's written instructions (**Handout: Devil 7**) so they know what to do next.

1. First, a large summoning circle must be inscribed. This may be done with chalk or simply traced in dust or soot on the floor. (The circle offers no further protection unless an Elder Sign spell is cast on it, in which case it must be inscribed or carved and not merely drawn.)

2. At least three people are required throughout the ritual, and they must all stand within the circle, with the fetish sitting in the center of the inscribed space.

3. More may participate and add to the ritual's effectiveness, but the total number of participants must always be divisible by three.

4. Others may stand by on guard, ready to step in and replace those "unable to continue," as the instructions put it.

5. Everyone participating must familiarize themselves with the strange syllables of the chant, requiring a successful **INT** roll—the Keeper should note down if any failed or fumbled the roll, as any number of failures impose one penalty die on the final opposed **POW** roll due to flubbed words, whereas any number of fumbled rolls imposes two penalty dice.

6. All active participants must pay 1D4+3 magic points as soon as they join the chant; they also immediately lose 1D4 Sanity points.

7. The chant must be kept up for at least one hour, by at least three of the participants at any one time. Shabelsky-Bork suggests maintaining the chant until sunrise for maximum effectiveness. (This actually does nothing, but Shabelsky-Bork does not know this.) Fortunately, as this is Midsummer's Eve, sunrise is only five hours away (see **The Demon Strikes**, page 136).

8. When the ritual concludes, the caster with the highest POW makes an opposed roll against the Demon-Großmann's total POW—this is normally 300 but may be less if any hosts have been completely destroyed in the course of the investigation, or if spirit-fragments possessing investigators have been successfully resisted and/or forced to flee (see Possession and Combat, **The Demon Großmann**, page 140, for further details). Remember, points of POW lost from the destruction of a vessel or resisting possession are gone for good. Apply the following modifiers (added to the investigator's POW) to the opposed POW roll:

- +10% for each full additional set of three casters.
- +15% if Großmann's doll is the fetish.
- +10% if the Tsarina's journal is the fetish.
- +50% if Großmann's journal is the fetish (see **A Very Bad Idea**, page 136).
- +10% if the ritual is taking place in Andreasplatz.
- +15% if the ritual is taking place in Großmann's apartment.
- +5% if the ritual is taking place at Großmann's shed.
- +5% for each sacrifice (complete destruction) of a treasured possession (as described in the investigator's backstory).
- +1% for each hit point lost from bloodletting, either directly from an investigator or from a living treasured possession (e.g., a pet).
- If the ritual is, for some reason, conducted indoors without any access to the open sky, the investigator's opposed POW roll is made with a penalty die.

Keeper note: remember, there should be a maximum of two penalty dice applied to any given skill roll. As this is an opposed roll, if it is subject to further penalty dice beyond that cap, ignore them.

The Ritual in Action

As the ritual is performed, the fetish takes on an increasingly fleshy and organic appearance; for example, the doll starts to look like a real, doll-sized girl, while the Tsarina's journal's leather binding slowly reverts to actual skin and becomes warm to the touch, with a palpable pulse. At the conclusion of the ritual, someone must ritually destroy the fetish; for example, by stabbing it with a knife, shooting it, or setting it on fire. Even one point of damage is sufficient to do the trick.

Keeper note: unless they have chosen to use Großmann's journal as the fetish, and while the investigators enact the ritual, refer to **The Demon Strikes** (see page 136), as the Demon-Großmann attempts to stop their magical rite.

If the caster wins the opposed POW roll, there is a great and terrible scream that seems to originate from all around, sending birds scattering into the sky and causing babies across the city to wail in their cribs. It is but an impotent gesture on the Demon-Großmann's part, for it has been beaten, quite literally, at its own game. Any possessed hosts who still have more than zero POW resume their old shapes, once again in control of their bodies. Those at zero POW drop dead, their spirits now at rest.

The ritual

Losing the opposed POW roll results in a disturbing anti-climax. The fetish is destroyed, but there is no scream; instead, a creeping sense of doom hangs over the space. All present have a nasty, lurking doubt in the back of their minds that the demon is still out there somewhere, biding its time—as indeed it is.

Unless the investigators take steps to relocate her to a safer location with a more responsible host, six days later Anna Tchaikovsky is finally murdered, alongside Baron Kleist and several of his guests. Kleist may be (reluctantly) persuaded to send Anna away; in this case, to the country estate of one Inspector Grünberg at Zossen, 20 miles (32 km) outside the city.

Finally, there is subsequently a noticeable uptick in cannibalistic spree killings across Germany over the remainder of the decade, as the demon spirit travels via possessed hosts: to Düsseldorf, Hanover, and beyond.

A VERY BAD IDEA

If the investigators opt to use Großmann's journal as the fetish, this vastly improves the odds of the ritual working, albeit in a way none could have predicted.

As the demon is pulled back into the very tome that gave it life, it is given physical form. At the conclusion of the ritual, if the caster wins the opposed POW roll, the creature erupts from the book's fleshy pages as a torrent of mouths and tentacles. Use the average statistics for a shoggoth given on pages 306–307 of the *Call of Cthulhu Rulebook*. Everyone within the protective circle is immediately subject to an engulf attack, as the globular blob of protean tissue pours out of the book. If the opposed POW roll was failed, mercifully, this "merely" has the same result as detailed in **Enacting the Ritual**: a lingering sense that all is not over.

THE DEMON STRIKES

Five hours is a long time—certainly long enough for the Demon-Großmann to realize what's going on. Unless Großmann's journal is being used as the fetish, it does not intend to allow the investigators and their allies to complete the ritual.

The Demon-Großmann currently possesses three hosts, including any possessed investigators. Choose any additional hosts required from the examples provided under **Sample Hosts** (page 142). As always, the demon aims to disrupt with shock and terror, and sends its hosts against the group in escalating degrees of mutation, culminating with an attack by the possessed investigator(s). Attacks occur two hours apart as the *Scheusals* travel back toward the site of the ritual, with the first commencing at 12:30 am.

A very bad idea

The investigators are obviously quite vulnerable during the the ritual. The summoning circle does nothing to prevent attacks on the participants. If the ritual is taking place at Großmann's apartment, it is easier to keep the marauding hosts from interfering through the simple expedient of blocking the door. In such cases, the Demon-Großmann alternates between trickery and brute force, sometimes trying to simply break down the door and, at other times, speaking in the host's original voice, *"Please help! There's a monster out here and it's coming for me! Save me, for God's sake! Open the door, I beg of you!"*

As long as at least an hour has passed, the ritual has a chance of succeeding, even if the *Scheusal* attacks disrupt it. After an hour, if the number of casters is ever reduced below three, immediately call for the opposed POW roll using the highest POW from among the remaining casters.

RATHENAU'S ASSASSINATION

Assuming he survives the night's proceedings, if present at the conclusion of the ritual (regardless of its outcome), Killinger asserts that the final ingredient of the banishment is the sacrifice of "Baldur."

Cagey investigators may see through Killinger's claims and realize that this sacrifice has no actual impact on the success of their banishment ritual—which a successful **Cthulhu Mythos** or Hard **Occult** roll confirms. They may even wish to prevent it, if they can discover the identity of the victim (assuming they don't already know it as a result of their dreams; **Dream Visions** and **Baldur's Sacrifice**, pages 104 and 131, respectively). If they don't know who the target is, Killinger will not willingly give up his victim's name; a successful **Intimidation** roll or actual physical violence (with the loss of 1 hit point or more) is required for him to spill the beans.

At this point, Killinger supplies further details: his stooge Erwin Kern, tricked into thinking Rathenau is one of the mythical Elders of Zion, is going to take a team of Consul assassins and gun down the minister on his way into the office. (Rathenau often works on weekends.) They will be waiting in a car near Rathenau's house in the Grunewald, then follow his vehicle, pull up alongside, and open fire on the car, tossing in a grenade for good measure.

With this information, the investigators have what they need to stop the assassination, if they can get there in time. Killinger will not stop it himself, but neither will he stand in the way of a determined band of investigators, choosing to save his own skin first. The fanatical Consul assassins will not go so quietly, either, and a gunfight is likely. See **Erwin Kern**, page 138, for the assassins' profiles.

If, of course, the investigators have already figured out who the victim is from their dreams, even if Killinger is killed at any point, they may still be able to stop the assassination. But, without that vital piece of information, the assassination goes off as planned, even if Killinger is dead.

CONCLUSION

Regardless of the investigators' success or failure, the *lustmord* spree winds down. Of course, the devil is in the details; a failed banishment results in many more deaths and incidents of cannibalism over the next decade than there would otherwise have been.

If Anna Tchaikovsky survives, she goes on maintaining her claim that she is the Grand Duchess Anastasia. Eventually changing her name to Anna Anderson, she is the most famous of the claimants to the Russian princess' identity, even having a movie made about her, starring Ingrid Bergman (*Anastasia*; Litvak, 1956).

If Rathenau is killed, the investigators realize that this was the "sacrifice" Killinger spoke of (if they didn't already know it). Within an hour of his death, the news has raced across Berlin, and hundreds of thousands of factory workers drop everything to fill the streets in protest. The neighborhoods around the Ku'damm swarm with streaming rivers of marchers carrying the red flag of Communism and the red-gold-black flag of the Republic, the sound of their marching feet the only accompaniment to the eerie procession.

Germany is plunged into economic chaos. The inflation of the German mark runs rampant, giving way to the *annus horibilis* of 1923, wherein the mark is so valueless that people burn stacks of the paper money to keep warm or use it to wallpaper their houses. The social disruption deeply scars the German psyche. In November 1923, Adolf Hitler attempts his "Beer Hall Putsch" in Munich. Although this fails, it provides him with a national platform during his trial and through the subsequent publication of his book, *Mein Kampf*, written in prison while serving an abbreviated sentence for attempted revolution. In many ways, the death of Rathenau is the beginning of the end for the Weimar Republic. The investigators may take cold comfort in the knowledge that they saved the city from a ravening horde of murder-happy cannibals—but at what cost?

If the investigators manage to save Rathenau, they have spared the country a great shock. They have also, somewhat unfortunately, prevented the one positive outcome of the murder, which is an all-encompassing crackdown on groups such as Organisation Consul. Right-wing terrorist groups, Consul at their forefront, continue their political assassinations and cryptic, vigilante *vehme* courts for years to come. Although Rathenau can prevent the worst of the economic collapse of 1923, the destabilization caused by the assassination squads has a net effect of cancelling out the Foreign Minister's efforts; the Republic is still doomed, but the country has at least been spared the wound of losing a politician who is, by all accounts, a genuinely compassionate and decent individual.

REWARDS

Grant the players an investigator development phase when they have completed this scenario and apply the following awards to each surviving investigator.

- Saving Anna Tchaikovsky: +1D4 Sanity points.
- Saving Walther Rathenau: +1D6 Sanity points.
- Banishing the Demon-Großmann: +1D10 Sanity points.
- Failing to save Anna Tchaikovsky: −1D6 Sanity points.
- Failing to save Walther Rathenau: −1D2 Sanity points.

CHARACTERS AND MONSTERS

NON-PLAYER CHARACTERS

Manfred Freiherr von Killinger, *36, assassin on a mission*

STR 50	CON 70	SIZ 75	DEX 55	INT 70
APP 50	POW 65	EDU 70	SAN 65	HP 14
DB: +1D4	Build: 1	Move: 7	MP: 13	

Combat

Brawl	70% (35/14), damage 1D3+1D4
Riding crop	70% (35/14), damage 1D3+½DB
Model P08 Luger	50% (25/10), damage 1D10
Dodge	27% (12/5)

Skills

Credit Rating 50%, Intimidate 65%, Language (English) 35%, Language (German) 70%, Law 45%, Mechanical Repair 25%, Navigate 55%, Occult 50%, Pilot (Boat) 70%, Psychology 35%, Spot Hidden 45%, Swim 60%, Throw 50%.

Erwin Kern, *23, Consul assassin*

Kern's accomplices are Hermann Fischer, Ernst von Solomon, and Ernst-Werner Techow. Use Kern's profile for these men as well.

STR 60	CON 60	SIZ 65	DEX 70	INT 55
APP 80	POW 65	EDU 60	SAN 65	HP 12
DB: +1D4	Build: 1	Move: 8	MP: 13	

Combat

Brawl	70% (35/14), damage 1D3+1D4
Bergmann MP18	55% (27/11), damage 1D10
"Potato Masher" grenade	50% (25/10), damage 4D10/3 yards/meters
Dodge	35% (17/7)

Skills

Climb 50%, Drive Auto 55%, Intimidate 60%, Jump 45%, Language (German) 60%, Law 50%, Sneer Menacingly 85%, Stealth 45%, Throw 50%.

Pyotr Shabelsky-Bork (aka Prince Gabriel Constantinovich), 29, conspirator

STR 65	CON 55	SIZ 60	DEX 65	INT 80
APP 45	POW 80	EDU 90	SAN 45	HP 11
DB: +1D4	Build: 1	Move: 9	MP: 16	

Combat
Brawl	60% (30/12), damage 1D3+1D4
.32 Automatic	65% (32/13), damage 1D8
Dodge	40% (20/8)

Skills
Art/Craft (Poetry) 45%, Charm 45%, Credit Rating 65%, Cthulhu Mythos 14%, Disguise 65%, Drive Auto 45%, Fast Talk 50%, Firearms (Rifle/Shotgun) 60%, First Aid 50%, History 55%, Intimidate 50%, Language (English) 45%, Language (French) 65%, Language (German) 75%, Language (Russian) 90%, Library Use 50%, Occult 60%, Persuade 70%, Psychology 60%, Ride 60%.

Spells: Banishment of Yde Etad, Prinn's Crux Ansata
Equipment: Crux Ansata

Red Mill Drunk

STR 65	CON 50	SIZ 75	DEX 55	INT 65
APP 45	POW 40	EDU 65	SAN 50	HP 12
DB: +1D4	Build: 1	Move: 7	MP: 10	

Combat
Brawl	60% (30/12), damage 1D3+1D4
Dodge	27% (12/5)

Anita Berber, 23, Berlin's naked goddess

STR 60	CON 55	SIZ 40	DEX 85	INT 75
APP 85	POW 90	EDU 55	SAN 80	HP 9
DB: 0	Build: 0	Move: 9	MP: 18	

Combat
Brawl	30% (15/6), damage 1D3
Dodge	45% (22/9)

Skills
Art/Craft (Acting) 35%, Art/Craft (Dance) 75%, Art/Craft (Poetry) 55%, Charm 65%, Fast Talk 55%, History 30%, Language (English) 20%, Language (French) 45%, Language (German) 55%, Language (Russian) 20%, Occult 25%, Persuade 65%, Sleight of Hand 30%, Stealth 40%.

Police Inspector Krieg, 54, hardboiled cop

STR 50	CON 40	SIZ 60	DEX 55	INT 85
APP 40	POW 70	EDU 75	SAN 60	HP 10
DB: 0	Build: 0	Move: 5		MP: 14

Combat
Brawl	45% (22/9), damage 1D3
.32 Automatic	45% (22/9), damage 1D8
Dodge	40% (20/8)

Skills
Accounting 35%, Climb 60%, Disguise 25%, Fast Talk 75%, Intimidate 45%, Language (English) 25%, Language (German) 75%, Language (Polish) 15%, Language (Russian) 20%, Law 65%, Listen 55%, Persuade 75%, Psychology 80%, Spot Hidden 80%, Stealth 45%, Throw 40%.

Baron Arthur von Kleist, 67, scheming monarchist

STR 50	CON 60	SIZ 50	DEX 65	INT 70
APP 45	POW 70	EDU 75	SAN 70	HP 11
DB: 0	Build: 0	Move: 5	MP: 14	

Combat
Brawl	25% (12/5), damage 1D3
Sword cane	60% (30/12), damage 1D6
Dodge	40% (20/8)

Skills
Credit Rating 75%, Intimidate 65%, Language (English) 15%, Language (German) 75%, Language (Russian) 25%, Law 45%, Persuade 65%, Psychology 60%, Spot Hidden 60%.

Franziska Schanzkovska (aka Anna Tchaikovsky), 26, Romanov pretender

STR 45	CON 40	SIZ 35	DEX 65	INT 50
APP 70	POW 50	EDU 60	SAN 32	HP 7
DB: −1	Build: −1	Move: 9	MP: 10	

Combat
Brawl	25% (12/5), damage 1D3−1
Dodge	32% (16/6)

Skills
Climb 50%, Disguise 30%, Intimidate 40%, Jump 40%, Language (English) 40%, Language (French) 50%, Language (German) 50%, Language (Polish) 60%, Language (Russian) 60%, Persuade 50%, Psychology 45%, Stealth 50%, Throw 35%.

RUSSIAN MONARCHISTS

Fyodor Viktorovich Vinberg

STR 50	CON 50	SIZ 50	DEX 60	INT 70
APP 50	POW 60	EDU 80	SAN 60	HP 10
DB: 0	Build: 0	Move: 6	MP: 12	

Combat

| Brawl | 45% (22/9), damage 1D3 |
| Dodge | 30% (15/6) |

Skills

Credit Rating 65%, History 45%, Language (German) 40%, Language (Russian) 80%.

Princess Natasha Alexandrovna

STR 35	CON 55	SIZ 45	DEX 65	INT 70
APP 65	POW 60	EDU 80	SAN 60	HP 10
DB: –1	Build: –1	Move: 8	MP: 12	

Combat

| Brawl | 25% (12/5), damage 1D3–1 |
| Dodge | 32% (15/6) |

Skills

Charm 45%, Credit Rating 75%, Language (German) 40%, Language (Russian) 80%.

MONSTERS

The Demon-Großmann, *murderous spirit*

STR —	CON —	SIZ —	DEX —	INT 65
APP —	POW 300	EDU —	SAN —	HP —
DB: —	Build: —	Move: —	MP: 60	

Combat

Attacks per round: 1

| Brawl | 70% (35/14), damage 1D3+DB* |
| Dodge | Use possessed host's skill |

Of the possessed host.

Skills

as per the possessed host.

Armor: none.

SPECIAL POWERS:

Possession: the spirit-form of Carl Großmann is a terrible entity indeed, able to possess those who unknowingly partook of Großmann's human meat products and turning them into monstrous caricatures of the killer. The more the spirit-fragment possesses the host, the less "human" the host becomes, until it is a walking avatar of *lustmord*.

The target must make an opposed **POW** roll when a fragment of the demon attempts to possess them. Fortunately for the victim, the demon's POW is divided evenly among the number of hosts currently possessed plus the current target—e.g. if the Demon-Großmann is inhabiting five other bodies and is trying to possess a sixth, its effective POW in each body is 50. The Demon-Großmann will not generally attempt to possess more than six hosts at a time and usually limits itself to no more than three. The spirit may abandon its hosts at any time and coalesce as it sees fit, even going so far as to reunite in a single host.

Failing the opposed POW roll means the victim is now possessed by the Demon-Großmann and they become completely subordinate to the demon's animate will. Horrifically, the victim remains aware of the actions they are taking and of the changes going on in their body.

The life force of the vessel is slowly consumed during the time of possession. Once per day while possessed, call for an opposed **POW** roll: if failed, the host body loses 3D10 POW. If the character can overcome the spirit, the demon loses 2D6 POW instead—these losses are permanent for both parties. The spirit will flee a host that causes it to lose half or more of the POW points it had when it possessed the host. If a host reaches zero POW, the vessel is effectively deceased and is only animated by the spirit. Once the spirit leaves, the host's body collapses in a dead heap. As POW is drained, the host takes on increasingly alarming characteristics of decay and monstrosity. In effect, the spirit-fragment inside is transforming the vessel to resemble the true form of the Demon-Großmann.

The demonic force possesses every cell of the vessel. Thus, dismemberment doesn't stop the vessel from continuing to act. Indeed, it simply guarantees that other, smaller parts of the host will now act independently! This cellular possession also fundamentally alters the vessel's biochemistry and physiognomy. This starts in the eyes: even without any other changes to the body, possessed hosts acquire Großmann's beady-eyed stare. Even more bizarrely, the shadow they cast is that of Carl Großmann (0/1 Sanity point loss when noticing this phenomenon). Blood and other fluids take on garish colors (white, dark or light red, black, or green) and, as APP is lost (see following), the victim's overall features become much more corpselike. The creature's voice is usually a demonic growl, although it can also take on other, disturbing forms, such as childlike singing.

For every 15 points of POW the host loses, they permanently lose 5 points of APP and should roll once on the **Demonic Mutation Table** (nearby) to see what bizarre changes take effect in their body.

Once a vessel is completely taken over, the Demon-Großmann may create the illusion of the vessel being restored to its full APP, speaking and appearing as it did before possession. The Demon-Großmann has full access to the vessel's memories, which it can use those to lull friends and loved ones into a false sense of security. These changes are entirely illusory. Furthermore, once a vessel's POW has reached zero, its body is putty in the hands of the possessing spirit. Bones may be broken and features completely reshaped—whatever the Demon-Großmann wishes to do to cause the maximum amount of terror—and it may even reshape the host's physical structure; essentially, any of the changes on the **Demonic Mutation Table** may now be applied at will.

If a host somehow survives their possession, they lose 1D3/1D6 Sanity points, +1 for each point of POW lost to the demon, the moment it leaves (or is expelled from) their body. APP and POW losses are permanent, but any mutations gained during possession disappear. APP loss manifests as scarring and a general "used-up" appearance.

Combat: unfortunately, the only way to stop a possessed host is to destroy the body or the head. Complete destruction through fire, explosion, or other sources of that nature will also do the trick. The Keeper should use the **Optional Hit Locations** rule (*Call of Cthulhu Rulebook*, pages 126–127) when investigators are fighting a possessed host. Each location can take a certain percentage of total hit points in damage before being severed/slashed open; excess damage from the blow is lost—see the **Hit Location Damage Percentages Table** (nearby). If a limb is severed, it now possesses that same percentage of its host's original total hit points and may act independently. It also reduces the host's *current* POW by the percentage given.

Example: the investigators are attacked by a possessed doctor with 12 hit points, containing a spirit-fragment of POW 100. An investigator strikes out with their fire axe and rolls "Right Arm" for the hit location. They inflict 6 points of damage with the strike.

The doctor loses 3 hit points (25% of his starting total); the remaining 3 points are wasted. The arm falls to the ground…and starts scuttling toward the investigators, trying to trip them up! The arm now has 3 hit points of its own. The possessing spirit's POW is reduced by 25 percent to 75, while the arm now has a spirit-fragment of its own with a POW of 25.

Investigators may target individual body parts by taking a penalty die on their attack—if the head is severed, the host is unable to see or hear. Strangely, the disembodied head is still able to talk and may even attempt to bite if an investigator gets too close, at least until the spirit-fragment flees (which

it does so as quickly as possible after the beheading to avoid being destroyed itself, either partially or completely).

The spirit-fragment may also elect to depart if the fight seems to be going against it. If it fails to do so before total bodily destruction, complete destruction of the head (as opposed to just severing it), or total dismemberment occurs, then the spirit-fragment contained within is destroyed, reducing the overall POW of the Demon-Großmann. Note that in cases of dismemberment (head or limbs), some fragment of the spirit may survive long enough to flee, with only a fraction being permanently destroyed. The spirit may choose to vacate a body temporarily before matters escalate too far, returning control to the host, only to come back and possess it again at a more opportune time.

Sanity loss: possession is incredibly traumatic; to be possessed by the Demon-Großmann is to experience the will of a monster made manifest by your own hands. Sanity should be lost for "witnessing" horrific acts committed by the possessing spirit-fragment. In addition, as already mentioned, should the host survive their possession, they lose 1D3/1D6 Sanity points, +1 for each point of POW lost

HIT LOCATION DAMAGE PERCENTAGES TABLE

Roll 1D10 to determine Location	Location	Total Hit Point Percentage (%)
1–3	Right Leg	30
4–6	Left Leg	30
7–10	Abdomen	30
11–15	Chest/Torso	40
16–17	Right Arm	25
18–19	Left Arm	25
20	Head	30

to the demon, the moment it departs, virtually guaranteeing indefinite insanity for all but the briefest possessions, even if the spirit-fragment flees the host before death.

The Sanity loss inflicted on those who witness a possessed host is dependent on their relationship to the host, as well as the degree to which the Demon-Großmann has taken over. Suggestions follow, but the Keeper should use their discretion, as not every possible permutation may be covered:

- Seeing Großmann's shadow: 0/1 Sanity loss.
- Noticing the change in the eyes: 1/1D2 Sanity loss.
- Mutations (minor) or seeing obvious signs of possession (decay, changed voice, etc.): 1/1D2 to 1/1D4 Sanity loss.
- Mutations (major): 1/1D6 Sanity loss.

Again, feel free to bump up these losses if the host is a loved one, a close friend, or a fellow investigator. Also, note that some mutations add to these losses (as noted on the **Demonic Mutation Table**).

Dormancy: a spirit-fragment, upon possessing a host, need not immediately show its hand. When a host is possessed by a dormant fragment, the victim should continue to make opposed **POW** rolls once every six hours and note the results (including mutations) but *should not apply them yet*. When the Demon-Großmann decides to manifest, apply *all* POW losses, Sanity losses, and mutations at once—this can result in quite striking transformations! The Demon-Großmann prefers to take action immediately upon possessing a host, but also sees the value in lying low for a time, particularly in the case of investigators.

SAMPLE HOSTS

Presented here are four luckless Berliners, each possessed by a spirit-fragment of the Demon-Großmann, each for a different length of time. All assume a possessing spirit-fragment of 100 POW (meaning that, as written, a maximum of three of them can be active together at any one time). Use these to assail investigators and as examples for creating your own.

Traudl, *maid*

STR 50	CON 50	SIZ 40	DEX 50	INT 45
APP 55	POW 40*	EDU 40	SAN 40	HP 9
DB: 0	Build: 0	Move: 9	MP: 8	

*100 **POW** for spirit-fragment

Combat

Attacks per round: 1

Brawl	70% (35/14), damage 1D3
Dodge	50% (25/10)

Skills

First Aid 50%, Language (German) 40%, Language (Russian) 20%, Listen 60%, Mechanical Repair 20%, Natural World 45%, Persuade 30%, Science (Pharmacy) 15%, Psychology 45%, Spot Hidden 55%.

Mutations: none.
Sanity loss: 1/1D2 Sanity points when possession is witnessed.

Anita Brandt, *half-silk prostitute*

Possession: 3 hours.

STR 40	CON 50	SIZ 35	DEX 65	INT 65
APP 60	POW 25*	EDU 60	SAN 25	HP 8
DB: −1	Build: −1	Move: 9	MP: 5	

*100 **POW** for spirit-fragment

Combat

Attacks per round: 1

Brawl	70% (35/14), damage 1D3−1
Dodge	65% (33/13)

Skills

Accounting 65%, Charm 35%, Climb 45%, Fast Talk 45%, Language (English) 25%, Language (German) 60%, Library Use 30%, Psychology 40%, Sleight of Hand 30%, Stealth 30%.

Mutations: extra-long tongue (5 feet long), bubbling skin.
Sanity loss: 1/1D4 Sanity points to see the mutated prostitute.

Sigfried Schröder, *member of Organisation Consul*

Possession: 1 hour.

STR 65	CON 60	SIZ 70	DEX 55	INT 50
APP 45	POW 39*	EDU 55	SAN 39	HP 13
DB: +1D4	Build: 1	Move: 7	MP: 7	

*100 **POW** for spirit-fragment

Combat

Attacks per round: 1

Brawl	70% (35/14), damage 1D3+1D4
Model P08 Luger	65% (32/13), damage 1D10
Dodge	50% (25/10)

Skills

Drive Auto 55%, First Aid 45%, Intimidate 65%, Language (English) 20%, Language (German) 60%, Language (Italian) 25%, Rifle 75%, Track 25%.

DEMONIC MUTATION TABLE

Roll 1D20	Mutation	Sanity Loss
1	**Multi-hinged mandibular jaw** (+1 biting damage)	**1/1D4**
2	**Long, craning neck** (extended reach; 1D4 feet* long)	**1/1D6**
3	**Clawed hands** (+1 brawling damage)	**1/1D2**
4	**Needle-like teeth** (+1 bite damage)	**1/1D2**
5	**Extra-long tongue** (1D6 feet* long)	**1/1D2**
6	**Spikes** (roll 1D6: 1–2 shoulder; 3–4 head; 5 chest; 6 legs)	**1/D4**
7	**Prehensile tail** (1D6 feet* long)	**1/1D6**
8	**Eye stalks** (360 degree vision)	**1/1D6**
9	**Multiple arms (1D3)** (one extra attack per arm)	**1/1D6**
10	**Multiple legs (1D4)** (add +1 to Movement per extra leg)	**1/1D6**
11	**Multiple eyes (1D20)** (scattered across head and upper torso; impossible to blind)	**1/1D6**
12	**Bubbling skin** (flesh ripples, bulges, and pulsates)	**1/1D4**
13	**Sucker-pads on hands and feet** (+1 Build when grappling; bonus die to Climb rolls)	**1/1D4**
14	**Second face** (a smaller version of Großmann's face manifests on the back of the head)	**1/1D6**
15	**Covered in suppurating sores** (pulsating sores, weeping sores)	**1/1D2**
16	**Smells of rotting meat** (opponent must make a successful CON roll when in melee or lose the first round of combat to retching)	**1/1D2**
17	**Extra-long fingers** (+1D6 inches**)	**1/1D2**
18	**Tentacle-like fingers** (combines Extra-long fingers and Sucker-pads)	**1/1D4**
19	**Bloody projectile vomit** (may target up to 5 feet away with 50% accuracy; those hit suffer 1/1D2 Sanity point loss and must make a successful CON roll or spend next round retching; those hit are vulnerable to possession)	**1/1D2**
20	**Screaming faces** (the faces of some of Großmann's previous victims press out against the flesh of the body from within; Stealth rolls impossible)	**1/1D6**

Note: Sanity loss may be increased a step for multiple mutations.
*1 foot = 30 cm
**1 inch = 2.5 cm

Mutations: bloody projectile vomit (may target up to 5 feet away with 50% accuracy; those hit suffer 1/1D2 Sanity loss and must make a successful CON roll or spend next round retching; those hit are vulnerable to possession).

Sanity loss: none, 1/1D2 Sanity points when witnessing projectile vomit.

Karlheinz Haas, *dockworker*

Possession: 15 hours.

STR 75	CON 70	SIZ 85	DEX 60	INT 50
APP 20	POW 00*	EDU 35	SAN 00	HP 15
DB: +1D4	Build: 1	Move: 10	MP: 0	

*100 **POW** for spirit-fragment

Combat

Attacks per round: 1

Brawl	70% (35/14), damage 1D3+1D4
Dodge	30% (15/6)

Skills

Climb 45%, Intimidate 40%, Language (German) 35%, Mechanical Repair 65%, Operate Heavy Machine 75%, Stealth 60%.

Mutations: long neck, suppurating sores, smells of rotting meat, three extra legs.

Sanity loss: 1/1D6 Sanity points to see the mutated dockworker.

Johann Caspersohn, *librarian*

Possession: 10 hours.

STR 50	CON 40	SIZ 60	DEX 55	INT 75
APP 30	POW 00*	EDU 80	SAN 00	HP 10
DB: 0	Build: 0	Move: 7	MP: 0	

Combat

Attacks per round: 1

Brawl	70% (35/14), damage 1D3
Dodge	27% (12/5)

Skills

History 45%, Language (Ancient Greek) 25%, Language (English) 45%, Language (French) 65%, Language (German) 80%, Language (Hebrew) 40%, Language (Latin) 35%, Language (Yiddish) 65%, Library Use 85%, Listen 55%, Occult 25%, Persuade 40%, Psychology 40%, Spot Hidden 45%, Stealth 35%.

Mutations: 12 extra eyes, screaming faces, prehensile tail (2 feet long), extra-long fingers (5 inches longer than normal), second face.

Sanity loss: 1/1D6 Sanity points to see the mutated librarian.

OTHER

Cassowary

STR 75	CON 50	SIZ 80	DEX 70	INT—
APP —	POW 50	EDU —	SAN —	HP 13
DB: +1D4	Build: 1	Move: 12	MP: —	

Combat

Attacks per round: 1 (claw, peck)

Fighting	60% (30/12), damage 1D6+1D4
Dodge	35% (17/7)

Skills

Listen 50%, Spot Hidden 30%, Stealth 50%.

TOME

Großmann's Journal

German, Carl Friedrich Wilhelm Großmann, 1917–1921

Großmann's journal not only contains a variety of sausage recipes and a record of his victims' names, but it also describes in unnerving detail the transformative power of consuming human flesh and of consuming the "necessary essence to transcend." Throughout, there are numerous notes and entries regarding some sort of "game" that only he seems to know how to play, along with strange charts in the style of chess diagrams, but clearly not referring to chess.

- **Sanity Loss:** 1D10
- **Cthulhu Mythos:** +2/+6 percentiles
- **Mythos Rating:** 30
- **Study:** 10 weeks
- **Spells:** Pawn Takes Whore (Consume Likeness), Pawn Promotion (Possess Corpse*), Endgame (Possession*)

*See **Spells**, below.

SPELLS

Pawn Promotion (Possess Corpse)

- **Cost:** 1 magic point; 1D8+2 Sanity points
- **Casting time:** 2 rounds

Enables the possession and animation of a dead thing for a period of up to 10 minutes. Dead things may include skeletons, animal corpses (including those that have undergone taxidermy or preserved in formaldehyde), animal skins, and human corpses. The caster's mind is transferred to the corpse for the duration of the spell and can command mobility in the corpse appropriate to its condition.

While the caster possesses the dead thing, their own body lies motionless and they no longer breathe (their heart stops pumping). When the caster returns to their own body, they must attempt a **CON** roll:

- If returning within 1–4 rounds: a bonus die is granted at Regular difficulty.
- If returning within 5–7 rounds: Regular difficulty.
- If returning within 8–9 rounds: Hard difficulty.
- If returning in 10+ rounds: Extreme difficulty.

If the CON roll is failed, the caster's body does not return to life; the caster's mind is entombed within their own (now dead) body. Another person may perform a successful **Medicine** or a **First Aid** roll to resuscitate the caster's body—the window of time in which resuscitation is possible is left to the discretion of the Keeper.

Note that if the corpse possessed is one of the living dead (a vampire, animated mummy, zombie, and so on) then an opposed **POW** roll should be made each round for the caster to remain in control of the body. If the caster loses an opposed roll, their mind is sent back to their own body (triggering a **CON** roll as detailed above). Generally, only one corpse can be possessed at any one time, although deeper magic (variant) versions may exist that allow for multiple or easier possessions.

Endgame (Possession)

- **Cost:** 15 magic points; 1D8 Sanity points
- **Casting time:** 4 rounds

Enables the possession of living human beings. By jumping from one body to the next, the caster can potentially ensure a very long lifespan. The high cost, however, means that it is used sparingly, with sorcerers preferring to stay in one body as long as possible.

The caster must be able to see their intended target with their naked eye. Words of possession are then spoken aloud to instigate the possession; the caster must win an opposed **POW** roll with the target to successfully transfer their consciousness. The possessor is unable to access any of their victim's memories while inhabiting their body. When the possessor leaves a body, the former victim has no recollection of the time when they were possessed—just a dark void in their memory.

CHAPTER 6

DANCES OF VICE, HORROR, AND ECSTACY

The infamous Anita Berber is back in town with her latest husband, but she is not long for this world. The mysterious Brotherhood of Saturn and an amateur sorcerer conspire to use the notorious dancer for their own blasphemous purposes. As a cold wind whips the streets of Berlin, death stalks the cradles and nurseries of the city, inhibitions fall away, and abominations and vermin clog its streets and clubs. The investigators must find a way to restore balance to the world before a new Babylon rises on the banks of the Spree.

KEEPER SUMMARY

Dances of Vice, Horror, and Ecstasy picks up, thematically speaking, where **The Devil Eats Flies** left off, delving deeper into Berlin's seedy underground, both occult and mundane. Split between two time periods (1926 and 1928), the bulk of the scenario presents a smorgasbord of threads the investigators may follow to one of several potential outcomes. The Keeper is provided with helpful non-player characters (NPCs) to assist with keeping the investigation on track. Be warned that this is a potentially complex scenario with extremely high stakes and should be handled appropriately.

In 1926, at a dance exhibition in the Friedrichstraße, the investigators encounter Anita Berber, deep into her self-destructive death spiral. She performs three numbers, culminating with "Astarte," a piece dedicated to the goddess of the same name with whom Berber strongly identifies— see **Astarte**, page 156, for another of Berber's *homages* to the goddess. This time, however, her performance seems to manifest something godlike on stage, much to the bemusement (or chagrin) of the audience.

The investigators, in attendance with noted occultist Albin Grau, are tasked by Grau to help unravel what occurred during the performance. Berber proves as difficult

AUTHOR NOTE

The theme of this scenario is Überschreitung ("transgression"). A coterie of mortals, attempting to create a god, get much more than they bargained for, leaving it up to the investigators to sort out the mess. The investigators themselves transgress to a shadowy reflection of Berlin and may transgress further still. In Stephen King's three-part analysis of horror, the primary type in this scenario is the Horror, which King defines as "the unnatural, spiders the size of bears, the dead waking up and walking around, it's when the lights go out and something with claws grabs you by the arm." In other words, plenty of visceral, supernatural thrills.

and drug-addled as always and seems genuinely unaware of any strange events caused by the exhibition.

The fact of the matter is that Berber's newest husband, Henri Châtin-Hofmann, is a wizard (albeit of the amateur variety), who is using his wife's considerable powers to fuel his castings. Unable to control his workings, he inadvertently sends the investigators into a parallel dimension filled with hordes of flesh-eating monsters.

The scenario then flashes forward two years to 1928. Berber has returned to Berlin, a used-up husk on the verge of death. Albin Grau, meanwhile, has been busy: after witnessing Berber's magical powers on the cabaret stage, he got in touch with his brethren in the Fraternitas Saturni, a powerful group of sex-magicians, with a plan to harness that energy into a working of tremendous power. Conspiring with Châtin-Hofmann prior to his departure, the pieces are put in place

Opposite: Abyzou watches over the reverie

for a great sacrifice. With Berber's passing, the ritual is carried out, and a newborn goddess walks the streets of Berlin—with disastrous consequences for the people of the city.

The investigators are pulled back into the scenario through a mysterious ally with connections to the conspirators, who feeds them clues via telephone. Over the course of the scenario, the investigators meet the new goddess, discover the sinister details of the ritual that brought her to Berlin, and uncover the means to send her back from whence she came. There's only one problem: the investigators must go with her to the Shadow City and save thousands of crazed Berliners from themselves, or else discover a way to destroy her corporeal body here on Earth. If they are successful, they will have banished a monstrous spirit and laid Anita Berber's soul to rest. If they fail—or, if they pay the ultimate sacrifice to succeed—then it is highly likely they are never seen again, at least not in the form they currently occupy...

INTRODUCING THE INVESTIGATORS

This scenario kicks off with an invitation from Albin Grau to one or more of the investigators to attend a dance performance at the *Weiße Maus* (White Mouse) club. Grau has enough free tickets for all the investigators to attend, either as direct invitees or as plus-ones.

If the investigators played through **The Devil Eats Flies** and ended on good terms with Baron Kleist, then it is he who recommends the investigators to Grau when the Baron is unable to attend. Alternatively, an investigator who is involved in the worlds of the fine arts, the movie industry, and Berlin's occult societies knows Grau via a mutual contact, in which case the tickets are simply a token of good will from an old friend.

If this is the investigators' first Berlin scenario, or if they are expatriates without any connection to the city, assume that they arrive at the Weiße Maus independently and are simply seated with Grau through the expedience of his table being the only one with places still available. The investigators may have come as part of a tour package, or they simply looking for some fun in the Friedrichstraße this evening. They will, of course, find much more than that.

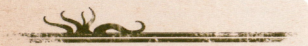

INVOLVING INVESTIGATOR ORGANIZATIONS

If the investigators belong to one of the organizations described earlier in this book (**Investigator Organizations**, page 16), please see the following suggestions for involving them in this scenario.

The Independent Order of Owls: it is only natural that a group of occult investigators would know Albin Grau, who has asked them to attend a show at the Weiße Maus tonight for more than mere fun and games. Grau suspects Anita Berber may be something other than a simple entertainer and wishes the opinion of a clutch of erudite Owls on the matter. He promises to get them backstage to interview her after the show.

Hilde-Film: another obvious connection, owing to Grau's history in the film industry. He and Hilde go way back, and, in lieu of pay this week, she has offered the tickets to some of her staff (i.e., the investigators) as compensation.

Landsberger Tenants' Association: the owner of the Landsberg tenement block, one Baron Grunau, is also one of Grau's old pals. It was the Baron who acquired the event tickets in the first place and gave them to Grau, who has decided to repay the Baron's largesse by holding a lottery for the tenants of his building; the investigators are the winners of that lottery.

The Apache Pathfinders: Albin Grau, finding himself with extra event tickets, decided to hold a radio contest to give away the extras. Too bad he didn't think to place an age limit on the winners! Decide which among the Pathfinders won the contest (perhaps the investigator with the highest Luck); the rest attend as guests of the winner.

SEXUAL CONTENT AND YOUR GROUP

This scenario involves a debased cult of Gnostic sex-magicians, teenage prostitutes, naked dancing, pregnancy as body horror, and a protean substance of alien fecundity.

As with the levels of violence and gore in **The Devil Eats Flies**, it is up to each Keeper and their players to determine their level of comfort with this type of content. We have endeavored to deal with these scenes in a way that allows Keepers to adjust the dial to what works best for them and their group, from "drawing a veil" up to "explicit content," but in all possible cases we have erred on the side of the former.

DRAMATIS PERSONAE

Albin Grau, *42, artist-occultist*

Visionary artist and producer of the 1922 Expressionist horror film *Nosferatu*, Albin Grau is the initial entry point for this scenario, providing the investigators with tickets to one of Anita Berber's shows and later enlisting them to help him find out more about the enigmatic performer. Grau also plays a major role in the ritual that transforms the dying Berber into the goddess Abyzou (**...and Rebirth**, page 164).

- **Description:** a bespectacled, mousy man, Grau does not look the part of the typical occultist. His buttoned-down exterior belies both his expansive artistic vision and his rather wild personal life.
- **Traits:** prior to his mind shattering as a result of Abyzou's incarnation, Grau is perfectly likeable in person, and he radiates the calm assurance of one who is well versed in a variety of disciplines. After he becomes a devoted member of Abyzou's cult, Grau has the bearing and mannerisms of a zealot, keen to recruit new members to the cause.
- **Roleplaying hooks:** unlike many of his fellow occultists, Grau does not put great stock in secrecy. Indeed, his past career as a filmmaker was built on his desire to promulgate occult information to the public (*Nosferatu* is sprinkled with esoteric Easter eggs throughout). He is always eager to talk on the topic of magic, the supernatural, and the unexplained.

Anita Berber, *27, priestess of depravity*

The central figure of this scenario, though her star has long since faded in the public's imagination. In the first part of the scenario (1926), Berber leaves a lasting impression on the investigators when one of her performances transcends this earthly plane. In the second part, her dying body is used as part of a ritual to create a living goddess on Earth, and it is through her influence even after death that a means of banishing said goddess presents itself.

- **Description:** after years of fast living and near-constant drug abuse, Anita Berber is beginning to show the effects of her reckless life. She is puffier around the face and now wears her theatrical makeup as much to cover the lines and wrinkles as for showy effect. Otherwise, she is still the same gap-toothed, androgynous, flaming-haired beauty she always was.
- **Traits:** still prone to outrageous behavior, Anita's cocaine and cognac habits ensure that the only thing predictable about her behavior is its unpredictability. Subject to fantastic mood swings, ill-considered soliloquies, and outbursts of violence, she is a tremendously difficult person to be around by this point in her life.
- **Roleplaying hooks:** increasingly banned from venues across Europe due to her violent outbursts and refusal to play by the rules, Berber is ever concerned with money. She has no qualms about selling her body and will do so at the drop of a hat. Investigators offering her cash or drugs will quickly find themselves her closest friend and will be treated to long digressions on the moon goddess, Astarte, and the beauty of white roses.

Albin Grau

Anita Berber

Henri Châtin-Hofmann, *26, dancer and dabbler*

Anita Berber's third and final husband (and amateur sorcerer), Henri Châtin-Hofmann is a man in over his head. Born Heinrich Hofmann in Baltimore, Maryland in 1900, the only son of a pastor at the Zion Lutheran Church there, Châtin-Hofmann changed the spelling of his name and added his mother's maiden name upon his confirmation at age 15. A few years later, despite speaking almost no German, he left home and took a ship to Berlin. There, in 1924, he met and married Berber.

- **Description:** possesses a boyish face, which only serves to accentuate his natural naïveté. He is handsome and slightly built, albeit extremely physically fit.
- **Traits:** generally quiet and retiring, Châtin-Hofmann is content to allow his wife to take the spotlight (both onstage and off). This is partly what comes naturally to him and partly due to not wanting to draw attention to his covert activities. Investigators talking to Châtin-Hofmann in 1926 find him to be an earnest, if somewhat clueless, young man. By 1928, two years of hard living and further explorations of unspeakable magical rites have left him easily rattled and suspicious.
- **Roleplaying hooks:** on the outside, he appears a devoted husband and artistic partner, constantly promoting his wife's career and attempting to minimize her bad press. In reality he is merely grooming her to take part in a great magical

working. Albin Grau, the occultist and cultist, draws Henri into a deadly plan to incarnate a goddess upon the Earth, beginning in 1926—one that is finally brought to fruition in 1928. Although Châtin-Hofmann pulls off the working, it leaves him a broken man, fleeing from that which he created.

Erma Kore, *appears 17, telephone-girl with a secret*

The adolescent Kore is a Telephone-Girl; a specialized sort of prostitute, she books clients only over the phone. These are clients who desire not only the illicit thrill of a pedophilic sexual encounter (some Telephone-Girls are as young as 14*) but who also wish to fulfill their modernistic obsessions with the cults of technology and celebrity; like all Telephone-Girls, Kore has adopted the looks and persona of a famous film actress—in her case, Marlene Dietrich.

*See **Age of Consent**, page 53.*

- **Description:** the soulful eyes and carven features of Dietrich, accentuated with a wig, makeup, and gender-bending sartorial choices. She also bears an uncomfortable resemblance to someone the investigators may have met in the past (**Meeting Erma**, page 181).
- **Traits:** although appearing to be only 17 years old, Kore, due to the nature of her work, possesses a world-weariness far beyond her years. Besides which, she is, in fact, an artificial creation of **Belshazzar the Doll Maker** (page 151; also

Henri Châtin-Hofmann

Erma Kore

Meeting Erma, page 181). Kore knows how to play off the sympathies of others, putting on a childlike voice for maximum effect when necessary. At other times, especially when meeting in person, she is cool and detached. Whatever mask she dons, her true personality is buried beneath so many layers that it is possible even she does not know what her "genuine" self looks like any longer.

- **Roleplaying hooks:** Kore works for a certain Baron Grunau, an associate of Albin Grau and is thus privy to much that the Borborite cultists would rather kept secret (**The Borborite Cult**, page 164). The accumulation of secrets has grown too much for her, and she turns to the investigators for help (see **Erma Kore: Telephone-Girl**, page 150, and **Erma's Connection**, page 168).

Belshazzar the Doll Maker,
90(?), Kabbalistic artisan

An ancient doll maker residing in Berlin's Jewish quarter, Belshazzar is also a master of Kabbalistic magic. These two fields of expertise intersect when he is commissioned by Albin Grau and his associates to make a series of *manikins* (living dolls) as part of their sinister summoning ritual. Although he agreed to do so, he now regrets the decision and may prove to be an ally to the investigators if treated sympathetically.

- **Description:** Belshazzar is a stooped old man of indeterminate antiquity. His spidery white hair sticks out in great puffs around the rim of his yarmulke, and a scraggly white beard dangles off the end of his chin. He wears a heavy cassock typical of those from the East but speaks fluent German.
- **Traits:** another sign of Belshazzar's exceeding age is his language: he speaks both German and Yiddish in an archaic dialect, full of outmoded grammatical constructions. He also displays a certain contempt for, and mystification with, modern technology (i.e., anything invented since the Napoleonic Wars). Investigators expecting a sly or dangerous sorcerer instead encounter an amiable, grandfatherly type who tends to ramble on about the old days while making winking jokes about how he is older than Methuselah.
- **Roleplaying hooks:** the creator of the *manikins* longs for death or oblivion as a result of the horror he helped inflict on the city, although he can be of great use to the investigators if they can convince him to share his secrets.

Gregor Gregorius, *38, occult bookstore owner*

Also known as Eugen Grosche, Gregorius is the owner of the **Occult Bookshop Inveha** (page 175), as well as the founder of the Fraternitas Saturni (FS; **Occult Societies**, page 60). Besides running his bookshop and attempting to disseminate esoteric knowledge to Berlin's masses, Gregorius is also present in Belshazzar's basement when the so-called "Berbelo Working" goes terribly wrong.

Belshazzar the Doll Maker

Gregor Gregorius

- **Description:** a quite striking appearance—a long, hooked nose, arched and furrowed brows, and large, penetrating eyes. He is nearly completely bald; what hair he retains has turned prematurely gray.
- **Traits:** the occultist is an intense, charismatic figure; he is not easily intimidated or swayed, especially after witnessing Abyzou's arrival.
- **Roleplaying hooks:** duped by his old friend Albin Grau into co-financing and participating in the attempt to bring the goddess Berbelo to Earth, Gregorius had no idea he was actually working on the Borborites' behalf up until it was too late, although he is both awed and horrified by the outcome. As a result of his involvement with Grau's insane scheme, Gregorius and his shop hold much that will help the investigators uncover the truth, although he is reticent to share it; however, if they first meet him in 1926, he has yet to become embroiled in the plan and can only confirm Châtin-Hoffman's purchase of his occult pamphlets.

Abyzou, *Whore of Babylon, Mother of Abominations*

A fragment of the Black Goat Shub-Niggurath given human form, Abyzou is simultaneously mother and whore, an irresistible force of nature that both creates and destroys all that she encounters. Her appearance in Berlin leads immediately to widespread deaths among the city's youth, as well as the appearance of shadowy monsters and unbridled vice around her Court of Sin, centered on the Großes Schauspielhaus Theater.

- **Description:** voluptuous and enticing, Abyzou's appearance recalls ancient Mesopotamian carvings of fertility goddesses. Her face, framed by spilling locks of golden-blonde hair, is almost androgynously beautiful. Her eyes are golden as well, and her breathy voice is as the sighing of a hot desert wind. The color of her skin changes with the phases of the moon: when the moon is new, as when she is incarnated upon Earth in this scenario, it is ebon black. As the moon waxes, her skin turns a steely gray. By the time of the full moon, it has turned milky white, almost luminescent; her golden hair shines against her skin regardless of its color—see **Phases of the Moon**, page 197, for details of when these conditions occur in November 1928.
- **Traits:** investigators meeting Abyzou face to face find her to be a highly charismatic and unique being with nerves of steel and unimaginable talents. She is wily, seductive, and wholly irresistible. Merely talking to her can bring an investigator under her spell, as many have discovered.
- **Roleplaying hooks:** for Abyzou, "the Sin Capital of the World" is precisely where she wishes to be. She exists to spread lunacy and lust, to take Berlin to new heights *and* depths of reckless abandon, and then to remake the city in her own image. Having done that, she will spread her power across the globe. Today Berlin, tomorrow…

START: BABYLON-ON-THE-SPREE (1926)

Anita Berber does not reveal vice lasciviously
Anita Berber does not coldly calculate the possibilities of lustful times
Anita Berber is vice
As much as she is horror
The horror and the ecstasy

—Sebastian Droste, *Dance as Form and Experience*

It is late summer in Berlin—August 7, 1926. Anita Berber is performing at the Weiße Maus, and the investigators have received tickets to the event, courtesy of Albin Grau, a failed movie executive. A successful **Know** roll recalls that it was his company, Prana Films, that produced the 1922 flop *Nosferatu* as its first movie.

It is nearly midnight as the investigators make their way from the Französische Straße U-Bahn station a block north of the club's Jägerstraße location. A fine summer rain is

Abyzou

falling, turning the Friedrichstraße into an obsidian mirror reflecting the bright lights of one of Berlin's most vibrant entertainment districts. Despite the weather, the sidewalks are still crowded.

As the group turns off Friedrichstraße at Jägerstraße, a marquee flashes in searing white light against the dark of night: the Weiße Maus, one of the hottest cabarets in the city. Passing into the cramped lobby, a hatcheck girl sits in a small cubicle just off to the right, idly French-inhaling the smoke from her cigarette in between taking *chapeaux*. The room is smoky and uncomfortably warm, ringing with raucous laughter. No doubt the investigators wish to push through to the main show area, but access is blocked by another young lady, this one wearing a sequin-fringed black and silver dress; she bears a large, shallow wicker bowl containing two rows of domino masks; one row black, the other white. "*If you would prefer anonymity, ladies and gentlemen,*" she croons, offering up the masks. It is up to each investigator whether they wish to take one.

Entering the main show area, the investigators see that most of the audience have chosen to conceal their identities. Twelve dinner tables are arranged around the room, seating close to 60 people. The investigators' table is waiting up near the curtained stage. Albin Grau is one of the few not wearing a mask; he is recognizable thanks to the red carnation in his lapel that he said he'd be wearing (should the investigators not know him already).

Picking their way through the murmuring crowd, the investigators see that the other attendees comprise an interesting mix. First, the investigators edge around a surplus of elderly and aging gentlemen, the masks sitting uneasily on their bony faces. Over there sits a group of sweaty salesmen out for a night on the town with the local company rep, their disguises doing little to hide their lascivious inebriation.

And here… Why, isn't that Manfred von Killinger? (If Killinger died during the events of **The Devil Eats Flies**, then this is someone who looks eerily like him.) The man is dressed in a paramilitary uniform once again, though it is different from the old Sportverein Olympia outfit. It is, instead, the uniform of the *Bund Wiking* (Viking League), a political organization founded in 1923 to bring together the disparate nationalist paramilitary groups that are now largely outlawed, Organisation Consul among them. Killinger is seated at a table with fellow Wiking compatriots and their *Nutte* (boyish teenage girl) prostitutes.

Keeper note: in among the Wikings is a young pimp named Horst Wessel; if the investigators make any overtly hostile moves toward the Wikings' table, he will not hesitate to don knuckledusters and start brawling. If required, use the **Ringverein Thug** profile (page 195) for Wessel; he later goes on

to become one of the Sturmabteilung's group leaders in Berlin before being shot to death in 1930 by members of the KPD.

As the investigators seat themselves, they note the table nearest them is occupied by happily chattering women. From the content of their loud conversation, their reason for being here quickly becomes obvious: this is a gathering of Berber's lesbian groupies.

Grau makes pleasant small talk with the investigators, the content depending on the circumstances of their invitation (**Involving the Investigators**, page 148). If this is his first time meeting them, he is polite and accommodating. He is happy to talk about art (he primarily makes his living as a painter these days), the movie industry, or matters occult or esoteric—he does not hide any side of his personality or interests.

The investigators have just enough time to get their drink orders in before the house lights dim, leaving only the light from the candle lamps at every table. The background chatter dies down. There is a moment of surpassing eeriness that comes from the sensation of being seated in a darkened room filled with mask-wearing strangers.

The cabaret's director walks out in front of the curtains, a small spotlight shakily following his progress. The audience applauds politely. "Madames et messieurs, Damen und Herren: *we have gathered here tonight because we all share a singular love. A love… of beauty. Yes! I say to you that we are here tonight to celebrate Beauty, to worship her for the goddess that she is.*"

The director's words are met with a ripple of laughter in the audience. Everyone is here to see scandalous naked dancing, and everyone—including the director—knows that.

"*Our featured dancers tonight, soon to depart the city for what is sure to be a well-received engagement in Amsterdam, are Frau Anita Berber and her husband and dance-partner, Henri Châtin-Hofmann. The first piece is a solo performance by Frau Berber entitled: 'Morphine.'*"

The director claps his way off stage, but the applause from the audience is somewhat muted. The heyday of Expressionistic nude dances already seems like lifetime away, a relic of the Inflation Years. Berber has been absent from Berlin, touring other parts of Europe—what could she know of the New Objectivity?

Keeper note: investigators may make a **Know** roll to recall reading in the papers about Berber's adventures abroad, including her scandalous turn in Yugoslavia, where she was arrested and briefly imprisoned on charges of being a German spy after insulting the country's young king, Peter II. Other more scurrilous reports maintain she and the king carried on a torrid affair.

Morphine

The curtain rises. An old armchair sits on the stage. A woman—Berber—lies back in its comforting arms, nearly lost in it. She wears a high-collared black dress that clings to her every curve and angle. Her hair is held down under a black diaphanous cap. In her hand is a syringe. She stares at her forearm.

SIGHTS OF THE CITY

1926: the Great Inflation is a rapidly fading memory. With the currency once again stabilized, those who can afford to do so are diving headfirst into Berlin's legendary nightlife. This is the classic era of Weimar Berlin, nestled unsteadily between the horrors of the post-war destabilization and the rise of the Nazis with the coming of the Great Depression.

Groups of drunken revelers stagger along, arm in arm, laughing like hyenas. Voices call out from the shadows of doorways and overhangs offering untold pleasures for pfennigs on the dollar. A young boy tugs at the sleeve of a passerby within earshot, "*Hey, you wanna come see an amputee sex show?*" Just as quickly, he disappears among the milling crowds. The sound of police whistles, shouting, and gunfire coming from somewhere nearby, perhaps just a block or two over. Is it growing closer? Better make yourselves scarce before the street violence spills over!

At night, every five minutes a pale beam swings over the rooftops: the signal of the brand-new *Funkturm* (Radio Tower), located out at the city's extreme western end. The light bothers some (who call it "wild lunacy" and a "luminous twitch") but stands as a signal to others of Berlin's arrival as a fully modern world capital.

On a wall, a weathered wheat-paste poster, its paper crinkled from exposure to the elements. The contents of the poster are perhaps cause for a double take: a skeleton dancing with a swooning woman in medieval garb, in the manner of old *Totentanz* (Death Dance) woodcut imagery. The text reads: *Berlin, halt ein! Befinne Dich. Dein Tänzer ist der Tod* (Berlin, stop! Come to your senses! Your dance partner is Death!)

1928: the sound of Joseph Goebbels on the radio, excoriating the "shameful dens of sin" (the clubs and movie theaters) that surround the Kaiser-Wilhelm-Memorial Church on Auguste-Viktoria-Platz.

Mischa Spoliansky's "Morphium" plays on a Vitaphone. Berber injects the syringe into her arm. As the music plays on, she sits, silent and unmoving. Then, explosively, she arches her body out of the chair. She begins to dance about the stage in jerking motions, ending in ecstatic poses. She returns to the chair, dancing around it. She looks out into the audience and smiles knowingly. Then, her face becomes a mask of contorted pain. She shudders and falls, her back arched painfully across the arms of the formerly welcoming chair. The curtain falls.

Her devoted fans explode in applause, but the response from the rest of the audience remains somewhat mixed. One of the drunken salesmen shouts, "*Take it off next time!*" From another table, a heckler shouts, "*Top swine!*"

This is too much for Berber, who comes exploding out from behind the curtains. She stalks over to the heckler, looming over him, sparks flying from her eyes, "*If you really think I'm top swine, why don't you come to my hotel room later for a closer inspection?*" The audience laughs its approval as the heckler shrinks back. Berber leaps back onto the stage and disappears behind the curtain.

Grau turns to the investigators, "*Well now. That was certainly… something. What did you all think?*" Encourage the investigators to proffer their thoughts on the subject before the director reappears onstage.

"*My dear audience, we are now going to witness the Beauty portion of the evening.*" His meaning is clear: here come the naked dances. "*First, a duet between Frau Berber and her husband entitled 'Salomé, Princess of Judah.'*" The director slides offstage as the curtain rises again.

Salomé, Princess of Judah

This time, a large bronze vessel sits upon the stage, its rim spattered with glistening globules of blood. A man enters from stage left, dressed in the garb of a Roman palace guard. He drags behind him a woman in a scarlet cloak who crawls upon the ground, beaten down. All in the audience can see that the woman is Berber, who crawls to the edge of the vessel and inhales the smell of the blood within.

Somehow, the scent of the blood seems to activate her. Twisting in a slow spiral, she rises. The Vitaphone now plays Richard Strauss' "Dance of the Seven Veils," and Berber-Salomé twirls about the vessel, her face lustful as she stares down into its gory depths. Beneath her cloak she is nude, but she dances with a large fan of ostrich feathers, which offers only tantalizing glimpses as she spins and swirls.

At last discarding the fan, Berber reaches down into the vessel and covers her hands in gore. Stretching back, she rubs her bloody hands across her naked abdomen, letting the crimson carnage run down over her thighs. She is transported by ecstasy, staggering about the stage, finally stopping to raise the cloak around her and disappearing inside it.

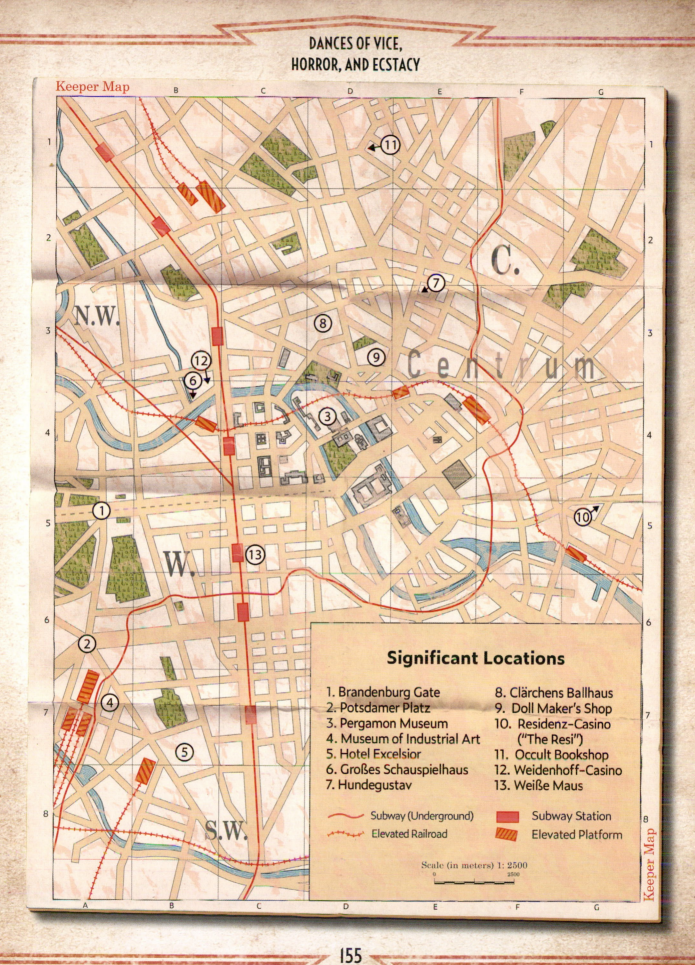

Keeper Map

N.W.

C.

C e n t r u m

W.

S.W.

Keeper Map

Significant locations of central Berlin Map

Significant Locations

1. Brandenburg Gate
2. Potsdamer Platz
3. Pergamon Museum
4. Museum of Industrial Art
5. Hotel Excelsior
6. Großes Schauspielhaus
7. Hundegustav

8. Clärchens Ballhaus
9. Doll Maker's Shop
10. Residenz-Casino ("The Resi")
11. Occult Bookshop
12. Weidenhoff-Casino
13. Weiße Maus

— Subway (Underground)   ▮ Subway Station

┄ Elevated Railroad   ▨ Elevated Platform

Scale (in meters) 1: 2500

0   2500

ASTARTE

Drip of silver, moon silver, muted silver
Rippling waves, blurred wafer
High over, the ether
Haze, noon, children at play
It is a godlike woman
She is not a woman,
She is not a boy
She is not an animal,
She is not a god
She is the moon, Silver
Hanging, dripping holy silver
Twenty-thousand pursuing women,
Bite through with furious voracity
Five thousand boys painted white
Lacerate with great desire
A brother murders his sister
A child lusts for blood
All slaves lust for lash marks
All stallions scream for mares
Silver drops from above, moon silver
Soft holy dripping silver
Lacerating, breathing out, evaporating
Astarte
She wears the coat of divine vice
She has the headdress of divine desire
She wears the emerald green of anguish
She flogs, she takes, she screams, she dances
All slaves cower, all whores wail
All boys groan, all stallions whinny
And the moonlight drips, and the silver shines
And Astarte smiles
Earth, altar, offering, incense,
Courtesans, rent boys, old men, animals
Plants, peelings, lotus, Nile
Astarte dances
Trembling outcry, naked
Headdress, emerald, hips
She dances the great dance
The boys offer themselves
The women kill themselves
The animals defile themselves
The plants tear themselves apart
Astarte dances
Then she takes desire's great bowl
Grips it with abrading hands
Takes the heads of the boys
The heads of the whores
The tails of the stallions
The leaves of the flowers
And laughs
Laughs and dances

—Anita Berber and Sebastian Droste, *Dances of Vice, Horror, and Ecstasy* (translation by Merrill Cole)

She rises again, dropping the cloak entirely now. She stands fully naked but for a crown of silver palm leaves on her head. She twirls back to the vessel and lays across it, letting her head dangle over the edge, while she arches her back and thrusts her blood-covered pelvis towards the sky. The curtain drops.

Now even the doubters have been pulled in. The applause is noticeably greater, and no heckling this time. Grau is among those applauding enthusiastically, "*She still has it!*" he enthuses. "*Wouldn't you say?*" Again, the investigators have an opportunity to discuss their reaction to the piece among themselves.

The director appears before the curtain, "*For our final piece of the evening, a solo number by Frau Berber entitled 'Astarte.'*"

Astarte

The curtain rises once more. The Vitaphone now plays a Tchaikovsky interlude. Berber comes out onto the stage wearing a long silver cape and a silver helmet, from which flutter many ostrich feathers; her face is covered by a black mask, not unlike the ones worn by those in the audience. Apart from these vestments, she wears nothing.

The effect is startling: with her face covered, her androgyny is emphasized even more. The feathers lend her a bird-like aspect, emphasized by her first moves of the dance, a piercing cry followed by a tinkling laugh. It should be ridiculous, but the audience is rapt.

The cape falls from Berber's shoulders as she dances first around the stage, then down into the audience; in the light of the pursuing spotlight, her lithe body seems to blaze like a magnesium torch. The mask drops, showing Berber's face, electrified with the frenzy of the dance. Every head turns to follow; here and there, some in the audience begin to rise from their chairs.

At this point, each investigator must succeed at an Extreme **POW** roll if they are to retain control of their own actions. If the investigator wears a mask, they make the roll with a penalty die—the anonymity of the mask makes one more likely to succumb to Berber's spell. Those who fail the roll are magically compelled to join in the revels to come.

Most of those present fall under Berber's sway. Some begin to dance in a wildly Bacchanalian fashion, tipping wine and champagne bottles over open mouths and shouting with unholy revelry. Others turn to those nearest them, tearing into each other with unbridled lust regardless of prior relationship, gender, or orientation. Berber laughs her tinkling laugh again. Genuflecting, she surmounts a table and holds a magnum of champagne aloft, "*To Astarte!*" she cries. Many in the crowd echo her toast. Berber leans back and pours the champagne down the front of her body—some of the revelers rush over to lap it from her.

Investigators caught up in the spell may be among those who do so, or they may be up to other shenanigans. Allow some leeway in players describing their investigators' actions, ideally tying their traits or other background information into their behavior. Alternatively, depending on the sensibilities of the group, draw a discreet veil over the night's festivities at this point.

The spell's effect on patrons and investigators lasts for 1D10 hours per person; those affected must succeed at a Hard **CON** roll or fall unconscious at the end of this duration, losing 1D4 magic points in the process. They also automatically lose 1D3 Sanity points due to the attendant feeling of helplessness that comes from falling under the spell's influence.

Investigators who have not been affected may, of course, choose to go at any time, though they must bodily carry their afflicted friends away with them if they wish to leave as a group. Even taken from the Weiße Maus, the spell continues to exert its effects for the indicated amount of time, though Berber gains no benefit from it (**Undying Revelry**, page 199).

Albin Grau is among those not affected, but he does not leave. He is fascinated by the spectacle before him; he does not tell anyone else at this moment, but he recognizes a magical working when he sees one. If they remained unaffected, one or more of the investigators may also realize what they have just witnessed if they succeed with a **Cthulhu Mythos** or **Occult** roll.

There is one other player in this scene, though he remains out of sight. Still dressed in his Roman costume, Anita's husband, Henri Châtin-Hofmann, watches smiling from backstage. This working, Unending Revelry, is his doing, and he is reaping the rewards. Every dancer that collapses inside the theater transfers 1D4 magic points to his wife and, as the night wears on, she waxes greatly in power, turning ever more into a living battery of magical energy. Thanks to his readings of pamphlets published by the Fraternitas Saturni (**Interviewing Berber**, page 158), Châtin-Hofmann knows that he can eventually tap into that power by sacrificing his wife in a magical ritual. What that ritual may be, he doesn't yet know, but he soon enough receives a suggestion from a certain Albin Grau.

Keeper note: the text of *Astarte* is nearby (page 156)

Anita Berber's performance of "Astarte"

GRAU'S REQUEST

The next morning, August 8, is a Saturday—a tender mercy for those who fell under Henri and Anita's spell. Those who did so awaken with a crushing hangover.

Any investigators who passed the night in the Weiße Maus due to ensorcellment, and who weren't carried out by friends, should make a **Luck** roll: if successful, they wake up in their own beds at home having somehow stumbled back there at some point. Failing the roll means the investigator wakes up somewhere else: in a heap of trash in a back-alley, at a church hostel, in one of the rooms of an upscale whorehouse, under a bush in the Tiergarten—be creative! A fumbled Luck roll means the investigator made enough trouble to get themselves thrown into the drunk tank at the Criminal Court complex (**The Tiergarten**, page 27) and must call upon fellow investigators or a contact to bail them out at a cost of 200 marks. Whatever the case, eventually everyone makes it home.

It is now 11:30 am. The sun shines too brightly; the leaves of every tree droop, as if panting. It promises to be a scorcher. Suddenly the phone rings. But whose phone? The Keeper should use their best discretion based on the circumstances in which the investigators found themselves at the Weiße Maus and the nature of their discussion with Grau prior to the show's start, for the man on the other end of the line is indeed Albin Grau. He wishes to talk about what happened the night before.

First, he asks the investigator for their opinion of what might have occurred. He listens attentively regardless of the answer; if the investigator suggests that it was some sort of magical working, he agrees enthusiastically; otherwise, he shares that theory with them.

"*Here is what I believe: something supernatural happened last night. Of this I have no doubt. Whether or not it was intentional is what I would like to discover. However, my interest in esoteric matters is well known. If there was an act of will behind last night's events, I may expose my intentions before the investigation can properly begin. And so we come to the purpose of my call: I wonder if whether you and your friends might attempt to… befriend Frau Berber? I realize it is quite a lot to ask…*"

Grau wants a detailed report on Anita Berber and her husband: their habits, their interests, how they spend their days and nights. He cannot offer financial compensation—remind the players that Grau is supremely well-connected, and that having him owe them a favor may come in handy. (As indeed it will over the course of this scenario.)

If the investigators agree, Grau sets up a meeting via an intermediary at the Hotel Excelsior, Châtin-Hofmann and Berber's current residence, in one hour's time (**Interviewing Berber**, following). The investigators are free to come up with their own cover story; otherwise, Grau makes the appointment under the pretense that they are fans of Berber's who simply wish to meet her and get her autograph.

"*See if you can find out whether she has any interest in the occult or magical practices while you're there,*" he says before hanging up. "*Anything you can turn up may be of use, so keep your eyes and ears open.*"

If the investigators turn Grau down, all is not lost: they are bound to encounter Châtin-Hofmann and Berber the next time they go out, invited by a contact or some other friend to attend a piano recital at the **Clärchens Ballhaus** (page 160).

INTERVIEWING BERBER

Investigators who agree to help Grau should follow his directions and present themselves at the Hotel Excelsior, across from Anhalter Station near the always-bustling Potsdamer Platz, shortly after noon.

The grandest hotel in Europe, the Excelsior boasts restaurant facilities sufficient to feed 15,000 patrons a day. The main lobby is an expansive, carpeted labyrinth of stout columns and overstuffed armchairs, many occupied by gruff-looking men smoking cigars and perusing the papers.

The front desk expects the investigators, and the receptionist directs them to Room 333 with an audible sniff—it is obvious the staff think little of Frau Berber. A ride in the brass-and-walnut elevator conveys the investigators to the third floor, where they find the happy couple's room. The door is answered seconds after their knock. It is Henri Châtin-Hofmann, still dressed in his robe and slippers. "*Ah, hello,*" he says in English. "*Please…*" He gestures for the investigators to enter.

Within, they find Anita Berber breakfasting on her preferred "morning elixir": a bowl of chloroform and ether into which she dips the petals of a white rose one at a time. She sits, cross-legged and naked, at a small table near the open balcony window, a warm breeze rustling the curtains. She is still wearing her stage makeup from last night, which by now is terrifically smudged and smeared. As she bites daintily into a frozen rose petal, she invites the investigators to have a seat anywhere they wish. This is easier said than done: the room is a disaster area. Clothes and costumes lie scattered across the floor. The bedclothes are heaped in a drooping pile at the foot of the bed. Countless cigarette butts spill out of filthy ashtrays. Empty liquor bottles are constantly underfoot and taking up most of every available surface.

Berber recognizes investigators whom she met during the events of **The Devil Eats Flies**, though her degree of recognition depends on the length of interaction she had with them at the Red Mill Cabaret—anything from a vague recollection to a happy reunion. She also remembers those investigators from the night before who directly engaged her in their debaucheries or who made notable spectacles of themselves.

If Berber does recall one or more of the investigators, then any interaction with her is made considerably easier: all social skill rolls are made with a bonus die. Her general attitude is altogether more accommodating, although she is just as susceptible as ever to wild mood swings, as the investigators soon discover.

If asked about her chimp, she relates the sad tale of how one night she felt its leathery grip around her neck slacken and turn cold. "*The poor creature had smothered under my wraps,*" she says with a melancholy air, then lets fly with her tinkling laugh and bites into another frozen rose petal.

Châtin-Hofmann, for his part, allows Berber to remain the center of attention. Stretched out across the hotel bed, he picks at the cold remains of a half-eaten Wiener schnitzel. Despite looking slightly despondent (and hungry), he is happy to speak glowingly of his wife's remarkable talents. If interviewed, he is guarded about his own past, admitting only that he is from Baltimore and that his father didn't approve of his dancing.

Keeper note: bear in mind Châtin-Hofmann's atrocious **Language (German)** skill; if no one speaks English, he can contribute only snippets of pidgin praise.

Investigators snooping around for evidence of occult or sorcerous material won't find much. Berber may be many things, but she is no sorceress. This should become clear in fairly short order through the successful use of a **Psychology** roll, as described below or, alternatively, use of the **Occult** skill to probe her understanding of esoteric matters.

A successful **Spot Hidden** roll notes books lying on the nightstand next to the bed on the topics of Babylonian and Egyptian mythology. If an investigator shows an interest in the books, Berber brightens, happily chattering away about the moon goddess Astarte, the fertility rites of her worshippers, and the temple-prostitutes of her cult. It seems to be mostly a pose on her part, although a successful **Psychology** roll discerns that she is genuinely interested in the subject, albeit on a superficial, non-academic level.

Another successful **Spot Hidden** roll turns up, buried among the liquor bottles and dirty clothes on the floor, a few scattered pamphlets entitled *Magische Briefe* (Magical Letters) penned by Gregor Gregorius. An address is given on the back of each pamphlet. The topics of the pamphlets (and their dates of publication) are: "Mirror- and Crystal-Magic" (May 15, 1925), "Splitting Magic" (October 16, 1925), and "Satanic Magic" (February 25, 1926).

If Berber is asked about the pamphlets, she laughs and says it's probably something one of their guests left lying around—a successful **Psychology** roll confirms she holds little if any interest in the pamphlets. Châtin-Hofmann also professes ignorance, but a separate successful **Psychology** roll exposes his deception. While he will under no circumstances admit in Berber's presence that he knows anything about the pamphlets, he will likewise not let them out of his sight once they've been discovered, jealously guarding them until the investigators leave. "*If they were indeed left here by a friend, he will no doubt want them back!*" is the excuse for his protectiveness.

Investigators who somehow manage to spirit the pamphlets away with a **Sleight of Hand** roll may find their contents useful later in the scenario—see also **At the Occult Bookshop Inveha**, page 175, for another opportunity to acquire copies of the Magical Letters in question. The books' utility as (non-Mythos) manuscripts is detailed in **Tomes and Spells** (pages 198-199).

Not long after the investigators arrive, the effects of Berber's breakfast start to take hold. She gets giggly and flirty, sitting on the lap of the shyest, most retiring investigator, tickling their nose. Châtin-Hofmann intervenes, "Liebchen, *come.* Wir mussen, *uh, bath you, eh?*" He takes her hand and guides her into the capacious white-tiled bathroom, and the sound of running water in the tub is soon heard, along with more giggles from Berber. Soon, Châtin-Hofmann re-emerges briefly, "*My apologies,*" he says in English. "*She shouldn't bathe unattended when she's like this. Please, take some…*"

He roots through a pile of detritus on the hall table and finds some half-crumpled flyers: he will be giving a piano exhibition that evening at the **Clärchens Ballhaus** (see following) on Auguststraße. "*Love to see you all there!*" he says with a strange gleam in his eye. He then disappears into the bathroom, closing the door behind him (and taking the Magical Letters with him if they were pointed out by the investigators earlier).

Reporting Back

If the investigators wish to contact Albin Grau to report on their interview, he is most interested in the Magical Letters. "*I know the author well,*" he says. "*Perhaps he remembers selling the pamphlets to Henri or Anita, if they are indeed the owners. I'll give him a call. I assume you are planning on attending this piano recital tonight?*"

If the investigators invite Grau to the piano recital, he politely demurs. "*I wish to maintain my anonymity in this matter for now.*"

THE CLÄRCHENS BALLHAUS

Located a few blocks north of the Alex in the heart of the Jewish Scheuenviertel (**The Doll Maker's Shop**, page 172), "Clara's Ballroom" inhabits an unassuming gray stone building set back from Auguststraße. The patio outside is crowded with café tables; over the entrance hangs a hand-painted sign (the work of Otto Dix) depicting a dancing couple and announcing the venue's name. Despite the event's late hour (8 pm), the heat of the day still hangs heavy in the gathering twilight.

Entering via a separate doorway to the right of the Ballhaus' main entrance, the investigators climb a creaking, angular stairway that leads to the famous *Spiegelsaal* (Mirror Room), where they find a grand piano sitting roughly in the center of the parquet dance floor. Two rows of mismatched chairs are arranged in a semi-circle around the instrument, where about a dozen folk sit or mingle; all are fanning themselves, for the heat in the ballroom is even more oppressive than outside.

The appointed time for the recital comes and goes. Some of the guests grow restless in the stuffy, hot room; a couple get up and leave, then a few more. Soon, only the investigators are left in the hall.

At 8:25 pm, shortly after the last of the audience leaves—but, perhaps, just before the investigators follow suit—

Châtin-Hofmann and Berber arrive. He is wearing evening clothes and sweating profusely. She is dressed in her black "Morphine" dress, accessorized with a monocle and a scowl.

Châtin-Hofmann attempts to guide Berber to her chair, but she imperiously bats him away. Without missing a beat or betraying any embarrassment, he proceeds to the piano, "Damen und Herren, danke schön für… *coming out this…* Abend." He clears his throat and takes a seat at the piano. It is utterly silent. The investigators, shifting in their chairs, can see their (no-doubt) uncomfortable, sweaty faces reflected in the massive mirrors that fill the upper three-quarters of the walls.

And then, Châtin-Hofmann begins to play. His chosen piece is Liszt's *Totentanz* (Dance of the Dead), a pounding, dynamic piece whose melody paraphrases the medieval Gregorian chant *Dies Irae* (Day of Judgment). The music explodes from the piano and fills the small ballroom; the pianist definitely has some chops.

As the 16-minute composition plays out, the investigators catch glimpses of themselves and Berber in the mirror. They notice something strange: everyone looks somehow different in the mirror's reflection. Berber's face looks much harsher and more haggard, far older than her 27 years. Her theatrical makeup looks like an artificial mask, her lips pinched and severe. Even more jarringly, her black "Morphine" dress is a deep crimson, like the color of viscera.

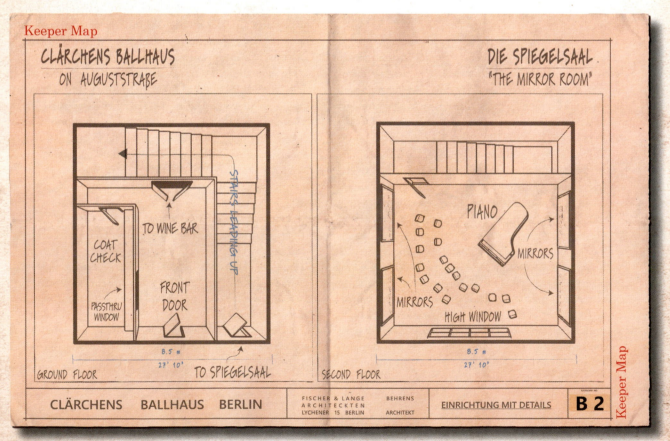

The investigators all look different as well. Go around the table and encourage each player to (briefly) describe what their investigator sees in the mirror. What ugly truths or repressed secrets are reflected in the unflinching objectivity of the enchanted mirror? Have their clothes changed at all? Their apparent age? Perhaps even their gender? These jarring visions threaten the investigators' mental well-being, provoking a **Sanity** roll (0/1 loss for seeing their inner selves reflected in the mirror).

The performance ends. As the final notes die away, the investigators suddenly realize that, in the blink of an eye, they have taken on the bizarre form of their reflections. Furthermore, Châtin-Hofmann and Berber are nowhere to be seen. The temperature in the room has fallen significantly, such that it now feels chilly rather than stifling. Call for another **Sanity** roll (1/1D4 loss).

The investigators further note that the door to the Mirror Room has been closed. The high windows now admit a milky, weak daylight rather than showing the night sky. Clambering up to look outside requires a successful **Climb** roll; the view through the windows is disturbing (see **Totentanz**, following, for details of what the investigator sees, and the attendant potential Sanity loss).

Keeper note: there is one way to immediately undo the effects of this enchantment: play *Totentanz* backward in its entirety. As Châtin-Hofmann did not use sheet music, it would have to be played from memory. An **Art/Craft (Piano)** roll may be attempted, but anything short of an Extreme success leaves the investigators stranded where they are. Smashing the mirrors or the piano does nothing but make a big mess. If the piece is successfully played backward, the story proceeds to **Home Again, Home Again** (page 163). The investigators have avoided potentially major Sanity losses, but at the cost of missing some valuable clues that become useful later in the scenario.

If the investigators decide to camp out in the room, they find the light coming in through the windows never changes. Night never comes. Soon they grow hungry. There's nothing for it but to venture outside…

TOTENTANZ

Heading back down the creaking stairway, the investigators emerge onto the café patio to find it utterly deserted. Bits of paper rubbish blow across the space in a stiff, steady wind, but there are otherwise no signs of life or movement. The silence is all pervasive and overwhelming.

The trees and vegetation around the square are all dead and lifeless, with one exception: here and there, white rose bushes bloom. The Clärchens Ballhaus sign is pitted and faded, hanging precariously on its mounting. The Clärchens building itself is streaked with age and neglect, with large chunks of stone chipped away from its façade.

Emerging onto Auguststraße, the scene is much the same. Under the gray, sunless sky, the street stretches off into illimitable, deserted dullness. There is no traffic, motorized or pedestrian. No voices call out, no birds sing. There is a palpable sense of complete isolation. Here and there, monumental, neo-Classical statues stand on plinths lining the street; nude, cold marble forms with featureless faces. Off to the west, a domed building of truly epic proportions rises up amidst the gloom, perhaps a half-mile (800 m) distant. Experiencing this unearthly vision calls for a **Sanity** roll (0/1D2 loss).

Which way do the investigators go? Whatever method of conveyance they used to get to the Ballhaus (tram, cab, bus, or private car) is no longer present, so they must walk. As they tromp on, they begin to hear a strange, rhythmic sound, like a thousand hinges creaking. Gradually they become aware that every window of every building on the block is opening and closing in unison, in a steady rhythm that matches their respiration, provoking a **Sanity** roll (0/1D4 loss). No sooner has the phenomenon been observed than it stops. The silence descends again. But wait—what was that?

Call for **Listen** rolls: those who succeed hear footfalls, like bare feet on cobblestones. Looking around, there is nothing to be seen. Now call for **Spot Hidden** rolls to note flashes of movement behind a window—there!—and over there in that alleyway! Perhaps the investigators aren't quite so alone after all!

The Rabisu Appear

A door creaks open on the front of a townhouse across the street. It is dark within, but the investigators can just make out a man-like shape lurking in the shadows, standing stock still in the doorway, as if watching the investigators pass. Calling out brings no response.

Now there can be no mistaking it, even for those who failed their rolls—this block is occupied. Moving with a shaky, unsteady gait, humanoid forms emerge from stairwells, deserted shop fronts, alleys, and squares. They wear black uniforms, silver skull pins glinting on their lapels, but they are not human. Their skin is pallid gray, their faces little more than gaping, lamprey-like maws ringed with jagged teeth. Lacking eyes and ears, they sniff at the air, catching the investigators' scent. They move forward, not speaking, not responding to calls. As they draw closer, their pace increases as they hone in on the smell of living flesh. At last, the assemblage begins to make a noise, but it is not speech. An unearthly chorus of guttural groans starts up, rumbling at first, then building to a cacophony of loud howls and screeches. And now they are running at the investigators, hands outstretched!

As the rabisu (**Creatures and Monsters**, page 195) pile out onto the street and start moving toward the investigators—a swarming, charging horde of monsters—call for one more **Sanity** roll (1/1D6 loss). No doubt, those investigators still in command of their faculties will wish to run for it, while those who have fallen insane also (ideally) flee in terror.

Run!

The pursuing horde forces the investigators inexorably toward the massive domed edifice to the west. They run along deserted streets flanked by monolithic, Futurist-style buildings, their gray glass windows and Brutalist façades looking down impassively. Skyways periodically connect upper stories across the boulevard. Is this a vision of Berlin's future? There is no time to seek shelter inside—the monstrous creatures are right on the investigators' heels!

Any investigator with a MOV of 7 or less is automatically caught by the horde and disappears as a knot of the creatures pause in their pursuit to tear the poor soul to pieces. Death comes mercifully quickly, with only a few seconds allowed for screaming. Investigators with MOV 8 must succeed at a Hard **DEX** roll; failure results in being caught and devoured. Investigators who try to stop and fight are similarly torn apart in short order. Those with MOV 9 are able to stay ahead of the pack of monsters.

Keeper note: those dying during this scene are not really dead; see **Home Again, Home Again** following.

The more fleet-footed investigators no doubt run, breath tearing at their lungs, as the howling, uniformed monstrosities bear down relentlessly on them from behind. All the while, the ludicrously outsized dome looms higher and higher ahead of them, like a Tower of Babel scraping the bottom of the gray, unmoving clouds overhead. A different sort of howling can be heard coming from that monumental structure, like a ceaseless wind pouring out of a bottomless pit, or the anguished cries of millions of voices.

Standing 10, 15, and 20 stories, the buildings surrounding the tower would be monumental in their own right if not dwarfed by the dome. From the sills and arches of these Futurist edifices hang limp, blood-red banners displaying strange symbols unknown to any of the investigators; they are reminiscent of Nordic runes, Hebrew letters, and Sumerian cuneiform, all at once.

A terrifying vision arises from the apex of the dome: a massive, tripartite woman's head with three faces, revolving slowly and glowing like the full moon. Even hundreds of feet up in the sky, it is a terrifying sight and calls for a **Sanity** roll (0/1D6 loss). The glow from the strange head grows in

Running from the rabisu

intensity until it blinds the investigators. The howling sounds of the pursuing rabisu, along with the roaring wind and screams, intensifies until it is all the investigators can hear. Then they feel the ground drop away beneath their feet—are they falling or rising?

As their vision begins to clear, they see central Berlin stretching out beneath them, its streets swarming with blind, uniformed rabisu. The massive dome and an equally huge public square lie just north of the Tiergarten, where the Königsplatz should be; the Siegesallee is also wider and grander as it bisects the park to the south, leading to another grand assemblage of structures. And where the Brandenburg Gate should stand, there is instead a strange complex of seven blue-tiled gates that look like a relic of ancient Mesopotamia.

Home Again, Home Again

With a jolt, the investigators wake up. It is November 10, 1928—the day before Armistice Day, the 10th anniversary of the Great War's end. Each investigator has had *that* dream again, although they can't quite shake the feeling that the preceding events were somewhere between a nightmare and a memory. It's been two years, yet they are still haunted by their encounter with Henri Châtin-Hofmann and Anita Berber. How much of that really happened? How much has been embellished in their dreams? It's impossible to say at this point.

Call for a **Sanity** roll; those who fail have passed the last two years in a sort of automatic state, their memories of the strange Shadow City somehow more real than their waking lives. As for those who succeed, their lives have gone on much as before, although tinged with a creeping sense of dread.

Conduct an investigator development phase now (*Call of Cthulhu Rulebook*, page 94), allowing those who wish it to engage in psychotherapy or self-help regimens to regain lost Sanity.

If any investigators suffered an indefinite insanity as a result of their time in the Shadow City, that character's player should decide whether they sought treatment in the intervening two years (**Treatment and Recovery from Insanity**, *Call of Cthulhu Rulebook*, pages 164–166). If they opt not to (whether out of concern for personal safety, career prospects, or simply a lack of desire to do so), remember to enforce the underlying insanity rules (*Call of Cthulhu Rulebook*, pages 158–159), as well as those for delusions and reality checks (*Call of Cthulhu Rulebook*, pages 162–163). Not only do delusions present many exciting opportunities for roleplaying in this scenario, but reality checks play a potentially much larger role in the next scenario (**Schreckfilm**, page 201), and players should become familiar with the mechanics now, if they are not already.

INTERLUDE: THE WOMAN WITH SEVEN MASKS (1928)

Oh she is the orchid
And the seven heads
Narrow wax heads
Opening, Tired grasping
Plotting, Tearing, Circling
And she is the orchid leafed through

—Anita Berber and Sebastian Droste,
"The Woman with Seven Masks" (translation by Merrill Cole)

Sadly, the investigators will never see Anita Berber again in her mortal form, for she dies on the day they rejoin the waking world. The following section details what happens "behind the scenes" while the investigators party at the Residenz-Casino, as well as providing the Keeper with an overview of the ongoing consequences of these actions and the stratagems of an unlikely ally. The remainder of the scenario proper picks up in **Restart: At The Resi** (page 168).

In 1926, after witnessing Anita Berber's "Astarte" routine at the Weiße Maus, Albin Grau begins to conceive his greatest working: an attempt to incarnate the goddess Berbelo upon the Earth, using Anita Berber's body as a vessel. He contacts her husband and enlists him, along with Gregor Gregorius. He also contacts a wizened old Jewish Kabbalist, Belshazzar the Doll Maker, to fashion a small company of *Manikinmenschen* (doll-people) that, animated by dark magic, disperse among Berlin's whorehouses, there to collect the necessary ingredients for use in the working.

In 1928, Grau, Gregorius, Châtin-Hofmann, and Belshazzar gather in the basement of the doll maker's shop and conduct the final stage of the Berbelo Working. Although the spell is a success, its outcome is completely unpredicted, summoning not the anticipated goddess Berbelo but instead the creature known as Abyzou.

BACKGROUND: BERBER'S DEATH...

On the afternoon of November 10, in a cold, antiseptic hotel room in Kreuzberg, Anita Berber dies a miserable death surrounded by icons of Christ and the Holy Virgin, brought in at her request. Her lips are crimson not with her trademark lipstick but from bloody spittle.

Henri Châtin-Hofmann sits in vigil beside her, a syringe in his hand. Inside the syringe is a strange substance, milky white shot through with streaks of red. As Anita's eyes roll back in her head, her husband mumbles words that sound like the rushing of a cold desert wind, while injecting the fluid into the cooling flesh of Anita's throat. He stands up, empty syringe in hand. Berber, in her final death throes, begins coughing violently. More blood foams on her lips, then a slimy, red-and-black mass the size and shape of a small mandrake root is expelled, dribbling out over her chin. Châtin-Hofmann scoops it up and places it in a jar, which he then drops into his coat pocket before summoning the nurse.

That night, his wife dead, he dances an engagement with his new partner, Helene Schelda, at the Weidenhof-Casino in the Friedrichstraße. Reviews note his manic energy but ascribe it to grief.

THE BORBORITE CULT

Albin Grau was only ever a half-hearted contributor to the Fraternitas Saturni. After the dissolution of the Pansophic Orient Lodge in the wake of the disastrous Weida Conference of 1925 (during which the question of whether or not to accept Aleister Crowley's religion of Thelema splintered the German occult community), Grau found himself drawn to a strange gnostic offshoot sect called the Borborites. Grau maintained cordial relations with Frater Gregorius and eventually joined the Fraternitas Saturni after its founding for expediency's sake.

The Borborite Cult was brought to Germany by Grau's friend and benefactor, Baron Grunau, who had himself first encountered it in the howling deserts of western Egypt while conducting archaeological digs around the Siwa Oasis. "Borborite" is derived from a Greek word meaning "mud" and is a reference to the cult's other name: "the Filthy Ones."

It is a name aptly applied, for the Borborites are libertine even by the standards of Gnosticism. Their despicable and depraved rites involve the consumption of blood and other bodily fluids, sex-magic rituals, and infant sacrifice. The cosmology of the Borborites maintains that there are three deities: the All-Father, Jesus Christ, and Berbelo, the androgynous bride of God who is the true mother of Christ.

Grau and Grunau use the magico-sexual rituals of the Fraternitas Saturni as a cover for their own rites, and as a recruiting ground. The Borborite cult in Berlin is tiny owing to their extreme caution when it comes to recruiting new members, who must be both despoiled and corrupted, yet simultaneously respectable and stable. The cult counts bankers, dilettantes, and artists among its members.

...and Rebirth

Berber is buried four days later at St. Thomas cemetery in Neukölln. By this time, Châtin-Hofmann's magical working, developed through a combination of Saturnian sex magic and ancient Egypto-Babylonian rites, has taken effect.

Before departing Berlin in 1926, Châtin-Hofmann—prompted by Grau—left instructions with a doll maker in the Scheuenviertel. Using a large chunk of Anita's drug money, supplemented by funding from Gregorius, he commissioned a series of dolls (actually life-sized *manikins* made of ceramics and real human hair) to be executed to the doll maker's highest standard. One of these *manikins* was to be reserved for later use. The others, at Châtin-Hofmann's instruction, were slowly but surely animated by the doll maker through an ancient Kabbalistic rite and sent out into the world, the magic of their creation giving them the appearance of living, breathing men and women.

For two years now, these *manikins* have worked the streets, brothels, and private backrooms of Berlin's underworld, stealing life essence from their clients. From this great battery of magical power, Châtin-Hofmann, upon returning to Berlin a week ago, prepared a serum, a derivative of the "*gestohlener Blitz*" ("stolen lightning") elixir used to animate the *manikins*. When the serum was injected into Berber at the moment of her death, it caused her to expel a small portion of her life essence, a living manifestation, like an unholy newborn.

Between the hospital and his dance engagement, Châtin-Hofmann paid a visit to the doll maker. There, in the old man's basement, with Grau and Gregorius in attendance, the homunculus-fragment of Anita Berber was placed into the chest of the final *manikin*, the *gestohlener Blitz* elixir was poured into its chest cavity, and ancient rites were performed by the unwitting quartet. Thus, Abyzou was incarnated, the Great Aeon and Triple-Androgynous Name who is the Mother of Abominations.

The sight of a darkly radiant goddess rising from the table drives the men mad in different ways. Châtin-Hofmann, an amateur sorcerer completely out of his depth, suffers hysterical amnesia and flees from the tumbledown shop. Grau and Gregorius, the two seasoned occultists, fall to their knees in open worship of the new goddess. While Grau thinks his plans have been fulfilled, he soon finds out how wrong he is (see **The Occult-Bookshop Inveha**, page 175). As for Belshazzar the Doll Maker, his fate is detailed in **The Doll Maker's Shop** (page 172).

And what of Abyzou? She emerges from the basement and heads off into the chill evening, a howling wind blowing wisps of foul miasma after her…

"THE CENTER CANNOT HOLD…"

Although there is no timeline in this scenario *per se*, the Keeper should keep track of the days that pass over the course of the investigation. Abyzou's corrupting influence (**Abyzou's Empire**, page 183), boosted by the howling wind that bears her pestilence across the city, exerts a noticeable effect within a week of her arrival, upon both the citizens of Berlin and the monstrosities that burst from the corpses of those who perish from their Bacchanalian exertions, brought into being by the Mother of Abominations.

- **Days 1–3 (November 10–12):** public drunkenness, exhibitionism, and swarms of flies. Funeral processions with tiny, infant-sized caskets. Police, flooded with calls for help, have their hands full 24 hours a day.
- **Days 4–5 (November 13–14):** brawls, public nudity, swarms of hissing cockroaches, and flocks of owls nesting everywhere. Quarantine markings on nearly every residence. Reports in the papers indicate that the media has been infiltrated (**Handout: Dances 1**). Police are hard-pressed to maintain order, and many have fallen under Abyzou's sway.

THE WIND

With Abyzou's arrival comes a relentless wind. Play this up as much as possible—the wind is as much a character in this scenario as any of the other allies and antagonists. Even while indoors, the wind reminds the investigators of its existence, rattling windows and blowing chill drafts through homes and businesses.

The foul miasmatic mist that accompanies the wind is most prominent at night, blowing up and down Berlin's broad boulevards, concealing Abyzou's loathsome fog-spawn. Use the mist to create a sense of eerie disconnection for investigators making their way around the city after sunset, as well as a real sense of danger if Abyzou targets them (**Abyzou's Reach**, page 187).

Below: Calendar for November, 1928

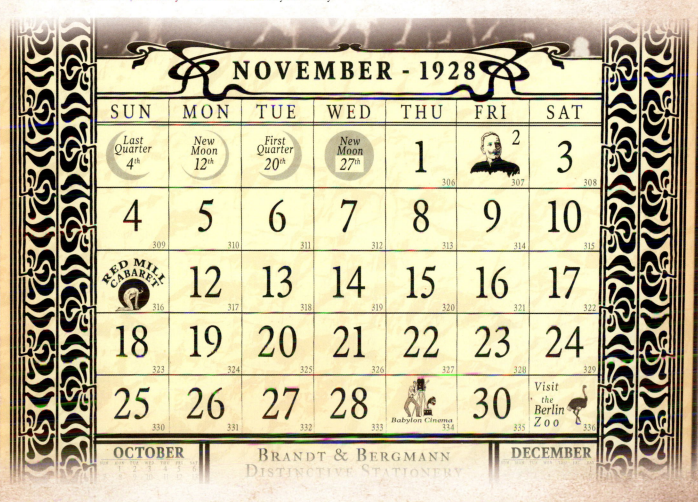

- **Days 6–7 (November 15–17):** by this point, the uptick in child deaths and illnesses has become noticeable and is reported on in the papers (**Handout: Dances 2**). Riots and street battles, public sex acts, hordes of rats, and packs of roving wild dogs. A minority of Kripo and Sipo units (**Beinls and Bulls**, page 37) still fight the good fight but are little better than vigilantes at this point, receiving no guidance or support from the thoroughly corrupted upper echelons.
- **Week Two and beyond:** parades of Bacchanalian revelers, drunk and fornicating, tearing apart the weak and helpless, who are unable to outrun them. Massive blood-sucking leeches oozing down the main boulevards. Men and women with the heads of dogs, bulls, and lions. Bodies of children and infants being dumped into mass graves. By this point, those police and jurists who haven't been corrupted by Abyzou's influence are at their wits' end and unable to cope with the flood of crime and strange stories—the rule of law has completely broken down.

The Culling of the Young

The arrival of Abyzou on Earth, unnatural and out of place, has a catastrophic effect. The winds, already cold and steady, now increase in intensity and do not let up; they blow and blow, 24 hours a day, seven days a week. The effect is to put the whole city on edge and leave tempers close to the breaking point. What's more, the winds blow a strange fog through the streets. Moving in great, cottony, billowing puffs, the mist is likely to remind more than a few veterans of poison gas. It is an apt comparison.

After Abyzou's arrival on the anniversary eve of the war's end, obstetricians at the city's hospitals start to report an increase in miscarriages. Priests and doctors are summoned to home after home, tending to panicked parents of young children suddenly fallen gravely ill. And always the wind blows and the fog creeps in through cracks in windows and doorways.

Keeper note: the mist is not actually causing the deaths, which are in fact caused by insubstantial creatures known as fog-spawn—see **Creatures and Monsters,** page 196, for more details. Though the fog-spawn may target anyone, they primarily go after the young. Do any of the investigators have a significant person who is vulnerable? Younger siblings, children of their own perhaps? Wives or sisters heavy with child? All may suffer at the hands of this new evil wind. Use the threat of death of a loved one as leverage and to increase tension—there is a palpable sense of danger that any night may be their last. Ultimately, the death of a child or infant closely related to one or more of the investigators should be contemplated only if the investigators tarry too long in dealing with Abyzou's threat.

Erma Kore: Telephone-Girl

"I am the daughter of Fortitude, and ravished every hour from my youth. For behold I am Understanding, and science dwelleth in me; and the heavens oppress me. They cover and desire me with infinite appetite; for none that are earthly have embraced me, for I am shadowed with the Circle of the Stars and covered with the morning clouds…. I am deflowered, yet a virgin; I sanctify and am not sanctified…. I am a harlot for such as ravish me, and a virgin with such as know me not."

—Excerpt from a letter received by Sir Edward Kelley and Dr. John Dee, May 23, 1587

Three blocks west of Potsdamer Platz, along a quiet stretch of Viktoria Straße, is a former ambassador's house, now remodeled into high-end apartments. One of these apartments, owned by Baron Grunau, is the residence of a 17-year-old "girl" (actually a *manikin*) called Erma Kore.

Baron Grunau, in addition to running a Telephone-Girl agency out of his Viktoria Straße apartments, is also a patron of the arts and something of an amateur archaeologist. It was on a dig at the Siwa Oasis in Egypt some 20 years ago that he discovered a set of moldering papyri, themselves copies of ancient clay tablets, which contained blasphemous rituals for incarnating a goddess upon the Earth.

Handout: Dances 1

And Why Not?
Editorial

Berliners have been seen engaging in some strange behaviors lately—and why not? Public drunkenness is on the rise over the last week, but who doesn't like a tipple from time to time? Exotic powders and concoctions are finding their way up our noses and into our veins, and it feels good! As the cold of winter closes in around us, we should all embrace and kiss and grind and tear into each other. It is time to finally cast off the last vestiges of Wilhemite-Prussian-Lutheran moralism. And why not?

Steuerzahler und

Grunau, in his capacity as a movie-lover, goes way back with Herr Albin Grau. It was mostly Grunau's money that funded Grau's Prana Films, and the two remain close to this day.

Erma Kore knows all of this. Like her filmic alter ego, Marlene Dietrich, she is wise and world-weary beyond her years, and she listens well to conversations that filter up from the downstairs parlor or that take place on telephone party lines. She knows about the Berbelo Working. She knows who funneled knowledge of the ritual and its methods to that naïve dancer-magician. She also knows of the "doll-people" that roam the streets of the city in great numbers (**… and Rebirth**, page 164), and that she is one of them. And she wishes to share all this information with the investigators.

Keeper note: although Grau's use of the rituals was sanctioned, encouraged, and secretly bankrolled by Grunau, the Baron was absent from the final working due to pressing business matters elsewhere—a narrow escape indeed.

It is Erma who phones the investigators' table at the Residenz-Casino—she is seated at a table set farther back in the recesses of the club, well out of sight—and who sneaks a small porcelain doll full of the *gestohlener Blitz* elixir into the tube system (see **Restart: At the Resi**, page 168, for these incidents).

Through her extensive network of clients (many of whom are also members of Berlin's occult underground), she keeps tabs on the investigators' progress. Although she initially she contacts them only via telephone, when the time is right she summons them for an eerie face-to-face interview (**Meeting Erma**, page 181).

Erma is the Keeper's secret weapon in this scenario. She is on hand to provide clues but cannot say too much—at least, not until they all meet in person—for fear of being overheard by unsympathetic ears on the telephone party line. Use her phone calls sparingly, particularly when the investigators are struggling; if they are racing along under their own steam, consider not using Erma at all until their meeting. Use the following cryptic clues for her to communicate over the phone.

- "The memory of Berber lives on."
- "Remember your old friend Grau."
- "The goddess of the moon is alive and well in Berlin."
- "Walter Andrae is a good man to know."
- "It's always a good time at the Hundegustav."

Handout: Dances 2

Plague in the City!

For the past week, Berlin has been bedeviled by unseasonable winds and blowing fog. As if carried on this foul miasma, a new epidemic is sweeping our neighborhoods. Tragically, it seems to be hitting our children and infants the hardest. Odds are that if you have not personally suffered a visitation in your own household, dear reader, you know someone who has.

Doctors at the Charité and other hospitals around the city have reported a distinct rise in infant mortality and serious illnesses among Berlin's youth. Symptoms so far have yet to manifest a distinct pattern: some suffer from fever, others from fits, still others from crippling intestinal complaints.

When contacted for comment, government hygiene and sanitation officials assured us that they are working as quickly as science allows in ascertaining and eliminating the source of the maladies.

RESTART: AT THE RESI

It is autumn in Berlin. The weather outside is clear but chilly, with periodic gusts of wind rattling the windows and sending unguarded hats flying. It is November 10, the same day as Berber's death.

ERMA'S CONNECTION

How does Erma Kore come to rely on the investigators for help in undoing the Berbelo plot? The investigators are sure to wonder that themselves.

Erma is a quietly mysterious figure. Her role in the scenario is to impress a sense of uncanny unease on the investigators, starting with the bizarre, unwholesome nature of her vocation. Play up the mystery of how she found out about them, but be ready with an answer, all the same.

If one or more of the investigators took part in **The Devil Eats Flies**, they will note an unmistakable resemblance between little Erma and the handsome assassin Erwin Kern, whom they encountered during the **Incident at Romanisches Square** (page 106) and possibly later in the scenario. Kern was the ringleader of the plot to assassinate Walther Rathenau and was ultimately caught and gunned down a month after the murder, unless the investigators killed him themselves during the scenario.

Erma is not a literal reincarnation of Kern, although her facial features were modeled from his (**The Doll Maker's Shop,** page 172); however, unlike Kern, she is a pitiable figure.

If the investigators did indeed encounter Kern in the past, Erma, due to the sympathetic magic inherent in the nature of her creation, has instinctively felt the urge to get in touch with these investigators, knowing that they could help her. Even *she* is at a loss to explain why this should be so.

If this scenario is being run as a one-off, or if no investigators present participated in **The Devil Eats Flies**, then Erma has heard of them while eavesdropping on Albin Grau discussing their unusual experiences at the Weiße Maus and the Clärchens Ballhaus two years ago. Realizing that they passed over to the Shadow City, domain of Abyzou, she sees in a flash that these are people with the necessary experience to help her cause.

The investigators are passing the time in their usual fashion. A small article in the back pages of the paper today (**Handout: Dances 3**), wedged in between large ads for theatrical revues with names like *Take It Off!*, *Houses of Love*, and *Goddammit—1,000 Naked Women!*, notes the return of Anita Berber, Berlin's own original naked dancer, to the city, which perhaps gives the investigators some pause as they no doubt recall their last interaction with her two years ago.

But such melancholy considerations are swiftly swept aside, for tonight the group has plans to meet up for drinks and entertainment at the Residenz-Casino, more commonly called simply "the Resi." Although it opened only last year, the Resi is already recognized as one of Berlin's premiere pleasure palaces, second only to **Haus Vaterland** (page 48).

The investigators arrive at the Blumenstraße address just south of Alexanderplatz around 10 pm. The wind is now blowing steadily and heavily, sending icy tendrils between coat buttons and up stockinged legs.

The building itself doesn't look terribly promising, being another of Berlin's *fin-de-siècle* Neo-Baroque excesses, but upon hustling in out of the cold night the investigators are struck by a surprisingly modern tableau: a multi-tiered club that gradually descends in stages toward a parquet dance floor with nearly 100 tables spread across all levels, each one surmounted by a small rotating mirror ball. Two orchestras, one all-male, the other all-female (both consisting entirely of remarkably attractive folk hired more for their looks than any actual musical talent) play foxtrots and American jazz at either end of the club; the mirror balls rotate and split open in time to the music. Elsewhere, small fountains throw lighted streams of colored water in graceful arcs and columns.

Craning their necks, the investigators see that the ceiling, too, is multi-tiered, the centerpiece being a motorized glass dome painted with Japanese-style cranes and orchids. The whole space is filled with laughing, happy people.

A *maître d'* appears and, after checking hats and coats, escorts the party to the tier just above dance-floor level, where they are seated at a table bearing a large placard, mounted just below the mirror ball and showing the number 58. From this vantage point, they have a good view of not only the dance floor but of most of the other tables and three of its four bars. Like every other table in this part of the club, this one features its own telephone mounted on the pole that holds up the spinning mirror ball, as well as a woven basket situated under what looks like a Rohrpost tube (**Media and Communication**, page 26). The phone may be used to call any other table in the club and initiate a conversation.

A waiter comes by with food and drink menus as well as a "gift menu"—this contains 135 little *tchotchkes* (small trinkets) that can be purchased and sent anonymously to any of the other numbered tables in the room via its system of pneumatic tubes.

The food on offer here is heavy and very Prussian: roasted pig knuckles on a bed of sauerkraut, and other dishes of a similar ilk. The drinks menu, however, is extensive, with a variety of beers, wines, liqueurs, and cocktails.

After drink orders are placed, the investigators settle in. Looking around, they note that there are approximately five women for every man in the club. What's more, most of these women look thoroughly middle-class—hardly the sort of ladies one would normally expect to see at a club this close to the Alex. Nothing is amiss; this is simply the kind of crowd the Resi draws most evenings. Allow whatever level of flirting, fun, and general revelry the investigators desire. They may place calls or send gifts to other tables, dance, drink and eat, or explore the club as they see fit before Erma Kore decides to call them.

In addition to the main dance floor area, which accommodates up to 1,000 dancers at a time, those poking around find two other sections of the club: the Carousel and Shooting Gallery, and the Wine Cellar. The latter is precisely what it says: a basement room with a few booths and tables where patrons may sample any of the Resi's many fine Rhinish wines, plus vintages imported from Austria, France, and Italy. The room is quite different in tone from the rest of the club, being quiet and private—a fine place to conduct clandestine meetings. Only half the tables down here have phones.

The Carousel and Shooting Gallery is a large room modeled on Luna Park in the Grunewald. Investigators who grew up in Berlin may have fond childhood memories of summer days spent at the now-crumbling water park, and this room does its best to recreate those memories in miniature. Drunken, giggling revelers try their skill at various small, water-powered shooting galleries. Others whoop and holler on the undersized eight-horse carousel that rotates gaily in the center of the space.

Ring Ring!

Once the players seem to have had their fill of frivolity, move the narrative forward. It's getting late—past 2 am—and the party is losing a bit of steam. Perhaps the investigators are starting to think of going home, or at least going somewhere a little less boisterous. Everyone has gathered back at Table #58 to check in and see how everyone else is doing. It's that uncomfortable part of the evening where no one wants to be the first to suggest going home, but everyone would very much like to do so.

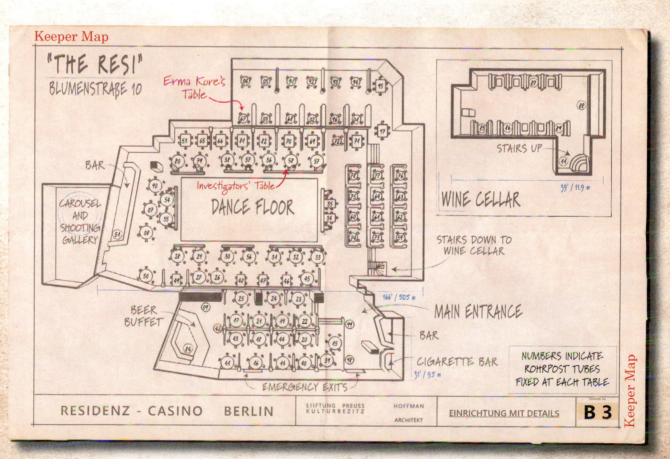

Suddenly, the table phone rings. Who picks it up? Answering, the voice on the other end sounds like no other this evening. There is no giggling, no clumsy drunken flirtation. Just a voice—that of a girl, saying, "She is coming. The Mother of Abominations. She brings death on black wings. All will suffer, but the young will suffer the most." The phone clicks off.

No sooner has this happened than the pneumatic tube roars to life and a small packet drops into the hanging net at the investigators' table. The packet opened, the investigators find a small, porcelain baby doll inside. It feels heavy, like its hollow interior is filled with something.

If the head or torso is smashed open, the investigators discover (to their disgust) that the doll is filled with a swirling mixture of a crimson and milky off-white substance that smells like congealed milk and looks like bloody pus— call for a Sanity roll (0/1 loss). If the investigator cracking the doll open fails a **Luck** roll, some of the substance splashes on their hand, causing 1 point of damage and instantly raising angry welts on their skin.

Examining the Doll

Examining the doll notes a maker's symbol just below the hairline at the nape of the neck (**Handout: Dances 4**). Investigators with **Language (Hebrew)** or those succeeding at a Hard **Know** roll recognize the symbols immediately: they spell the word *emet*, meaning "truth." Jewish investigators making a subsequent successful **History** or **Occult** roll recall that this is the word supposedly written on the forehead of the legendary Golem of Prague—non-Jewish investigators may make this roll as well, but they require a Hard success to recall such a fact.

If the Resi staff is alerted to this bizarre gift, they apologize abjectly, comping the investigators' bill for the evening. They are at quite a loss to explain how this could have happened; the doll isn't even on the gift menu, and none of the Resi's staff admit to sending it. If the investigators wish to trace the location of the doll's manufacturer, see **The Doll Maker's Shop**, page 172.

Examining the doll

DEAD ENDS

After their visit to the Resi and Erma's unnerving phone call and gift, the investigators may wish to seek out some of their old comrades from their visit to the Weiße Maus.

Contacting Grau

Albin Grau, their old occultist friend, is listed (number and address) in the telephone directory, but calls to his residence go unanswered. A personal visit finds no one home, his nosy landlady telling investigators that she hasn't seen Herr Grau for some days.

Visiting Berber

Investigators may wish to seek out Berber at her hospital bedside in Kreuzberg. Of course, by the time they read the notice in the paper (**Handout: Dances 3**), she is already dead.

Her body is held in the hospital morgue for four days prior to burial (a pauper's grave at St. Thomas Cemetery in Neukölln). Investigators with an occupation in the medical or police field, or those with **Credit Rating** 50% or higher, may arrange a viewing of the body.

What they find on the cold slab is a ravaged specimen of humanity: underweight, with sunken eyes and cheeks, looking much older than her 29 years. Track marks cover her arms. Flecks of blood still stain her lips and chin. A successful **Medicine** or **Science (Forensics)** roll notes that she also has a needle wound on her throat that appears relatively recent, although probably inflicted prior to death.

Discussions with the charge nurse or doctor on duty on the day of her death indicate she wasn't administered anything via her neck. Cause of death is listed as consumption (tuberculosis).

Handout: Dances 3

Handout: Dances 4

Berber back in Berlin!

Notorious dancer and actress Anita Berber, once called "the Dresden Madonna" but now largely forgotten in this city, has at last made her way back to Berlin, where she began her career nearly ten years ago.

For some time now, Berber has been traveling abroad with her husband, Henri Châtin-Hofmann, performing in Egypt, the Levant, and even in the shadows of once-mighty Babylon itself.

Reports have reached this writer that Berber has returned via the Orient Express in ill health and has been hospitalized for a week at the Bethanien Hospital. Although this is distressing news, we are sure that, at 29 years old and still in the prime of her life, she will recover swiftly and be back on the dancing stage in short order!

THE DOLL MAKER'S SHOP

One of the investigators' first leads is the marking on the doll's head from the Resi. Using this symbol, it is possible to trace the location of the manufacturer, though it requires a bit of footwork.

Referencing the Doll Maker's Mark

The library of the Museum of Industrial Art (**Berlin's Libraries and Museums**, page 45) houses several reference volumes collating marks of doll makers going all the way back to the 17th century. Investigators with an arts background can think of this automatically; others may be aware of the resource with a successful **Know** roll. Investigators may also come to the doll maker's shop via leads from interviewing Henri Châtin-Hofmann (**Regarding Henri**, page 180), snooping around the **Inveha Bookshop** (page 175), by visiting a more commercial doll shop and inquiring about the mark, or—if all else fails—through a direct prompt from **Erma Kore: Telephone-Girl** (page 166).

Finding the mark in the catalogs at the Industrial Art library requires a successful **Library Use** roll and one hour of searching. Once located in the index, the mark gives an address but no name: Rosenthaler Straße 39—just north of Hackescher Markt, deep in the city's "Barn Quarter" (*Scheuenviertel*); a down-at-heel neighborhood in the Alex that's home both to *Ringvereine* criminals and most of Berlin's Jewish population, both native and immigrant.

Rosenthaler Straße

At nearly any time of the day or night, Rosenthaler Straße is a typically broad and bustling avenue, with three- and four-story buildings looming over both sides of the street. Currently, the talk of the neighborhood seems to revolve around what happened at the **Hundegustav** (page 183) the other night. If asked, the locals—mostly Eastern European Jews—happily volunteer the information about the dive bar on Linienstraße that seems to have taken a dive all its own. "*Some sort of riot, they say. All sorts of strange rumors! A black-skinned lady shows up and the whole place gets turned upside-down, or so they tell it. I might stroll over later and have a look myself, but I won't get too close. A pretty rough crowd usually hangs around there. Ach, this wind! When is it going to let up?*"

Number 39

As for the doll shop, Number 39 is located down a damp alley that provides some relief from the steady wind, offset by the eerie whistling of the breeze as it blows over the courtyard within. Blank windows stare down at the investigators; dead ivy climbs up crumbling stucco and exposed brickwork.

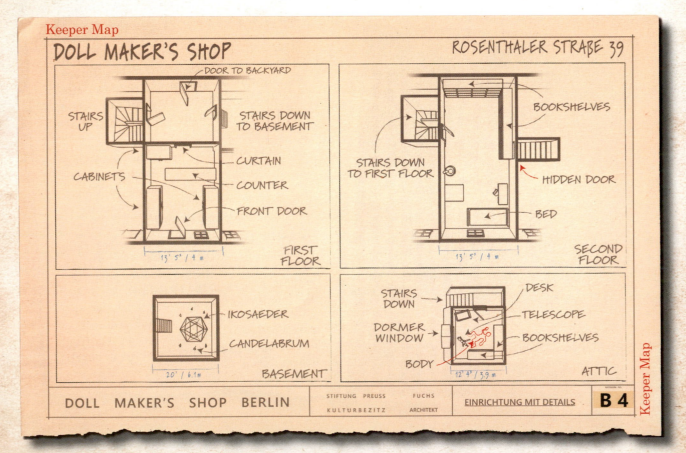

Several doors promise access to spaces beyond, but one grabs the investigators' attention, or rather the sign hanging above it does: the doll maker's symbol and the word (repeated twice, once in Roman and then again in Hebrew letters): *Belshazzar*. Regardless of the time of day or night the investigators visit, they find the door unlocked. Entering the shop, the interior is unlit and chilly. Perhaps no one is home?

A dirty window is the only source of outside light, with no electrical or gas lights inside. If the investigators lack light sources of their own, a quick search turns up three candles in various wax-encrusted candleholders.

The investigators can see that they are in a tiny shop front. Porcelain dolls of various sizes sit upon shelves in the numerous open-fronted cabinets dotted around the premises, staring down on the visitors with their dead eyes. Other ceramic pieces may be seen here and there, including a garden gnome or two. A successful **Spot Hidden** roll notices a doll that has fallen from one of the shelves, its once-pretty face now cracked open.

Keeper note: Châtin-Hofmann, in his rush to flee from the Berbelo ritual, smashed into the cabinet and sent the doll tumbling.

Calling out brings no response. A curtained door provides access to the rear of the shop; stepping through, the investigators find themselves in a hallway. To their left, a stairway ascends and quickly turns out of sight. To their right is a small door, only about 5 feet high and 2 feet wide (1.5 m by 0.6 m). Directly ahead is a normal-sized door, its small window of colored glass indicating that this one leads outside.

The outside door opens onto a small, quaint courtyard, the sky overhead nothing more than a small gray patch just visible beyond the surrounding walls. Here may be found a large kiln, suitable for firing porcelain and other ceramics. If an investigator possesses **Art/Craft (Ceramics)** or **Mechanical Repair**, they can tell that the kiln has been fired within the past week.

Back in the hall, the small door across from the base of the stairs is unlocked. Opening it reveals a steep set of steps disappearing into pitch darkness. If the investigators have been relying on ambient light up until this point, they have no choice but to find a light source or risk falling and breaking their necks on the steep descent.

Down in the Basement

The basement below smells of moist earth and mildew. The walls are of fitted granite, quite ancient, perhaps of medieval vintage; the floor is unfinished packed dirt. The space, barely 100 square feet (9 square meters), is unfurnished save for half a dozen wrought iron candelabra and an odd, metal frame-like structure in the center of the room. It is obvious from their remains that the candles in the candelabra were allowed to burn all the way down, their blood-red wax now dried in copious rivulets along the stands and in large puddles on the ground.

The frame-like structure is a 6 foot (1.8 m) tall polyhedron made up of 20 equilateral triangles (i.e., identical in appearance to a hollow 20-sided die). Those with **Art/Craft (Dance)** recognize the frame at once as a creation of the iconoclastic dance theorist Rudolf von Laban. It is called an *Ikosaeder* (icosahedron) and is used in some of Laban's dance exercises. What it is doing in the basement of a doll maker's shop is anybody's guess. It must be completely disassembled (a task requiring a blowtorch and lots of time) to move it out of the basement's narrow exit.

Keeper note: should the investigators wish to look into the *Ikosaeder* and its maker, see **Rudolf Von Laban**, page 179.

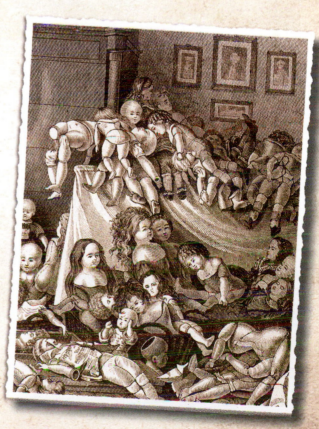

There are signs of recent activity, with many fresh footprints on the earthen floor—a successful Hard **Track** roll estimates that as many as half a dozen people were in here at one time. The tracks are all of men's shoes with one exception: a set of slim, bare footprints, likely of a woman or a youth, that lead from the center of the room to the staircase.

There is one other (easily spotted) odd artifact in the room: a glass jar with a screw-on cap. Although the jar is empty, the interior is streaked with what is unmistakably a viscous organic substance, not unlike bloody mucous. A successful **Medicine** roll surmises the goo is at least partially made of lung tissue. There is otherwise nothing else to find in the room.

Upstairs

Investigators who follow the stairs leading up from the hallway reach a modest bedroom and living quarters. Here the investigators find a rumpled bed, a small vanity, and a makeshift dining area set up next to a wood-burning stove. A window next to the bed looks out over the front courtyard. Most of the wall space in this room is given over to bookshelves. The subject matter ranges over a wide variety of topics, from mathematics to history to geography to books on ceramic-firing techniques, in languages including Latin, Greek, German, and Hebrew. If any of the investigators know the latter, they note that many of the tomes in that language appear to be on extremely esoteric subjects having to do with the study of the Kabbalah.

One of the few bits of art on the wall is an unframed, slightly curled 17th-century print depicting an old man, seated on a chair, holding a 10-pointed symbol inscribed with various Hebrew letters. A successful **Occult** roll identifies this symbol as the Sephirah, the ten "emanations" in Kabbalah. A successful **Spot Hidden** roll, or if studying the print closely, reveals that it flutters from time to time, as if a draft is blowing through the room. Alerted to this, the investigators may determine (using candle flames or simply their own sense of touch) the direction the draft is blowing from. It seems to originate along the edge of one of the bookcases opposite the entrance to the room. Sure enough, this portion of the bookcase is a narrow false door. Pushing hard on the side nearest the wall sets the case moving on its counterbalanced pivot, uncovering another set of stairs leading still farther up.

Down in the basement

Heading up the Hidden Stairs

Following these stairs brings the investigators to a small room with a dormer window that looks out over the Scheuenviertel. The window is open, and the damnable wind blows through in whistling gusts. A brass telescope stands next to the window (it is pointed at the constellation Virgo, as a successful **Science (Astronomy)** roll reveals). The room contains many more books, most in Hebrew, Ancient Greek, and Latin, as well as a tall desk (not unlike a monk's desk) and piles of papers and parchment, most now scattered about by the breeze.

A successful **Spot Hidden** roll notes a manila folder that contains several dozen photographs of men and women, all in their teens and twenties—some candid street shots, some clipped out of newspapers. Among the photos is a newspaper image of Erwin Kern (**Erma Kore: Telephone-Girl**, page 166). Though the investigators cannot know it, these were the reference photos used by Belshazzar in his construction of the *manikins*.

As the investigators move into the room, they see something: almost out of sight, lying half-covered by the swirling, wind-blown papers in the corner of the room, is a prone, unmoving man. A ream's-worth of the papers is stuck to him, soaked through with the man's congealed blood.

The Old Man

The man is extremely aged, at least 90 years old. He wears a yarmulke skullcap and a long cassock, perhaps marking him out as an immigrant from the East. It is obvious that he has slit his wrists—a bloodstained knife is still clutched in one hand. He is pale and cold to the touch, but miraculously he is still alive. Apparently, the scattered papers on the floor, adhering to his seeping wounds, acted as *ersatz* bandages and kept him from bleeding out.

Attending to the man brings him to consciousness (a successful **First Aid** roll aids his recovery but is not essential). The man is, of course, quite weak, but he keeps croaking out the same words over and over again. It requires a successful **Language (Yiddish)** roll to understand their meaning: "Let me die, Lord. Let me die." If none of the investigators speak Yiddish, then German speakers get the general gist of the statement. The injured man is, thankfully, bilingual and responds to anyone speaking to him in German or Yiddish.

This is Belshazzar the Doll Maker, or so he calls himself. His exact age and actual name are impossible to determine, but his German and Yiddish are both of an archaic dialect. With a bit of coaxing and help, Belshazzar can be induced to descend from his observatory to the bedroom and be put to bed. He adamantly refuses transport to a hospital, though he will consent to an examination from a doctor making a house call (or from an investigator with a medical background).

With his wounds dressed and after an hour of rest and some hot tea, Belshazzar is in more of a mood to talk, though he won't admit to much beyond being a doll maker with an interest in esoteric Biblical studies; however, if shown the doll from the Resi, or if a successful **Persuade** or **Charm** roll is made, he realizes that the jig is up and reveals more.

- Two years ago, he was commissioned by a man calling himself "Pacitius" to make two-dozen life-sized dolls. He will not be drawn on what these dolls were used for, though a successful **Psychology** roll reveals furtive glances at the doll from the Resi, if it is visible while he talks.
- Earlier this week (on November 10) he participated in a magical ritual in the basement of this building. Pacitius was in attendance, along with two other men: one, a youthful American dancer, the other older and harsher-looking, with great, piercing eyes.
- The object of the ritual was to create "something not of this Earth," as he puts it. He will not volunteer more information than that, though another successful **Psychology** roll detects great feelings of regret just beneath the surface.
- "*What I laid eyes upon was a vision too wondrous to contemplate. I am content to die. I wish to die! For I shall never look upon another visage like that. O Ashtoreth!*"

At this point he suffers a seizure that sends him into raving fits. Although he eventually recovers, he refuses to speak any more on the subject, begging instead only for sleep.

Investigators who don't otherwise think of it may attempt an **INT** roll: success connects the old man's description of the "youthful American dancer" with Henri Châtin-Hofmann. A successful **Occult** or **Anthropology** roll recalls that Ashtoreth is the Hebrew spelling of the goddess Astarte, later ascribed to the demon-king Astaroth.

THE OCCULT BOOKSHOP INVEHA

The bookshop opened in 1926 on a quiet north Berlin side street called *Zionskirchstraße* (Zion Church Street) at the intersection of Anklamer Straße. The simple storefront welcomes visitors into a modest space crammed with overfull bookshelves and tables. A tinkling bell rings when the front door opens. The air inside is pungent with the odor of burning incense.

Book subjects range from Egyptian architecture and Peruvian sacrificial rites to psychoanalysis, hypnotism, and non-Euclidean physics. There are also books on yoga, the Kabbalah, electro-magnetism, and astrology, among much more. Any investigator taking a half-hour to browse the shelves in-depth and making a successful **Library Use** roll notes quite a few books on Gnosticism, particularly the Gnostic Gospel of St. John and something called "the Berbelo Gnostics." A successful **Occult** or **Anthropology** roll applied to this latter topic recalls something about a tripartite god, the wife of Yahweh, and heretical cults during the earliest years of Christianity.

Keeper note: further information may be gleaned through purchase of these books or research at the Prussian State Library (**Berlin's Libraries and Museums**, page 45). A successful **Library Use** roll at the State Library finds information about the Borborites contained within the pages of *Von denen Verdammten* and summarized in the box **The Borborite Cult** (page 164).

Researching Astarte, Ishtar, or Lilith

Investigators may also wish to look for information on Astarte, Ishtar, and Lilith. There are several easily located books within the shop containing general information on Near Eastern moon goddesses, which impart roughly the same information provided by Walter Andrae (**The Pergamon Museum**, page 179). One of the books contains a reproduction of a photograph of a relief carving from the ruins of Babylon. The carving depicts a naked, winged goddess figure with bird talons for feet, standing upon two lions (or hyenas?) flanked by owls. The caption below the picture identifies the goddess as Lilith.

Pamphlets

Several wire racks on the front counter display various pamphlets published by the Fraternitas Saturni, pamphlets that look familiar to those who saw similar copies at the Hotel Excelsior two years ago. Among various tracts on astrology, pendulum forecasts, and sacred coitus, there are also copies of a large-format magazine called *Saturn Gnosis*, printed on heavy paper with tipped-in color plates. The magazine's editor and illustrator are listed as Albin Grau. Lastly, there is a neat stack of flyers advertising the next Fraternitas Saturni lecture, to be presented by a Brother Leonardo on the topic of "Spiritual Leadership as a Magical Reality," to be held at this bookstore two nights from now.

The Owner

As the investigators browse the books, a man emerges from the back. "*May I help you?*" This is Gregor Gregorius, shop owner, occultist, and author of the pamphlets now on display at the sales counter. Likely the investigators are here to get some answers; the following points detail what Gregorius is willing to offer up on likely topics of inquiry. Note that a successful **Psychology** roll detects his lies.

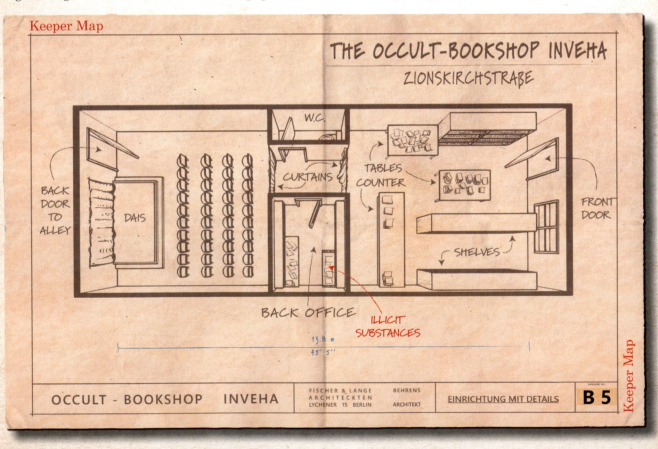

Keeper Map

THE OCCULT-BOOKSHOP INVEHA
ZIONSKIRCHSTRAßE

W.C.

BACK DOOR TO ALLEY

DAIS

CURTAINS

TABLES
COUNTER

FRONT DOOR

SHELVES

BACK OFFICE

ILLICIT SUBSTANCES

13.8 m
45' 5''

OCCULT - BOOKSHOP INVEHA

FISCHER & LANGE ARCHITECKTEN LYCHENER 15 BERLIN

BEHRENS ARCHITEKT

EINRICHTUNG MIT DETAILS

B 5

- **Albin Grau:** "*Herr Grau is an old friend of mine. I believe he is engaged in a new artistic project right now—we haven't spoken for some months, as is usual for him when he gets inspired.*" (This is partly a lie, Gregorius remains in regular contact with Grau.)
- **Henri Châtin-Hofmann:** "*Yes, I believe he's been in here a few times. Bought some of my pamphlets. An amateur dabbler and nothing more, I think—I hope he hasn't gotten himself mixed up in anything untoward?*" (Another partial lie, Gregorius last saw Châtin-Hofmann at Abyzou's summoning ritual; however, his contempt for the youth, apparent from his tone of voice, is real.)
- **Fraternitas Saturni:** "*Ah, an esoteric study group that I run. We offer lectures on matters of secret knowledge, classes on deeper occult subjects, and general education in these topics, all right here in the lecture hall out back. Would you be interested in joining?*"

Investigators demonstrating a faculty for **Occult** studies via a successful skill roll, and particularly those who also show an interest in the Fraternitas Saturni, are most likely to make a good impression on Gregorius. If they have also inquired about Grau, Gregorius volunteers, "*I believe that he is planning to attend our next ceremony. It's two evenings from now, starting at 7 pm.*" He then hands out a flyer detailing the topic, location, and time, as previously described.

The Back Office

Entrance to the back of the store is gained via passing through a glittering purple and gold curtain hanging over an open doorway. Beyond is a narrow hall that eventually leads to the "lecture hall" (**Attending the Lecture,** following). To the left is a simple door with a frosted glass window marked "Manager"—this is Gregorius' office and study.

Ambitious investigators may wish to attempt a break-in. Gregorius keeps his office door locked when he isn't inside; it requires a successful **Locksmith** roll to pick the lock, or the investigators can simply smash the glass if subtlety is not required.

Beyond the door is a small room mostly taken up by a scuffed writing desk. Light is provided by a Tiffany desk lamp, as well as a naked bulb hanging from the ceiling. The walls are completely concealed behind bookshelves and cubbyholes; the shelves sag under the weight of books, while the cubbyholes all overflow with papers, letters, receipts, and notes. If there is any system of organization here, it is entirely in Gregorius' head.

Searching Gregorius' office for incriminating evidence takes at least an hour. Reduce this time by 10 minutes per extra investigator participating, but keep in mind that, due to the cramped dimensions of the office, only four investigators

Gregor Gregorius in his store

in total can cram in at once and still effectively search the place; thus, the minimum amount of time required to search the office is 20 minutes.

A successful **Spot Hidden** roll finds several small drawers stuffed with various illicit substances. Depending on their background, or with a successful **Science (Chemistry** or **Pharmacy)** roll, the investigators may identify cocaine, hashish, and peyote, all in significant quantities.

A successful **Library Use** roll finds reams of scattered notes, apparently translating a Medieval Latin tome into German (see **Das Necronomicon** in the Tomes and Spells section, page 198, for details).

A successful **Accounting** roll turns up several receipts dating from as recently as two weeks ago and as far back as 1926, all made out to "Belshazzar the Doll Maker" for "*manikins.*" Adding up the receipts, it appears that 26 *manikins* were purchased over the two-year period. About half the receipts are signed by either Grau or Gregorius, the balance by Châtin-Hofmann.

Unless the investigators go out of their way to ensure their security, for every 10 minutes spent in the office call for a group **Luck** roll (based on the Luck of those investigators present); failure means that Gregorius turns up. He does not hesitate to use magic to exact his revenge on the interlopers, using Dominate, Implant Fear, or Mental Suggestion at first, resorting to the use of Shrivelling if attacked or if his initial spells fail (see **Gregor Gregorius' profile**, page 195).

Attending the Lecture

Depending on the impression the investigators made on Gregorius, they may have received an invitation to the next Fraternitas Saturni lecture. Alternatively, having seen the flyers around the shop, they may decide independently to show up to the event. It is not critical to the investigation that the characters attend, but several blanks may be filled in with the evening's events.

Returning to the bookstore on the appointed evening at 8 pm (two nights after they first visited the venue), the investigators proceed through the back hallway and enter a large, high-ceilinged room that stands in glaring contrast to the cramped spaces found elsewhere in the building. A small stage is backed by a purple curtain displaying a silver lamé, six-pointed star with the head of a bull in the center. A successful **Occult** roll identifies the symbol as a Talisman of Saturn, used in ritual magic.

Several rows of chairs are set up facing the stage, which also has a rickety lectern. About 40 people are in attendance, evenly split between men and women. The crowd consists of aristocrats and middle-class types, of professors and politicians. Perhaps one or two personalities from **Oh! You Pretty Things** (page 71) are here as well, at the Keeper's discretion.

A door in the back of the lecture hall opens, and Gregorius, Grau, and another man enter. The conversation dies down and people take their seats. Gregorius makes some preparatory remarks and then introduces "Frater Pacitius"— who is, of course, none other than Albin Grau himself. Grau looks somewhat crazed, his shirt collar unbuttoned and his hair a wild mass atop his head. He looks like he has aged greatly since the investigators last saw him.

"Pacitius" takes the stage and introduces Frater Leonardo, "*One of our most talented members and a master of mirror-magic.*"

The third man, Brother Leonardo, now steps up and begins his talk. Grau sits and listens politely.

"*I have always been missing something when so often within our circle the impulse of the new age has been discussed,*" Leonardo begins. "*I am missing the absolute becoming aware, the radical articulation which everyone of us has to feel within their flesh and blood. With regards to this matter, we cannot look often enough at the similarities between our situation today and that of the first Gnostics in classical Rome. From all the countless catacombs, a mysterious admonition is coming toward us! During these days when they lived their lives in absolute truthfulness, a whole world was shattered. It was with the downfall of Rome that the last of the classical empires sank down into dust. Yet even back then the few initiated felt everything passing by like a huge wind.*"

The speech goes on in this vein for about a half-hour. At last, Brother Leonardo concludes, "*The clock of the world is advancing to its last hour! Who knows if the good and harmonic forces will prevail and spare us the imminent bitter chalice of another war? Because it would result in the downfall of whole cultures. Or might even this suffering be necessary—according to a higher resolution—to further mature humanity? We do not know.*"

By the time the lecture wraps up (to general applause), Gregorius has retired to his office, but Grau is still present and the investigators may approach him, although what they find may be rather unexpected.

"*My good friends!*" Grau says, a cracked smile upon his face. "*So good to see you again!*" Grau is in what can best be described as an elevated mood; nothing seems to faze him. "*I am so pleased to see you here. Truly, you are on the right path! Brother Leonardo is right: a new wind is blowing. Surely you have noticed? It gusts all day and night, now that She is here.*"

If the investigators ask who "She" is, Grau's response is simply, "*Come to the Schauspielhaus, my friends, and be transformed, as I have been!*" He is positively manic in his evangelism by this point. "*The word will spread to the whole city. She rules the night, holding court between sunset and sunrise. Soon all shall be night…*" he continues, giggling.

If grilled about Belshazzar the Doll Maker and what took place in his basement, or if asked directly about the details of the Berbelo Working, Grau merely laughs, *"Yes, that's right. I helped with the working. But what came to us is far greater than anything I could have anticipated!"* Grau's eyes light up with a private vision and he shudders with paroxysms of laughing ecstasy. *"Sup of Her milk and be transformed!"* he says, as the investigators are pushed aside by others in the crowd, drawn by Grau's ravings.

If the investigators wish to stick with Grau, he happily takes them to **The Großes Schauspielhaus** (page 184) and introduces them to Abyzou.

RUDOLF VON LABAN

Investigators may wish to follow up on the *Ikosaeder* in Belshazzar's basement (**The Doll Maker's Shop**, page 172) by contacting its inventor, Rudolf von Laban. They find the Hungarian by looking up his name in the Berlin directory, which provides an address for *Tanzschule Laban* (Laban's Dance School) at Gillstraße 10, Grunewald.

On arrival, Laban appears to be in a terrible rush. He and his company are departing for a tour of Germany and Italy on the morrow of whichever day the investigators first pay him a visit, and there is much for him to do before he leaves. It requires a successful **Fast Talk**, **Charm**, or **Persuade** roll to even get him to stop for a few minutes to answer questions—an investigator with **Art/Craft (Dance)** may, instead, roll against that skill to catch Laban's ear.

Laban's helpfulness depends on how well the investigator rolls. A success at the indicated level (below) uncovers the information given, plus everything from the prior levels—potentially up to four tidbits. He has no time for extended conversations, so only one roll (including a pushed attempt) is permitted.

- **Regular success:** Laban confirms that he sold an *Ikosaeder* recently, but he won't say when or to whom.
- **Hard success:** Laban pins down the time, saying he sold it two weeks ago.
- **Extreme success:** Laban lets slip that he sold it to Albin Grau but will not reveal why.
- **Critical success:** with a gleam in his eye, Laban says, *"I believe Grau and his associates are planning to use it to transcend the sexual fourth dimension. Now good day to you!"*

THE PERGAMON MUSEUM

Investigators following a clue from Erma (**Erma Kore: Telephone-Girl** page 166) and looking up Walter Andrae find him in the phone directory; his occupation is listed as "Director of the Pergamon Museum's Near Eastern Department." Another route to Andrae is available to those who research "Astarte" or "Ashtoreth" at the library, where they are directed by the librarian to Andrae as the best person to provide information about ancient Near Eastern deities.

On Museum Island, between the National Gallery and a Stadtbahn line that crosses the island and the river, is a large construction site. Here the Pergamon Museum is nearing completion after nearly two decades of work interrupted by war and economic crises.

The museum is constructed specifically to hold the Pergamon Altar, excavated from the acropolis of the same name during the years 1878–1886 by Carl Humann. The first such museum, opened in 1901, quickly proved inadequate, and plans were drawn up for a larger facility that would hold not just the altar but also many of Berlin's greatest artifacts from the ancient Near East and Mediterranean. The museum's plans include a Near Eastern Department, where currently a monumental installation is taking shape.

The archaeologist Robert Koldeway conducted extensive excavations at the site of ancient Babylon around the turn of the century. Among his many notable finds was the so-called Ishtar Gate, a gatehouse and grand processional entrance, situated on Babylon's northern walls and constructed by King Nebuchadnezzar II 2,500 years previous. The entirety of the gate complex was broken down and shipped to Berlin, where its intricate lapis lazuli and gold brickwork was reconstructed by Koldeway and his assistants, chief among them Walter Andrae.

Now, after years of work, the great Gate nears completion, restored to its former glory under the watchful eye of Andrae, promoted to Director of the Near Eastern Department of the Pergamon after Koldeway's death in 1925. It takes 1D3 days to arrange a meeting with the extremely busy director, although a successful **Archaeology** roll, or **Credit Rating 50%** or higher, reduces this time to 1D3 hours.

Arriving at the museum site for their appointment, the investigators are ushered beyond the wooden fencing that surrounds the property by a junior-level functionary. He escorts the group to a wing of the massive complex, which even now rings with the symphony of a hundred hammers and scores of saws. Passing into the wing, the investigators find themselves staring at a most incongruous sight: a massive, Babylonian gate complex housed entirely indoors under the diffused illumination of skylights. A man in his fifties with a deep bronzed tan, a shock of silver hair, and intense, probing eyes is supervising work on the gatehouse, where a team of workers on scaffolding is busily laying in lapis lazuli-glazed tiles. Almost all the walls and towers of the complex have been set with these tiles, broken only by gold-glazed bricks depicting bulls, lions, and strange hybrid creatures. With a jolt, the investigators recognize the seven gates from their dream vision of the Shadow City, provoking a **Sanity** roll (0/1 loss.) These are, in part, the strange walls and towers that replaced the Brandenburg Gate in their dream-memories.

Walter Andrae hands his clipboard to an assistant, then approaches the investigators and pumps their hands in greeting. He is friendly enough but clearly slightly irked to be taking time away from this most important project. "*We are nearly complete. Of course, there is not room enough in this space to reconstruct the whole complex, but I think the overall effect comes across, don't you?*"

It's a good idea for the investigators to keep their questions brief and to the point. Following are the answers he provides to the most salient questions.

- **About the Ishtar Gate:** they were unearthed from the ruins of Babylon and are called the Gates of Ishtar (see previous for more details). Andrae says they originally had seven cedar gates, which were called the Seven Gates of Heaven. "*Those gates long since rotted away, and we have room for only one gate here at the museum.*"
- **About "Astarte" and "Ashtoreth":** these are, respectively, the Greek and Hebrew names for the Mesopotamian goddess Ishtar (also called Inanna).
- **About Ishtar/Inanna:** the Babylonian/Sumerian goddess of fertility, love, and beauty. She was associated with the moon and had an active clergy of sacred temple-prostitutes. Later, when Ishtar became Astarte, she was linked with two other goddesses in a tripartite incarnation. Those two goddesses were Anat and Qudshu—the former a virginal war goddess, the latter a goddess of sexual pleasure and ecstasy. Some latter-day scholars link Ishtar/Astarte with the Talmudic mythological figure Lilith, the Mother of Abominations, or else the Whore of Babylon. "*These remain fringe theories at best,*" Dr. Andrae sniffs. Later legends tie in Lilith with the vampire myth, making her a true creature of the night. "*In such tales, Lilith loses most of her powers during the day, becoming weak and vulnerable so long as the sun shines in the sky.*"
- **About the Borborites:** Andrae is only passingly familiar with the Borborites and refuses to believe they may be active in modern-day Berlin.

REGARDING HENRI

Investigators recalling their encounters with Henri Châtin-Hofmann in 1926, or else prompted by their visit to Belshazzar or a clue from Erma (**Erma Kore: Telephone-Girl**, page 166), may wish to seek him out once more.

As an entertainer and public figure, finding Châtin-Hofmann is initially no problem: he is in residence at the Weidenhoff-Casino. Getting him to talk about anything of substance is a much tougher prospect.

By the time of his 1928 return to Berlin, Châtin-Hofmann has a new dance partner, Helene Schelda, and is booking shows in clubs and cabarets around the city. Finding him in his dressing room after one such performance reveals a man already desperately trying to distance himself from his past. Unfortunately for him, that past is catching up with him quickly indeed.

Depending on their level of interaction in 1926, Châtin-Hofmann may well remember the investigators; however, if they ask about his performance at the **Clärchens Ballhaus** (page 160), he claims no such recital ever took place. A successful **Psychology** roll reveals he is telling the truth or at least firmly believes he is.

Châtin-Hofmann's madness drives him to forget his sordid past, to distance himself as much as possible from the terrible bargains he struck and the compromises he made. He was convinced that the Berbelo Working was the best way to save his beloved Anita. In the wake of it backfiring so spectacularly, he wants nothing to do with it nor with any of his magical workings. The day after the ritual, he burned all of his occult and esoteric texts, and has cut off all communication with Grau and Gregorius.

If contacted on Day 2 (November 11), Châtin-Hofmann puts up a cool, diffident façade to the investigators but cracks under the slightest pressure: showing him the doll from the Resi, confronting him with Belshazzar's tale, or even referencing the events of two years ago at the Weiße Maus—these are all sufficient to turn him into a blubbering wreck.

"*We didn't know! We didn't know!*" he wails in English, holding his head in his hands. "*We thought we were doing good. I thought I was doing good—that I could restore her, make her more than she was! She wanted to be Astarte, and I thought I could help!*" He looks up at the investigators, wild-eyed. "*But I was fooled, you see? Just a patsy. A lousy patsy. It was those no-good bums at the bookstore. The Inveha. Oh, I wish I'd never found that place! Curse them all and their filthy, degenerate heresies!*"

At this point, Helene Schelda intervenes and threatens to fetch the theater director and call the police if the investigators don't leave. Their last sight of Châtin-Hofmann is that of a pathetic, broken man, curled up on the couch of his dressing room, weeping inconsolably. "*Nothing I could do… Nothing I could do…*"

Post Meeting

Spooked by his encounter with the investigators, Châtin-Hofmann packs up and flees with Schelda, taking a cheap hotel in the Alex where he begins to consider his next move. Unfortunately, Abyzou finds him first.

Spurred by the fragment of her that used to be Anita Berber, Abyzou wishes to find her "husband" as well. On the night following his meeting with the investigators, her fog-spawn locates him. Schelda is killed in the ensuing attack, but Châtin-Hofmann makes it out alive. For the next 24 hours, he is a man on the run, subject to repeated close calls with Abyzou's "pets." The only reason he survives is that the fog-spawn are sent to capture rather than kill him, but they aren't quite intelligent enough to pull off the job. Eventually, insensate and raving, he finds his way to Erma Kore's apartment (**Erma's Guest**, page 183), where investigators may encounter him again.

Investigators may, no doubt, find Châtin-Hofmann to be something of a sad specimen, but his role in bringing doom to Berlin should not be overlooked. Later in the scenario, the investigators find Châtin-Hofmann to be a potential key to banishing Abyzou from our world for good.

MEETING ERMA

The time the investigators meet Erma Kore face to face is left to the Keeper. Ideally, they have used her clues and their own inquiries to put together an idea of the peril that now stalks Berlin's streets and are trying to figure out a way to put a stop to it. Under no circumstances should the meeting take place earlier than the evening of November 12, giving Châtin-Hofmann time to show up at her apartment first (**Erma's Guest**, page 183). Furthermore, the meeting most likely takes place after dark.

When the time comes, a dark Ford sedan pulls up as the investigators are setting off for some destination or another. One of the tough, scarred men in the front passenger seats rolls down the window, greeting them with, "*If you oppose the evil that festers in this city, you will get in.*"

It's clear both men are criminals of some sort, likely members of a local *Ringverein*. It's up to the investigators whether they take the risk and get in the car. If they do, they are whisked away to a quiet, tree-lined stretch of Viktoria Straße (located off Potsdamer Platz) filled with upscale row houses.

The car's chauffeur remains in the vehicle, but the other man escorts the investigators inside, up a lushly carpeted flight of stairs to a second-floor landing. He gives a discrete knock; from within, a youthful, familiar voice calls, "*Enter.*"

Keeper note: the key to the following scene is to emphasize the beyond-her-years maturity and *Weltschmerz* (melancholy and world-weariness) of the girl behind the door. While Erma Kore is a victim of a supernatural plot, she is equally a victim of a depraved society that trades so willingly in adolescent flesh.

"If you oppose the evil that festers in this city, you will get in."

The investigators find themselves in a sumptuously decorated living room, laid out with fine French antiques (mostly Louis XIV- and XV-era). Standing at a window overlooking the street, gazing down through diaphanous curtains, is a petite girl dressed in a flowing robe and negligee. She cannot be more than 17 years old. Her golden-blonde hair is cut shoulder-length, and her makeup is expertly applied. She resembles nothing so much as a teenaged Marlene Dietrich. She simultaneously looks eerily familiar to certain investigators—those who met Erwin Kern during the events of **The Devil Eats Flies** might even swear that she is his little sister.

Their escort bows his way out. He waits on the landing for Erma's signal to escort the investigators away.

"*Please, have a seat,*" says the girl. Her childlike voice contrasts harshly with her sophisticated bedroom attire. As the investigators seat themselves on the couch and chairs near the marble fireplace, she crosses the room and picks up an old box, flips it open, and takes out a pre-rolled cigarette, fitting it into a cigarette holder. She then waits for an investigator (preferably male) to light it for her. "*Please, help yourselves,*" she adds, and then positions herself next to the fireplace.

"*It's a pleasure finally to meet you all in the flesh,*" she says, exhaling smoke. "*I know all of you already, but I should introduce myself. My clients call me Marlene, but my real name is Erma. Erma Kore.*"

By now it should be obvious to any investigator with even passing familiarity with Berlin's sex industry that Erma is a prostitute, a particular type known as a "Telephone-Girl"—always young (14–18 years of age) and made up to look like a famous movie star, their engagements are arranged exclusively over the telephone.

Erma has summoned the investigators here to lay everything out, to the best of her knowledge. She may be able to fill in some gaps in the investigators' understanding, but she mainly functions as a means to communicate to the group just what they're up against, if they haven't figured it out already.

Moving around the room, Erma greets each of the investigators by name. "*I must apologize; I have been watching you from afar,*" she explains. She asks them what they know of the *Manikinmenschen*. As the investigators are unlikely to be familiar with this term, she explains further.

"*Belshazzar the Doll Maker. He made these… creatures. They begin as human-sized porcelain dolls, but he uses sorcery to infuse them with life. They take on the appearance of people—flesh and blood people, I mean.*"

If asked how she knows this, she only smiles grimly before carrying on. "*The manikins, after being given life—or the semblance of it—were sent out into the city to collect ritual ingredients, which they call 'gestohlener Blitz'—'stolen lightning'—that the Baron's cult needed for the great working. Who is the Baron? Never mind that for now. The cult needed great quantities of these ingredients*

to make their elixir. You have seen some of this already, perhaps?" Investigators who broke open the doll at the Resi sense recognize she is referring to this substance. "*The manikins, they work the streets or the brothels, do you follow? These ingredients… are best collected by prostitutes. This was crucial to their magical rites, and to the working.*"

She crosses to and kneels before the investigator with the highest **POW**. Looking up with searching eyes, outlined in false lashes and painted-on eyebrows, she broadcasts a stomach-turning impression of someone who has seen far more than a child her age should have.

"*You wonder how I know all this, yes?*"

She turns around on her knees and reaches back, lifting her hair and baring her neck. Visible just at the hairline is the familiar maker's mark of Belshazzar the Doll Maker (**Handout: Dances 4**). Seeing this unmistakable mark in this context provokes a **Sanity** roll (0/1D2 loss).

"*I was one of the ones who worked for the past two years to collect the* gestohlener Blitz," she continues. "*I am a Telephone-Girl and I work for Baron Grunau, leader of the Borborite cult. Now that I know what my work has wrought, I turn to outsiders—you—to help set it right.*" Erma stands again and resumes her place near the fireplace. She flings her half-smoked cigarette into the fire. "*So, what do you want to know?*"

Like all the other *Manikinmenschen*, Erma feels an intrinsic connection to Abyzou. While most of the doll-people have happily fallen under the goddess' sway, Erma holds out, tortured by a sense of conscience—this would come as quite a surprise to Belshazzar and the Borborites, as they assume the *manikins* lack consciences.

Because of her connection to the goddess, Erma can provide some useful details.

- Abyzou possesses an otherworldly charm. Those who are apt to fall in love with a beautiful woman will almost certainly come under her spell upon seeing her.
- She brings with her a great pestilence that causes sickness and death. It begins by afflicting the youngest and most vulnerable members of the community, but eventually it lays all to waste. The longer she is in one place, the deadlier the epidemic becomes.
- She was summoned from another place, a dimension darkly reflecting our own, and ultimately wishes to make our world look like hers.
- The best chance for ridding the world of her curse is to travel to her home dimension and, once there, find a way to draw her back. There are no banishing rituals here on Earth that could send her back.
- How may this be accomplished? "*You must drink of the sacred milk that is in her chalice then pass through the Seven Gates of Heaven, though what those gates may be is unknown to me.*"

Erma's Guest

Whether or not the investigators have already sought out and interviewed Châtin-Hofmann, he is now here, sheltering in Erma's bedchamber. He has been attacked three times by fog-spawn, barely escaping with his life, and now suffers from agoraphobia as a result.

Upon concluding her initial interview with the investigators, Erma excuses herself and disappears into the bedroom. The investigators hear a man's voice, quavering and fearful, and Erma's soothing voice in reply. Then, leading him by his hand like a child, Erma escorts Châtin-Hofmann into the main apartment.

"*Henri, these are the people I was telling you about,*" Erma says consolingly in accented English. If the investigators interviewed Châtin-Hofmann prior to the attacks, he scarcely looks like the same man: his eyes are bloodshot and red-rimmed, his face unshaven. He wears trousers, suspenders, and an undershirt, but his bare feet and hands are caked with dirt, the knees of his pants torn up and revealing bloody abrasions beneath. Erma turns to the investigators, speaking German. "*He showed up here this afternoon, ranting about 'monsters in the fog.' I think he's too scared to venture back outside, but he mustn't remain here.*"

Investigators may attempt a **Charm**, **Fast Talk**, **Intimidate**, or **Persuade** roll to get Châtin-Hofmann to come with them, but they only get one chance per skill (including a pushed attempt); failure results in his adamant refusal to leave. He may, of course, be bodily carried out—Erma summons Pesch the gunsel to help if the investigators wish to resort to physical means.

If the investigators cannot entice him or choose to leave without Châtin-Hofmann, he disappears from the scenario, a victim of the Baron's wrath along with Erma (**A Tearful Farewell**, following). Their task of banishing Abyzou from this world is now markedly more difficult and will require considerable sacrifice on one or more of the investigators' parts.

A Tearful Farewell

Once she has answered the investigators' questions to the best of her abilities and re-introduced them to Châtin-Hofmann, Erma calls out to her man, "*Pesch! These kind people are ready to depart.*"

Pesch takes the investigators back to the car. As the car drives off, they notice Pesch and the chauffeur (a man named Georg) weeping quietly. If asked why they cry, Georg speaks up, "*That is the last we shall ever see of that saintly girl. Baron Grunau has eyes all up and down this street and is bound to find out about your visit. It won't take him long to put the pieces together. And then...*" An icy silence descends over the vehicle.

From this point on, the investigators are on their own. Within hours, Erma Kore is no more, her shattered porcelain body dumped into a rubbish bin behind her former Viktoria Straße residence. If Châtin-Hofmann remained behind, his body turns up floating in the Havel River later that night, dead through suffocation.

ABYZOU'S EMPIRE

When Abyzou awoke in the basement of Belshazzar's doll shop, she knew little of the world around her. An evening spent in the underground clubs and cabarets of Berlin changed all that. Whatever Abyzou was at her inception, she has become a beacon of vice, criminality, and depravity, her very presence creating a feedback loop that serves only to amplify the city's indulgences.

Beginning on the first day of her existence, Abyzou gathers around her a coterie of worshippers from across Berlin's upper and lower castes: petty thugs and *Ringverein* crime bosses, judges and lawyers, vice cops and prostitutes. Overnight, Abyzou becomes the most powerful underworld figure in the city.

THE HUNDEGUSTAV

After her incarnation on the night of November 10, Abyzou walked out into the chill Berlin night and, following some desultory walking about the cramped streets of the Scheuenviertel, found herself outside the sturdy iron door of the Hundegustav, one of the city's most notorious underground dives (**Food and Drink**, page 56).

Heading in, the nude goddess, with her black skin and blonde hair, naturally attracted the attention of the bar's drunken patrons, a mix of *beinls* and bulls, many of whom fell over themselves in immediate prostration. This was Abyzou's first victory and the seed from which she grew her increasingly extensive criminal network. And, although Abyzou is now gone from this place, sitting instead in residence at the **Großes Schauspielhaus** (following), the wake of her disruption remains.

Investigators may have been directed to the Hundegustav by a telephone clue from Erma (**Erma Kore: Telephone-Girl**, page 166); alternatively, as detailed in the **Doll Maker's Shop** (page 172), snooping around the neighborhoods adjacent to Belshazzar's home leads them here as well.

The door to the club hangs open, its doorman nowhere to be seen. Heading down into the old coal cellar, the investigators find the space in total disarray. Chairs and tables are overturned, while several men and women lie passed out, or possibly dead, in the corners. The bar is empty and untended, all the drinks bottles looted or smashed. The air is uncomfortably stuffy and hangs thick with smoke and an unwholesome mist. A few rather dissipated men and women sit around, holding their heads in their hands or quietly puffing on cigarettes. The investigators are met with universally hostile looks from these patrons.

Each passing moment spent in the bar risks physical violence. Only one patron is the least bit sympathetic to the investigators, a Cameroonian called Emil, and even he tries his best to usher the investigators out before things turn ugly. "*Bar's closed, mates. Best keep moving,*" he says in his thick West African accent. "*No, seriously. Nothing to see or do here. Move on. Now!*"

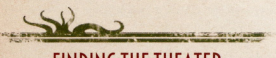

FINDING THE THEATER

Initially, the changes Abyzou exerts are not immediately obvious to an outsider passing by the Großes Schauspielhaus' rather drab exterior, which still resembles the brick marketplace it originally was. Thus, Abyzou's presence is likely to go unnoticed, at least at first.

Fast-moving investigators may gain clues to the goddess's whereabouts from several sources: **Attending the Lecture** (page 178) results in an encounter with the mad Albin Grau, who raves about the theater; he even offers to take the investigators there directly. Visiting the **Hundegustav** (page 183) also provides a lead, either in the form of Emil's warning or the *Immertreu* thugs' capturing the investigators and dragging them there.

Even without these clues, the theater gradually begins to show its new character. By Day 3 ("**The Center Cannot Hold…,**" page 165), it is obvious that *something* is going on at the theater: people go in but hardly ever leave, cars are abandoned on the street outside, drunken wretches lie splayed out, half-naked, in the gutter. After a week, Abyzou's influence is clear to all, as the non-stop party spills out of the theater and turns the blocks around it into a 24-hour revel of Bacchanalian proportions.

Of course, investigators with an eye out for strange happenings receive indications of the happenings at the Great Playhouse well before that. An investigator prone to being invited to parties (dilettantes, artists, and the like) is sure to receive a call from a *very* excited friend within 24 hours of Abyzou taking residence (which she does at 3 am on the morning of November 11), inviting them to come to, "The best party you'll ever see."

A successful **Fast Talk**, **Charm**, or **Intimidate** roll garners a bit of information from Emil, whispered through gritted teeth, "*She's not here. She's at the Großes Schauspielhaus over near the Passage. Stay away, if you can.*"

Investigators who insist on lingering are at serious risk of a beating. Unless someone succeeds with a **Listen** or **Spot Hidden** roll, the investigators remain oblivious to the fact that several pock-marked, beefy gentlemen, each wearing a large pinkie ring that reads *Immertreu* (Always Faithful), have stood up and moved into position, forming a circle around them, while another one moves to block the stairs. Any investigator who succeeds on their roll sees (or hears) this happening with enough time to make a quick exit before being cut off. There are a number of these **Ringverein Thugs** (see profile, page 195) equal to the number of investigators plus two.

During any ensuing tumult, one of the *beinls* cheering on the thugs gets violently knocked aside. She smashes into the corner of the bar, cracking her skull—and then some! Half her head shatters open like a porcelain doll. But, instead of brains, only a flow of blood-flecked *gestohlener Blitz* elixir oozes out: a *manikin*! Call for a **Sanity** roll (1/1D6 loss) and a group **Luck** roll to see whether the thugs are also affected; if so, they momentarily pause, providing the investigators with an opportunity to make a run for it (the thugs do not give chase). Otherwise, the thugs won't stop until they've beaten all of the investigators unconscious or at least captured them, at which point they are brought to the Großes Schauspielhaus and dumped in the main theater, within sight of Abyzou (**The Großes Schauspielhaus**, following).

THE GROßES SCHAUSPIELHAUS

And desert creatures shall meet with hyenas,
and a goat-demon shall call to his neighbor;
surely there Lilith shall repose,
and she shall find a resting place for herself.

—Isaiah 34:14 (LEB)

The locus of Abyzou's empire is the Großes Schauspielhaus (**The Alex**, page 28). Here, beneath the soaring, stalactite dome of the theater, Abyzou reigns supreme. Her most debased worshipers, the **Maenads** (page 196), swarm around her, engaged in a constant orgy of debased revelry.

All are welcome at Abyzou's temple; they need only show a willingness to give into the vice that surrounds them as soon as they pass through the theater's doors. Drinks are proffered, while bumps of cocaine and lit hash pipes are thrust into the

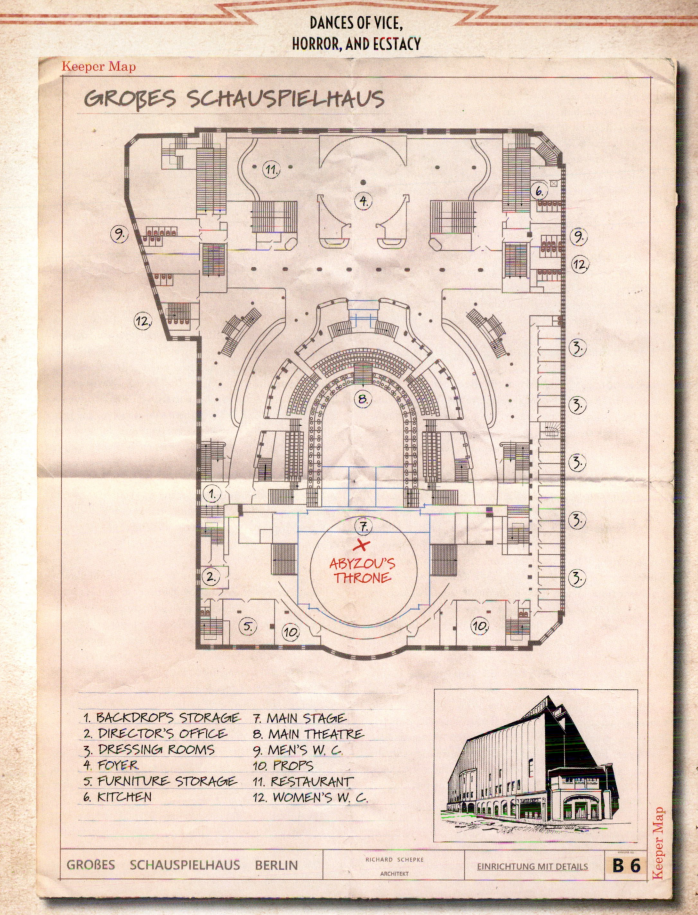

GROßES SCHAUSPIELHAUS

ABYZOU'S
THRONE

1. BACKDROPS STORAGE
2. DIRECTOR'S OFFICE
3. DRESSING ROOMS
4. FOYER
5. FURNITURE STORAGE
6. KITCHEN

7. MAIN STAGE
8. MAIN THEATRE
9. MEN'S W. C.
10. PROPS
11. RESTAURANT
12. WOMEN'S W. C.

GROßES SCHAUSPIELHAUS BERLIN

RICHARD SCHEPKE
ARCHITEKT

EINRICHTUNG MIT DETAILS

B 6

investigators' faces. Men and women, overcome with lustful joy, throw their arms around the newcomers, laughing and kissing them, unbuttoning shirts and blouses.

The hot, humid air reeks of sweat and sex. The atmosphere is a billowing swamp of condensed perspiration, cigarette and opium smoke, and Abyzou's own strange, intoxicating, deadly fog. War veterans are reminded of clouds of mustard gas in No Man's Land, clinging like vaporous oil to skin and clothing.

Pressing through to the main theater, the investigators witness a breathtaking vista. The theater itself, with its expressionistic, cave-like décor, now enfolds a roiling, squirming, rutting orgy, like a nightmare vision from a Bosch painting. Quite a few of the maenads wear masquerade garb, even in states of half-dress or undress, lending the scene an even more surreal edge: Pierrot masks, towering powdered wigs, turbans, oversized and grotesque papier-mâché masks, domino masks, and feathered headdresses decorate many of the revelers.

The stage, which projects out into the center of the round theatrical space, is Abyzou's throne room. There she sits, one leg hooked over the arm of the gold-embossed throne provided for her from the basement, laughing and caressing the heads of those who swarm around her, naked and sweaty, crawling about like animals.

She is clothed only in a scarlet wrap that enfolds her voluptuous hips. A trickle of milk oozes from her nipples, forming glistening, blood-flecked rivulets that run from her bare breasts to her belly and thighs. Honey-golden hair cascades down over her shoulders. Upon her head is a ten-pointed crown, a prop from the theater's costume department. In one hand she holds another prop, a "gold" goblet, from which she occasionally sips, wiping its opalescent fluid from her lips each time she does so. From time to time, she refills the goblet with her breast milk. The whole scene is so striking, so revolting, that it calls for a **Sanity** roll (0/1D4 loss).

Abyzou was incarnated from the flesh of Anita Berber, and so some of Berber's consciousness lives on within the goddess. This is most obvious when Abyzou smiles, for she has the same gap-toothed grin as Berber. This is immediately apparent to any investigator who encounters Abyzou up close and sups from her goblet, for she always smiles when she brings another supplicant under her sway. Those who knew Berber in life see that there is something of the Dresden Madonna within this Whore of Babylon.

Keeper note: see **Abyzou's** profile (page 196); all investigators who are sexually attracted to women must make an Extreme **POW** roll as soon as they see her or else fall under her soporific spell, staring slack-jawed at her beauty. They are now easy prey for the swarming masses around them and their many temptations, but Abyzou has greater plans for them.

- If they have brought Châtin-Hofmann with them, refer to **Through the Seven Gates** (page 187).
- If they have come without Châtin-Hofmann, Abyzou picks the ensorcelled investigators, seemingly at random, from the crowd. In a silken, purring voice not unlike the susurrus of a wind whistling through the ruins of hoary Babylon, she commands them to seek out and find "her no-good husband Henri," and bring him before her. An image of Châtin-Hofmann's face forms in the mind of each afflicted investigator. "*But first,*" she coos, "*come forth and sup of my goblet…*"

Only overt physical removal from the premises or a good, solid punch to the face or other source of intense pain (enough to cause the loss of 1 hit point) breaks the goddess' hold on an investigator. Should such an intervention fail, once Abyzou issues a command to an afflicted investigator, only being the subject of a successful **Psychoanalysis** roll brings them back to their rational mind prior to their completion of the task. Until such time, they risk all to carry out the goddess' wishes, though they are still otherwise in command of their mental faculties. Attempting an action that contravenes an order from Abyzou triggers a Hard **POW** roll; if successful, the investigator may act as desired but loses 1D3 Sanity points from the ensuing stress and mental strain.

What happens now greatly depends on why the investigators came here.

- If they have come to sup the "milk of Shub-Niggurath" from Abyzou's grail, either voluntarily or at her command, they may do so: she beckons supplicants to come before her and kneel, and she tips the contents of the goblet into their mouths. Those who drink are immediately impregnated with a clutch of Abyzou's abominations, which they feel writhing and kicking inside their abdomens (**Sanity** roll; 1/1D6 loss); should the investigator die, their corpse bursts open, releasing the larvae within. See the nearby box, **The Milk of Abyzou**, for more details.
- More militantly minded investigators may have come with the intention of killing Abyzou. If their trip to **The Shadow City** (page 188) ended in failure, this may be their only remaining option. This is, of course, much easier said than done. First, between dusk and dawn Abyzou is normally invulnerable to physical attacks. Second, the moment she senses danger (from physical or magical attacks), she commands her faithful maenads to rise up and protect her. Assume that there are 100+3D100 maenads in the theater at any one time. Lastly, if she is reduced to zero hit

points, she crumples to the ground—only to split apart, unleashing her monstrous form, that of a massive gug-like creature (**Abyzou**, page 196). The horrifying beast sends Abyzou's maenads into a frenzied flight as it sweeps forward, devouring all it can snatch up in its claws (including any unfortunate investigators that might get in its way) for 1D6+1 rounds before winking out of existence (see **Abyzou Returns,** page 191, for more details).

Abyzou's Reach

Although Abyzou spends her nights and days holding court at the Großes Schauspielhaus, she projects her will across Berlin at all times. Her chief instruments for doing so are her fog-spawn, loathsome invisible entities Abyzou births at will, rising from her skin like vapor. These creatures, which exist within the mists also conjured by Abyzou, obey her direct wishes and, when not directly commanded, go about their own malicious ends, choking infants and small children in the night while they slumber in their cribs.

Once Abyzou becomes cognizant of the investigators' threat to her, she will not hesitate to send her "children" against them—see the **Fog-Spawn** profile, page 196.

THROUGH THE SEVEN GATES

If thou openest not the gate to let me enter,
I will break the door, I will wrench the lock,
I will smash the door-posts, I will force the doors.
I will bring up the dead to eat the living.
And the dead will outnumber the living.

—*Descent of the Goddess Ishtar Into the Lower World*
(translated by M. Jastrow, 1915)

All roads eventually lead to Abyzou and her court of madness at the Großes Schauspielhaus. Although all may seem lost in the presence of such a mighty supernatural force, there is one weakness within the Mother of Abominations the investigators may exploit.

As described, Abyzou was incarnated from the flesh of Anita Berber, manifested in her gap-toothed grin. Berber's will manifests also in Abyzou's strange obsession with Châtin-Hofmann. Were it up to the goddess, she wouldn't be bothered with just another flea-speck mortal, but the part of her that is Berber, however muted and suppressed, still wishes to see her old husband again.

Châtin-Hofmann, for his part, is terrified of such a reunion and does everything in his power to prevent it: if the

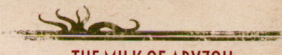

THE MILK OF ABYZOU

Abyzou's ambrosia, a version of the milk of Shub-Niggurath, is possessed of remarkably fecund life-giving properties; Belshazzar and Grau's *gestohlener Blitz* is but a pale imitation. Plants watered with the milk grow to quadruple their normal size but also begin to develop their own, wholly alien (and not altogether friendly) intelligences.

The milk is both highly addictive and terrifically toxic to mortal drinkers. Its substance is corrosive, causing 1 point of damage each time it is touched or swallowed. Those who consume the milk more than 1D3 times become addicted to it with the same intensity as a heroin addiction (**Drugs**, page 40). Over time and with repeated use, the milk works both as an aphrodisiac and soporific, reducing its users to an animal-like cycle of sleeping, eating, and copulating, with little thought for anything else.

Worst of all, however, is that the milk, once ingested, begins transforming the very biology of the subject, literally creating monstrosities within. After 1D10+1 days, those who have supped the milk of Abyzou die in screaming agony as their body bursts open, spilling forth countless larval abominations. These vary from subject to subject, but typical examples include massive, foot-long leeches or maggots, black rats, oversized tarantulas, swarms of horseflies, slimy owls, and so forth. Seeing someone give "birth" to Abyzou's larvae calls for a **Sanity** roll (1/1D6 loss; if the subject was known to the viewer, the loss increases to 2/1D8+1).

Larva inside a living body require periodic "feeding" from more doses of milk but will eventually die naturally to be reabsorbed into the subject's tissues if they go more than a week between feedings—assuming, of course, that the host manages to live that long.

investigators speak openly of their plans to visit Abyzou and do not guard him closely, he attempts to flee. If allowed to get away from the investigators, he is as good as dead.

Assuming Châtin-Hofmann can be tricked, cajoled, or physically conveyed to the Großes Schauspielhaus, he is brought, screaming, before the goddess, although he falls silent as soon as Abyzou presses his lips to her breast, forcing him to suckle her milk direct from its source. After staring intently into his eyes, her brow furrowing, she turns to the investigators, *"Tell me: did this man mourn the death of his wife?"*

If they answer "yes," she replies, "*In what ways did he mourn?*" Allow a single Hard **Persuade** or **Art/Craft (Acting)** roll to evoke the depths of Châtin-Hofmann's heartbreak and regret over his wife's death.

- Investigators able to convince Abyzou of Châtin-Hofmann's grief defuse the situation: she rises, taking Châtin-Hofmann by the hands. "*My dear husband, I know you acted out of sympathy for my condition. But as you see, I have transcended the mortal realm and its petty sufferings. Come, I wish to introduce you to my mistress in her realm.*"
- Failing the roll, or simply answering "no," enrages Abyzou. A pushed roll is allowed, but a failure here indicates the investigator lets slip Châtin-Hofmann's part in Anita's death and her transformation (to the extent the investigators are aware of it).

In either event, she rises from her throne. "*I know not the way to the lower world, but I wish to journey thence. I must pass through the Seven Gates. Tell me where they are to be found.*"

Investigators who have talked to Walter Andrae (**The Pergamon Museum**, page 179), or who remember their dream vision of the transformed Brandenburg Gate (**Totentanz**, page 235), recall that the structure had seven gates. Indeed, the Brandenburg Gate contains five routes through it, plus one on either side—seven gates! The Keeper may allow an **INT** roll to make this connection from the old dream visions if none of the investigators think of it. Failing this, if the investigators are still drawing a blank, the Keeper may have a nearby reveler provide the connection the Brandenburg Gate.

Once provided with this information, Abyzou announces to the whole assembly, "*Come, my faithful! We journey to the City of Shadows!*" She then walks regally from the Schauspielhaus, regardless of time of day, pulling a cowed and compliant Châtin-Hofmann behind her.

What follows is a truly remarkable spectacle, as the naked goddess emerges for the first time onto Friedrichstraße and walks openly down the middle of the street, bringing traffic to a standstill. Her faithful followers pour out after her, cheering and hollering and carrying on. Many on the street immediately fall under Abyzou's spell and fall in with the crowd, while others flee screaming.

Do the investigators follow? Those under the goddess' spell have no choice but to do so. If none of the investigators are afflicted, they may choose to remain behind, of course. The Keeper should make it clear to the investigators that hundreds, if not thousands, of Berliners are traipsing off to what could very well be their doom.

Abyzou's procession moves down the Friedrichstraße and across the grand 200-foot (61 m) wrought-iron expanse of the Weidendammer Bridge, bedecked with imperial eagles and ornate lamps, spanning the Spree. At Unter den Linden, the procession turns right. By now, thousands of Berliners follow in Abyzou's wake as the wind howls and great gouts of foul mists blow down the avenue. The whole tableau is like something out of a nightmare.

Ahead sits the Brandenburg Gate. Only those who have supped from Abyzou's grail may pass through with her—everyone understands this on an instinctual level. Have any investigators not partaken? Now is their last chance. Likewise, if the investigators wish to try and stop Abyzou with physical force, now is their last chance before she reaches the Gate.

Abyzou stands before the Brandenburg Gate, beckoning her followers to pass through the seven passageways, offering her goblet to those who need to sup. Investigators who pause to look note that the revelers seem to disappear before they reach the far side, provoking a **Sanity** roll (0/1D3 loss). Investigators who have not taken any milk from Abyzou's goblet may do so now. Those that do not must remain behind, for good or ill.

Finally passing through the portal, each investigator loses 1D6 magic points and sees before them a massive cedar gate at the far end of the passageway. It stands open, admitting the flow of revelers, but beyond lies only shadow and mist.

THE SHADOW CITY

Emerging through the cedar gate brings the investigators back to the Shadow City of their old nightmares. This automatically costs 1 point of Sanity, as memories of the last trip come bubbling back.

Although they should be standing on the far side of the Brandenburg Gate, looking back over their shoulders, the investigators see that it now resembles the Ishtar Gate from the Pergamon, albeit how it must have looked when it was brand new in the days of ancient Babylon.

Ahead of them stretches Charlottenburger Chausee, the main east-west road through the Tiergarten. On the north side of the street, however, massive Futurist façades rise, just as in their old nightmares. From the buildings' rooflines, blood-red banners hang limply in the eerily still air. Niches set periodically at ground level depict idealized nude sculptures, their faces featureless.

The thousands of revelers accompanying Abyzou look around in wonder, hardly knowing what to think. "*Come, my children!*" the goddess cries as she leads them through a canyon-like passage between two of the outsized buildings.

Assuming the investigators follow, they enter a staggeringly massive plaza square some 3.7 million square feet (85 acres) in size (34,400 square meters/34.4 hectares). Even with its great numbers of revelers, the sheer scale of this space dwarfs the crowd's size.

The Great Tree

With a start, the investigators see that, every 30 yards/meters around the square's perimeter, lamprey-mouthed rabisu stand guard in their black uniforms. Fortunately, they remain standing at attention and seem uninterested in Abyzou or her party.

On the other side of the huge square is a building that matches it in sheer scale. Towering to a height of nearly 1,000 feet (around 300 m) is a great dome, immediately recognizable to the investigators from their prior visit to the Shadow City; glimpsed only from afar until now, it is overwhelming in its sheer size.

Beneath the dome is a colonnaded entrance flanked by two huge statues, both depicting a woman with three faces, garbed in Grecian-style robes. Abyzou leads the assembly across the square and up the stairs to the temple beyond. Entering, the investigators see an enclosed space so huge in dimension that clouds hover up near the top of the dome. The oculus at the dome's apex seems tiny from 1,000 feet (300 m) below but is in fact 150 feet (46 m) across. Silvery moonlight shines in, though no such light source was visible outside.

There is little in the way of a floor under the dome; at the chamber's center lies only a dark abyss. Floating above the abyss, rotating slowly, is a monumental tree in full leaf, complete with a dangling root system, blackened and lifeless, that descends some ways into the pit.

As their eyes adjust to the dim half-light, the investigators can see that the tree is composed of a fleshy, organic substance. The "leaves" are lobe-like flaps; the dead roots are desiccated, mummified flesh.

The tree stops spinning. At the point where the trunk turns into the root system, a massive three-lobed eye opens, flooding the hall with orange light. Other smaller, single-lobed eyes, nine above and nine below, also open now, adding their feeble light to the overall glow. Movement may be discerned among the tree's branches, where a serpentine shape larger than the greatest anaconda slithers, oozing among the tree's soft, pulsating limbs. One end of the enormous, undulating worm splits into seven heads, each of which ends in a gaping, lamprey-like mouth reminiscent of the rabisu.

The final shock comes as the three-lobed eye seems to focus and intensify its light, blinding the investigators. The glare diminishes, and, as their vision returns, the investigators see floating before them, above the tree, a most singular apparition: a woman's head, colossal in scale, with three faces, each pointing in a different direction. The faces each share an eye, meaning there are only three eyes in total—a most eerie sight. The head, in the manner of the tree, rotates slowly but in the opposite direction. Call for a **Sanity** roll for witnessing this bizarre vision (1D3/1D8+2 loss).

Many of those present cannot cope with what they see and go mad. Some flee screaming, others faint dead away, and still others hurl themselves laughing towards the tree, plummeting instead into the blackness of the abyss. As they fall screaming into the pit, a great chorus of eerie wails rises from below. Investigators who dare to look into the abyss are in for quite a sight.

The Pit of the Dead

Measuring 300 feet (91 m) in diameter, the abyss is a massive pit, whose sides gradually incline to form a long cone, seemingly bottomless. The walls of the pit give it its name, composed as they are of 11 million corpses, all dressed in a variety of military uniforms. Stacked and pressed together by the weight of their decaying comrades, the cadavers' arms reach out from the walls of the pit, their rotting throats giving voice to a mournful moan. These are the dead of the Great War, and they hunger for the flesh of the living.

Those looking into the pit must make a **Sanity** roll (1/1D10 loss). Anyone falling into the pit eventually hits the sloping wall, where they are grabbed by the hands of the dead, pulled in, and devoured. Even Abyzou is vulnerable to this fate.

The Three-Lobed Eye

A successful **Cthulhu Mythos** roll recognizes the three-lobed burning eye at the center of the great tree as a possible aspect of Nyarlathotep, the tree as some form of the Dark Mother, Shub-Niggurath.

Abyzou raises her arms imploringly. "*Mother! Mistress! I beseech thee! Give me the power and I shall bring the two worlds together. I have brought with me the blood sacrifice thou desirest.*"

Abyzou is speaking, of course, of the thousands of Berliners who now crowd the hall around the Pit of the Dead. With a word, she may order them all to plunge headfirst into the abyss, along with any investigators who are under her power. There are several possible outcomes in this moment.

- Abyzou is standing near the edge of the pit, and the investigators may attempt to push her in. This is a **Fighting (Brawl)** maneuver opposed by Abyzou's Dodge of 50%. The investigators may try to rush her all at once: determine which investigator has the best **Fighting (Brawl)** skill and apply a bonus die for each investigator in beyond the first (up to a maximum of two bonus dice). Investigators who are under Abyzou's influence must succeed at a Hard **POW** roll to attempt this action or else shrink back, unable to act. Although this approach is probably the best option overall, there is one catch: to hit Abyzou hard enough to pitch her over the edge, the investigator(s) must go over with her. Allow each falling investigator a **DEX** roll to grab the edge of the pit, as well as an opposed **STR** roll against the grasping hands inside the pit (STR 65). If either roll fails, the investigator tumbles to their doom. Should Abyzou fall, there comes a tremendous shriek from the triple-headed goddess above the tree. The whole temple begins to implode, only to be interrupted by a sudden howling noise and the sensation of a malign intelligence clutching at the investigators' minds; moments later, those who did not go into the pit each wake up in their beds (see **Conclusion**, page 192).

- If the investigators prefer to save their own skins and have gathered enough information about Châtin-Hofmann's role in the Berbelo Working, then simply notifying Abyzou (and the tiny fragment of Berber-consciousness within) about his role in Anita's death and "resurrection" is enough to turn the goddess's wrath wholly upon the poor wretch trembling at her feet. She unceremoniously casts him into the pit. Consigning someone, no matter how despicable, to such a fate requires a **Sanity** roll by all investigators present (0/1D3 loss). While this saves thousands of lives, it leaves Abyzou willing and able to return to Berlin to continue her evil work (see **Abyzou Returns**, nearby); however, the death of Châtin-Hofmann in the Pit of the Dead weakens the magic connecting Abyzou to our world and she loses her magical nighttime invulnerability, although she does not know this. She also forgets about her plan to sacrifice her followers, consumed with anger over Châtin-Hofmann's betrayal. She returns to Berlin, along with the citizens who came with her.

- Driven by madness or craven self-preservation, the investigators may try to flee from the temple. When they do so, the rabisu guards outside spring into action and give chase in a terrifying recreation of their old nightmare—almost. This time, if the creatures catch them, there will be no waking up safe in their beds. The rabisu chase the investigators out of the massive square and toward the Ishtar/Brandenburg Gate. Passing through, the investigators reemerge into 1928 Berlin—but with the rabisu hot on their heels! Keepers may wish to use the chase rules (**Chapter Seven**, *Call of Cthulhu Rulebook*) to determine the outcome of this pursuit or else simply describe the rabisu falling upon the local citizenry, tearing their throats out and howling with unholy pleasure while the investigators get away. Meanwhile, those maenads who followed Abyzou to the Shadow City now willingly march over the edge of the abyss and to their doom, constituting a blood sacrifice on a massive scale. The offering complete, a permanent Gate opens, allowing more monstrosities to spill through into an unsuspecting Berlin.

- Investigators who fled due to madness suffer no further Sanity loss, but those who ran due to self-motivated cowardice should now make a **Sanity** roll, with 1D8/2D10 loss as they realize what they have allowed to happen. See **Abyzou Returns** (nearby) for the continuing effects.

What If Henri Is Dead?

Investigators who failed to save Henri Châtin-Hofmann from Baron Grunau's wrath (**A Tearful Farewell**, page 183) or who allowed him to escape their custody (**Through the Seven Gates**, page 187) must deal with an angry goddess. Abyzou, in speaking with investigators at the **Großes Schauspielhaus** (page 184), can sense their failure to protect Châtin-Hofmann and wishes to see them pay for their sin.

Proceed through the events described in the sections above, but any references to Châtin-Hofmann are instead applied to the investigators—including Abyzou's insistence that they hurl themselves into the Pit of the Dead.

Fortunately for the others, Abyzou's anger is sated after the first investigator jumps in—but how to choose the unlucky one? That is for the investigators to work out among themselves.

If none of the investigators are willing to sacrifice themselves, they may of course choose to flee instead, with grave consequences for the city (**Abyzou Returns**, following).

ABYZOU RETURNS

If the investigators fail to destroy Abyzou in the Shadow City, then they have no choice but to try and destroy her back in Berlin.

Upon her return, Abyzou rules openly from her throne at the Großes Schauspielhaus. If Châtin-Hofmann died, her Berber-fragment has been banished for good, and with it any traces of mortal sympathy. If it hasn't happened already, she begins working toward opening a permanent connection between the Shadow City and Berlin via the Brandenburg Gate, a task she completes in 1D6 days.

The investigators should bring everything they can to bear against Abyzou. This may include contacts in the military or law enforcement who remain independent of the goddess' influence, or even paramilitary forces. Consulting with Belshazzar is an excellent way to find out details about Abyzou's strengths and weaknesses, including her nocturnal invulnerability—remember that if Châtin-Hofmann died in the Pit of the Dead, Abyzou has lost this valuable protection.

As noted previously, Abyzou does not die when she reaches zero hit points. Instead, she spawns an abomination of her own, a terrifying monstrous giant similar to the gugs of the Dreamlands. This creature has only two hands instead of four, but it possesses a massive, fanged mouth that originates in the crotch between its stumpy legs and proceeds vertically up the middle of the torso. Rampaging, it scoops victims up with its claw attacks and stuffs them into its gaping maw. The monstrous abomination cannot last long in our world, however. After 1D6+1 rounds, it blinks out of existence, effectively ending Abyzou's presence on Earth.

Abyzou's Victory?

If the investigators fail to stop Abyzou, other forces eventually do the job, albeit at great cost. Akin to the raid that takes place in Lovecraft's story "The Shadow Over Innsmouth," the Reichswehr is called in to put an end to the grotesque chaos, and after much fighting against crazed maenads and unholy monstrosities, Abyzou's empire is crushed, leaving thousands dead or mentally broken. Berlin's buildings acquire a new set of bullet scars as well—although not for the last time. Officially, the whole incident is recorded as one more political uprising. The Republic traipses further toward collapse as the Nazi Party seizes upon this unprecedented level of unrest to gain yet more seats in the next round of elections.

Closing the Gate for Good

If Abyzou manages to open a Gate between Berlin and the Shadow City, she may be stymied in her plans by closing off the connection, although this option is probably available only to seasoned investigators by dint of their greater occult (and Mythos) knowledge and experience. A successful **Cthulhu Mythos** roll divines that the connection between the Shadow City and Berlin may be severed by placing an Elder Sign at each of the seven passageways of the Brandenburg Gate. The Sign must be inscribed and set permanently; allow the players to be creative in coming up with a plan to do so. This act also has the benefit of ending the investigators' nightmares of the events of August 1926 for good.

CONCLUSION

Investigators defeating Abyzou, either in the Shadow City or our own realm, are left with something of a mess on their hands. The goddess' spell is broken immediately, which makes for hundreds of shocked and ashamed former maenads. Many lose their minds, broken by the depths of excess to which they sank. Others run screaming into the streets, covering their faces in shame. The strange incident of Abyzou's tenure on Earth is quietly swept under the rug by an embarrassed citizenry. At least there aren't any more flocks of owls or swarms of hissing cockroaches to contend with.

Investigators who destroyed Abyzou in the Shadow City wake in their beds at home, an eerie parallel to the waking nightmare that started this part of the scenario. A month has passed. Did all that really happen? Are their jobs in jeopardy? After all, no one has seen or heard from them in all this time. The wind no longer rattles the windows, and—although Berlin remains a city of sin—things seem to be back to normal. The Großes Schauspielhaus has returned to showing plays and light opera with nary a word of its brief tenure as a locus for criminal vice and murder.

Investigators asking after Erma Kore discover that she has no records on file, being apparently an unregistered resident. Going to her apartment finds an old retired couple who have just moved in; they know nothing of the previous occupant.

As a final postscript, describe the following scene to one of the investigators.

Two days before Christmas, they are riding a tram or bus line back home after doing some Christmas shopping. The big article in the paper today relates to a strange death at

Handout: Dances 5

Berliner Herold

Zeitung in Berlin | Nachrichten * Theater * Film * Sport * Finanziell * | Seiten der Werbung

Vol. 2 | 23 Dezember 1926 | 10 Pfennig

Murder in the Library

Police report that a young man, an employee of the Prussian State Library by the name of Ralf Schneider, was found dead at the library this morning when other employees arrived for work. Poor Mr. Schneider was discovered on the floor of the Rare Books and Manuscripts wing. Police inform us that foul play is suspected and ask any members of the public with

information that may pertain to this case to contact Inspector Krieg of the Criminal Police straight away.

Dr. F. Milkau, director of the Prussian State Library, reports that nothing seems to have gone missing from the Rare Books and Manuscripts wing, although as the wing contains many thousands of volumes, it will take some time to

make absolutely certain.

"Mr. Schneider was one of our brightest young librarians with a promising career ahead of him. His death is an absolute tragedy, and has proven quite a blow to our staff," Dr. Milkau said in a statement to our reporter.

We will, naturally, bring you further details of this shocking case as they become known to us.

the Prussian State Library (**Handout: Dances 5**; the report foreshadows the events of the final scenario in this book, **Schreckfilm** (page 201), although the investigator is not to know this). Outside the steamy windows, fat flakes of snow are beginning to fall, presaging a big winter storm due to blow in tonight. Most of the folks on the bus are doing their holiday shopping and getting ready for Christmas. The vehicle pulls to a stop. Idly, the investigator notices a man getting up out of his seat a few rows up. Something catches the investigator's eye: right at the hairline on the back of his neck, the man bears a mark—that of Belshazzar the Doll Maker! As the man stands up, he looks back at the investigator—he has their face! Winking at the investigator, their *dopplegänger* alights from the conveyance. The car is too crowded with holiday shoppers to pursue, and now the conveyance is on its way again. Could it have simply been the investigator's imagination? Surely that must be it…

REWARDS

Grant the players an investigator development phase when they have completed this scenario and apply the following awards to each surviving investigator.

- Defeating/destroying Abyzou: +1D10+2 Sanity points.
- Permanently closing the gate to the Shadow City: +1D6+1 Sanity points.
- For each week that passed while Abyzou remained on Earth: −1D2 Sanity points.
- Failing entirely to stop Abyzou: −2D10 Sanity points.

For Investigators Who Fell into the Abyss

This section is presented as an option for characters sacrificing themselves in the Pit of the Dead. The Keeper may decide whether those deaths should remain permanent or if the characters deserve redemption of a sort.

If any investigators ended the scenario on good terms with the doll maker, Belshazzar does his best to repay their heroism. Unfortunately, the best he can manage is to craft a *manikin* in the image of the deceased investigator(s). After the surviving characters complete their investigator development phases and receive their final Sanity rewards, relate the following to those who fell into the pit.

You wake up with a jolt. You are back in your bed at home! Your time in the Shadow City seems an ever-dimming memory. Indeed, you can scarcely recall it even now, as it quickly fades like a half-remembered dream. Sitting up, you can see that your bedroom is a little dusty, the air stuffy, as if you have been away for a while.

The investigators find they have been gone for a month. They are possibly out of a job and have many other logistical headaches to sort out, far too many to worry about how

MANIKIN-INVESTIGATORS

Manikins are, as a general rule, unaware of their status, thinking themselves regular flesh-and-blood creatures. For all intents and purposes, they are. Characters "re-born" as *manikins* have their original Sanity points (equal to one-fifth POW) restored, regardless of what they were at the time of their living counterpart's death. Any skill checks acquired over the course of the scenario are, however, erased.

Clues to the character's true nature are few but significant. First, they experience frequent episodes of *déjà vu*, as Belshazzar has filled in gaps in their personalities with his own day-to-day experiences. Secondly, they don't ever remember their dreams—in truth, they are incapable of dreaming now. In campaigns featuring trips to the Dreamlands, *manikin*-investigators may only cross over physically, never through dreams. *Manikin*-investigators otherwise function mechanically exactly as per their flesh-and-blood fellows—they sweat, bleed, eat, and excrete just like normal—with one important exception.

If a *manikin*-investigator ever takes a major wound, their true nature is revealed for all to see. Keepers may wish to use the **Optional Hit Locations** rule (*Call of Cthulhu Rulebook*, pages 126) when a *manikin*-investigator takes such an injury. The result indicates where the hit took place and where there is now a massive gaping hole in the ceramic of the doll's body, which leaks a milky-white substance shot through with blood. Eerily, the investigator is still able to move, walk, and talk as normal. Although minor wounds heal normally, a major wound requires Belshazzar's skills of to fix; until that happens, the investigator may never heal more than half their total hit points, and has a rather obvious hole in their body, limb, or head! The Sanity loss to witness a *manikin*-investigator take this sort of wound is 1/1D6 points. To experience this type of wound is, no pun intended, a potentially shattering moment as the *manikin* realizes their true nature, incurring 2/2D10+1 Sanity loss.

One final note: if this scenario is being run as a one-shot, or one or more of the players needs to generate a replacement character at the start or during the course of the scenario, it may be a fun idea to have them play a *Manikinmensch*.

exactly they made it back after their fall into that dreadful pit. See the nearby box **Manikin-Investigators** for further details relating to their new state.

CHARACTERS AND MONSTERS

NON-PLAYER CHARACTERS

Assume that all statistics provided refer to the 1926 version of the non-player character (NPC), unless that person is first (or only) encountered in 1928.

Albin Grau, *42, artist-occultist*

STR 55	CON 50	SIZ 50	DEX 60	INT 85
APP 55	POW 80	EDU 85	SAN 73	HP 10
DB: 0	Build: 0	Move: 8	MP: 16	

Combat
Brawl	30% (15/6), damage 1D3
Dodge	30% (15/6)

Skills
Art/Craft (Painting) 75%, Cthulhu Mythos 12%, Electrical Repair 45%, Fast Talk 55%, History 40%, Language (English) 20%, Language (French) 50%, Language (German) 85%, Library Use 55%, Mechanical Repair 55%, Occult 85%, Psychology 50%, Stealth 50%.

Spells: Chant of Thoth, Elder Sign, Prinn's Crux Ansata, plus 1D4 other spells of the Keeper's choosing.

Anita Berber, *27, priestess of depravity*

STR 60	CON 40	SIZ 40	DEX 85	INT 75
APP 70	POW 90	EDU 55	SAN 80	HP 8
DB: 0	Build: 0	Move: 9	MP: 32*	

Berber's magic points have been artificially inflated through magical rituals enacted by Châtin-Hofmann, turning her into a living battery of magical energy.

Combat
Brawl	30% (15/6), damage 1D3
Dodge	42% (21/8)

Skills
Art/Craft (Acting) 35%, Art/Craft (Dance) 80%, Art/Craft (Poetry) 55%, Charm 60%, Fast Talk 65%, History 30%, Language (English) 20%, Language (French) 45%, Language (German) 55%, Language (Russian) 20%, Occult 35%, Psychology 40%, Sleight of Hand 30%, Stealth 40%, Throw 45%.

Henri Châtin-Hofmann, *26, dancer and dabbler*

STR 60	CON 70	SIZ 55	DEX 75	INT 50
APP 60	POW 55	EDU 60	SAN 45	HP 12
DB: 0	Build: 0	Move: 9	MP: 11	

Combat
Brawl	30% (15/6), damage 1D3
Dodge	37% (18/7)

Skills
Art/Craft (Dance) 70%, Art/Craft (Piano) 75%, Cthulhu Mythos 5%, Fast Talk 65%, Language (English 60%, Language (German) 15%, Medicine 15%, Occult 40%, Persuade 50%, Psychology 35%, Sleight of Hand 30%, Stealth 35%.

Spells: The Unending Revelry (Dionysian Revels)*, Enthrall Victim.

*See **Spells** (page 199).

Erma Kore, *17, telephone-girl with a secret*

STR 35	CON 65	SIZ 35	DEX 60	INT 65
APP 90	POW 60	EDU 50	SAN 54	HP 10
DB: −1	Build: −1	Move: 8	MP: 12	

Combat
Brawl	25% (12/5), damage 1D3−1
Dodge	30% (15/6)

Skills
Art/Craft (Acting) 75%, Charm 75%, Disguise 50%, Fast Talk 55%, Language (Dutch) 20%, Language (English) 20%, Language (German) 50%, Listen 60%, Occult 25%, Persuade 65%, Psychology 80%, Sleight of Hand 35%, Stealth 55%, Throw 50%.

Belshazzar the Doll Maker, *90(?), Kabbalistic artisan*

STR 40	CON 45	SIZ 50	DEX 65	INT 75
APP 40	POW 80	EDU 80	SAN 70	HP 9
DB: 0	Build: 0	Move: 2	MP: 16	

Combat
Brawl	25% (12/5), damage 1D3
Dodge	32% (16/6)

Skills

Art/Craft (Doll Making) 95%, Cthulhu Mythos 8%, History 70%, Language (Ancient Greek) 35%, Language (Akkadian) 20%, Language (German) 75%, Language (Hebrew) 75%, Language (Latin) 45%, Language (Yiddish) 80%, Library Use 65%, Occult 85%, Psychoanalysis 30%, Psychology 45%.

Spells: Create Living Doll*, Elder Sign.
*See **Spells** (page 199).

Gregor Gregorius, *38, occult bookstore owner*

STR 50	CON 70	SIZ 55	DEX 50	INT 65
APP 45	POW 90	EDU 75	SAN 63	HP 12
DB: 0	Build: 0	Move: 7	MP: 18	

Combat

Brawl	25% (12/5), damage 1D3
Dodge	25% (12/5)

Skills

Appraise 35%, Archaeology 40%, Fast Talk 50%, Intimidate 65%, Language (English) 15%, Language (Enochian) 15%, Language (German) 75%, Language (Italian) 25%, Library Use 70%, Natural World 45%, Occult 85%, Psychology 65%, Spot Hidden 45%.

Spells: Contact Deity (Tsathoggua), Dominate, Elder Sign, Enthrall Victim, Implant Fear, Mental Suggestion, Mirror of Tarkhun Atep, Shrivelling.

Walter Andrae, *53, architect and archaeologist*

STR 60	CON 65	SIZ 60	DEX 60	INT 65
APP 60	POW 55	EDU 80	SAN 55	HP 12
DB: 0	Build: 0	Move: 6	MP: 11	

Combat

Brawl	45% (22/9), damage 1D3
Dodge	30% (15/6)

Skills

Anthropology 25%, Archaeology 75%, First Aid 45%, History 60%, Language (Akkadian) 40%, Language (Arabic) 45%, Language (English) 15%, Language (French) 65%, Language (German) 80%, Language (Sumerian) 40%, Library Use 70%, Navigate 35%, Occult 20%, Persuade 55%, Survival (Desert) 40%.

Ringverein Thug

Use this profile for any thugs, guards, and general hoodlums as needed.

STR 70	CON 65	SIZ 85	DEX 55	INT 45
APP 45	POW 50	EDU 40	SAN 50	HP 15
DB: +1D4	Build: 1	Move: 7	MP: 10	

Combat

Brawl	70% (35/14), damage 1D3+1D4
Dodge	40% (20/8)

Skills

Climb 50%, Fast Talk 35%, Intimidate 50%, Language (German) 40%, Look Menacing 65%, Psychology 30%, Stealth 40%, Throw 50%.

CREATURES AND MONSTERS

Rabisu,
famished cannibal residents of the Shadow City

Use this profile for all rabisu. Their skin is a pallid gray and they are without eyes or ears; their faces are little more than gaping, lamprey-like maws ringed with jagged teeth. They sense prey by smell and vibration.

STR 35	CON 55	SIZ 50	DEX 55	INT 35
APP —	POW 50	EDU —	SAN —	HP 10
DB: 0	Build: 0	Move: 8	MP: 10	

Combat

Attacks per round: 1 (bite, claw, kick, kiss)

Kiss: with a successful kiss attack, the rabisu latches onto the target, draining 1D10 magic points in the following round unless the target can succeed in an opposed **POW** roll (roll each round). If magic points are drained to zero, the rabisu detaches from the unconscious target. Breaking free of a rabisu's kiss requires a successful **STR** roll.

Kiss	80% (40/16), damage 1D10 MP drain
Claws	85% (42/17), damage 1D6
Dodge	50% (25/10)

Skills

Stealth 55%, Track by Scent 95%.

Armor: none.
Sanity loss: 0/1D3 Sanity points to see a single rabisu; 1/1D6 points to see a whole swarm.

Fog-Spawn, *instruments of Abyzou's dark will*

Near invisible and shrouded in fog, these monsters are comprised of other-dimensional matter and are insubstantial in earthly terms. Though insubstantial, they might be seen momentarily in bright light as a sparkling gray cloud with thin, whip-like tentacles. Fog-spawn give off a strange odor of burning hair (noticeable when within 25 feet; 8 m) and rarely venture forth out of darkness, as they are averse to bright light.

STR 150	CON 150	SIZ 150	DEX 90	INT 5
APP —	POW 125	EDU —	SAN —	HP n/a
DB: n/a	Build: n/a	Move: 10	MP: 25	

Combat

Attacks per round: 6 tentacles of mist, each with a reach of 35 feet (10.5 m)

Fighting: the fog-spawn inserts pliable tentacles into the nostrils and mouth of the target—up to six victims simultaneously—inflicting choking damage, which increases each round: 1 point of damage in first round, 2 points of damage in second round, 3 points of damage in third round, and so on. If the target can win an opposed **STR** roll versus the STR of the tentacles, they may break free and escape. Each tentacle has STR 25, multiplied by the number of tentacles attacking the individual; thus, if the fog-spawn performs three successful attacks on one target, the opposed roll is versus STR 75, and so on.

Investigators suffer a penalty die to all attempts to hit the monster (they must essentially make wild attacks), with fumbles meaning they have hit an ally or the fog-spawn's victim instead.

Insubstantial: immune to physical attacks. Direct sunlight dispels the fog-spawn back to its native dimension (transition takes ten minutes), from whence it cannot return. Strong beams of light may cause a fog-spawn to retreat. If it can find a perpetually dark place, such as a deep sewer or a cave, the fog-spawn might stay on Earth for some time.

Fighting	50% (25/10), treat as surprise attack, see Fighting for damage details
Dodge	n/a

Skills

Hunt for Victim 65%, Stealth 95%.

Armor: none—the fog-spawn is insubstantial, and nothing material can harm it. Bright light can drive it away but does not actually harm it.

Sanity loss: 1/1D10 Sanity points to see a fog-spawn. Automatically lose 1D8 Sanity points upon the fog-spawn's first successful attack.

Maenads, *crazed mortal followers of Abyzou*

STR 75*	CON 75	SIZ 60	DEX 55	INT 25*
APP —	POW 50	EDU —	SAN —	HP 13*
DB: +1D4	Build: 1	Move: 8	MP: 10	

Attributes are artificially altered due to constant adrenaline rush caused by Abyzou's influence.

Combat

Attacks per round: 2 (claw, or grab and bite)

Fighting: may attack twice with their bare hands, attempting to claw the flesh from opponents' bones, or alternatively may attempt a grab and bite fighting maneuver—roll to grab; if successful, roll to bite with a bonus die (bite bonus is applicable for each round following if target is still held). Target may break free of grab with opposed **STR** or **DEX** roll.

Claw	50% (25/10), damage 1D3+1D4
Grab (mnvr)	50% (25/10), roll to bite with bonus die
Bite	35% (17/7), damage 1D3+1D4
Dodge	27% (13/5)

Skills

Gibber and Rut 85%, Listen 40%, Spot Hidden 50%.

Armor: none.

Sanity loss: none, or 1/1D4 Sanity points if pursued by a large horde of maenads out for blood.

Abyzou,
Whore of Babylon, Mother of Abominations

STR 150	CON 265	SIZ 45	DEX 100	INT 125
APP 125	POW 175	EDU —	SAN —	HP 31
DB: +1D6	Build: 2	Move: 9	MP: 35	

Combat

Attacks per round: 1 (claw, kiss)

Fighting: may attempt to kiss one helpless or willing victim per round; alternatively, she attacks with her preternaturally sharp fingernails, clawing for the softest and most vulnerable parts of her target.

Enthrall: all who are sexually aroused by the female form (i.e. straight men, lesbian women, bisexual men or women) must make an opposed **POW** roll when they see Abyzou; those failing may do nothing more than stare in dumbfounded stupefaction, overcome by Abyzou's beauty (those who succeed are free to act). Abyzou may then command anyone under her sway to do her bidding; such commands are executed eagerly, even if leading to suicidal or dangerous situations. Attempting an action in contravention of Abyzou's orders triggers a Hard **POW** roll; if successful, the investigator may act as desired but loses 1D3 Sanity points from the ensuing stress. Breaking Abyzou's hold requires the target to suffer at least 1 point of damage or receive a successful **Psychoanalysis** roll.

Kiss: anyone kissed must win an opposed **POW** roll to avoid losing 1D10 magic points, which are gained by Abyzou.

Kiss	100% (50/20), damage 1D10 MP drain
Claw	85% (42/17), damage 1D6+1D6
Dodge	50% (25/10)

Skills
Charm 100%, Inspire Others 100%, Stealth 100%.

Armor: cannot be harmed by any physical attack between sunset and sunrise. During daylight hours, may be harmed normally. Abyzou may also regenerate 1 hit point for every magic point she spends. If reduced to zero hit points, Abyzou rises in her monstrous form (see following).
Spells: Clutch of Nyogtha, Flesh Ward, Melt Flesh, Quicken Fog-Spawn*, Shrivelling, Steal Life, Wither Limb.
Sanity loss: 0/1D4 to see Abyzou.

Abyzou's Monstrous Form

STR 225	CON 140	SIZ 285	DEX 50	INT 65
APP —	POW 50	EDU —	SAN —	HP 42
DB: +5D6	Build: 6	Move: 7	MP: 10	

Combat
Attacks per round: 1 or 2 (1 bite or 2 claw)

Fighting	40% (20/8), damage 4D6+5D6
Bite	60% (30/12), damage 1D10
Dodge	25% (12/5)

Armor: 8 points of wrinkly hide. If reduced to zero hit points Abyzou exits this dimension.
Sanity loss: 1/1D10 Sanity points to see Abyzou in her monstrous form.

Rabisu

PHASES OF THE MOON

Because Abyzou's complexion moves from midnight black to silvery white over the course of a lunar month, Keepers may wish to reference the following chart for phases of the moon in November 1928 for an idea of how she'll appear on any given day.

- November 12: new moon—Abyzou appears ebon black.
- November 20: first quarter—Abyzou appears steely gray.
- November 27: full moon—Abyzou appears milky white, almost luminescent.
- December 3: third quarter—Abyzou appears steely gray.

TOMES

Fraternitas Saturni Magical Letters

German, by Gregor Gregorius, c. 1926

These pamphlets are part of an ongoing series produced by Gregor Gregorius, head of the *Fraternitas Saturni* (Brotherhood of Saturn), a brand-new but increasingly influential association of magicians and occultists in Berlin. Gregorius is producing these pamphlets as a means of disseminating magical knowledge to the public; as such, each pamphlet contains a small tract of esoteric knowledge and a minor magical working (non-Mythos)—though the magic contained within is of little practical use.

- **Sanity Loss:** none
- **Occult:** +1 percentile
- **Study:** 3 days for each pamphlet

Das Necronomicon

German, translated by Gregor Gregorius, 1926–28

Gregor Gregorius is slowly translating a copy of Olaus Wormius' Latin *Necronomicon* into German. The original book is held at the Prussian State Library, but Gregorius keeps his scattered and incomplete notes located in his office at Inveha. Assembling these notes into a single volume creates an *ersatz* tome.

- **Sanity Loss:** 1D6
- **Cthulhu Mythos:** +1/+3
- **Mythos Rating:** 12
- **Study:** 30 weeks
- **Suggested Spells:** Call/Dismiss Yog-Sothoth, Contact Deity/Nyarlathotep, Dominate, Dread Curse of Azathoth, Resurrection, Shrivelling, Voorish Sign.

SPELLS

Create Living Doll (Create Golem variant)

- **Cost:** 15 magic points; 25 POW; 1D6 Sanity points
- **Casting time:** 1D6+4 days

Fashions and brings to life an artificial being made of porcelain: a *Manikinmensch*. Unlike a golem, these "doll-people" can understand and speak a rich variety of language and carry on an autonomous lifestyle if given the opportunity.

Once the *manikin* has been constructed from porcelain and human hair, the *gestohlener Blitz* elixir, along with the activation word (in the case of Belshazzar's creations, his maker's mark: *emet*) and the necessary arcane incantations, give it life. Creation of the *manikin* requires at least one week, a successful Art/Craft (Doll making) roll, and the necessary spell costs.

These living dolls are unaware of their true nature unless they receive a major wound, which instantly makes visible their manufactured status. The only way to "kill" a *manikin* is to smash it to pieces, thus draining it completely of the elixir and destroying the word animating it.

Undying Revelry (Dionysian Revels)

- **Cost:** 2 magic points; 1D6 Sanity points
- **Casting time:** 5 minutes

To cast this spell originally used by priests of Dionysius to whip worshippers into a frenzy, the caster must make a successful Art/Craft (Sing, Dance, Musical Instrument, and so on) roll to begin their dance. They then begin casting the spell as they weave their way through the revelers. Each person witnessing this dance must make an opposed POW roll against the caster or they too begin dancing without heed to their surroundings or circumstances for 1D10 hours. For each hour of such exertion, a reveler must make a Hard CON roll or fall unconscious.

Once satisfied with the revels they have engendered, the caster may sacrifice an additional magic point to break free of the dance; the other dancers must continue until the spell expires or they collapse. For every dancer collapsing, the caster gains 1D4 magic points as long as they remain within sight of the revelry.

Quicken Fog-Spawn (variant)

- **Cost:** 25 magic points; 10 POW; 1D6 Sanity points
- **Casting time:** 5 rounds

Usually, this spell requires the larva of an other-dimensional Mythos entity (sometime known as "Gish-rla" but which has many conflicting names). The spell must be cast within dense fog through which no bright light can penetrate. A drop of the caster's blood must be smeared on the larva and the spell's cost paid. In Abyzou's case, however, she can summon both the necessary fog and the larvae from her skin via this spell instantaneously and at no cost.

The creatures summoned may be mentally commanded by the caster to move in any direction and to act as the caster chooses (usually it is directed to kill, as the creature has limited mental faculties). While mere mortals must remain within 200 feet of the creature or it will go free, Abyzou is under no such limitations. If she cares to think about it, then she can sense her "children's" approximate location wherever they might be in the city; however, while she can control her pets for as long as she wishes, the fog-spawn will still flee if faced with bright light, and direct sunlight dispels the creatures, although they possess sufficient intelligence to find a place of darkness to lurk in during daylight hours. Once released from Abyzou's control, the creatures vanish back to their own realm.

SCHRECKFILM

An aristocratic witch cult is intent on filming a movie adaptation of the Necronomicon. *Their magical machinations cast a pall of menace over Berlin. After a reporter involves them in her deadly caper, the investigators infiltrate both Berlin's film industry and the witch cult that runs part of it, courting disaster and eternal servitude in so doing.*

KEEPER SUMMARY

This is the final scenario of the *Berlin: The Wicked City* trilogy and is intended to be the most personal. Unlike the previous two adventures, the city at large is not endangered directly. This is a tale of the investigators facing the demons in their own minds, of experiencing total isolation in the middle of a city of four million souls.

There are two separate factions at play in this scenario, and thwarting one faction does not necessarily stop the other. On the one hand, the investigators are personally threatened by the attentions of Countess Ágnes Esterházy and her witch cult. The only way to resolve this situation is to destroy the former noblewoman. Ironically, the investigators have the means to do so in their hands from the very start of the scenario but won't necessarily realize it right away. On the other hand, the investigators should wish, for the good of the world, to prevent Baron Grunau's latest film, *Das Necronomicon,* from ever reaching completion, for once it does it will unleash a time "with laws and morals thrown aside and all men shouting and killing and reveling in joy." Unfortunately for the investigators, shutting down the film's production may prove to be their ultimate undoing.

With a few exceptions, this scenario does not operate on an absolute timeline. The investigators are free to pursue their ends however they choose.

AUTHOR NOTE

The underlying theme of this scenario is algolagnia (the craving of pain for sexual pleasure), expressed through the machinations of a witch cult that has sunk its claws deep into the power structures of Berlin through its ring of Dominas operating out of the Salon Kitty brothel. In Stephen King's Danse Macabre analysis of horror, the primary category featured in this scenario is Terror, which he defines as, "when the lights go out and you feel something behind you, you hear it, you feel its breath against your ear, but when you turn around, there's nothing there…"

BACKGROUND

It is a frozen night in Berlin. The city's lights mock the icy darkness in hollow defiance. The good-time party atmosphere rolls on but has taken on an indifferent atmosphere to mirror the weather. It is January 1, 1932—a Friday, and New Year's Day. After a respite of six years following the end of the Great Inflation in 1924, the economy has tanked again thanks to the knock-on effects of the American stock market crash in October 1929. There are more than half-a-million unemployed people in the city, and street violence between right- and left-wing militias is nearly constant. Despair lies over the city like a stifling blanket.

Opposite: Agnes, the puppeteer

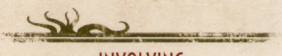

INVOLVING INVESTIGATOR ORGANIZATIONS

Although, as mentioned, the immediate hook for this scenario should work for just about any investigator group, individual organizations are bound to have different motivations for continuing the investigation. Following are suggestions for investigators who are all members of one of the groups outlined under **Investigator Organizations** (page 16).

The Independent Order of Owls: this scenario is a home run for the Owls—finding evidence of an actual witch coven operating among the upper classes of Berlin society is exactly the reason the Owls were founded! Indeed, Keepers may decide that the Sapient Screecher and assorted other high-ranking officials (possibly including one or more of the investigators) have had their suspicions about Countess Esterházy for some time, although she seems to have disappeared from the public eye.

Hilde-Film: the hook here is Baron Grunau and his film production. As a studio in the business of making occult-centered films themselves, Hilde-Film no doubt sees Grunau's efforts as direct competition. Discovery of Grunau's strange alchemical techniques of film processing only further motivates investigation.

Landsberger Tenants' Association: as established in **Dances of Vice, Horror, and Ecstasy,** Baron Grunau is owner of the residential flats where the Tenants' Association resides. A shadowy figure in the former scenario, he comes into his full menace here. Indeed, once the investigators' role in the mystery becomes known to him and his allies (**The Coven's Activity**, page 213), eviction notices are sure to follow, carried out with extreme prejudice at the hands of the Criminal Police.

The Apache Pathfinders: in many ways, this is a classic scenario for the "youngsters solving creepy mysteries" genre. Adolescents already tend to be suspicious of adults in positions of power, so uncovering a wide-ranging conspiracy among the city's elite is bound to feed existing suspicions.

Suicides are way up this winter. Driven by personal grief, political crisis, or simple *ennui*, Berliners choose to end it all in record numbers. One favored method is an icy plunge into the waters in and around Berlin, chiefly the Spree and Havel Rivers and their canals. Many of these bodies, washed downstream toward the Grunewald, are fetching up near the Friedhof Grunewald-Forst, also called "the Graveyard of the Nameless" (see **Berlin's Cemeteries**, page 67). The Keeper should give the players **Handout: Schreckfilm 1** at the beginning of the scenario to establish the grim mood currently gripping Berlin.

Every day of the scenario, the Keeper should ask each investigator to make a **Luck** roll. With a failure, they receive word that someone they know has committed suicide. This may be a contact, a friendly non-player character met in a previous scenario, or even a significant person (provided they are not also the investigator's key connection, of course). Alternately, the Keeper may simply choose a different investigator each day to be the recipient of such bad news. These "background suicides" serve to create an overall feeling of gloom and mournful loss. They also potentially come back to haunt the investigators, quite literally, in the final portion of the scenario.

INTRODUCING THE INVESTIGATORS

The photograph that leads Lina Desmond to the investigators (**Going Over the Dossier: 3-by-5 Photograph**, page 210) means that every type of player character can become embroiled in the plot, regardless of whether they know each other at the outset—after all, despite its fading grandeur, **Luna Park** (page 208) is still a favorite location for an evening stroll for both residents and visitors to Berlin. Even if the investigators are complete strangers, serendipity has undoubtedly brought them together in the park for their New Year's Day revels, ready to uncover the truth behind Fräulein Desmond's dropped dossier.

While this initial hook is all-encompassing, there are several potential reasons why investigators may wish to remain involved, besides the imminent threat to their safety. Perhaps a reporter knows of Lina Desmond and, although they may not have worked together, is aware of the quality of her work, meaning they are more likely to believe even her most outlandish claims. Or perhaps one or more investigators know girls who've gone to work for Madam Kitty and have heard whispers of the strange goings-on at this infamous bordello.

Of course, if the investigators survived the events of their previous two adventures with their bodies and minds largely intact, then they know (or are aware of) at least one of the antagonists in this scenario: Baron Grunau. This could mean that, despite appearances, the investigators' entanglement in this latest escapade may be anything but accidental, the baron's motives in involving them may be are left to the Keeper to decide.

DRAMATIS PERSONAE

Lina Desmond, *27, investigative reporter*

The mystery woman who kick-starts the scenario, Desmond is an investigative reporter in way over her head. On the trail of Berlin's witch cult, she was considered nothing more than a petty nuisance until she laid hands on Countess Esterházy's most treasured possession: a seemingly innocuous cutting of 35mm film.

- **Description:** fair-haired in contrast to her sister's dark aspect, she still retains some traces of her once-refined beauty, although months of living rough have taken their toll. She is noticeably underweight and sleep-deprived, and hasn't had the time or motivation to purchase a proper winter wardrobe and is, therefore, obliged to wear summer frocks in spite of the freezing temperatures.
- **Traits:** a clearly determined woman, evident in her steely gaze and firm-set jaw. Once fixed on a goal, she lets nothing deter her from pursuing it, even if it means her own undoing. Feeling guilty for involving the investigators in her deadly pursuit, Desmond does what she can to make amends. She is also secretly relieved to have more people helping—she wasn't sure how much longer she was going to be able to stay on the run.
- **Roleplaying Hooks:** Desmond is committed to printing her story and is devastated by the loss of her dossier. She seeks out the investigators just as doggedly as her foes do, praying she reaches them first. Once she finds them, she proves a valuable ally, albeit one with a potentially deadly secret: "Lina Desmond" is Ágnes Esterházy's sister, Alma!

Baron Grunau, *58, occultist and filmmaker*

Amateur archaeologist, dissipated dilettante, debased occultist, and movie producer. After the failure of Albin Grau's Prana Films (which Grunau largely financed) in 1922, the baron began looking for a new way to bring his interest in the occult to the masses. He found it in the pages of Gregor Gregorius' translation of the *Necronomicon* (see **Das Necronomicon**, page 198), and his wish to consult the primary source led to bloody murder at the Prussian State Library, as revealed at the end of **Dances of Vice, Horror, and Ecstasy** (**Handout: Dances 5**, page 192).

Eventually, Grunau took it upon himself to write a film treatment of certain elements in that blasted tome, in something of the manner of Benjamin Christensen's 1922 pseudo-documentary *Häxan* (*Witches*). But Grunau continually found his creative efforts falling far short of his madness-tinged vision, so he turned to the witch-cult of Ágnes Esterházy for help—assistance she was only too ready to provide.

Grunau functions as one of the two primary antagonists in this scenario, alongside Ágnes Esterházy. As the only one of the duo who is also still living flesh and blood, he takes a hands-on approach to stymying the investigators' efforts, though they may not realize he is a snake in the grass until it is too late.

- **Description:** a rosy-cheeked man of considerable girth approaching his twilight years, the old baron looks like nothing so much as a beardless Father Christmas.

Handout: Schreckfilm 1

Seite 4

Suicide Waves

The editorial board need not remind our gentle readers that this has been a particularly bitter winter in more ways than one. In addition to the chill winds and icy frosts, many a Berliner feels the cold grip of uncertainty. As a new round of elections approaches, what is to become of our dear Republic? What of the economy? Why can the police not control the violence increasingly seen on city streets in a terrible callback to the lawless days of '18 and '19?

As Germans, we must persevere through such doubtful times as best we can. Sadly, according to the latest statistics released by central government officials, suicides are at an all-time high in the city. Many good folk—far too many—have fallen into the ultimate despair clutching the pill bottle or the gun barrel, or with a one-way trip to the riverside. The gravediggers of the Friedhof Grunewald-Forst have had their hands full fishing bodies out of the Havel and placing them into the cold, half-frozen ground.

The editors of this paper heartily enjoin any who may be reading this not to make the dishonorable choice. Although dark times are here today, we remind you that a sunnier tomorrow awaits us all. Better times are just around the corner. Persevere.

Haben wir mehr öffentliche Bibliotheken?

Es besteht kein Zweifel, dass wir Berliner die herausragende Bibliothek Europas beherbergen, und niemand würde die preußische Staatsbibliothek, die jetzt ihr achtzehntes Betriebsjahr beginnt, bestreiten oder herabsetzen. Unter seiner Kuppeldecke im öffentlichen Lesesaal zu sitzen, ist sowohl für das intellektuelle als auch für das künstlerische Empfinden eine Freude. Und wo befinden sich die kleineren Bibliotheken, die weniger öffentlichen Freuden mit ihren attraktiven Tageszeitungen, populären Fiktionen und illustrierten Kapitelbüchern für die Kinder?

- **Traits:** a sociopath, using his charm and apparently harmless appearance to his advantage. His rosy-cheeked smile quickly fades when away from mixed company, and his eyes flash with a devilish light when presented with a chance to destroy those who would stand in his way (such as the investigators).
- **Roleplaying Hooks:** Grunau is the consummate host, whether the investigators are visiting him on the film set or at home; however, he turns on a dime when threatened or if he senses vulnerability, deploying every trick his box—political favors, poison, brute force, even magic—to silence them.

Ágnes Esterházy, *33, witch and movie star*

Born to a Hungarian noble family of great antiquity, Esterházy is both a movie star and a full-blooded countess. After the collapse of the Austro-Hungarian Empire and concomitant decline in her family's fortunes, she turned to film acting to earn her daily bread. Her first roles were in minor Hungarian films, but soon she was landing jobs in Vienna, Munich, and Berlin.

Esterházy enjoyed regular if undistinguished work throughout the 1920s. Sometime in the mid-1920s, shortly after starring in the classic occult-horror film *The Student of Prague* (Galeen, 1926), she fell in with elements of Berlin's occult underground, and her name began to circulate in connection to Satanic masses and black-magic rituals. Naturally, this only boosted her appeal among jaded Berliners! She now commands a coven of thirteen witches.

After the simultaneous disasters of the Great Crash and the ascension of talkies, Esterházy's career went into severe decline. Her last major role was in 1930—an age and a day ago in the fast-moving German film industry. Fortunately for the countess, thanks to her latest magical workings, she will never be parted from the celluloid dreams of cinema again.

Approached by Baron Grunau, a long-time acquaintance in the darker circles of Berlin's occult societies, Countess Esterházy fabricated a special potion to use in the processing of his film *Das Necronomicon*, one calculated to bring the film's nightmare visions a startling vitality to all who witness them. In creating the brew, she also discovered a way to achieve literal immortality on the silver screen: by intoning a certain spell over a strip of nitrate featuring her image, she has become a walking, talking, three-dimensional film projection, immune to physical harm, sickness, and aging.

- **Description:** to see Countess Esterházy in person is a truly striking experience. She appears like a silver nitrate hologram, fully three-dimensional yet completely immaterial and insubstantial. Curiously, even her voice has the tinny, somewhat scratched quality of early talkies. Observing her is, for all intents and purposes, like watching a film projection, albeit a completely autonomous one—see her profile in **Creatures and Monsters**, page 240, for the Sanity loss resulting from encountering Esterházy "in the flesh."

Lina Desmond

Baron Grunau

- **Traits:** like many born to a life of privilege and comfort only to have everything yanked away in the wake of 1918, Esterházy hasn't been quite right since the end of the Great War. Her transcendence to immaterial film-creature took away what was left of her fragile sanity. She is completely megalomaniacal and overconfident, character flaws that savvy investigators may exploit to their benefit.

- **Roleplaying Hooks:** the reason Esterházy is so intent on retrieving the stolen folder (see **Handout: Schreckfilm 2**) is that her one weakness, the short strip of fragile film that holds her soul, is tucked inside! She unhesitatingly kills any investigator holding the folder if she feels she can do so without endangering that precious fragment of film. Dealing with Esterházy while in possession of the strip is the equivalent of dancing with a cobra—one slip-up, however slight, and it's all over.

Wolf-Heinrich Graf von Helldorff,
35, leader of the Berlin SA

Debased and dissipated scion of an ancient Thuringian noble family, Wolf-Heinrich, Count Helldorff, is a rising star in the firmament of the Berlin chapter of the Nazi Party. After serving in the Great War, he joined a number of different Freikorps outfits and participated in the 1920 Kapp Putsch. He has been a member of the NSDAP since 1924 and, since his arrival in Berlin with Goebbels, has taken an active role in organizing anti-Semitic attacks throughout the city (including the riot that kicks off this scenario). These days he spends most of his time mooching off the hospitality of the psychic Erik Jan Hanussen or else enjoying the convivial atmosphere of Salon Kitty.

- **Description:** Helldorff is possessed of a cherubic visage that belies his debased habits.

- **Traits:** the Sturmabteilung (SA) leader is addicted to many pleasures: horse and dog racing, fine food and drink, and pain administered at the hands of domineering mistresses. These addictions are always simmering just below the surface, ready to come roaring up at a moment's notice. His habits have one thing in common: they are all quite expensive. Helldorff is not shy about hitting others up for money or even brazenly stealing valuables (infamously, he once drove a Mercedes off a car lot after "forgetting" to pay for it). In public, Helldorff is the consummate Nazi, dour and imposing in his SA uniform. Behind closed doors, he is a wretched sight—when he isn't drunkenly gambling away his meager savings, he is submitting to pain and humiliation from various favored Dominas and Boot-Girls (**Prostitution**, page 53).

- **Roleplaying Hooks:** Helldorff represents a weak link in Berlin's occult underground, one the investigators may exploit to their benefit. He is close with Hanussen and, through him, Baron Grunau and Countess Esterházy. His extensive debts and hedonistic addictions make him vulnerable; for the right price, he happily turns on his so-called friends.

Ágnes Esterházy

Wolf-Heinrich Graf von Helldorff

Aleister Crowley,
56, occult impresario and struggling artist

The self-styled "Great Beast 666," dubbed by his eternal enemies in the British press as "the wickedest man in the world," the chess-playing, mountain-climbing artist-*cum*-occultist Aleister Crowley has been residing in Berlin for nearly two years.

Although he has achieved some recognition for his paintings among the members of Berlin's decadent art scene, the perennially cash-strapped Crowley is always on the lookout for new ways to make a buck. For some time now, that has included efforts to produce a *Schreckfilm* (horror movie) based on one of his short stories, "The Testament of Magdalen Blair". To this end, he has been in contact with Baron Grunau in a so-far fruitless search for funding. He is also dimly aware of the activities of Berlin's witch coven.

- **Description:** thanks to a lifetime's devotion to hedonistic pleasures, as well as an addiction to the heroin used to control his asthma attacks, Crowley looks about ten years older than his actual age of 56. He is mostly bald, with wisps of gray hair around the ears, and is somewhat overweight. His eyes, often puffy and baggy, are nevertheless entrancing in their intensity. Crowley is an inveterate pipe smoker and often has one in hand. Even when not smoking, the lingering smell of tobacco smoke clings to his clothes and skin.
- **Traits:** investigators expecting a dangerous madman may be

surprised to find themselves in conversation with an aging Edwardian gentleman, run down by a lifetime of chasing after the next big score and disillusioned by the modern world. He is polite, respectful, and refined in his manners, and he expects the same from others. If he does not receive courtesy, he can be relied upon to do his best socially to alienate and attack those who offend him, but he is not generally given over to physical violence.

- **Roleplaying Hooks:** Crowley makes for a potentially powerful ally to the investigators. Unfortunately, his personal life is about to take a sour turn, and if they delay in contacting him, they lose their opportunity. Also, even if the investigators successfully enlist his help, the man who also goes by the name Baphomet never does anything without expecting something in return.

Police Inspector Krieg, *63, burned-out cop*

First encountered nearly ten years ago during the events of **The Devil Eats Flies** (page 97), Inspector Krieg is, today, a man broken in body and spirit—just as he likes it.

Krieg fell under the sway of Ágnes Esterházy some years ago and has served her faithfully ever since. A career of policing the mean streets of Berlin shook his sanity to its core, making him a willing victim of the countess' black magic. Today, his greatest ambition is to be reborn as one of Esterházy's demonic familiars—but only once she has used him up and discarded his mortal shell.

Aleister Crowley

Police Inspector Krieg

- **Description:** investigators who remember Krieg from their investigation of Karl Großmann are not surprised to see that the old inspector has not aged well at all. His hair has almost completely fallen out; what little remains is snowy white. His skin is sallow and sunken, his fingers stained yellow with nicotine. His eyes, bloodshot and limpid, swim with a quiet menace.
- **Traits:** Krieg still smokes like a chimney but now has a hacking smoker's cough to show for it.
- **Roleplaying Hooks:** as a loyal minion of the countess, he follows her orders to the letter, relentlessly pursuing any enemies of the cult (i.e., the investigators), applying a lifetime of criminology and legalistic knowledge to making their lives a living hell. There is only one way to neuter his aggression: show him the photograph where he is collared and leashed (**Handout: Schreckfilm 2**); this evidence completely disarms him, due both to his embarrassment and the presence of the investigators in the photo.

Margo Lion, *31, androgyne chanteuse*

Born to French parents in Constantinople as Marguerite Hélène Barbe Elisabeth Constantine Lion, Margo first comes to Berlin in 1921 to study ballet. Once in the city, she meets Marcellus Schiffer, an artist and illustrator who is beginning to dabble in the world of cabaret.

Lion makes her stage debut in 1923 in one of Schiffer's revues, "The Wild Stage" (*Wild Buhne*) and goes on to star in many stage productions, the most famous of which is *Es Liegt In Der Luft* (1928), where she creates a sensation in her duet "Wenn Die Beste Freundin" with the up-and-coming Marlene Dietrich. Indeed, Lion's distinctive androgynous style is said to have been a huge influence on Dietrich. Starting in 1926, Lion parlays her stage success to the silver screen, and appears in ten films over the next eight years. Lion marries Schiffer in 1928 and the two become one of the power couples of Berlin nightlife.

At the start of this scenario, she is in talks to take the role of Jenny in the French-language cinematic adaptation of Brecht and Weill's *Threepenny Opera*.

- **Description:** there is no mistaking Margo Lion; she is slender, with long sinuous limbs and an aquiline Gallic nose. She accentuates her natural lines with tailored clothing (both suits and dresses), jewelry, and short bobbed hair.
- **Traits:** Lion views all of life as a performance, never missing an opportunity to make an impression through her looks or performance. On a personal note, lately she has been concerned about the well-being of her beloved husband Marcellus, whose depressive episodes have become more frequent and darker.
- **Roleplaying Hooks:** Lion is the consummate cabaret star, having seen everything that Berlin nightlife can offer (or so she believes); it takes a lot to impress Frau Lion, and she is usually detached and aloof around those who have not earned her trust or interest.

Margo Lion

Kitty Schmidt

Kitty Schmidt, *50, madam and witch*

The daughter of a butcher in Berlin, Kitty Schmidt was born Katharina Zammit; nowadays, she is known to almost everyone simply as Madam Kitty.

At the orders of Ágnes Esterhazy, Schmidt opens Salon Kitty in 1930 in a high-class part of Charlottenburg and quickly makes a name for herself catering to Nazi Brownshirts and other far-right clientele—all part of the coven's plans to produce compromising material for later use in blackmail schemes, plans which have succeeded beyond the Countess's wildest dreams. Schmidt has thus earned her place as Esterhazy's right-hand witch, and handles most of the coven's "real world" tasks of pulling strings and making sure the right people remain paid off or compromised. For the most junior members of the coven, Kitty *is* their leader as far as they're concerned.

- **Description:** a woman of middle years, with platinum blond marcelled hair and an over-the-top opulence. She is rarely seen not dripping in jewels and furs, a smoldering cigarette at the end of a long ivory holder. Although she has used magic to keep the signs of age at bay, she still covers her face in too much makeup.
- **Traits:** extremely vain and responds easily to flattery. In spite of her elevated position within the coven, she is paranoid and opportunistic.
- **Roleplaying Hooks:** an equal measure of sass and crass, Schmidt knows her role as madam requires her to possess a quick wit and a sharp tongue. She is nigh-unflappable, and always gives back better than she gets. If the winds of fate turned against her, she would be on the first train out of town with hardly a second thought.

Use the **Coven Witch** profile, page 240, for Kitty.

START: LUNA PARK

On this chilly New Year's Day night, the investigators are trying their best to forget their troubles with dinner and amusements at Luna Park, but this once-great destination, situated at the end of the Ku'damm adjacent to a small lake called the Halensee in the Grunewald—much like the rest of Berlin—has seen better days.

The park's façades, executed in the once fashionable oddly angled Expressionistic style, are battered and peeling. The park's most famous feature, the water slide (currently closed for the season), is streaked with rust and mold. Trash sits in sodden piles against fence posts and in forgotten corners.

As twilight creeps in, the investigators share a meal at one of the park's many restaurants. This being the off-season, the venue is half-empty. From their window seats, the investigators look out at the Swivel House, a notably strange attraction: a full-sized two-story house that rocks back and forth on a central pivot, tilting up to 45 degrees in either direction. Right now, with nobody inside it, the house sits at an impossible angle, looking like it is on the verge of tumbling over the side of an unseen cliff.

As they pay their bill, the chill air outside gives way to a freezing fog. Darkness has fallen as the investigators depart from the restaurant, the park managers doggedly proceeding with the nightly fireworks show despite the cloudy skies. Overhead, as the rockets streak into the heavens, the grey clouds are intermittently lit up with flashes of green, red, and gold, the reports of the exploding fireworks muffled and distant.

Nevertheless, the jaded crowd of park attendees stop to watch; the investigators, surrounded, are obliged by the press of people to crane their necks at the invisible show as well. Suddenly, one of the investigators is nearly knocked to the ground by the impact of someone pushing through the throng. All is momentarily chaos. As other bystanders jostle and shout, the fireworks overhead reach a crescendo that paints the whole scene in a strobe-like light.

There is brief moment of eye contact between the investigator and their assailant; she is a young woman, probably in her mid-twenties. She is underdressed for the weather, wearing only a light raincoat, skirt, and a small black hat. Her mascara runs dramatically down over her cheeks. Her eyes bear the look of one who is hunted and barely managing to stay one step ahead of their pursuer. Then she is off among the crowd again, quickly disappearing from view. Attempts to call after her bring no response, and she is immediately lost amid the darkness and milling attendees under the strobe-like flashes of the fireworks overhead; using the **Track** or **Spot Hidden** skills in such an environment is doomed to automatic failure.

Looking down, the investigators see that she dropped something: lying on the wet ground is a folder made of

WESTEND

Luna Park is situated in a district of Berlin known as Westend. Located out beyond Charlottenburg, at the extreme end of the Ku'damm and hard up against the Grunewald, Westend is one of the city's most elegant and tony neighborhoods. Here may be found a colony of new villas, a hospital, and two beer gardens in addition to the amusement park.

heavy card, the sort that is used to collect papers for dossiers and such. Flipping open the folder, they see something startling: a photograph showing the entire investigator group in the company of several people they've never seen before in their lives!

In addition, inside the folder are a glossy 8-by-10-inch (20-by-25-cm) photograph of an attractive woman, a calling card, a postcard, a yellowed newspaper clipping, and a short strip of film. Though the investigators have no way of knowing it yet, this folder contains all the clues necessary for unraveling the mysteries of this scenario.

GHOSTS IN THE FOG

The investigators no doubt wish to retire to a more private locale to go over the contents of this slightly waterlogged dossier. This may be one of their residences, a nearby hotel, bar, restaurant, or other destination. One thing is for sure: as the crowd breaks up after the lackluster fireworks show, an announcement goes out on the public-address system that the park is closing in 15 minutes.

Leaving Luna Park by way of a long sweeping bridge that takes them out of this manufactured fantasy land and back into the city, they find the Ku'damm a surrealistic dreamscape of neon lights and street lamps shining through the freezing

mist. Then, quite suddenly, out of the fog come the sounds of police whistles, shouts, and shattering glass. Running feet can be heard, and many shapes seen moving about in the murk. A brick comes arcing out of the fog, skidding along the pavement only a few feet from the investigators!

A street battle has broken out here on the Ku'damm. Several hundred Brownshirts of the NSDAP's Sturmabteilung paramilitary wing clash with a like number of members of the newly formed *Eiserne Front* (Iron Front), a coalition of anti-Nazi, anti-monarchist, and anti-Bolshevik paramilitary groups put together in December 1931 specifically to oppose the growing power of the NSDAP in Berlin. The city's policemen are impotently attempting to break up the fight, only adding to the chaos. At a loss, they open fire with their rifles.

No doubt the investigators are already looking for a way to distance themselves from the foggy melee. Emphasize the pandemonium that reigns at this moment as street fighters come surging out of the mist. Three factions grapple with each other, throwing fists and bricks, in an environment with visibility limited to about 10 feet (3 m).

Keeper note: the Brownshirts, acting on Goebbels' orders, have come out to this part of town—which they despise for its large Jewish population and many "degenerate" entertainment venues—to conduct a provocative march,

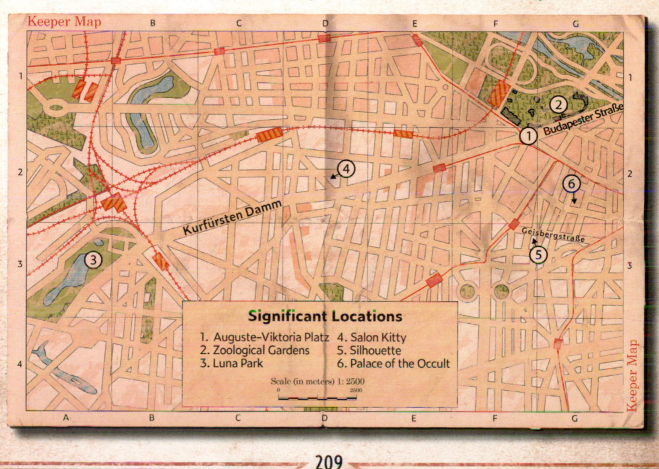

Keeper Map

Significant Locations

1. Auguste-Viktoria Platz
2. Zoological Gardens
3. Luna Park
4. Salon Kitty
5. Silhouette
6. Palace of the Occult

Scale (in meters) 1: 2500

smashing the windows of cafés and Jewish-owned businesses. Their tactic worked, drawing out the Iron Front in a counter-demonstration that quickly degenerated to violence. If any of the investigators have contacts in the SA or in labor or socialist groups, they may know of these plans and understand what is going on.

Running back over the bridge to Luna Park is a bad idea, as the gates have already been shut. If an investigator isn't crushed by the stampeding herd of fleeing citizens who had the same idea (a successful **DEX** roll or suffer 1D4 points of damage), they will instead tumble over the bridge into the Halensee, requiring a successful **Swim** roll—or assistance—to reach land.

If an investigator is foolish enough to linger on the Ku'damm, the sound of gunfire echoes in the air. Unless they state they are diving to the ground or taking cover, call for a **Luck** roll: a fumbled result means they may be shot. If they do fumble, roll the policeman's Firearms (Rifle) skill of 45% to see if the investigator has been hit (apply a penalty die to the roll for the poor visibility). Shot investigators suffer 1D6 damage from a ricocheting bullet. A profile for a sample **Berlin Police Officer** can be found on page 239, if required.

A far safer approach is to simply scatter and head for a side street; call for a **Navigate** roll from anyone who does so. Those who succeed may choose to keep close to one other investigator, while those who fail find themselves parted from their companions by the surging crowds and, subsequently, on their own.

Strange Pursuit

Pick an investigator, preferably one who is alone. Describe their flight down a quiet side street, the sounds of the street battle quickly fading behind them. Now all they can hear in the freezing fog is their own footsteps. The mist crowds in closer, turning the nearby residential flats into ghostly ruins, their windows staring down like hollow eye sockets. Visibility is 5 feet (1.5 m) or less. Suddenly, from out of the mist, there comes another sound: the pitter-patter of little feet. Something—a small animal, by the sound of it—is paralleling the investigator's progress. If the investigator stops, so do the other footfalls. As soon as they start walking again, the pursuer moves as well. Does the investigator break into a run?

Call for a Hard **Spot Hidden** roll (make this Extreme if the investigator is running): if failed, the investigator falls over a trio of aluminum garbage cans, scattering their contents over the sidewalk and hitting themselves hard on the pavement (1 point of damage). A pack of stray cats bolts away from the scene, screeching angrily in human-like voices. Even if the investigator manages to avoid the trashcans, they can see the mangy cats luxuriating among the frosted filth

in the cans, their bottlebrush tails swinging about as they change perches.

Either way, at this point the investigator's pursuer catches up. It is, at first glance, a naked, hairless cat. With a hiss, it bounds out of the fog. There is a glimpse of the thing as it jumps toward the investigator, its human-like face twisted into an expression of pure malice, its tiny, human-like hands extended to grab onto the investigator's face! Call for a **Sanity** roll for seeing this terrifying creature (0/1D6 loss).

This is a **Cat-Thing** (see profile, page 240), a servant of the Berlin coven that has been pursuing the investigators since Luna Park. It was trailing Lina Desmond but switched its quarry when it saw the investigators pick up the dossier. The cat-thing believes this investigator (rightly or wrongly) to be in possession of the dossier and intends to kill them and take the folder back to its masters.

The cat-thing fights savagely but flees if reduced to half its hit points or less. If it is killed or incapacitated, the investigator now has a tangible relic of the strange forces arrayed against them—if they hang onto the corpse.

Keeper note: if the cat-thing is shown to Aleister Crowley, he finds it a most fascinating specimen (see **Consulting Crowley**, page 215).

If the investigator somehow falls victim to the cat-thing's attack, they later turn up as a cat-thing themselves. If the investigator was indeed carrying the dossier, it goes back to the coven. The remaining investigators now have less to go on, certainly, but all is not lost. Lina Desmond comes looking for the dossier, and her presence can help steer the investigation back on track (see **Lina Turns Up**, page 213, for more details).

GOING OVER THE DOSSIER

After being scattered to the four winds, the investigators presumably rendezvous later at their agreed-upon location. Once safely away from street battles and stalking monstrosities, give them **Handout: Schreckfilm 2** as they settle in and begin going over the contents of the folder in greater detail.

3-by-5 Photograph

The investigators have no way of knowing this, but the photograph in which they feature was taken at the residence of noted Berlin psychic Erik Jan Hanussen (**The Palace of the Occult**, page 220). Apart from the investigators, the other people in the photo are Hanussen, his friend Count Wolf-Heinrich Helldorff, and noted cabaret singer Margo Lion. Just visible at the bottom of the frame are a black poodle of sinister aspect and a man, shirtless, with a ball gag

3×5 (7.6 × 12.7 cm) photograph: shows the investigators in the company of two men and a woman, none of whom the investigators have ever met before.

Glossy 8×10 (20 × 25 cm) photograph: showing the actress Ágnes Esterházy, signed by her and dedicated to "Count von Helldorff."

Calling card: with no name, merely an odd sequence of letters and symbols—"A∴A∴"—and a phone number. On the back, written in fading pencil, is a note: "May be able to help?"

Postcard: depicting a tall brick tower looming up from woodland surrounding a lake.

Newspaper clipping: dated four years ago, its headline reads, "Murder in the Library."

Filmstrip: about 6 inches (15 cm) long.

STASHING THE GOODS

Once the investigators realize the magnitude of the hot *kartoffel* (potato) that has landed in their laps—particularly after Krieg and the SA start coming down on them (**The Coven's Activity**, page 213)—they may think to place the dossier and its valuable contents in a strong box or vault.

As may be expected of a world capital, Berlin boasts many large and esteemed banks. These are clustered along the Unter den Linden and down the streets adjoining the Friedrichstraße. All are open from 9 am to 1 pm every day except Sundays and holidays. Sample banks and their locations include: Reichsbank (Jägerstraße 34), Deutsche Bank (Behrenstraße 9–13), S. Bleichröder (Unter den Linden 13), Delbrück, Schickler & Co. (Mauerstraße 61–65), and Hugo Oppenheim & Sohn (Pariser Platz 1). A safe deposit box may be secured with a successful **Credit Rating** roll and may be subsequently accessed during banking hours.

It should also be noted that all reputable hotels have their own safes that guests may keep valuables in, and Wertheim's department store on Leipziger Platz has its own bank and vault as well. Both of these options offer greater access to the goods but at the cost of being easier to compromise owing to less scrupulous employees. It is left to the Keeper's discretion whether the Coven's reach extends to the normally unimpeachable members of the German banking industry.

in his mouth and a dog collar identical to the poodle's around his neck. The man is held on a tight leash by Hanussen, the poodle by Helldorff.

Keeper note: if the investigators have been resident in Berlin for longer than a few months, they may attempt a **Know** roll to recognize Margo Lion (see **The Cabaret Singer,** page 218, for more information). If the investigators have met Inspector Krieg in a previous scenario, they recognize him as the man on the leash. As for the investigator's appearance in the image, there is no explanation.

8-by-10 Glossy Photograph

Countess Ágnes Esterházy is a successful Hungarian actress who has starred in movies since the early 1920s. She is probably in her mid-thirties by now, and her career has seemingly stalled—she hasn't been in a movie in over two years.

Keeper note: those with a background in film or who succeed with a Hard **Know** roll recall this information. Investigators reading the dedication on the signed photo and who possess a **Credit Rating** of 50% or higher know of a Count Helldorff active in right-wing politics here in Berlin.

Calling Card

The symbol on the calling card refers to the spiritualist organization Argentum Astrum, founded by British occultist Aleister Crowley.

Keeper note: a successful **Occult** roll recognizes the symbol (those with **Occult** 50% or higher recognize it automatically). There are no lodges or public venues for the A∴A∴ in Berlin. Those who know the symbol are also aware that Aleister Crowley has been residing in Berlin for the past couple of years.

Postcard

Any resident of Berlin recognizes the tall brick tower as the Kaiser-Wilhelm-Turm, a local landmark in the Grunewald district. If the investigators are new to Berlin, showing the postcard around quickly identifies its subject.

Newspaper Clipping

This is **Handout: Dances 5** from **Dances of Vice, Horror, and Ecstasy** (page 192).

Film Strip

The strip is 35mm nitrate film, indicating a professional production. The cells on the strip represent about one-third of a second of real time—not enough to depict any action. Holding the film up to the light, the cells show a standing woman, holding a hand to her throat and looking concerned. A shadowy figure in the background is out of focus and impossible to identify, though he looks male. It's apparent that the woman is the same one as in the 8-by-10 glossy photograph, namely Countess Ágnes Esterházy.

Keeper note: investigators involved in the film industry, or self-professed movie fans, may attempt an **INT** roll to recognize the scene; if successful, they know it comes from the 1926 picture *The Student of Prague*, directed by Henrik Galeen and starring Countess Esterházy alongside Conrad Veidt and Werner Krauss. The film, also released under the title *The Man Who Cheated Life*, concerns a man who sells his soul to the Devil for material wealth and is then confronted with an evil mirror reflection of himself. The filmstrip cannot be cut or destroyed by any means short of throwing it in a fire. Successful analysis using **Art/Craft (Photography)** or **Science (Chemistry)** reveals the film was developed with an unknown agent.

THE COVEN'S ACTIVITY

The investigators are now embroiled in a race against time, and it won't be long from the moment they pick up the dossier until the witch cult discovers their existence and their knowledge of Lina Desmond's investigation. This could happen the very night the investigators get the dossier if the cat-thing survives to give its report, although they may manage to conceal their involvement until they decide to tip their hand (or not, as the case may be). Although it is possible to get through most of the scenario while remaining out of the coven's sight, it is unlikely; after all, the coven has its eyes and ears everywhere. Once the coven finds out about the investigators, they bring to bear all the same tricks they've been using against Desmond.

- The coven deploys their connections inside the Criminal Police (**Beinls and Bulls**, page 37) to hound and persecute the investigators. Their willing slave, Inspector Krieg, is dogged in his pursuit of the investigators, not hesitating to frame them for serious crimes like burglary and murder. Unless the investigators give the Inspector suitable ammunition, none of these charges will stick, but they will prove incredibly inconvenient, with constant calls to come in for questioning and such like. Investigators who *do* get up to activities like breaking and entering, assault, or murder are well advised to remember that they have a hostile police inspector actively looking to catch them and send them to prison.
- Likewise, the coven has its claws deep into the city's judiciary, ensuring that any investigators arrested is facing a brutal prison term if matters ever get to court. Obviously, things should not get to this point—being sentenced to five years' hard labor on trumped-up charges of disturbing the peace is no way to conduct an investigation—but it should be an obvious threat that sows the seeds of paranoia and isolation among the investigators. No institution is safe or trustworthy, and turning to the authorities is a surefire way to never to be heard from again. Even without being arrested, investigators going to the powers that be find their pleas ignored, their attempts to gain help met with hostility and veiled threats. Lina Desmond can make this threat clear if the investigators don't figure it out for themselves.
- Through a combination of blackmail of the queer members of its leadership and influence wielded through Joseph Goebbels (one of the coven's most enthusiastic patrons at Salon Kitty), the witch cult can send *Rotte* (teams) of SA men to harass and intimidate the investigators. The number of bully boys in these groups is equal to the total number of investigators plus two, and to accomplish their ends they will do everything short of murder—and even that isn't

out of the question if they think they can get away with it. Furthermore, if they are met with lethal force from the investigators they will unhesitatingly respond in kind. The witch cult will not abuse this privilege, sending no more than three *Rotte* against the investigators before turning to more arcane means. A sample **Rotte Member's** profile can be found page 239.

The coven has powerful magic at its disposal and terrible creatures. The Keeper may deploy these threats as appropriate; see the **Coven Witch** and **Cat-Thing** profiles (page 240) for details.

THE COVEN'S STOOGES

Countess Esterházy's coven uses the local Nazi Party apparatus as its cat's paw; this is a fundamentally unequal power dynamic. Goebbels and his goons *do not* have access to any of the coven's magic or Mythos secrets. The countess possesses extensive files on Goebbels and the SA, and she uses this extortion material as leverage. When facing off against a *Rotte* of Brownshirts, the investigators need only fear the Nazis' knuckledusters, truncheons, blades, pistols, and so on, rather than any magical shenanigans.

LINA TURNS UP

Regardless of what other scrapes they get themselves into, Lina Desmond eventually reappears in the investigators' lives. When precisely this occurs is left to the Keeper. If the investigators are struggling with the clue trail, she provides a welcome boost to their efforts. Or perhaps there is a slow moment in the action that could use a touch of the uncanny, in which case Desmond's new appearance does the job quite nicely.

Although she now has an effective disguise, Desmond is still incredibly cautious to the point of paranoia; the process of getting her new face only exacerbated her tenuous hold on reality. Preferably, she shows up in the middle of the night or in the small hours of the morning, knocking on one of the investigators' doors.

If the investigator is understandably reluctant to open their door to a total stranger, Desmond informs them of who she is: "*My name is Lina Desmond. I'm a newspaper reporter. I believe you or one of your friends has a folder that I dropped in*

Luna Park. *You must know by now that you are in grave danger. I can help you.*" A successful **Psychology** roll reveals that she is telling the truth; however, the woman calling herself Lina Desmond no longer looks like the woman encountered at Luna Park. Although she is of similar build and still wearing clothes far too light for the chill season, her face is completely different. This is obvious to anyone who saw her at the park.

If asked about her change in appearance, Desmond brightens. "*This is one of the ways I think I can help you. I know a man who, for a price, can change your face, no questions asked.*" If pressed, she gives the investigators Aleister Crowley's name and contact information—the number matches that on the calling card from **Handout 2: Schreckfilm**—see **Crowley's Offer**, page 218, for more information.

Desmond then opens up to the investigators, telling them of her ongoing scrutiny of a coven of witches operating among the highest echelons of Berlin society. "*They pull the strings of the police and the judiciary. They operate through a variety of* Ringvereine *to sell drugs and traffic in sex slavery. The Nazis here in Berlin are completely under their thumb, either indirectly—like Goebbels—or directly—like Count Helldorff and his SA men. In fact, they do much of their recruiting through Salon Kitty, that high-class whorehouse over on Giesebrechtstraße that the SA men like so well.*"

If asked, she volunteers that the contents of her dossier were collected over the course of her investigation, mostly from various contacts around the city. She doesn't know every source, though she has suspicions—see bullet points, following.

Desmond explains that she was trailing the investigators at Luna Park after recognizing their faces from the photo in the dossier. She wishes to know how they figure into the mystery, where the photo was taken, and why they were there. She is most alarmed by the fact that they do not remember being in that photo.

Assuming the investigators have questions, Desmond can relate the following information.

- The witch cult worships Hecate, the triple-headed goddess of witches.
- Countess Ágnes Esterházy is definitely one of the coven leaders.
- Esterházy has not been seen by anyone, as far as Desmond can ascertain, in over a year.
- Nevertheless, there seems to be some sort of connection between Esterházy and the film producer Baron Grunau (who produced *The Student of Prague*).
- She saved the newspaper clipping because she heard rumors that the *Necronomicon* was stolen from the Prussian State Library, although she hasn't yet been able to confirm this.

- The Kaiser-Wilhelm-Turm seems to hold some sort of important ritual significance for the coven—she witnessed a ritual being carried out atop the tower on the Winter Solstice (December 21).

- If asked about the photo of the investigators and where she acquired it, she wrinkles her brow in consternation. "*I… don't remember,*" she says. "*I recognize the photo, of course, but I can't for the life of me place where I acquired it or from whom…*" If necessary, she can identify Erik Jan Hanussen, Count Wolf-Heinrich von Helldorff, and Margo Lion in the image.

- There's something significant about that filmstrip. It was slipped through the mail slot in her apartment inside a wax envelope. She's been on the run ever since. It seems that, with her acquisition of that piece of film, she immediately became a top-priority target for the coven, which had been ignoring her up until to that point. She can only assume that someone close to the coven heard about her investigation and decided to pass the filmstrip to her, although how they got hold of it, and what its significance is, she has no idea.

The Keeper may use Lina Desmond as they see fit from this point on. Some suggestions for her possible interactions in the scenario are as follows.

- **Ally:** Desmond is a capable investigator in her own right and makes for an excellent replacement should the worst happen to one of the existing player characters. For smaller groups, her skill set may prove an invaluable asset.

- **Victim:** Desmond may disappear again only to turn up dead in an investigator's bed, with Inspector Krieg bursting through the door to arrest the hapless investigator on murder charges. Or she may disappear only to turn up as a horribly mutated cat-thing. Alternately, Desmond may suffer the ill effects of one of her sister's blasphemous spells right before the investigators' eyes, a warning of the power of the witches.

- **Turncoat:** Desmond's dark secret is that she is actually Ágnes Esterházy's sister, Alma. Although Ágnes won't recognize her sister any longer thanks to her new face, Alma retains filial fondness in spite of her sister's wicked deeds and transhuman transformation. At the Keeper's option, Alma is merely a patsy, a willing accomplice in the inscrutable plots of the witch cult. In this option, "Desmond" targeted the investigators on purpose, drawing them into the web and leading them to their own destruction. Of course, if this is the case, a successful Hard Psychology roll reveals that Desmond knows more about the filmstrip and where it came from than she's letting on. This option works best with a group of seasoned investigators who may possess tomes, artifacts, or dangerous knowledge of their own—something the witch cult is interested in acquiring.

If any of the investigators suggest returning the dossier to Desmond to end their woes, she makes it clear that, having had the dossier in their possession, they are now tainted and a target in the eyes of the coven. "*If you wish to make it out of this alive, you must help me destroy this foul conspiracy. The pieces are in place, but we must move quickly and—above all—cautiously!*"

THE DOLL MAKER

Another potential ally in this scenario comes in the form of Belshazzar the Doll Maker from **Dances of Vice, Horror, and Ecstasy.** Assuming he made it through the events of that scenario, Belshazzar may prove vital in helping the investigators survive the attentions of Countess Esterházy and Baron Grunau.

Belshazzar is aware of the Hecate-worshipping coven's activities in the city, and he knows that Countess Esterházy resides at Salon Kitty where unwholesome rituals and sacrifices take place. He is not yet aware of her transformation, but if told of it he may intuit why she is so concerned about the filmstrip. He is less interested in destroying her than in using the possession of the strip as a bargaining chip, but he will not object if the investigators wish to incinerate the film instead.

CONSULTING CROWLEY

Keeper note: this is a time-sensitive clue. Aleister Crowley's life grows considerably more complicated after January 4, when he has a falling-out with his friend and assistant, Karl Germer. Once this occurs, Crowley has no time to spare for helping a bunch of amateur occultists.

Following up on the calling card, the investigators may attempt to call the phone number on the card (**Handout: Schreckfilm 2**, page 211)—or Lina Desmond may have given them Crowley's number. If they call after 6 pm, the phone rings and rings but no one picks up; however, if they call during the day, after far too many rings a gruff, male voice comes on the other end of the line. In English, speaking with a distinctly English accent, he says, "*Yes, what is it?*"

The investigators soon find out that they have made contact with perhaps the most notorious occultist in Europe,

Opposite: Lina turns up

if not the world: Aleister Crowley. Although Crowley is hung over and not in the best of moods, he is willing to talk. First and foremost, he wishes to know how the caller got his number, as their name and voice are unfamiliar to him. The best strategy an investigator can adopt in this situation is to be honest, telling Crowley of the dossier and its strange clues. Mentioning Desmond, if they have met her already, is also a good way to catch Crowley's interest, particularly if the investigators mention Desmond's new face.

Crowley is intrigued by the mystery, even more so if the investigators have begun to uncover the occult connections associated with the contents of the dossier or have a cat-thing corpse in their possession (**Ghosts in the Fog**, page 209). Those attempting to prevaricate must succeed at a Hard **Charm** or **Persuade** roll, as Crowley is adept at seeing through such fabrications. If they have piqued his interest, Crowley gives them an address on Bülowplatz, telling the investigators that he'll see them there in an hour—see **Dinner With The Beast**, following.

DINNER WITH THE BEAST

The address proves to be a large movie house called the Babylon Cinema—investigators who survived **Dances of Vice, Horror, and Ecstasy** may be given some pause by the name. The five-story building is constructed in a rounded, Modernist style with a mustard-yellow stucco exterior. The interior continues the *Neue Sachlichkeit* (New Objectivity) motif of the exterior, with clean lines and colorful forms in gray, red, and yellow.

After a few minutes of standing around in the winter chill, watching occasional flecks of snow drift down from the leaden sky, Crowley emerges from within the theater, taking some preliminary puffs on a freshly lit pipe. "*Nice place, eh?*" he asks. "*Chap who built it, name of Poelzig, is also a theatrical architect. He's been consulting with me on a recent film project. But enough chit-chat. I believe you promised me dinner?*"

This is Crowley's way of getting a free meal out of what he suspects is otherwise a waste of his time. He wishes to dine at Gourmania Palast, one of the city's newer restaurants (having opened in 1929), located near Auguste-Viktoria-Platz and the Zoological Gardens. Magnanimously, he offers to cover cab fare (unless the investigators brought their own vehicle). During the trip, Crowley makes small talk with the investigators, attempting to get a read on their personalities and motives.

Unter den Linden map

Keeper Map

Oranienburger Straße

Unter den Linden

Significant Locations

1. Prussian State Library
2. Babylon Cinema

Scale (in meters) 1: 800

Keeper Map

The drive takes the investigators through the Tiergarten, with its leafless trees and dead, frost-flecked lawns. Pulling up outside Gourmania, the investigators can see that it is located inside a long, low, sleekly modern building that runs along the northern side of Budapester Straße. The spire of the Kaiser-Wilhelm-Memorial Church can be seen stretching toward the heavens above the roof of the Romanisches Café, just to the west.

Entering the restaurant brings warm relief from the outside chill. The interior is a grand, three-story space lit by a ceiling of skylights arranged in geometric patterns. In pleasing contrast to the dead world of the Tiergarten, the dining area here is alive with potted tropical plants.

With the dining party seated and wine lists perused, Crowley is ready to get down to business, particularly if the investigators indicated that they have information of an occult nature in their possession or if they mentioned any connection to the film industry. In the latter case, he has in his valise a treatment for an adaptation of a short story he wrote about 30 years ago. "*Imagine that you can read others' minds and that your loved one dies. What do you find when you read the mind of a dying man?*" he says in a well-oiled pitch.

Crowley has the following reactions to pieces of evidence presented to him; use this information to form a dialogue and a conversational tone for the meeting.

- **3-by-5 photograph:** Crowley recognizes the room in the photograph featuring the investigators. "This is at Hanussen's residence, I'm quite sure. I believe he's holding a séance there this week. If you'd like to attend, I can arrange for invitations to be sent out. My treat." (See **The Palace of the Occult**, page 220, if the investigators attend Hanussen's séance.) While Crowley can identify Erik Jan Hanussen and Margo Lion in the image, he does not know Count Helldorff by sight.

- If the investigators query how they could be in the photograph, Crowley smiles and suggests their memory could have been affected by "copious drug taking and intoxication."

- **8-by-10 glossy photograph:** Crowley merely gives a knowing chuckle at the photo of Esterházy. "*Stay out of her way, hm? She worships the triple-headed goddess.*" Whether this is a good or bad thing in his book, Crowley does not say.

- **Filmstrip:** he lingers over the fragment of nitrate. "*There's something to this, but I can't quite put my finger on it.*"

- **Cat-thing:** if the investigators have the body of the cat-thing, Crowley is quite intrigued. "*What a bizarre specimen! A homunculus, perhaps? Or a qlippoth? I wonder…*" He requests the carcass for further study.

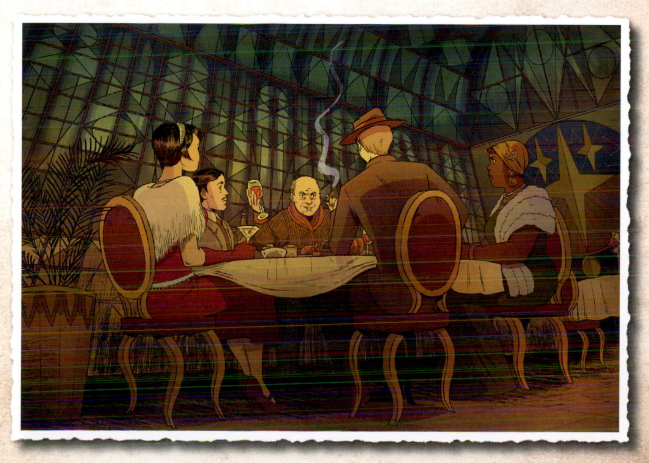

Dinner with the Beast

Crowley can arrange an invitation to Hanussen's séance. He refuses to have anything to do with the filmstrip, saying only that there is something gravely unsettling about it.

Crowley's Offer

If the investigators have mentioned Lina Desmond's new face or are otherwise discussing disguises, hiding from the coven, or other related matters, Crowley, sensing a chance to make some money, offers to teach the investigators a magical working. This is the same one he taught to Desmond, who then used it as a way to shake the witch cult.

Keeper note: in the event the investigators do not meet with Crowley, they may still learn this ritual from Lina Desmond, who, if pressed, teaches it to them for free (either out of the goodness of her heart or as part of the witch cult's subtle machinations, depending on her true motives).

"*I must warn you: this is one of the darkest, most vile rituals with which I have come into contact. I only offer the knowledge to you because I can see how desperate you are.*" Crowley's price is 5,000 marks (equivalent to £350 or $1,750). With a successful Hard **Charm** or **Persuade** roll, he may be bargained down to 4,000 marks (£280/$1,400).

Learning the spell is relatively easy, as its ritual components are quite straightforward. An hour of study with the teacher (Crowley or Desmond) and a successful Hard **INT** roll are all that are required. Only one investigator need learn the ritual, as it may be cast on another.

The ritual is known as Guise of the Other (**Spells**, page 242) and requires the freshly flayed face of another person, either living or recently deceased. The skin so taken loses efficacy if more than 24 hours have passed between removal and use.

If asked, Desmond says she obtained hers from a body in the morgue of the Westend Hospital (paying off an attendant to do so). Investigators may, of course, come up with their own plans for how to acquire new faces of their own. Flaying flesh from a face provokes a **Sanity** roll (1/1D3 loss) for anyone save a medical professional. Using a live specimen—even a member of the witch cult or other nominal "bad guy"—requires the investigator to fail a **Sanity** roll even to undertake the grisly act, which automatically costs 1D6+1 Sanity points per victim for committing cold-blooded murder and mutilation.

If the investigators learn the spell from Desmond, she neglects to teach them the reversal ritual (again, either due to an oversight on her part or due to intentional malice).

This spell is here to be used or ignored as the investigators see fit. It is not necessary to use it to get out of the scenario alive, and the scenario's climax does not presume the spell's use; however, its utility should be obvious to the investigators. With it, the investigators can escape the heat of the witch cult's pursuit and even infiltrate cult meetings, but at a significant cost. In the end, the investigators may be the engine of their own undoing, which may be precisely what Countess Esterházy and her minions wish.

THE CABARET SINGER

Investigators may wish to seek out the cabaret star pictured in the photograph from Desmond's dossier: Margo Lion. Those with contacts in the world of Berlin nightlife, or who have the **Art/Craft (Singing)** or another entertainment specialty skill, learn quickly that Frau Lion may be found at Silhouette, a well-known cross-dressing bar on Geisbergstraße in Wilmersdorf, not far from Nürnberger Platz.

The bar's entrance is situated at the corner of its building, flanked by artful drapery. Entering, the investigators move into a long, narrow room illuminated in soft pink lighting from Japanese paper lanterns. A thick haze of blue tobacco smoke hangs in the air. Two bars, each backed by a mirror, flank the entrance, both manned by handsome, slick-haired youths who frequently ignore customers in favor of checking out their own reflections in the mirror of the bar opposite.

A small, red-carpeted dance floor provides space to move to the rhythms of a modest orchestra, but most of the clientele are here to relax, sip their drinks, and gossip. Looking around, it is clear that at least half the guests are either men in women's garb or women wearing men's clothes.

The dance floor is lined on both sides by low sofas. Closed off by a velvet rope and an attendant, a set of stairs in the back provide access to a bank of private booths protected behind a balustrade. It is in one of these booths that Margo Lion currently reposes, along with her husband Marcellus Schiffer. Getting access to Lion requires a chat with the attendant at the foot of the stairs and either a successful **Charm** or **Fast Talk** roll, while those with **Credit Rating** 60% or higher may be admitted without a roll.

Lion is striking in appearance, being noticeably thin of build and possessed of a large Gallic nose. Born in Constantinople in 1898, she is now in her mid-thirties and has been living in Berlin for more than ten years; her native French accent is, at this point, slight. She is probably best known to Berliners for her 1928 duet with the up-and-coming star Marlene Dietrich, "Wenn Die Beste Freundin"— an ode to lady-love that quickly became an anthem for the city's lesbian community. Tonight, she wears a somewhat androgynous outfit consisting of a hunting jacket, jodhpurs, and a broad-brimmed man's hat. Her husband, Marcellus, is already nearly pass-out drunk despite the early hour.

As a drag performer strikes up a rhapsody down below, Lion welcomes the investigators to her booth. A little tipsy, she is in a gregarious mood and happy to answer the investigators' questions. Use the following points to direct the conversation.

- No, she does not recognize the investigators, if they care to ask.
- If shown the **3-by-5 photograph**, she apologizes for not knowing who they are. "*I meet so many people, you must understand.*"
- She is quite sure, however, that the picture was taken at the residence of the famous psychic and medium Erik Jan Hanussen. She happily provides the address, if asked. "*He often opens up his apartments in the evening to conduct séances. It is quite the establishment,*" she says with a giggle. "*I believe he's holding a séance this week—you should go! Terrific fun.*" (See **The Palace of the Occult**, page 220, if the investigators attend Hanussen's séance.)

THE PRUSSIAN STATE LIBRARY

Investigators following up on the lead from the newspaper article about the murder in the State Library (**Handout: Dances 5**) find little to go on—this is a four-year-old cold case, after all. If an investigator thinks to ask to see the Wormius *Necronomicon*, they must pass a combined **Credit Rating** and **Library Use** roll: if failed, access is denied; with success, they may come back the following morning for an hour of research time with the notorious tome.

Arriving, the investigators are escorted to a high-ceilinged study hung with tapestries and containing many locked book cases. There, on the large oak table in the room's center, lies the *Necronomicon*. Or so it seems. Upon opening the book's clasps, it is revealed to be a clever forgery. Externally, the book looks the part, but internally the pages are simply copies of Newton's *Principia*. Perfidy!

Keeper note: although the investigators may never find this out, Baron Grunau was behind the theft and replacement of the *Necronomicon*, and the murder of the hapless librarian, Ralph Schneider. The real book is currently hidden away inside an elaborate "dreamland" constructed by Countess Esterházy, as revealed in **Inside the Church**, page 235.

MALLEUS MALEFICARUM AND OTHER RESEARCH

The State Library archives also hold an original printing of the *Malleus Maleficarum* (*Call of Cthulhu Rulebook*, page 236), the infamous "Hammer of Witches"—a late medieval guide to witch-hunting. The Keeper may use this tome to disseminate basic information on witches—such as the fact that covens traditionally number 13 members, magical power is derived from a pact with the Devil, and so on—although there are several more pertinent pieces of evidence to be found within.

Investigators who have begun to piece together clues as to the nature of their enemies may wish to consult this tome. While there is not enough time for an in-depth reading, investigators who have encountered the countess' cat-things will no doubt be startled to find within the book's pages an engraving of a crone feeding a trunk full of familiars who look quite, well, familiar: foul, cat-like creatures with human faces. The accompanying text (requiring a successful **Language (German)** roll to read, even for native speakers) talks of how some witches possess the power to turn their enemies into abominations to serve as spies and assassins. Chillingly, the text makes note of the fact that, even after transformation, the wretched victim retains a small sense of their former self.

Investigators who wish to find more information on the goddess Hecate may discover one or more of the following facts with a successful **Library Use** roll.

- Hecate is a Greek triple-goddess associated with darkness, crossroads, spirits, the moon, and witchcraft.
- Her three faces are said to represent the three phases of womanhood: maiden, mother, and crone.
- Hecate rules over the Earth, Sky, and Sea. Furthermore, as the daughter of Titans, she is not bound by the restrictions that hold back the Olympian gods from overt interference with mortal affairs.
- Her association with witches was sealed for good with her appearance in Shakespeare's *Macbeth*.
- Hecate is sometimes associated with Lilith, but these connections are weak at best.

If the investigators have yet to work out the names of the people in the **3-by-5 photograph**, a successful **Library Use** roll enables them to identify Erik Jan Hanussen, Margo Lion, and Count Helldorff from various newspaper stories.

THE PALACE OF THE OCCULT

Introduced to Erik Jan Hanussen's "Palace of the Occult" by either Aleister Crowley or Margo Lion, the investigators are invited to attend a midnight séance for Berlin's elite.

Located at Lietzenburger Straße 18 in the Ku'damm, just south of the famous KaDeWe shopping emporium (**The Ku'Damm,** page 30), Hanussen's apartment takes up the top two stories of the Neo-Baroque residence block. The investigators arrive around 11:30 pm, bracing themselves against the frigid nighttime air.

The entry hall is dominated by a massive bronze Buddha surrounded by a halo of astrological symbols painted on the wall behind. Moving on into the apartment, the investigators' senses are assailed. A mosaic rainbow set into the floor guides them into the dimly lit interior, through the ballroom, the séance room, the animal menagerie, and the lounge, wending its way around gurgling fountains and bubbling aquaria.

In the animal menagerie room, a massive floor-to-ceiling cage houses a flock of chirping finches. Over here is a hothouse with slithering snakes and blinking lizards moving among tropical foliage, while over there is a globe of the world standing taller than a man. The recessed lighting casts yellow and green hues through the rambling space, and yet more astrological signs glare down from the high ceilings, lit with red neon tubes.

In the séance room there are massive couches, seemingly built for giants, framing a circular glass table. A bright light shines down from above, causing the glass to sparkle with its own inner radiance. The table's center is hollow and therein sits a massive swivel chair, unoccupied for now.

The Palace is crowded with chattering guests. Investigators with particularly high **Credit Ratings** (75%+) recognize (and are recognized by) various princes and counts. The failed author and Nazi sympathizer Hans Heinz Ewers (writer of the novel *Alraune* and the screenplay of the original 1913 *Student of Prague,* directed by Wegener and Rye) holds a small court in the lounge, entertaining a gaggle of admirers with tales of decadent Berlin in the years before the Great War. Throughout, there are men in Nazi Party uniforms.

Margo Lion is in the ballroom near the massive marble fireplace, wearing a candy-striped black-and-white dress and monocle, laughing. Her outfit looks familiar; it is the one she wears in the **3-by-5 photograph** found in Desmond's dossier!

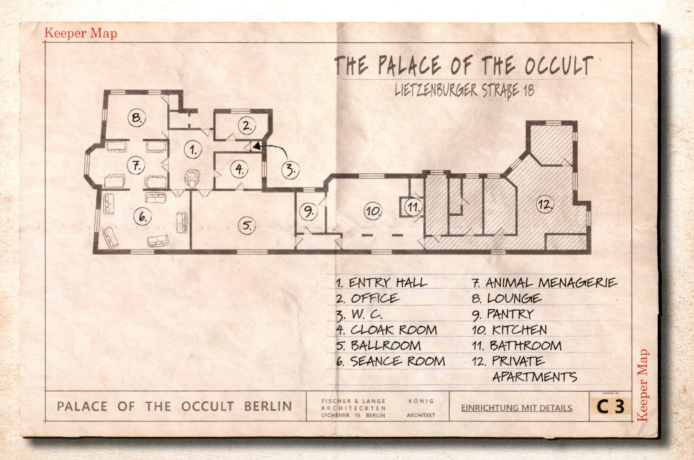

Keeper Map

THE PALACE OF THE OCCULT
LIETZENBURGER STRASSE 18

1. ENTRY HALL
2. OFFICE
3. W. C.
4. CLOAK ROOM
5. BALLROOM
6. SEANCE ROOM
7. ANIMAL MENAGERIE
8. LOUNGE
9. PANTRY
10. KITCHEN
11. BATHROOM
12. PRIVATE APARTMENTS

PALACE OF THE OCCULT BERLIN

FISCHER & LANGE ARCHITECKTEN LYCHENER 15 BERLIN | KÖNIG ARCHITEKT | EINRICHTUNG MIT DETAILS | C 3

The Palace of the Occult map

Keeper Map

If Anna Tchaikovsky survived the events of **The Devil Eats Flies**, she is in the ballroom as well, recently returned from an extended residence in America and now going by the name of Anna Anderson. She is with her lawyer, Edward Fallows, and her latest royal supporter, Prince Frederick of Saxe-Altenburg. Should the investigators greet her, she remembers them and reacts in accordance with how they treated her in the former scenario. Regardless, she seems more stable now, and more confident. Her hair is cut in a fashionable bob, her clothes clearly bought from the finest New York boutiques—refer to her profile in **The Devil Eats Flies**, page 139.

The door to the kitchen swings back and forth incessantly, disgorging waiters carrying platters of hors d'oeuvres and flutes of champagne. As the investigators mingle and move through the rooms of the palace, have everyone make a **Psychology** roll: success indicates a distinct feeling of unease, as if everyone is staring at them and gossiping behind their backs. Yet, whenever the investigator tries to pick out snatches of conversation or catch someone staring, they come up with nothing. This feeling of creeping paranoia garners unease but does not cost any Sanity points.

Enter Erik Jan Hanussen

Presently, the man of the hour emerges from his private apartments. Erik Jan Hanussen is a gentleman of middling build with dramatically bushy eyebrows and large ears. His eyes are the immediate focus: deep-set and intense. The piercing beam of his gaze passes over everyone present, taking in his guests with a single sweeping look. Perhaps to the alarm of the investigators, he leads a black poodle on a short leash. As the witching hour grows near, everyone knows to converge on the séance room, where Hanussen gives his welcoming speech.

"*Ladies and gentlemen,*" he says with a slight accent, "*I thank you all for attending tonight's event. As always, I am here to offer my humble talents to those seeking answers.*" As he moves among the guests, he places a finger to his temple. "*Already I see the truth shining forth from some of you. One here tonight claims to be the Grand Duchess Anastasia Romanov. I can confirm these claims are correct.*" (If Anna Anderson is not present, assume this is one of the many other claimants.) "*We should all be honored by her presence.*" An appreciative murmur ripples through the crowd.

He pauses before a group of Nazis. "*My dear Count Helldorff,*" he says, addressing a man wearing the uniform of the Stormtroopers. "*Your party will do quite well in the upcoming elections. Quite well indeed.*" With a start, the investigators realize Hanussen is speaking with the other man from the mysterious photo in the dossier!

Hanussen continues to move among the crowd. Eventually, he introduces himself to the investigators and thanks them for coming. As Hanussen moves on to speak to some other guests, the investigators see a man, nearly naked, being led around on a leash, a gag in his mouth. It is Inspector Krieg of the Criminal Police. Much laughter ensues at the man's pathetic predicament. Helldorff takes the man's leash. "*Look, Erik! Now I have a dog too!*" More laughter.

A photographer is present. The investigators find themselves in the shot as Hanussen poses with Helldorff, Margo Lion, Inspector Krieg, and the poodle—it is the very photograph they already hold in their figurative hands! As the camera's flash bursts forth, call for a **Sanity** roll for experiencing this surreal time distortion (1/1D3 loss).

Keeper note: if the investigators went out of their way to wear different clothes, have changed faces, or otherwise taken steps, inadvertently or otherwise, to make themselves look different, a quick check of the "original" photo nevertheless shows the investigators in their current garb and appearances—this realization adds an additional point of Sanity loss.

Before the investigators can do anything else, the psychic moves over to his glass round table and seats himself in the great chair at its center. The overhead light shines down on him, while another light set into the chair's headrest gives him a beatific halo. "*Please come to the table if there are questions you wish answered,*" he says. As he speaks, he looks at each of the investigators in turn (regardless of where they are situated), a quizzical look upon his face as if trying to place where he has seen them before. He motions to each of them, "*I think you all need to come up to the table.*"

The Séance

Joining the investigators are Count Helldorff and sufficient other partygoers to make up a total of twelve. Once seated, Hanussen instructs everyone to place their hands on the table, fingers splayed. The light overhead dims, along with the house lights, and an interior light under the frosted glass of the table comes up, giving everyone seated for the séance a ghostly, underlit glow. The light behind Hanussen's head continues to shine as well, and the investigators now note that his chair is set slightly higher than theirs, giving him a commanding position.

Slowly Hanussen rotates, staring at each participant, his eyes flashing and intense. Finally, he stops. He is staring at an investigator (choose randomly or pick the one with the lowest **Luck**). "*You: close your eyes. What do you see?*"

Presuming the investigator does as instructed, initially they see nothing. They feel Hanussen's fingers moving just in front of their face as he begins to hypnotize them. Ask the investigator to make a Hard **POW** roll: if successful, the investigator is resistant to Hanussen's attempt to put them in a deep hypnotic state and he moves on to another investigator. Keep going until all the investigators have succeeded with their POW roll or if one of them fails. With a failed roll, the following scene takes place.

Gradually, all sound and tactile sense drops away from the investigator; they feel like they are floating in an endless, cold void. There is no sense of up or down. The investigator's eyes cannot open, no matter how much they struggle. Suddenly, almost instantaneously, the investigator feels their mind under a terrific psychic assault, as if icy fingers are reaching into their skull and attempting to wrench their brain free. There is a momentary glimpse of a laughing face, as if projected in a black and white film—Countess Esterházy! Her laughter ends abruptly, her face now a steely mask of fury. "*Hand back the folder and I shall suffer you to live. Do not, and you will* beg *me for death!*"

Keeper note: if the investigators have somehow lost the dossier, the countess insists they turn Lina Desmond over to her instead.

The other guests at the table witness the investigator, at first sweating and mumbling, suddenly stiffen in their seat and then begin screaming uncontrollably. The afflicted investigator automatically loses 5 Sanity points and falls temporarily insane, suffering a bout of madness: psychosomatic disabilities, fainting, or physical hysterics are all especially appropriate. The séance collapses into chaos.

Even after the afflicted investigator recovers from their bout of madness, they continue to see Countess Esterházy's laughing face everywhere: in the mirrored reflection of shop windows, among the clouds and mist hanging over the city, and especially in their dreams. For the remainder of the scenario, the investigator loses 1 Sanity point per night owing to disturbed sleep.

What Happens If All Pass the POW Roll?

If all of the investigators passed the Hard POW roll, Hanussen hypnotizes another guest, who then experiences the terrifying vision of the countess. When they are brought back to their senses, they immediately seek out the investigators and relate the countess's demand: "*She said if you didn't do as she instructs, she will strike me dead!*"

The séance

The countess is as bad as her word, and the hapless partygoer's corpse turns up 24 hours later if the investigators don't turn over the dossier (or Lina Desmond). Inspector Krieg uses this death as probable cause to bring one of the investigators up on murder charges and has a judge issue an order of arrest—if he can plant the body in one of the investigator's homes, all the better!

THE STRANGE CASE OF THE PHOTOGRAPH

So, what's the deal with *that* photograph, anyway? The answer is left ambiguous. The point of the image is to create a sense of unease, unreality, and time distortion; to offer a pat explanation is to undo that effect. Suffice to say that Countess Esterházy's magic seems to be having a deleterious impact on the fabric of reality here in Berlin.

Cagey investigators may think to look up Albert Einstein at his residence in **Schöneberg** (page 32). The professor is often abroad for lecture tours and academic business trips, and at the Keeper's discretion may be away at this time. Otherwise, investigators with suitable academic credentials or a high **Credit Rating** (50%+) may sit for an hour or two in Einstein's comfortable loft apartment, discussing the intricacies of space-time and wormholes; this may even be a fine opportunity to drop some dark hints about the existence of other realities within our own. There is little practical information to be gleaned, though Einstein is certainly fascinated by the photograph and the story behind it, if the investigators share it. Those with the **Science (Physics)** skill above base gain a free skill check for this illuminating discussion.

RESEARCHING COUNT HELLDORFF

If they have not yet identified Count Helldorff in the **3-by-5 photograph**, the investigators get a chance to meet him at séance (**Palace of the Occult**, page 220). Should they wish to conduct research on Helldorff, the following information can be gleaned from a search of recent newspapers (**Library Use**) or by asking around (social skill roll at the Keeper's discretion).

Born in 1896, during the Great War Helldorff served as a lieutenant from 1915 and became a member of the Freikorps in 1919. He later became a member of the Prussian Parliament from 1924 to 1928, and also joined the National Socialist Freedom Party (NSFP), which became the NSDAP in 1926. In 1931, Helldorff joined the Sturmabteilung (SA), leading the group in Berlin. Subsequently, Helldorff has directed the SA in numerous anti-Semitic attacks, as well as street fights and altercations with left-wing political groups. His connection to Joesph Goebbels is well known.

Asking questions about a man like Helldorff is likely to lead to trouble. As an active member of the Nazi party and friend of Goebbels, he is liable to frown on a bunch of nosy investigators asking questions, should their interest in him come to his attention. If they are careless about who they speak to about Helldorff, ask for a group **Luck** roll to determine whether word reaches the count about the investigators. Depending on the approach taken by the investigators, the Keeper is at liberty to have a group of Brownshirts come calling to inquire as to their interest in the count. Use the **Rotte Member** profile (page 239) for these thugs, who prefer to let their fists do the talking.

Investigators may attempt to follow the count, either following the séance or when noticing him near a SA bar or rally. Such an endeavor won't reveal anything out of the ordinary but should lead the investigators to **Salon Kitty** (following), which Helldorff frequents on a regular basis.

SALON KITTY

The investigators may have shadowed Wolf-Heinrich Graf Helldorff to Salon Kitty or, more likely, discovered from Lina Desmond that Count Helldorff frequents the brothel, renowned for its Dominas (**Prostitution**, page 53). What neither the investigators nor Desmond know is that Salon Kitty is where Countess Esterházy has resided ever since she transcended into her current form.

Located at Giesebrechtstrasse 11 on a street that branches off at an odd angle from the Ku'damm, this bordello matches the surrounding neighborhood's air of high-class charm. Inside, fragrant with the odor of cigar smoke and expensive facial creams, the decor recalls a *fin de siècle* literary salon or Wilhelmian drawing room.

The salon is run by the eponymous Kitty Schmidt. A Mae-West-esque voluptuous woman who just turned 50, she uses her native charm and wit to put her guests at ease. She is always on hand to greet visitors and guide them into the front parlor, where they are presented with a picture book of the 20 girls working at the bordello. Kitty encourages the client to select the best girl to meet their needs; she then telephones the one chosen, who then meets the client in the back parlor, where they sit and converse. After drinks and small talk, they retire to one of the rooms on the third or fourth floors.

The second, third, and fourth floors of the building comprise private quarters for some of the salon's residents (as well as Ágnes Esterházy), while the fifth floor, with its large skylights, has been cleared for witches' sabbats, sacrifices, and other rituals. The floorboards still bear the bloody stains of past sacrifices. This is also the place where new cat-things are created using the cult's blackest magic. A brief description of Salon Kitty follows; refer to the plan of the establishment on page 225.

Keeper note: Keep in mind that not all women at the brothel are witches or even aware of the coven's activities. Only Kitty and eleven of the working girls (out of 20) are coven members.

Paying a Visit

If the investigators pay the salon a visit in the evening, there are 1D6 men in the front and back parlors, smoking, drinking, and conversing with some of the girls. They are a mix of high-society types, foreign diplomats (chiefly Italian and Romanian), and Nazi Party members. If this is a random visit, there is a 25% chance that Baron Grunau is among them and a 75% chance that Count Helldorff is there. Visiting in daylight hours finds the Salon much quieter.

Kitty is happy to entertain visitors who wish to talk business but stonewalls those who come simply to snoop and ask prying questions. Furthermore, if the countess is aware of the investigators and they come to the salon looking for answers, she does not hesitate to rally the witches in her coven (calling first on the few who work at Salon Kitty), as well as her familiars, to corral and interrogate the hapless dupes. Soporific hallucinogens slipped into drinks from the bar (a successful Hard **CON** or suffer hallucinations and a penalty die to all skill and attribute rolls for 1D6 hours) are just the tip of the iceberg. Remember, she will not rest until she gets her filmstrip back and does not hesitate to torture or kill in order to achieve this goal.

There are 2D4 cat-things in and around the property at any given time, acting as both a sort of surveillance system and security for the building. Investigators looking around may, at the Keeper's discretion, cross paths with one or more of the disturbing creatures.

Keeper note: investigators confronting the countess and managing to destroy the filmstrip (either here or elsewhere) will have rid themselves of the most immediate threat. They may wonder, however, about the mysterious Baron Grunau. Soon enough, the newspapers provide a lead in the form of a **Cattle Call** (page 230).

Parlor Floor

The ground floor of Salon Kitty, and the only part of the building non-paying customers and casual visitors see (unless they're very unlucky).

Entry Vestibule

An elegantly swept flight of steps leads up off the street to a set of double doors with frosted glass windows. A brass buzzer summons one of the coven initiates to the doors to escort visitors inside; here they may hang coats and hats before stepping through a second door to the salon beyond.

Mudroom

A back entrance provides access to the salon from an alleyway running behind the building. Most of the girls use this door for coming and going.

Back Parlor

This is where clients retire with their girl(s) for the evening before heading upstairs. The lighting in here is low and intimate, with couches and armchairs interspersed between potted plants to provide some measure of privacy. A large bar is tended by the prettiest coven initiates and provides libations (beer, French wine, champagne, coffee, or hard liquor) and German canapés.

Front Parlor

The main entertaining room contains overstuffed armchairs, a grand piano, velvet curtains and Persian carpets, satin flock wallpaper in a deep burgundy with gold filigrees, potted ferns, and tasteful Art Nouveau knick-knacks. In one of the corners stands a plaster copy of an ancient Hellenistic statue depicting a goddess with three faces. Investigators who survived **Dances of Vice, Horror, and Ecstasy** and witnessed the triple-headed creature in the Shadow City are likely to notice this right away. A successful **History** or **Archaeology** roll identifies the goddess as Hecate, while a successful **Occult** roll recalls that she is the goddess of light and entryways, but also of sorcery, witchcraft, and herb lore. If the investigators ask Kitty about the Hecate imagery around the Salon, she claims it was a gift from a wealthy client. "*Some sort of old Roman goddess, I think,*" she says, feigning ignorance.

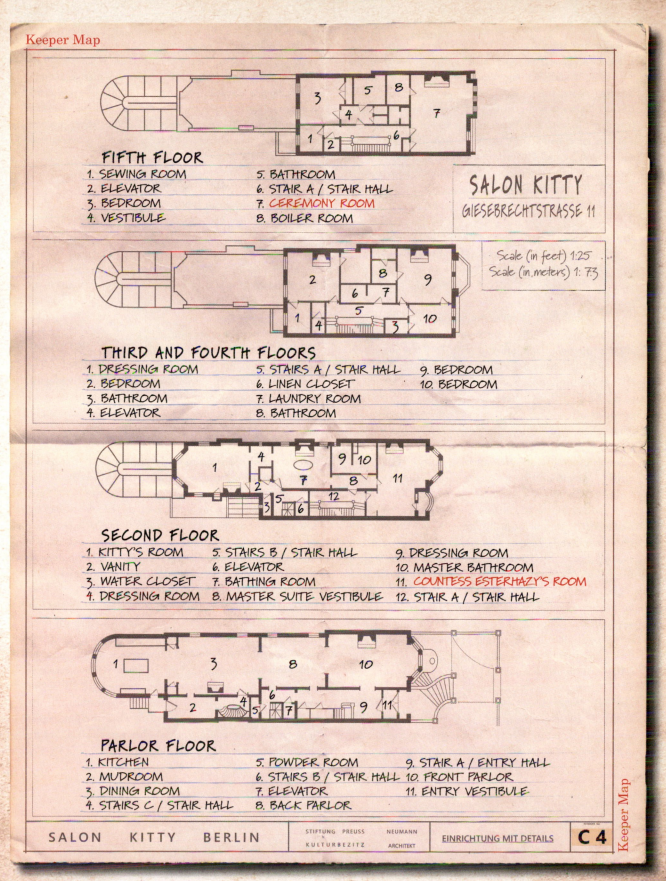

FIFTH FLOOR

1. SEWING ROOM
2. ELEVATOR
3. BEDROOM
4. VESTIBULE
5. BATHROOM
6. STAIR A / STAIR HALL
7. CEREMONY ROOM
8. BOILER ROOM

SALON KITTY
GIESEBRECHTSTRASSE 11

THIRD AND FOURTH FLOORS

1. DRESSING ROOM
2. BEDROOM
3. BATHROOM
4. ELEVATOR
5. STAIRS A / STAIR HALL
6. LINEN CLOSET
7. LAUNDRY ROOM
8. BATHROOM
9. BEDROOM
10. BEDROOM

Scale (in feet) 1:25
Scale (in meters) 1: 7.3

SECOND FLOOR

1. KITTY'S ROOM
2. VANITY
3. WATER CLOSET
4. DRESSING ROOM
5. STAIRS B / STAIR HALL
6. ELEVATOR
7. BATHING ROOM
8. MASTER SUITE VESTIBULE
9. DRESSING ROOM
10. MASTER BATHROOM
11. COUNTESS ESTERHAZY'S ROOM
12. STAIR A / STAIR HALL

PARLOR FLOOR

1. KITCHEN
2. MUDROOM
3. DINING ROOM
4. STAIRS C / STAIR HALL
5. POWDER ROOM
6. STAIRS B / STAIR HALL
7. ELEVATOR
8. BACK PARLOR
9. STAIR A / ENTRY HALL
10. FRONT PARLOR
11. ENTRY VESTIBULE

SALON KITTY BERLIN

STIFTUNG PREUSS
KULTURBEZITZ

NEUMANN
ARCHITEKT

EINRICHTUNG MIT DETAILS

C 4

Elevator and Stairs

There are three sets of stairs in the building (noted on the plan as A, B, and C). Stair A is a large and grand staircase wending its way up through all five floors of the salon. Stair B is the "back stairs" for use by staff; it goes up to the fourth floor. Stair C leads down to the cellar, where produce, meat, and coal are stored for use in the kitchen. The general staff and coven initiates also maintain private apartments down here. An old brass elevator, somewhat clunky and rattling—using it with stealth is impossible—goes all the way up to the fifth floor.

Second Floor

This floor comprises the private apartments for Countess Esterházy and Kitty Schmidt.

Kitty's Room

A richly appointed suite, complete with canopied bed, marble fireplace, leather armchairs, bookshelves, and an antique dining set. A roll-top desk contains dozens of reels of sound recordings made of compromising pillow talk, as well as hundreds of incriminating photographs of city officials, judges, police detectives, and high-ranking members of the Nazi Party. A successful **Accounting** roll made when investigating the ledgers reveals hundreds of thousands of marks in income per month. A successful **Library Use** roll while investigating Kitty's bookshelves turns up dozens of volumes on the history and practice of witchcraft (including a reprint of the *Malleus Maleficarum*, a second edition of *Thaumaturgical Prodigies in the New-England Canaan*, and a heavily annotated copy of Murray's *The Witch-Cult in Western Europe*), as well as other occult and Mythos tomes (among them Frazer's *Golden Bough*, Blavatsky's *Isis Unveiled*, and an original printing of Juntz's *Unaussprechlichen Kulten*; see *Call of Cthulhu Rulebook* for further information on all of these manuscripts). Kitty's bedroom looks out over the glass roof of the kitchen below to the back alley and adjoining properties—if Kitty is in this room, there's a good chance she'll spot investigators acting suspiciously behind the salon.

Dressing Room

Kitty's extensive wardrobe of sequined dresses, expensive furs, Italian shoes, and Parisian hats is contained within this massive walk-in closet.

Bathing Room

A huge tiled room with sky blue satin wallpaper, brass fixtures, and large mirrors. A fireplace and a marble bathtub (large enough to seat five or six people) dominate this room. Count Helldorff frequently rents out this room to entertain two or three of his favorite girls. Like every other place of assignation, it has been wired to record the conversations taking place within.

Second Dressing Room

Another walk-in closet, similar in scope to Kitty's, but oddly empty. No clothes, hats, or shoes are to be found here.

Master Bathroom

A finely appointed bathroom that, much like the dressing room, shows signs of disuse—a thin layer of dust sits upon the countertops and toilet seat.

Countess Esterházy's Room

Decked out in classic bordello fashion, with a fire blazing in a red marble fireplace, this is the countess' residence. She dwells here most of the time, taking visitors from across the city come to pledge their loyalty and seek out her magical assistance. She often takes note of visitors from her window seat, shielded from view by a set of fine lace curtains.

Keeper note: if alerted to an investigator's approach, she stands behind a Japanese paper screen when the visitor first enters, addressing them from there—a successful **Spot Hidden** roll notices the light from the fireplace casts no shadow on the paper screen. If the filmstrip is proffered as a bargaining chip, the countess emerges, revealing her unearthly condition to all present, provoking a **Sanity** roll (0/1D6 loss to see her three-dimensional projection). She demands not only the film but also the total obeisance of the investigators, commanding them to bow down at her feet and swear fealty to the coven—she intends to turn any male investigators into cat-things and put any female investigators to work at the brothel while they serve as coven initiates. This is a tense moment. The roaring fire presents an excellent opportunity to destroy the countess on the spot, should an investigator think to fling the filmstrip into the blaze. If any moves are made toward the fireplace while the filmstrip is in view, the countess cannot hide her nervousness, casting anxious glances at the roaring flames.

Third and Fourth Floors

These floors are identical in layout and comprise the "business end" of Salon Kitty. Here, the coven witches and their uninitiated sisters entertain paying guests.

Dressing Room

A place for the salon's working girls to retire to change outfits, wash up, and otherwise relax in private.

Bedrooms

Each of the bedrooms sleeps two; a large paper screen provides some measure of privacy between the two bedsteads. The numerous whips, paddles, and restraints found in each bedroom certainly belie the plush, unthreatening comfort of the downstairs parlors. Unless otherwise requested by a client, Kitty schedules one girl per room during operating hours.

Fifth Floor

This floor is a mix of utility rooms, the last of the bedroom suites, and the coven's ceremonial magic space.

Sewing Room

Two sewing machines, several dress forms, and bolts of fabric provide the ladies of the salon with the means to mend and create their own wardrobe.

Bedrooms

As per the third- and fourth-floor bedrooms, although only ever used by coven members and those allied to them.

Ceremony Room

A large space, once perhaps a master suite complete with its own fireplace; nowadays, the fireplace is cold, the floors bloodstained and bare. The walls are lined with cabinets full of various strange ritual artifacts (a weathered skull inscribed with unearthly runes, a copper dagger, lengths of red silken rope, and so on).

Keeper note: investigators captured by the coven (either inside the salon or elsewhere in the city) are taken here, tied to simple wooden chairs, and interrogated by the countess and a number of witches equal to the *total* number of investigators in the group (regardless of how many have come to the salon). Using both physical and magical torture, the interrogations are designed to find out where the filmstrip and Lina Desmond are—see the **Characters and Monsters** section at the end of this scenario for the spells available to the coven. If Desmond has been operating as a patsy, this is a dramatic time for her to reveal herself.

THE TOWER IN THE WOODS

The Kaiser-Wilhelm-Turm, shown on the **postcard** in Lina Desmond's dossier (**Going Over the Dossier**, page 210) may draw the investigators' interest. Desmond reinforces the importance of the tower when she speaks to the investigators (**Lina Turns Up**, page 213). It is likely that the investigators journey out to the Grunewald to take a look at the tower the prior to its use as a film location. There's not much to find there, initially at least.

The tower is open to the public 24 hours a day, seven days a week. If visiting during daylight hours (between 8 am and 4 pm at this time of year), a few scattered day-trippers linger in the area or stand up on the observation deck. If visited at night, the atrium is the domain of a gang of wild-boys (see box, nearby; a **Wild-Boy** profile can be found on page 239).

The tower sits atop a platform of red porphyry and is built of red brick in a Gothic Revival style, reminiscent of north German castle construction. The tower's base is a large atrium containing a life-sized marble statue of Kaiser Wilhelm I, founder of the German Empire. The vaulted ceiling overhead is decorated with a neo-Byzantine mural, and iron reliefs of the Kaiser's closest advisors (Albrecht von Roon, Helmuth von Moltke, Otto von Bismarck, and Prince Friedrich Karl of Prussia) stand in the four corners.

A spiral staircase wends its way up the center of the tower to the observation platform, 150 feet (46 m) above the summit of the Karlsberg hill upon which the tower sits. From here, sweeping views of the Grunewald and the Havel may be taken in. Regardless, there are no signs of anything untoward or sinister.

WILD-BOYS

An unusual offshoot of the Wandervogel movement (**The Apache Pathfinders**, page 18), the Wild-Boys of Berlin are a loosely affiliated group of all-male bohemian prostitutes. Composed of adolescents between the ages of 14 and 18, usually runaways, they exist on the peripheries of the city, both literally and figuratively. They may be found, leading a lifestyle reminiscent of Peter Pan and his Lost Boys, in public parks, abandoned warehouses near the riverfront, squatting in tenements, or living wild out in the Grunewald.

Gangs are led by a "Bull," the eldest member. New recruits are initiated through sadistic or scatological hazing rituals, culminating in a blood oath of loyalty. Each gang (with names like "The Wild and Free Gang," "Fear No Death," "The Forest Pirates," "Wild West," "Santa Fe," "Gypsy Love," and "The Dirty Boys"—more than 200 in all) sports a distinctive appearance. Insofar as it exists, the default Wild-

Boy "look" is a motley assortment of bangles, hoop earrings, colorful scarves, Tyrolean hats, and lederhosen. Other gangs opt for a more distinctive unified look; some examples include tuxedos and top hats, mortar boards and scholar's robes, or even papier-mâché buffalo masks.

Wild-Boys are generally considered a scourge on the city, as they make their money exclusively through criminal activity: pick-pocketing and mugging, breaking and entering, car theft, cat burglary, and (most notoriously) prostitution. Often, the youngest members of the gang are sent out by the Bulls to walk the Alex or ply underground *Dielen* looking for willing suitors.

As with the fictional Lost Boys, "growing up" means an end to life as a Wild-Boy, though a certain rough fraternity remains among former members who now walk the city streets in suits and ties or the paramilitary uniforms of the SA.

Cars & Trucks

Ezterhazy's Car

Extras

Circle marks Von Grunau's position

Cameras & Film Crews

SPANDAU

KAISER WILHELM TOWER

HAVEL RIVER

ZEHLENDORF

TELTOW

OBSERVATION PLATFORM

180' / 55 m

KAISER WILHELM TOWER

GRUNEWALD FOREST

5   10   20 m

KAISER WILHELM TURM GRUNEWALD

TELTOW GEMEINDEAMT BRANDENBURG

PFEIFFER ARCHITEKT

EINRICHTUNG MIT DETAILS

C 5

CATTLE CALL

Up till now, the investigators have only heard of, rather than met, Baron Grunau; either in conversation with Lina Desmond (**Lina Turns Up**, page 213) or, possibly in passing, by Aleister Crowley (**Dramatis Personae: Aleister Crowley**, page 206). A slim chance exists for the investigators coming across the baron if they visit **Salon Kitty** (page 223), although it is assumed that they do not get a proper chance to entertain a dialogue with the man.

Investigators attempting to seek out the baron find a lead in due course, likely through an unexpected channel: on the morning of January 4, an article appears in the local papers (**Handout: Schreckfilm 3**). Should the investigators decide to take on the role of film extras, they must arrive at the Kaiser-Wilhelm-Turm at the time stated in the news story. A perimeter of security guards posted a quarter-mile (400 m) from the film set intercept the merely curious, unless they can con their way in using press credentials or some other plausible cover.

Arriving for the Casting Call

It is still dark outside when the investigators arrive at the tower for the casting call. It is also frigidly cold, with another freezing mist encasing the forest. As the sky overhead begins to lighten, the tower's various spires can be seen but dimly through the gloom. It is an altogether eerie scene.

About 100 other brave individuals have ventured out in response to the newspaper advertisement, mostly desperate souls attracted by the promise of a hot meal and some spending money—poor immigrants, migrant workers, homeless veterans, and so forth. If the investigators have been out to the tower already and met the local Wild-Boys, they recognize their faces in the crowd as well.

The flat summit around the tower is now crowded with cars, lorries, and film equipment, including three cameras. The director, Henrik Galeen, is moving around, consulting on camera positioning and directing his crew. A successful **Spot Hidden** roll picks out a limousine—perhaps a famous movie star is here? (See **Countess Esterházy**, following.)

Keeper note: investigators who identified the filmstrip in Desmond's dossier recall that Galeen directed the 1926 version of *The Student of Prague* depicted in it.

COUNTESS ESTERHÁZY

Assuming she has not already suffered a fatal confrontation with the investigators (**Salon Kitty**, page 223), watching these events from behind a curtained window in the backseat of her luxury sedan is none other than Countess Esterházy. In

her company is her favorite cat-thing (a former investigator, perhaps?).

Peeking from behind the curtains, it takes her a while to pick the investigators' faces out of the crowd, but soon the countess notices they are in attendance. That is unless, of course, they have taken steps to disguise themselves, through means mundane or arcane (**Guise of the Other**, page 242, for example).

If she does recognize the investigators and hasn't yet retrieved her filmstrip, then the countess makes one last desperate bid to do so. She directs one of the film crew to collect one of the investigators and bring them to her car—if one suffered a vision of the countess at Hanussen's séance, she chooses that investigator; otherwise, decide randomly.

8

Casting Call

Producers working on a new Schreckfilm have issued a casting call for extras. The film, tentatively entitled "Das Necronomicon," is to be a documentary style fictionalization of the occult secrets contained within "one of the most infamous tomes of all time," according to the movie's financier, Baron von Grunau. The film has had a troubled production, being stalled in development for over two years now. Von Grunau assures our reporter that, thanks to some recent technological and creative breakthroughs, the production is back on track and that he hopes to see the film ready for release before Easter.

Those wishing to appear as extras in the film must report to the Kaiser-Wilhelm-Turm in Grunewald tomorrow morning at 6:00 a.m. for a day of shooting in and around the location. Food and a nominal stipend will be provided.

Stellenangebote

Sofortige Ablehnung der neu geschaffenen Position des Produktionsmanagers zu planen

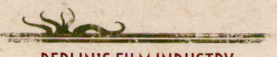

BERLIN'S FILM INDUSTRY

Berlin is the center of the European film industry, with the studio lots at Babelsburg rivaling those of Hollywood in the United States. Although films had been shot in Berlin almost from the inception of moving pictures, Berlin doesn't begin its ascendancy until 1912 with the filming of *Der Totentanz* (*The Dance of Death*), starring Asta Nielsen, at Babelsburg. Other studios are established in the suburbs of Weißensee and Tempelhof, as well as farther outside the city at Woltersdorf.

Without question, the biggest film production company is Ufa, which is actually a consortium of smaller film production companies, as well as the owner of a string of movie theaters in Berlin and across Germany. In addition to the lots and soundstages at Babelsburg, Ufa rents hangars at Tempelhof Airport for some of its film projects. By the mid-1920s, Ufa is large enough that its films find international distribution deals with Paramount and MGM, with a large segment of Berlin's local economy devoted to film production and its many ancillary businesses.

Ufa's near-monopoly of the German film industry is only one key to Berlin's emergence as an important cinematic center. The other factor at play is the enormous pool of talent drawn to Berlin to make films. Directors like Fritz Lang, F. W. Murnau, Josef von Sternberg, and G.W. Pabst work with actors such as Conrad Veidt, Emil Jannings, Pola Negri, Lya de Putti, Greta Garbo, Marlene Dietrich, and even American imports like Louise Brooks, to create some of the most memorable visions of silent and early sound cinema: *The Cabinet of Dr. Caligari* (Wiene, 1920), *Nosferatu* (Murnau, 1922), *The Niebelungen* (Lang, 1924), *The Last Man* (Murnau, 1924), *Metropolis* (Lang, 1927), *Pandora's Box* (Pabst, 1929), *The Blue Angel* (Sternberg, 1930), *M* (Lang, 1931), and many more.

There, she threatens to stop the investigator's beating heart (**Spells: Stop Heart**, page 242) and then do the same to the investigator's companions, at the rate of one per day, starting today at sunset, unless they hand over the filmstrip. Counter-threats are met with derisive laughter and warnings of even worse retribution. "*You have met my familiars, have you not? They were all once my enemies, just like you. Now they serve me for eternity. And soon you will join them if you don't do as I demand.*"

Of course, larger events are about to render Countess Esterházy's attempts at coercion null and void, but the investigators don't know that yet. If Countess Esterházy gets her filmstrip back, she leaves the investigators alone—for now.

LIGHTS, CAMERA...

After an hour of milling about, during which time hot coffee is distributed to the shuffling, shivering extras, Galeen surmounts the porphyry base of the tower, megaphone in hand. The sky overhead is now a steely gray, with sunrise proper still about an hour away.

Through his megaphone, Galeen lays out the plans for the day's shooting. The extras are to portray worshippers of an ancient god, participating in a ritual of supplication. Over the next hour, costumes are handed out along with a page from the script. The costumes are those of medieval peasants, ill-fitting and shoddily made. Curtains inside the tower's atrium have been put up to allow some privacy for changing. The script is a chant that the extras must intone while the cameras are rolling. Schnitzel and more coffee is handed out as final preparations get under way for the shoot.

Investigators wishing to snoop around, perhaps hoping to find the purloined *Necronomicon*, discover nothing of the sort. Today is just for filming the big crowd scene—no props required.

Camera Equipment

Three cameras, each loaded with enchanted film, are put into position. One is stationary, its lens dialed in for close-ups on Grunau. The second is mounted on a mobile platform with four large, rubber tires, to be used to capture tracking shots. The third is mounted atop a goose-necked crane, to be used for wide shots. Due to the nature of the camera setup, only those taking extraordinary precautions are able to stay out of the baleful influence of the enchanted film—essentially, an investigator must be on the far side of the Kaiser-Wilhelm-Turm once filming starts. Even then, the Keeper may call for a **Luck** roll if the investigator is doing anything other than staying stationary and out of sight.

The Baron Arrives

Once the camera equipment is set, another limousine pulls up and Baron Grunau emerges, garbed in a much better-made costume that looks reminiscent of a medieval bishop, albeit completely lacking in Christian iconography. Instead, his robes are woven with bizarre symbols; a successful **Cthulhu Mythos** roll identifies them as those associated with the god Yog-Sothoth. The tip of his crozier depicts a triple-headed goddess.

Grunau moves around to the "rear" of the tower set to the grand stairs leading up to the tower proper. After disappearing behind the porphyry base for a minute, he reappears, sweeping around the side of the tower to take up his mark at its base, looking down onto the sea of extras below.

Keeper note: if the investigators wish to get close to him, they may each attempt a **Charm** or **Fast Talk** roll to convince the assistant director to position them toward the front, within 10 yards/meters of Grunau. The base of the tower rises 15 feet (4.6 m), so an investigator who wishes to actually physically assault the baron must pass around to the stairs on the far side, just as the baron did.

Finally, after hours of nothing much happening, all is suddenly a flurry of activity. Large, powerful lights blaze into life, large boom microphones swing out, Galeen calls for quiet on set, then…*ACTION!*

The sound of the cameras rolling can be heard briefly before the extras start in with their chant. All within direct view of the cameras lose 1D6 magic points. Those who are right beside the cameras, or who can trace a line of sight to the cameras without being caught in the shot, lose 1 magic point.

Grunau turns toward the tower, arms held wide, staff pointing away from his body and held horizontally. "*Yog-Sothoth knows the Gate. Yog-Sothoth is the Gate. Yog-Sothoth is the key and guardian of the Gate…*"

Anyone being filmed by the cameras now loses a further 1D6+2 magic points; everyone else loses 1D3 magic points instead (unless they are completely hidden behind the tower, as already described). Here and there some of the more frail-looking extras faint.

Strange, rippling clouds begin to form over the tower. After a minute of filming, as Grunau and the crowd continue their chant, all who are under the cameras' eyes lose a further 2D6 magic points; those nearest the cameras lose 1D6 instead. Dozens of extras begin to faint, as does some of the film crew.

With the enchanted film growing in power, draining the assemblage's life essence, every subsequent minute of filming drains away 2D6 more magic points from cast and crew alike until all lay unconscious, the whirring of the cameras now the only noise filling the glade around the tower.

Filming at the tower

As long as even one camera continues to roll, magic points continue to plummet. Soon, the entire cast of extras are swooning and collapsing. Strangely compelled by the magical energies of the film, Galeen refuses to yell cut.

Keeper note: one clue that the problem lies not with the baron but with some other source is the fact that the investigators continue to lose magic points even if the baron is silenced. Everyone within sight of the three cameras is subject to this draining effect, including Grunau, so killing or subduing the baron (or his simply fainting) has no discernable effect on their own growing weakness.

Magical Film

The true enemy is, of course, the specially treated film in the cameras. Should the investigators think to destroy the cameras and burn the film, they spare themselves the unpleasantness that is about to transpire and should be congratulated for their perspicacity. Assuming both the countess and the baron are neutralized as well, proceed to **Rewards** (page 237). However, such a drastic course of action is not entirely without consequence. The three cameras in operation are all a classic "mouse-eared" model with 10 hit points each; it requires a certain amount of violence to render them inoperable. Any disruption to the filming brings the attention of 1D6+1 teamsters (**Beefy Teamster**, page 239) who do their best to neutralize the vandals.

Gunfire or explosions cause the crowd of any extras still awake to panic and stampede like a herd of frightened cattle—the Keeper may call for a **DEX** roll from the investigators to avoid falling under the crowd's rushing feet and suffering 1D6+3 points of damage. And, naturally, if either the baron or the countess are still active and present, they will use every trick in their considerable arcane arsenals to eliminate those investigators who dare to interfere with their evil scheme.

If Countess Esterházy is present in the limousine, anyone making a move toward Galeen or the cameras risks being the target of one of her spells, Power Drain (**Spells**, page 242) to hasten the loss of magic points—this spell takes 2 rounds to cast and pits Esterházy's formidable POW 120 in an opposed roll against the target investigator's POW. If she wins, she drains 1D6 magic points from her victim; if she loses, the reverse occurs. In addition, the countess can also call upon the spells Mindblast, Spectral Razor, Stop Heart, and Wither Limb as necessary.

As soon as all of the investigators reach zero magic points, proceed to **The Deep, Dark Woods** (following). If some investigators retain consciousness, they do not journey to the strange dream-woods whence their comrades are now bound and are free to carry out whatever plan they can concoct to bring the surrounding chaos to an end. It should be noted, though, that burning the film currently being shot once anyone has fallen unconscious due to its effects is an extremely bad idea (see **Conclusion**, page 237, for the reasons why).

THE DEEP, DARK WOODS

The enchantment placed on the film in the cameras attempts to steal the souls of all whose image it captures. Due to its powers, the investigators pass through a transformation similar to that undergone by Countess Esterházy, but with the crucial difference that their continued existence is imperiled rather than immortalized.

After falling unconscious at the Kaiser-Wilhelm-Turm, each investigator awakens alone, in what at first seems to be a section of the Grunewald. Bare trees loom all around, while beneath them is a layer of dead leaves and humus. A dense, low-lying fog creeps across the forest floor.

As the investigators begin to stand, they notice that this forest boasts some strange features. First, and most immediately, noticeable is the complete lack of color. Although they may have mistaken it for dusk or early morning, the investigators soon realize they are, quite literally, in a black-and-white world. Looking down, they see that they still wear the garb of a medieval peasant but that they, like Countess Esterházy, are now black and white as well. Call for a **Sanity** roll (1/1D6 loss).

Keeper note: if the countess has been burned up in the waking world, everything has a slightly charred look to it—the trees are scorched, the church blackened. The smell of acrid smoke is heavy in the air.

Looking around the woods, the investigators notice that the trees are clearly not real. Constructed of trunks and branches as if real trees, the joins and nails on these specimens are obvious once examined up close. The trees do not have a root system, being mounted instead on wooden beams concealed beneath a couple of inches of forest loam. Furthermore, the shapes of the trees themselves are clearly artificial, being closer to caricatures of actual trees—limbs jut in a riot of strange, impossible angles, dark and foreboding, creating a bracken-like effect that seems to press in from all directions.

Those who glance up see no sky—just diffused light and an overarching darkness without stars. The overall sensation is of being on a giant soundstage, albeit one without any visible boundaries—there is just endless, fake forest all around.

A powerful, dream-like sensation pervades the entire scene. The woods are utterly silent. No animals stir, no breeze blows. The temperature is mild rather than frigid, again suggesting an artificial environment. Gradually, the investigator becomes aware of ghostly shapes moving in the mist. Whether the investigators remain standing still or begin to move, one of the shapes draws ever nearer.

Then out of the mists comes a terrifying vision. The nature of the vision varies from investigator to investigator and should be personalized based on the character's backstory from events within this scenario or those experienced in previous adventures—some suggestions follow.

- If the investigator used Crowley's ritual to obtain a new face, the face's former owner wants it back. The corpse's facial muscles and tissues shine in the dim-half light, its lidless eyes staring. Through lipless teeth it gibbers, crying for its skin, clawing at the investigator's stolen face (see **Vengeful Corpse** profile, page 241). If the creature inflicts 4 or more points of damage in a single hit, it sinks its nails into the investigator's forehead and begins to peel—any "damage" done here in the dream world is deducted from the investigator's Sanity, not from their hit points (see **Reality Checks**, following). Strangely, the investigator's old face, bloody, tender, and raw like sub dermal flesh, lies below. At the conclusion of this encounter, possibly with the investigator running away, move to **Totentanz Noch Einmal**, page 235.

- Did the investigator lose a friend or contact to suicide during the course of the scenario? If so, this person appears out of the mists, their clothes sodden, their skin bloated and livid with innumerable small lacerations and lesions courtesy of the fish in the Havel nibbling at their dead flesh. These vengeful corpses do not attack the investigator physically; instead, from waterlogged lungs, they sob and wail, asking the investigator why they did nothing to save them. Call for the investigator to make a Hard **POW** roll; if failed, the investigator loses 1D8 Sanity points. The corpse continues to follow and harangue the investigator in this manner unless the investigator bodily attacks them; it flees after losing half or more of its hit points in damage (remember, any damage dealt to the investigator is taken from their Sanity points and not their hit points). Alternately, if the investigator lost a close friend or loved one in the past to other causes, they appear now as a vengeful corpse, crying out in the same manner. Use the **Vengeful Corpse** profile on page 241, and at the conclusion of this encounter, move on to **Totentanz Noch Einmal**, page 235

- The investigator may encounter one of their significant people (per their backstory), who now has the waxen pallor of the recently deceased. Mournfully, the significant person claims they are dead, killed as a result of the investigator's actions or negligence—whether true or false, the corpse accuses the investigator—this may in and of itself be a spur

toward making a **reality check**: if the investigator refuses to believe this news, they may make a **Sanity** roll; with a success, they snap out of the dream (see **Conclusion**, page 237), while a failure causes them to lose 1D8 Sanity points—if they suffer a bout of madness, refer to **Alone and Mad in the Woods**, page 235; otherwise, move on to **Totentanz Noch Einmal**, page 235.

- Finally, the investigator may come face to face with themselves! This doppelganger is dressed in something more typical of their everyday wardrobe and seems quite perturbed by the investigator's presence. They claim that *they* are the real person, and that they are trapped in a dream and the "original" investigator is but a dream manifestation. "*Look at your clothes! You look like an extra in a bad movie!*" Again, this may spur the investigator to make a **reality check** roll, with the same outcomes as with the significant person option, above. Otherwise, at the conclusion of this scene, move on to **Totentanz Noch Einmal**, page 235.

REALITY CHECKS

The artificial, black-and-white nature of the woods may serve as an indicator to cagey investigators that they are in a land of the unreal. The magic of Countess Esterházy's specially treated movie film has trapped them inside a dreamland of her own making. Even if the countess was destroyed earlier in the scenario, the visions here persist.

The only respite, for the moment, is to realize this is all a terrible illusion and nothing more. Indeed, the investigators cannot be physically harmed while in this dream-forest; all damage done to them in this realm is deducted from Sanity instead of hit points.

The only way to escape the dream woods before permanent madness sets in is to make a successful **reality check** (*Call of Cthulhu Rulebook*, page 162). Reality checks are always voluntary, and a failed roll results in the loss of 1 Sanity point, while a successful roll brings the investigator back to reality (see **Conclusion**, page 237).

Because the investigators are not likely to be suffering from a bout of madness at the outset of the vision, the use of a reality check may not occur to them. Generous Keepers may wish to drop increasing hints about the unreal, nightmarish, and constructed nature of the woods and its inhabitants. Alternatively, mechanical clues (such as losing Sanity points instead of hit points) may provide the necessary insight. Lastly, if an investigator does suffer a bout of madness while within the woods, the effect (somewhat ironically) leads them to believe that what they are experiencing is a hallucination, thereby suggesting a reality check is in order. If all fails, a successful **INT** roll helps the investigator to understand the situation.

Investigators who make their reality checks are out of the game for now. The Keeper should *not* reveal their fate right away, simply telling them: "*You shut your eyes tight. All is black and silent.*"

Alone and Mad in the Woods

If an investigator suffers a bout of madness while alone in the woods, they pass out. When they awaken, an indeterminate period of time has passed. They are first aware of lying on their back, followed by a gentle swaying motion. Opening their eyes, they see only pitch blackness. Attempting to move their arms and legs quickly reveals that they are in a coffin, with the muted sound of drum and fife coming in through the walls of the pine board casket.

Suddenly, they are set down rather roughly. Then comes the sound of earth hitting the coffin lid—they are being buried alive! Call for a **Sanity** roll (1D3/1D6 loss.) The unwitting investigator is still in the dream world and may attempt a **reality check**, if they think to do so; otherwise, escape from the coffin is impossible—for details on what is going on outside, see **Totentanz Noch Einmal** (following).

Totentanz Noch Einmal

After their eerie encounter in the woods (or perhaps while fleeing from it), the investigator hears the distant tolling of a church bell. Following the sound through the artificial forest, they catch sight of a medieval church situated on a craggy hill. The dimensions and proportions of the church are exaggerated in a twisted, angular fashion reminiscent of old Expressionist film sets from ten years ago: the angles are all subtly wrong, leaning crazily and ending in sharp, dagger-like points. The bell tower twists and turns in on itself, rising up to the featureless sky, the belfry tilting so severely that it looks like it could collapse at any moment.

The church is ringed by a low stone wall, within which lies a graveyard. The gravestones sit like rows of shattered teeth, leaning and sagging at a variety of crazy angles just like the nearby church. Among the stones traipse animated skeletons. They move with a herky-jerky motion, as if being controlled by a puppeteer lurking just out of sight. (The motions of the skeletons and the Expressionistic architecture of the churchyard are yet more clues about the unreality of the situation.)

Some skeletons wear the robes of priests, others the garb of medieval townsfolk. A group of skeletons play fifes made of femurs and bang on drums with bone drumsticks. Their melody is dirge-like and mournful; a successful **Art/ Craft (Music)** roll identifies it as a 15th-century *Totentanz* ("Dance of the Dead").

No doubt with a degree of relief, the remaining investigators catch sight of each other at this point, all emerging from the woods at different points. The investigators see a procession entering the graveyard. It bears at least one coffin and possibly more; if any investigators suffered a bout of madness in the woods, there is an additional coffin in the procession per investigator so afflicted. The entire eerie scene provokes a **Sanity** roll, with a loss of 0/1D3 Sanity points.

The first coffin being borne forth is not going quietly. From within comes the muffled sound of a man screaming and thrashing, desperate to get out—if any investigators are also encased within a coffin, they are no doubt adding to the cacophony as well.

Fortunately, rescue is a relatively straightforward affair. The skeletons are susceptible to physical damage (**Skeletons**, page 241) and are easily scattered—after the first one or two are destroyed, the rest collapse into piles of bones and grave dust.

Prying open the top of the casket reveals none other than Baron Grunau. Still in his strange ecclesiastical robes, he is drenched in sweat, his eyes bulging out of their sockets, half-mad with fear. If the investigators killed him prior to passing out, he bears evidence of the wounds they inflicted upon him, yet otherwise seems quite alive and well. Clambering out of the casket, he looks about, as if sure that he is being pursued. "*Quickly, into the chapel!*"

If the investigators hesitate, Grunau pauses at the door. "*I believe the means of our escape lie within. Follow me if you will or remain out here at your peril!*" With that, he disappears inside, the hem of his robes whipping out of sight. If other investigators are trapped in coffins, now is the time to free them.

Keeper note: if the countess has been burned up in the waking world, she may, at the Keeper's option, reappear here, for this is where she now dwells—inside her own personal dreamland. She is once again flesh (though still black and white like everything else here), but her skin is horrifically charred, her features terrible to look upon, provoking a **Sanity** roll (1/1D4 loss); the investigator who actually lit the film on fire loses an additional point of Sanity. The countess may not be killed inside her own dream; however, inflicting one point of damage to her "dispels" her long enough for the following events to transpire. As in the waking world, the countess does not hold back in her wrath but, again, any damage she inflicts is to the investigator's Sanity rather than their hit points.

Inside the Church

The interior of the church is empty: no pews, no altar, no icons, no pulpit. Just a bare stone floor and, at the far end of the nave, a large lectern. The walls, floor, and ceiling are clearly wood painted to look like stone—there's even a slight lingering odor of fresh paint in the air. Upon the stand is an ancient folio several hundred pages thick; the binding appears to be some sort of dark leather, now cracked and flaking.

When the investigators enter, Grunau calls out, "*Countess Esterházy helped me hide the* Necronomicon *when I stole it from the State Library. Such a shame that young man intruded upon us when he did, but then, it seems this book demands a payment in blood from all who seek to use it.*"

If queried about the hiding place, the baron explains, "*Yes, this is a space outside our normal realm of existence. The film in the cameras, you see, it creates a bridge to this world of dreams. The dreams of the countess, as it happens. She lives on here, in this land.*" He looks around, shuddering slightly, then walks over to the book. "*All that ritual today was so much nonsense, play-acted for the cameras. But clearly it had some sort of effect, for here we undoubtedly are. That wasn't supposed to happen. Well, not to me, at least…*"

The baron unclasps the leaden locks on the book cover. With obvious effort, he opens it to a marked spot somewhere in the middle, then runs his finger down the illuminated page. Curious investigators looking over the baron's shoulder see images of a great toothed maw opening in the heavens and men below kneeling in supplication.

"*This is the original ritual. The Yah-Zek Channeling. It calls upon the Key and the Gate. As we are currently somewhere other than our own dimension, I think our best hope for escape is to call upon… it.*"

The investigators may agree to this or they may not. This is their last chance to invoke a **reality check** and easily escape the dream. No manner of convincing will compel the baron to do the same; he is locked into this reality far too deeply to simply will himself out of it. For him, it is Yog-Sothoth or nothing.

If the investigators agree to assist the baron, he is delighted. "*Excellent! You already know your part: the ritual chant from your scripts. You can help by shedding blood, as well. Not to worry—only a bit! Or a bit more, if you like.*" He giggles, his mind becoming unhinged. "*Shatter yonder stained-glass panes and mortify your flesh, my disciples!*"

If the investigators agree to do so, they may contribute as many hit points as they care to the success pool—remember, they have no magic points to contribute at the moment; however, if they have avoided taking any "physical" damage so far in the dream world, they now find that, as they cut themselves, they lose Sanity points rather than hit points, even though they are clearly bleeding. Investigators who are not already suffering from a bout of madness may not sacrifice more than 5 Sanity points in this manner. Every Sanity point so sacrificed adds +1% to the chance of the spell's success. Baron Grunau, by now quite mad, sacrifices

the remainder of his Sanity, slashing at his flesh in a bloody orgy while he shouts the intonation to Yog-Sothoth.

By the moon-eye, By the imprisoned, By the free,
By Samas, Gibil and Nusuku, By the High Name of Ea,
By the Seven Demons, Guardian, let the Gate be opened!
By Chaos, By the Void, By the Light, By the Darkness,
By the Air, By the Fire, By the Water, By the Earth,
Key, open the Gate!
By my sacred oath,
Let those who want to leave come out!
Let those who want to enter come in!
Let us see into the Hiding Light!
Let us see into the Blinding Darkness!
Rend the Veil! Crush the Mirror! Reveal the Illusion!
See, the Gate opens!"

Soon his flesh hangs in ribbons, his robes in blood-soaked tatters. Witnessing this terrible ritual demands a **Sanity** roll (1/1D6 loss). As the baron's chant reaches a crescendo, a terrific rending sound comes from the roof beams overhead. Then, with a great wrenching, the entire roof of the church flies away as if caught in a tornado.

Indeed, a terrific wind now blows overhead, swirling down into the church. High above, great coruscating clouds gather, rippling and bubbling. Unlike everywhere else in this dream-reality, these are seen in vibrant color: greens, yellows, oranges, and browns. Among the clouds, multitudinous eyes bubble and churn. Then a great-toothed maw begins to open, sucking in the wind, the artificial trees, the gravestones, the skeletons, the church itself.

Witnessing this apparition of the dread Yog-Sothoth requires a **Sanity** roll (1D10/1D100 loss); however, the ritual works! In the chaos and confusion, the investigators return to the real world. Everyone, that is, save those investigators reduced to zero Sanity. These luckless souls are forever trapped inside a dream vision of their own making; their minds reset to the last happy memory before all this turmoil came down upon them. Completely catatonic in the waking world, they nonetheless retain a beatific smile upon their faces until their dying day, while in their mind they shoot the water slides and ride the roller coasters of a dreamscape of Luna Park. Perhaps it was better this way.

One final note: if Countess Esterházy has not yet been destroyed, summoning Yog-Sothoth inside her own dreamland is more than sufficient to overcome her own petty magic. As the investigators are sucked up into Yog-Sothoth's toothy maw, they hear the countess unleash a blood-curdling scream as her own essence is torn to shreds and flung out to countless corners of the universe as her dream world collapses in on itself.

CONCLUSION

Investigators waking from the dream with their Sanity intact find themselves once more at the foot of the Kaiser-Wilhelm-Turm. All around, men and women lie unconscious or groaning, some slowly coming to and gazing around in a panic. The crew look on in stunned silence; Galeen has at last yelled "*CUT!*" Only a few seconds have passed in real time.

What the investigators do now is obviously somewhat contingent on whether Countess Esterházy is present. If she is still "alive" (possible if the baron has somehow failed to summon the Key and the Gate to facilitate his escape—for example, having been buried by the skeletons without being rescued), now is the time she unleashes the full fury of her magical powers, as well as calling forth assistance from her favored cat-thing.

If the investigators killed Grunau prior to passing out, he remains dead, his soul torn apart as the dream-church collapses around him. If still alive, Grunau slowly struggles to his feet as well. He looks at the investigators, then to the cameras, his face a mask of madness, "*You must… You must burn the film. All of it.* DESTROY IT ALL!" His last statement comes out as a throat-rending screech. Flames begin to lick his face, bursting forth from beneath his robes. Within seconds he is consumed in a pillar of fire—a final act of vengeance on the countess' part as her dream world and spirit are torn asunder thanks to the baron's summoning of Yog-Sothoth.

If the investigators have dealt with the countess already, or if they came back via Grunau's ritual and have thus destroyed the countess indirectly, they are now free to burn the film without opposition, as the sight of the baron's immolation causes everyone else present to run screaming into the woods.

The film is nitrate and so catches fire with an almost willful intensity. Did the investigators make sure to awaken all of the extras, as well as their own friends who may still be unconscious? If not, then a terrible event accompanies what should be a cathartic moment: all around them, the slumbering extras begin to scream and writhe, smoke pouring off their bodies. Then, all at once, they catch fire just like the baron, burning up from the inside out. All in all, if the investigators didn't bother to wake them up, 6D10 people were still unconscious and trapped inside the dream-forest. See **Rewards** (following) for the full repercussions of this thoughtless act.

With Grunau dead and the film stock of *Das Necronomicon* destroyed, the investigators, scarred mentally and perhaps forever changed physically, may console themselves that they have prevented a disaster on a global scale. They may think to collect all extant copies of the script, too, and they would be well-advised to do so. Grunau may no longer be around, but others may wish to take up his creative mantle and try their hand at making this strange film. Henrik Galeen, in particular, was left with a strange compulsion to do so thanks to his exposure to the enchanted film and the strange events he witnessed at the base of the tower. If he can gain access to the script, he could attempt to carry on making the movie.

What of the Countess?

It is just conceivable that Countess Esterházy could survive the scenario. If further adventures await our doughty investigators at this, the teetering end of the Weimar Republic, she may continue to pop up as a foil or outright adversary. After the Nazi *Machtergreifung* (seizure of power) from January to March of 1933, Countess Esterházy slowly and cannily ingratiates herself behind the scenes, forming a close working relationship with Goebbels and Himmler; Salon Kitty becomes a rich source of intelligence for the Gestapo and the Sicherheitsdienst (the intelligence wing of the SS). We wish the investigators the best of luck in their efforts to stop the countess after this point.

THE REEL DEAL

Just what would the film do, if completed and released? Well, in the spirit of Lovecraft's short story, *Nyarlathotep*, and the maddening *King in Yellow* play written about by Robert Chambers, those witnessing the bizarre spectacle are never quite the same again, and not in a good way. Nowhere is safe from its influence and, yet, despite knowing the horror it brings, people are drawn to its screenings like moths to a flame. Slowly, the film spreads madness and despair, a pale yet potent reflection of the destabilizing truths contained within the real *Necronomicon*, and the world descends ever further into chaos and bloodshed.

REWARDS

Grant the players an investigator development phase when they have completed this scenario and apply the following awards to each surviving investigator.

- For destroying the enchanted film: +1D10 Sanity points.
- For letting the film extras be burned alive in the dream-woods: −2D6+2 Sanity points.
- For destroying Countess Esterházy: +1D8 Sanity points.
- For destroying all extant copies of the film's script: +1D6 Sanity points.

CHARACTERS AND MONSTERS

NON-PLAYER CHARACTERS

Lina Desmond, *27, investigative reporter*

STR 55	CON 75	SIZ 45	DEX 60	INT 60
APP 65/50*	POW 70	EDU 75	SAN 52	HP 12
DB: 0	Build: 0	Move: 9	MP: 14	

Before and after her face transferal.

Combat

Brawl	25% (12/5), damage 1D3
Dodge	30% (15/6)

Skills

Art/Craft (Writing) 65%, Charm 50%, Credit Rating 45%, Cthulhu Mythos 4%, Disguise 65%, Fast Talk 70%, Language (English) 20%, Language (French) 40%, Language (German) 75%, Library Use 60%, Listen 50%, Locksmith 30%, Occult 35%, Persuade 70%, Psychology 50%, Stealth 30%, Throw 40%.

Aleister Crowley, *56, occultist and struggling artist*

STR 45	CON 30	SIZ 65	DEX 50	INT 85
APP 40	POW 93	EDU 80	SAN 76	HP 9
DB: 0	Build: 0	Move: 5	MP: 18	

Combat

Brawl	35% (17/7), damage 1D3
Dodge	40% (20/8)

Skills

Art/Craft (Painting) 65%, Art/Craft (Poetry) 50%, Climb 75%, Cthulhu Mythos 18%, Fast Talk 70%, History 50%, Language (Ancient Greek) 45%, Language (English) 80%, Language (German) 20%, Language (Italian) 20%, Language (Latin) 65%, Language (Sanskrit) 15%, Library Use 55%, Natural World 50%, Navigate 45%, Occult 85%, Persuade 65%, Photography 40%, Psychology 75%, Survival (Mountains) 50%, Track 35%.

Spells: Guise of the Other*, plus any other spells of the Keeper's choosing.

*See **Spells**, page 242.

Erik Jan Hanussen, *42, clairvoyant performer and psychic*

STR 55	CON 55	SIZ 75	DEX 50	INT 50
APP 40	POW 90	EDU 50	SAN 90	HP 13
DB: +1D4	Build: 1	Move: 6	MP: 18	

Combat

Brawl	25% (12/5), damage 1D3+1D4
Dodge	25% (12/5)

Skills

Art/Craft (Acting) 65%, Charm 50%, Fast Talk 75%, Hypnosis 75%, Language (Danish) 10%, Language (German) 50%, Language (Italian) 30%, Language (Yiddish) 45%, Occult 45%, Psychology 60%, Sleight of Hand 45%, Spot Hidden 50%.

Wolf-Heinrich Graf von Helldorff, *35, leader of the Berlin SA*

STR 70	CON 65	SIZ 75	DEX 70	INT 55
APP 55	POW 60	EDU 60	SAN 50	HP 14
DB: +1D4	Build: 1	Move: 7	MP: 12	

Combat

Brawl	65% (32/13), damage 1D3+1D4
Model P08 Luger	75% (37/15), damage 1D10
Dodge	50% (25/10)

Skills

Credit Rating 65%, Intimidate 70%, Language (French) 20%, Language (German) 60%, Law 40%, Occult 35%, Ride 50%, Throw 40%.

Inspector Krieg, *63, burned-out cop*

STR 50	CON 30	SIZ 60	DEX 55	INT 85
APP 35	POW 65	EDU 75	SAN 55	HP 9
DB: 0	Build: 0	Move: 4	MP: 13	

Combat

Brawl	45% (22/9), damage 1D3
.32 automatic	45% (22/9), damage 1D8
Dodge	40% (20/8)

Skills

Accounting 40%, Disguise 25%, Fast Talk 75%, Intimidate 55%, Language (English) 25%, Language (German) 75%, Language (Polish) 15%, Language (Russian) 20%, Law 70%, Listen 60%, Persuade 75%, Psychology 85%, Spot Hidden 85%, Stealth 45%.

Baron Grunau, *58, occultist and filmmaker*

STR 65	CON 65	SIZ 85	DEX 40	INT 75
APP 50	POW 80	EDU 70	SAN 42	HP 15
DB: +1D4	Build: 1	Move: 5	MP: 16	

Combat
Brawl	50% (25/10), damage 1D3+1D4
Dodge	20% (10/4)

Skills
Archaeology 70%, Charm 40%, Credit Rating 75%, Cthulhu Mythos 27%, Firearms (Rifle/Shotgun) 40%, Intimidate 50%, Language (Arabic) 40%, Language (English) 15%, Language (French) 40%, Language (German) 70%, Occult 70%.

Spells: Call Yog-Sothoth, Contact Tsathoggua.

Berlin Police Officer

STR 55	CON 65	SIZ 55	DEX 55	INT 60
APP 55	POW 60	EDU 60	SAN 60	HP 12
DB: 0	Build: 0	Move: 8	MP: 12	

Combat
Brawl	45% (22/9), damage 1D3
Model P08 Luger	50% (25/10), damage 1D10
Gewehr-98 rifle	45% (22/9), damage 2D6+4
Dodge	40% (20/8)

Skills
Accounting 20%, Climb 40%, Drive Auto 40%, First Aid 50%, Intimidate 35%, Language (German) 60%, Law 50%, Listen 40%, Psychology 50%, Ride 25%, Spot Hidden 65%, Track 35%.

Rotte Member

STR 65	CON 55	SIZ 65	DEX 50	INT 45
APP 45	POW 45	EDU 50	SAN 45	HP 12
DB: +1D4	Build: 1	Move: 8	MP: 9	

Combat
Brawl	70% (35/14), damage 1D3+1D4, or brass knuckles 1D3+1+1D4
Small club	70% (35/14), damage 1D6+1D4
*Nahkampfmesser**	70% (35/14), damage 1D4+2+1D4
Dodge	30% (15/6)

*German for trench knife.

Skills
Intimidate 65%, Language (German) 50%, Spout Nazi Ideology 55%, Throw 40%.

Wild-Boy, *17, gang member*
Use this profile for all wild-boys.

STR 50	CON 50	SIZ 55	DEX 55	INT 60
APP 60	POW 50	EDU 50	SAN 50	HP 10
DB: 0	Build: 0	Move: 8	MP: 10	

Brawl	50% (25/10), damage 1D3 or knife 1D4 or club 1D6
Dodge	30% (15/6)

Skills
Charm 40%, Climb 60%, Fast Talk 50%, Intimidate 30%, Language (German) 50%, Psychology 35%, Stealth 50%, Throw 50%.

Beefy Teamster

STR 75	CON 60	SIZ 85	DEX 50	INT 65
APP 55	POW 80	EDU 55	SAN 80	HP 14
DB: +1D4	Build: 1	Move: 7	MP: 16	

Combat
Brawl	60% (30/12), damage 1D3
Dodge	25% (12/5)

A Wild-Boy

ADVERSARIES AND MONSTERS

Cat-Thing, *unwholesome feline*

These loathsome creatures look like hairless cats, albeit with a human-like face and forepaws that resemble human hands. The Berlin coven uses its darkest arts to turn enemies and servants who fail them into cat-things, who then serve the witches faithfully. Cat-things are particularly fond of the taste of feline flesh and attack domestic cats on sight with an eye toward devouring them.

char.	average	roll
STR	10	1D3×5
CON	40	2D6×5
SIZ	10	1D3×5
DEX	90	(4D6+4)×5
INT	50	3D6
POW	35	2D6

Average Hit Points: 5
Average Damage Bonus (DB): –2
Average Build: –2
Average Move: 9
Average Magic Points: 7

Combat

Attacks per round: 1 (claws or teeth)

Grab (mnvr): cat-things attack by pouncing on their opponents, preferably from a height. They use their human-like forepaws to grab tight onto their target, granting a bonus die to bite & claw attacks on subsequent rounds as they sink in their needle-like teeth and rake with their back claws. If multiple cats grab onto a single target, they gain 2 bonus dice to subsequent attacks, per the outnumbered rule. If grabbed, a target may attempt to pull the cat-thing off with a successful STR roll.

Fighting	40% (20/8), damage 1D3–2
Grab (mnvr)	40% (20/8), holds onto target, grants bonus die to bite & claw attacks
Bite & Claw	35% (17/7), damage 1D4+1–2
Dodge	45% (22/9)

Skills

Climb 80%, Listen 50%, Stealth 80%.

Armor: none, but attacks to hit a running cat-thing are made with one penalty die.

Spells: cat-things have a 30% chance of knowing 1D3 spells; those who knew spells in life retain that knowledge as cat-things.

Sanity loss: 0/1D6 Sanity points to see a cat-thing; if the cat-thing was known to the observer in life, it costs 1/1D8 Sanity points to see it.

Coven Witch

There are thirteen witches in Esterházy's coven, comprised of Kitty Schmidt plus eleven Salon Kitty employees; Agnes Esterházy is the thirteenth member.

STR 50	CON 55	SIZ 45	DEX 65	INT 70
APP 75	POW 75	EDU 60	SAN 00	HP 10
DB: 0	Build: 0	Move: 9	MP: 15	

Combat

Brawl	35% (17/7), damage 1D3
Dodge	35% (17/7)

Skills

Charm 75%, Cthulhu Mythos 25%, Language (English) 20%, Language (French) 25%, Language (German) 60%, Language (Russian) 35%, Listen 45%, Occult 45%, Persuade 65%, Psychology 50%, Sleight of Hand 25%, Spot Hidden 65%, Stealth 40%, Throw 35%.

Spells: Dominate, plus 1D3 spells of the Keeper's choosing.

Ágnes Esterházy, *33, countess, witch, movie star*

STR —	CON —	SIZ 40	DEX 70	INT 60
APP 90	POW 120	EDU 60	SAN 00	HP —
DB: —	Build: —	Move: 9	MP: 24	

Attacks per round: 1

Fighting: as she is non-corporeal, the countess can engage in combat only through her ability to wield magic.

Brawl	25% (12/5), damage as per the Spectral Razor spell*
Dodge	35% (17/7)

Skills

Art/Craft (Acting) 60%, Charm 75%, Cthulhu Mythos 35%, Language (English) 40%, Language (French) 50%, Language (German) 50%, Language (Hungarian) 60%, Language (Russian) 30%, Occult 85%, Persuade 55%, Psychology 45%.

Armor: none, she is immune to physical attacks and can be destroyed only by burning the strip of film in which her life essence is "recorded."

Spells: Curse of the Cat-thing*, Dominate, Dread Curse of Azathoth, Elder Sign, Mindblast, Power Drain*, Spectral Razor*, Stop Heart*, Wither Limb.

Sanity loss: 0/1D6 Sanity points to see Ágnes Esterházy, a three-dimensional film projection.

*See **Spells**, page 242.

Vengeful Corpse

STR 80	CON 80	SIZ 65	DEX 35	INT —
APP —	POW 05	EDU —	SAN –	HP 14
DB: +1D4	Build: 1	Move: 8	MP: 1	

Combat

Attacks per round: 1 (claw, bite)

Fighting	30% (15/6), damage 1D3+1D4
Dodge	Lacking volition, this is not an option

Armor: major wounds delivered to the body will result in loss of a limb. Otherwise, ignore damage except to the head (one penalty die on rolls to target the head).

Sanity loss: 0/1D8 Sanity points to see a vengeful corpse.

Skeletons

STR 50	CON —	SIZ 65	DEX 50	INT 50
APP —	POW 5	EDU —	SAN —	HP n/a
DB: 0	Build: 0	Move: 7		MP: 1

Combat

Attacks per round: 1 (claw, bite)

Resistant to Harm: dried bones are fairly brittle, snapping and splintering easily from a heavy blow; however, no area of a skeleton is more vulnerable than any other. Any blow striking a skeleton has a chance of destroying it equal to or less than the damage done × 5 (as rolled on 1D100). For example, if an axe hit a skeleton and did 8 points of damage, there would be a 40% chance of destroying the skeleton by shattering it. Unless the skeleton shatters, it remains totally undamaged. Apply one penalty die on attacks made with an impaling weapon (including bullets), since much of the target is simply air.

Claw	45% (22/9), damage 1D3
Dodge	30% (15/6)

Armor: resistant to harm (see above).

Sanity loss: 0/1D6 Sanity points to see a skeleton.

Cat-Thing

SPELLS

Curse of the Cat-Thing (variant)
- **Cost:** 20 magic points; 5 POW; 1D10 Sanity points
- **Casting time:** 1 day

A variant of the more common spell, Curse of the Rat-thing, when cast upon a corpse, dead within 24 hours, it causes the target's spiritual essence to settle into the newly created body of a cat-thing.

The disintegrating corpse forms the substance of the cat-thing. The cat-thing's face closely resembles a malevolent version of the target's own face. As the Keeper wishes, being reborn as a cat-thing may cost a person's total Sanity and perhaps force full-fledged membership in that evil species (considering the target was already dead, this seems highly likely).

Guise of the Other
- **Cost:** 10 magic points; 5 POW; 1D6 Sanity points
- **Casting time:** 2 rounds

Enables the caster or another to assume the face of someone else. The caster must have access to the flayed facial skin of another person, which must be fresh (i.e., the face has been removed within the last 24 hours). As the caster places the bloody skin over their own face they recite a short prayer to Nyarlathotep. The flayed flesh melds with the caster's face, giving them the appearance of the person from which the flesh was removed (APP changes accordingly). The new face is permanent but can be removed if the spell's prayer is reversed and the cost paid again.

Keeper note: unfortunately, unbeknownst to Aleister Crowley, the new face is good only for a number of days equal to the wearer's POW multiplied by two. After this time the new face begins to rot, reducing APP by 5 points per day thereafter. Unless the spell is reversed and the new face removed, the wearer begins to look like a walking corpse, which may provoke **Sanity** rolls in others (0/1D3 loss). If the wearer cannot remove the new face and their APP falls to zero, they suffer the loss of 1 Sanity point per day until permanently insane.

Power Drain
- **Cost:** 1D8 Sanity points
- **Casting time:** 2 rounds

Leeches magic points from a target. For the spell to take effect the caster must win an opposed POW roll with the target: if the caster is successful, the target loses 1D6 magic points and the caster gains them; if the caster fails to overcome the target, the caster loses 1D6 magic points to the target. If all magic points are depleted, the spell then drains hit points (if all hit points are drained, the target falls unconscious—this spell lacks the power to kill).

Spectral Razor
- **Cost:** variable magic points; 2 Sanity points
- **Casting time:** 1 round

Creates an invisible blade that can be used as an offensive weapon. The spell costs 2 magic points per round to maintain the effect. The immaterial knife is used with the caster's Fighting (Brawl) skill, as if they were holding a real blade (i.e., the caster makes cutting and stabbing motions with the hand in which they are "holding" the immaterial knife). The magical blade inflicts 1D6 damage in successful attacks, can impale (but receives no damage bonus), and can damage creatures affected only by magical means. The spectral weapon cannot become stuck in the victim.

Should the caster go insane while wielding the spectral razor, the weapon takes on a life of its own, spinning out of the caster's hand and proceeding to fly about the area, randomly attacking those nearby. Attempts to dodge the blade are made with one penalty die; if the dodge is unsuccessful the blade automatically hits the target. The weapon will carry on in this fashion for 1D4+1 rounds before vanishing.

Stop Heart (deeper magic variant)
- **Cost:** 14 magic points; 2D6 Sanity points
- **Casting time:** 2 rounds

Causes the target of this spell to suffer a massive heart attack. For the spell to take effect the caster must succeed in an opposed **POW** roll with the target, who must be in the caster's line of sight. If successful, the target loses 4D6 hit points and, if still alive, is incapacitated for 2D10 rounds.

INSPIRATIONAL MEDIA

The following books and other media provided direct or thematic inspiration during the creation of *Berlin: The Wicked City* and may do so again for interested Keepers and players.

PUBLICATIONS

Baedeker, Karl. *Berlin and Its Environs: Handbook for Travellers*. London: George Allen & Unwin, 1923.

Baum, Vicki. *Menschen im Hotel*, 1929.

Churton, Tobias. *Aleister Crowley: The Beast in Berlin: Art, Sex, and Magick in the Weimar Republic*. Rochester, Vermont: Inner Traditions, 2014.

Flowers, Stephen E. *The Fraternitas Saturni—or Brotherhood of Saturn: An Introduction to Its History, Philosophy and Rituals*. Smithville, TX: Runa-Raven, 2006.

Gill, Anton. *A Dance between Flames: Berlin between the Wars*. New York: Carroll & Graf, 1994.

Gordon, Mel, Sebastian Droste, and Anita Berber. *The Seven Addictions and Five Professions of Anita Berber: Weimar Berlin's Priestess of Depravity*. Los Angeles, CA: Feral House, 2006.

Gordon, Mel. *Voluptuous Panic: The Erotic World of Weimar Berlin*. Los Angeles: Feral House, 2000.

Isherwood, Christopher. *Goodbye to Berlin*. New York: James Laughlin, 1954.

Jung, Carl Gustav, Sonu Shamdasani, Mark Kyburz, and John Peck. *The Red Book*. New York (NY): W. W. Norton, 2009.

Levenda, Peter. *Unholy Alliance: A History of Nazi Involvement with the Occult*. New York: Continuum, 2002.

Lutes, Jason. *Berlin: City of Smoke*. Montreal, Quebec: Drawn & Quarterly, 2011.

Lutes, Jason. *Berlin: City of Stones*. Montreal, Quebec: Drawn & Quarterly, 2001.

Magida, Arthur J. *The Nazi Séance: The Strange Story of the Jewish Psychic in Hitler's Circle*. New York: Palgrave Macmillan, 2011.

Metzger, Rainer, and Christian Brandstätter. *Berlin: The Twenties*. New York: Abrams, 2007.

Nabokov, Vladimir, and Dmitri Nabokov. "A Guide to Berlin." *Details of a Sunset and Other Stories*. London: Penguin, 1994.

Roth, Joseph, Michael Hofmann, and Michael Bienert. *What I Saw: Reports from Berlin, 1920–1933*. New York: Norton, 2003.

Tucholsky, Kurt, and Eva C. Schweitzer. *Berlin! Berlin!: Dispatches from the Weimar Republic, 1907–1932*. New York, NY: Berlinica LLC, 2013.

Ulrich, Barbara. *Hot Girls of Weimar Berlin*. Los Angeles, CA: Feral House, 2002.

Yeats, W. B. "The Second Coming." *The Collected Poems of W.B. Yeats*. New York: Macmillan, 1956.

MOVIES AND TELEVISION

Alraune, Henrik Galeen (Director), 1928

Asphalt, Joe May (Director), 1929

Babylon Berlin, Tom Tykwer, Achim von Borries, Henk Handloegten (Creators), 2017

Berlin Alexanderplatz, Phil Jutzi (Director), 1931

Berlin: Symphony of a Great City, Walter Ruttmann (Director), 1927

Cabaret, Bob Fosse (Director), 1972

Christopher and His Kind, Geoffrey Sax (Director), 2011

Diary of a Lost Girl, G.W. Pabst (Director), 1929

Dr. Mabuse, the Gambler, Fritz Lang (Director), 1922

Grand Hotel, Edmund Goulding (Director), 1932

Invincible, Werner Herzog (Director), 2001

M–Eine Stadt sucht einen Mörder, Fritz Lang (Director), 1931

Metropolis, Fritz Lang (Director), 1927

People on Sunday, Robert Siodmak & Edward G. Ulmer (Directors), 1930

The Cabinet of Dr. Caligari, Robert Wiene (Director), 1920

The Serpent's Egg, Ingmar Bergman (Director), 1977

The Testament of Dr. Mabuse, Fritz Lang (Director), 1933

MUSIC AND VISUAL ART

Otto Dix

Max Ernst

George Grosz

Raoul Hausmann

John Heartfield

Hannah Höch

Käthe Kollwitz

Münz, Lori, Rudolf Nelson, Friedrich Hollaender, Ralph Benatzky, Werner Heymann Richard, and Mischa Spoliansky. *Cabaret Berlin*. Hamburg, Germany: Ear, 2005.

Dmitry Vorsin

COLLECTED HANDOUTS

Handout: Devil 1

B·Z·am Mittag

Morgen-Ausgabe.

| XXXIX. Jahrgang | Donnerstag, 22 Juni 1922 | 10 Pfennig |

Carl Großmann found Dead in his Cell

Who among our readers will not shudder at the memory of the infamous and outrageous acts of the Beast of the Silesian Station, Carl Großmann? Arrested 10 months ago in his flat at Lange Straße 88/89, the fiend was found with the body of a murdered woman—a destitute thing, lured into the spider's lair with promises of cash and food. Instead, she met her death, but not before her screams and thrashing attracted the notice of the building's neighbors. Police found the poor creature in Großmann's kitchen, stripped naked and trussed up like a hog for butchering.

Indeed, Inspector Krieg of the Criminal Police noted extensive apparatus for meat processing and sausage-making in Großmann's apartment. The Devil-Carl claimed that this was merely owing to his career as a butcher, but persistent rumors claim otherwise. His neighbors recall that, during the starving days of 1917–18, Großmann seemed to do quite well for himself selling homemade sausages at the Silesian Station. At the time, there was much speculation as to where he procured his meat, but nowadays most shudder to contemplate the question.

Inspector Krieg found evidence in the form of blood stains sufficient for the courts to charge Großmann with two other "lust murders," and the perverted criminal, who spent 14 years in jail prior to the War on charges of illicit activities with children, went on trial four days ago. Today, the judge was expected to announce a guilty verdict in the matter of three murders committed at Großmann's hands, but the reprobate was found hanging from his bed sheet inside his jail cell this very morning.

Handout: Devil 2

013 Telegramm   *Deutsche Reichstelegraph*

aus   BERLIN : 182 +26 +10- +12 56 3

	Aufgenommen					Übermittelt	
Tag: 21	Monat: 06	Jahr: 22	Zeit :		Tag :		Zeit :
vom: Hmb		durch : 035			an		durch

Amt Memel

PRINCE GABRIEL CONSTANTINOVICH DESIRES THE PLEASURE OF YOUR
COMPANY TONIGHT AT 8:00 PM TO DISCUSS A MATTER OF EXTREME
DELICACY. ROOM 415, EDEN HOTEL. KURFÜRSTENDAMM 246/247.

Für dienstliche Rückfragen

OBP 8. 39   X C 187 DIN A 5 (Kl. 29)

Handout: Devil 3

Handout: Devil 4

Handout: Devil 5

Grand Duchess Anastasia Alive and well in Berlin?

The city's White Russian community is humming with the news that a woman claiming to be the Grand Duchess Anastasia Romanov is living here in Berlin. The woman, who calls herself Anna Tchaikovsky, was recently released from the Dalldorf Asylum and remanded into the care of Baron Arthur von Kleist, who served the Tsar honorably as Chief of Police of Russian Poland until the Revolutions of 1917 forced him to flee, like many of his compatriots, to Germany.

Miss Tchaikovsky, who is said to resemble the Grand Duchess in appearance and bearing, was admitted to Dalldorf in 1920, having lost her wits in a fall into the Landwehr Canal in February of that year. She claims that her memory is slowly returning to her, although many details remain unclear.

The Baron, who resides in a spacious third-floor apartment off Savignyplatz at Carmerstraße 11, asks that the public respect Miss Tchaikovsky's privacy at this time as he attempts to help sort out the truth of the matter.

DISTURBANCE IN CHARLOTTENBURG

Readers of this paper may recall our report of one Anna Tchaikovsky, currently in residence at the home of Baron Arthur von Kleist, Carmerstraße 11, Charlottenburg. Scandalous as it is, it is our sad duty to report that Fräulein Tchaikovsky was this past evening attacked in her residence by a servant of the Baron's household. The maid, who has subsequently been dismissed, came at Fräulein Tchaikovsky with a knife, but was fended off by friendlier hands present at the time. Fräulein Tchaikovsky is reported to be uninjured but quite rattled, as is understandable given the circumstances.

Handout: Devil 6

DEATH STALKS BERLIN!

Police have reported three separate murders in and around the Friedrichshain neighborhood in the last 24 hours. One body, that of a woman known only to locals as "Lulu," was found by students of the Andreas-Gymnasium school (Koppenstraße 76), up among the branches of a tree. "If we didn't know better, we would say she climbed the tree to escape a wild animal, but was pursued and torn apart up there," one of the officers informed our reporter. We now must ask: is there a bear in Berlin?

Two other bodies were pulled from the Spree River. Inspector Krieg of the Criminal Police has refused to comment on the ongoing case but notes that both women were far too mangled to make a positive identification at this time. Reports of missing persons in the Friedrichshain district will be forwarded to Inspector Krieg while the case remains open, but many of the residents are unregistered immigrants and there seems little hope that these "Ladies Unknown" will be identified anytime soon.

The Ritual Performance

First, prepare the area. Inscribe a summoning circle using chalk, or may be traced in dust or soot on the floor. At minimum, three are required throughout the ritual. They must all stand within the circle, with the fetish sitting in the center of the inscribed space. More may participate but the number of participants must be divisible by three. Others may stand by, guarding the sacred area, ready to step in and replace those unable to continue.

i. Facing East, assume the Wand Posture. Declare: "GEH."

ii. Raise the arms at the sides. Declare: "LONDOH."

iii. Touch right shoulder with left hand. Declare: "OD MICALZO."

iv. Touch left shoulder with right hand. Declare: "OD BUSD."

v. Keeping arms crossed, bow head and declare: "GOHED."

vi. Make the Gesture Cervus: at the first point, declare "EXARP;" at the second point declare "ORO IBAH AOZPI."

vii. Turn to face North: make the Gesture, declaring "NANTA" at the first point, "MOR DIAL HCTGA" at the second.

viii. Turn to face West: make the Gesture, declaring "HCOMA" at the first point, "MPH ARSL GAIOL" at the second.

ix. Turn to face South: make the Gesture, declaring "BITOM" at the first point, and "OIP TEAA PDOCE" at the second.

Repeat these steps until the sun rises in the East.

Handout: Dances 1

Handout: Dances 4

angege-
ten der
angsam
l wurde
es gab
ss der
etragen
Armit-
eine
nahm,
te ihn
die
Mut
iuften,
ierung
valde-
Ende
tt lag,

And Why Not?
Editorial

Berliners have been seen engaging in some strange behaviors lately—and why not? Public drunkenness is on the rise over the last week, but who doesn't like a tipple from time to time? Exotic powders and concoctions are finding their way up our noses and into our veins, and it feels good! As the cold of winter closes in around us, we should all embrace and kiss and grind and tear into each other. It is time to finally cast off the last vestiges of Wilhemite-Prussian-Lutheran moralism. And why not?

Steuerzahler
und

Handout: Dances 2

Plague in the City!

For the past week, Berlin has been bedeviled by unseasonable winds and blowing fog. As if carried on this foul miasma, a new epidemic is sweeping our neighborhoods. Tragically, it seems to be hitting our children and infants the hardest. Odds are that if you have not personally suffered a visitation in your own household, dear reader, you know someone who has.

Doctors at the Charité and other hospitals around the city have reported a distinct rise in infant mortality and serious illnesses among Berlin's youth. Symptoms so far have yet to manifest a distinct pattern: some suffer from fever, others from fits, still others from crippling intestinal complaints.

When contacted for comment, government hygiene and sanitation officials assured us that they are working as quickly as science allows in ascertaining and eliminating the source of the maladies.

Handout: Dances 3

Berber back in Berlin!

Notorious dancer and actress Anita Berber, once called "the Dresden Madonna" but now largely forgotten in this city, has at last made her way back to Berlin, where she began her career nearly ten years ago.

For some time now, Berber has been traveling abroad with her husband, Henri Châtin-Hofmann, performing in Egypt, the Levant, and even in the shadows of once-mighty Babylon itself.

Reports have reached this writer that Berber has returned via the Orient Express in ill health and has been hospitalized for a week at the Bethanien hospital. Although this is distressing news, we are sure that, at 29 years old and still in the prime of her life, she will recover swiftly and be back on the dancing stage in short order!

Handout: Dances 5

Zeitung in Berlin		Seiten der Werbung

Berliner Herold
Nachrichten * Theater * Film * Sport * Finanziell *

Vol. 2	23 Dezember 1926	10 Pfennig

Murder in the Library

Police report that a young man, an employee of the Prussian State Library by the name of Ralf Schneider, was found dead at the library this morning when other employees arrived for work. Poor Mr. Schneider was discovered on the floor of the Rare Books and Manuscripts wing. Police inform us that foul play is suspected and ask any members of the public with information that may pertain to this case to contact Inspector Krieg of the Criminal Police straight away.

Dr. F. Milkau, director of the Prussian State Library, reports that nothing seems to have gone missing from the Rare Books and Manuscripts wing, although as the wing contains many thousands of volumes, it will take some time to make absolutely certain.

"Mr. Schneider was one of our brightest young librarians with a promising career ahead of him. His death is an absolute tragedy, and has proven quite a blow to our staff," Dr. Milkau said in a statement to our reporter.

We will, naturally, bring you further details of this shocking case as they become known to us.

Handout: Schreckfilm 1

Seite 4

Suicide Waves

The editorial board need not remind our gentle readers that this has been a particularly bitter winter in more ways than one. In addition to the chill winds and icy frosts, many a Berliner feels the cold grip of uncertainty. As a new round of elections approaches, what is to become of our dear Republic? What of the economy? Why can the police not control the violence increasingly seen on city streets in a terrible callback to the lawless days of '18 and '19?

As Germans, we must persevere through such doubtful times as best we can. Sadly, according to the latest statistics released by central government officials, suicides are at an all-time high in the city. Many good folk—far too many—have fallen into the ultimate despair clutching the pill bottle or the gun barrel, or with a one-way trip to the riverside. The gravediggers of the Friedhof Grunewald-Forst have had their hands full fishing bodies out of the Havel and placing them into the cold, half-frozen ground.

The editors of this paper heartily enjoin any who may be reading this not to make the dishonorable choice. Although dark times are here today, we remind you that a sunnier tomorrow awaits us all. Better times are just around the corner. Persevere.

Haben wir mehr öffentliche Bibliotheken?

Es besteht kein Zweifel, dass wir Berliner die herausragende Bibliothek Europas beherbergen, und niemand würde die preußische Staatsbibliothek, die jetzt ihr achtzehntes Betriebsjahr beginnt, bestreiten oder herabsetzen. Unter seiner Kuppeldecke im öffentlichen Lesesaal zu sitzen, ist sowohl für das intellektuelle als auch für das künstlerische Empfinden eine Freude. Und wo befinden sich die kleineren Bibliotheken, die weniger öffentlichen Freuden mit ihren attraktiven Tageszeitungen, populären Fiktionen und illustrierten Kapitelbüchern für die Kinder?

Handout: Schreckfilm 3

8

Casting Call

Producers working on a new Schreckfilm have issued a casting call for extras. The film, tentatively entitled "Das Necronomicon," is to be a documentary style fictionalization of the occult secrets contained within "one of the most infamous tomes of all time," according to the movie's financier, Baron von Grunau. The film has had a troubled production, being stalled in development for over two years now. Von Grunau assures our reporter that, thanks to some recent technological and creative breakthroughs, the production is back on track and that he hopes to see the film ready for release before Easter.

Those wishing to appear as extras in the film must report to the Kaiser-Wilhelm-Turm in Grunewald tomorrow morning at 6:00 a.m. for a day of shooting in and around the location. Food and a nominal stipend will be provided.

Stellenangebote

Sofortige Ablehnung der neu geschaffenen Position des Produktionsmanagers zu planen

El Di
stellt t
Woch
Mitto

Keine
Cons
Woch
Schre
besitz
Bewe

Pr

Die P
wurde
Aufga
Elekt
Kostü
Zigare
persön

Handout: Schreckfilm 2

3×5 (7.6 × 12.7 cm) photograph: shows the investigators in the company of two men and a woman, none of whom the investigators have ever met before.

Glossy 8×10 (20 × 25 cm) photograph: showing the actress Ágnes Esterházy, signed by her and dedicated to "Count von Helldorff."

Calling card: with no name, merely an odd sequence of letters and symbols—"A∴A∴"—and a phone number. On the back, written in fading pencil, is a note: "May be able to help?"

Postcard: depicting a tall brick tower looming up from woodland surrounding a lake.

Newspaper clipping: dated four years ago, its headline reads, "Murder in the Library."

Filmstrip: about 6 inches (15 cm) long.

The Ku'damm Map

1. Berlin Zoo – Elephant Gate
2. Berlin Zoo – Ostrich House
3. Romanisches Café
4. Eden Hotel

Subway (Underground)
Elevated Railroad
Subway Station
Elevated Platform

Scale (in meters) 1: 1000

Player Map

Devil Eats Flies map 1

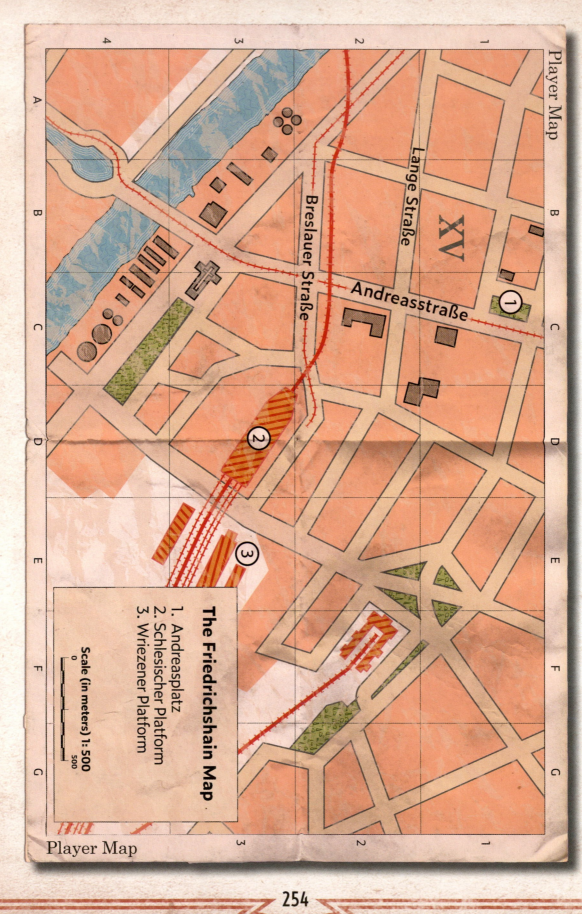

Player Map

Devil Eats Flies map 2

The Friedrichshain Map

1. Andreasplatz
2. Schlesischer Platform
3. Wriezener Platform

Scale (in meters) 1: 500

0

500

Lange Straße

Breslauer Straße

Andreasstraße

XV

Player Map

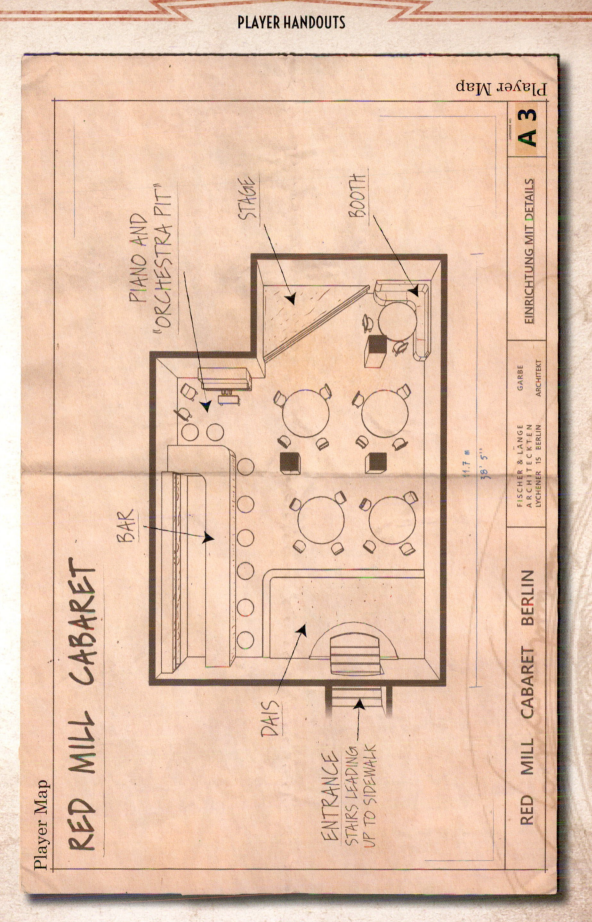

Player Map

RED MILL CABARET

PIANO AND "ORCHESTRA PIT"

STAGE

BOOTH

BAR

DAIS

ENTRANCE
STAIRS LEADING UP TO SIDEWALK

Player Map

A 3

EINRICHTUNG MIT DETAILS

FISCHER & LÄNGE
ARCHITECKTEN
LYCHENER 15 BERLIN

GARBE
ARCHITEKT

11.7 m

38' 5''

RED MILL CABARET BERLIN

Devil Eats Flies map 3

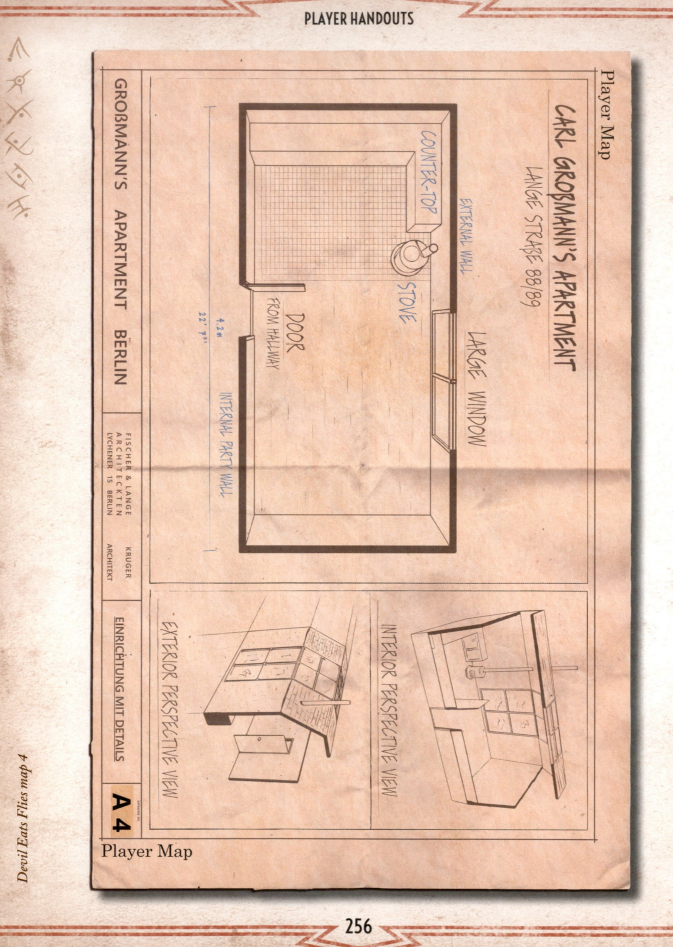

Player Map

CARL GROßMANN'S APARTMENT

LANGE STRAßE 88/89

EXTERNAL WALL

COUNTER-TOP

STOVE

LARGE WINDOW

DOOR
FROM HALLWAY

4.2m
22' 7"¹

INTERNAL PARTY WALL

GROßMANN'S   APARTMENT   BERLIN

FISCHER & LANGE
ARCHITECTEN
LYCHENER 15 BERLIN

KRUGER
ARCHITEKT

EINRICHTUNG MIT DETAILS

EXTERIOR PERSPECTIVE VIEW

INTERIOR PERSPECTIVE VIEW

A 4

Player Map

Player Map

The Zoological Gardens

Player Map

Selected Zoo Highlights

1. Administration Offices
2. Antelope House
3. Aquarium
4. Bird House
5. Elephant Gate
6. Large Predator House
7. Monkey House
8. Ostrich House
9. Palace
10. Restaurant

Scale (in meters) 1: 333

0   300

Devil Eats Flies map 5

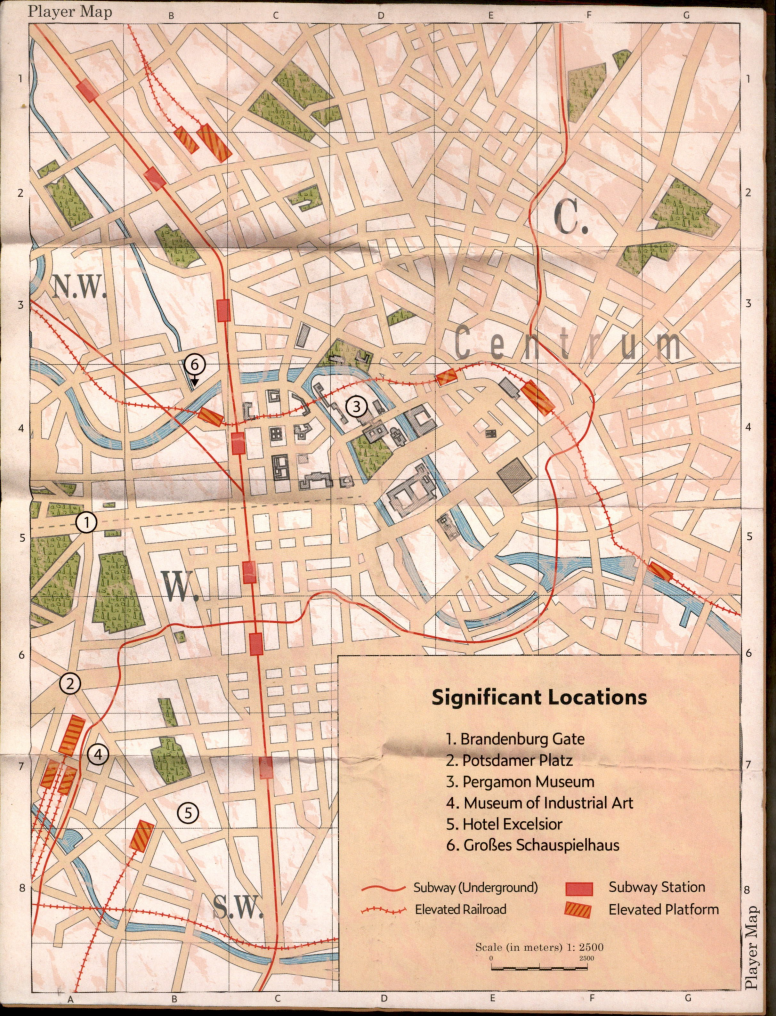

Significant Locations

1. Brandenburg Gate
2. Potsdamer Platz
3. Pergamon Museum
4. Museum of Industrial Art
5. Hotel Excelsior
6. Großes Schauspielhaus

Subway (Underground) · Subway Station

Elevated Railroad · Elevated Platform

Scale (in meters) 1: 2500

0   2500

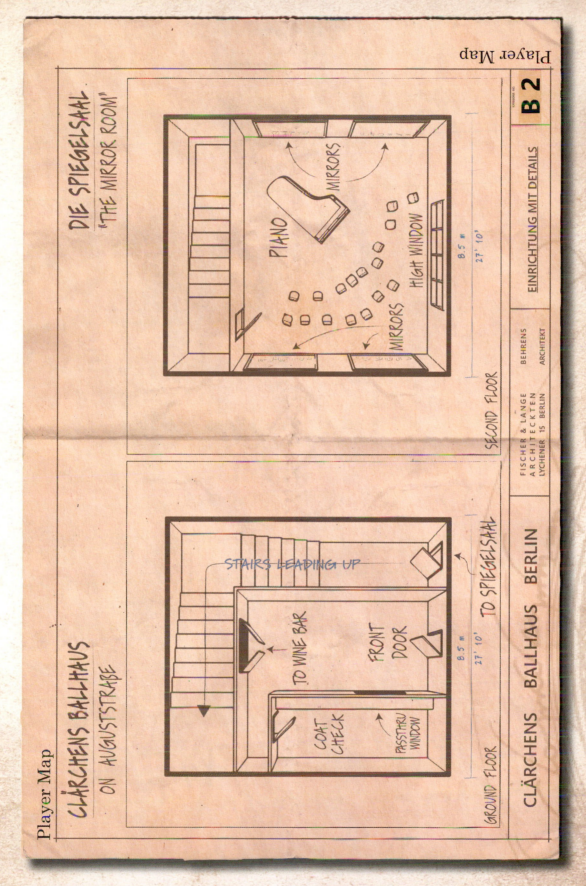

Player Map

CLÄRCHENS BALLHAUS
ON AUGUSTSTRAßE

DIE SPIEGELSAAL
"THE MIRROR ROOM"

Player Map

B 2

EINRICHTUNG MIT DETAILS

PIANO

MIRRORS

MIRRORS

HIGH WINDOW

8.5 m
27' 10"

SECOND FLOOR

FISCHER & LANGE
ARCHITECKTEN
LYCHENER 15 BERLIN

BEHRENS
ARCHITEKT

STAIRS LEADING UP

TO SPIEGELSAAL

TO WINE BAR

FRONT DOOR

COAT CHECK

PASSTHRU WINDOW

8.5 m
27' 10"

GROUND FLOOR

CLÄRCHENS BALLHAUS BERLIN

Opposite: Dances of Vice, Horror, and Ecstasy map 1
Right page: Dances of Vice, Horror, and Ecstasy map 2

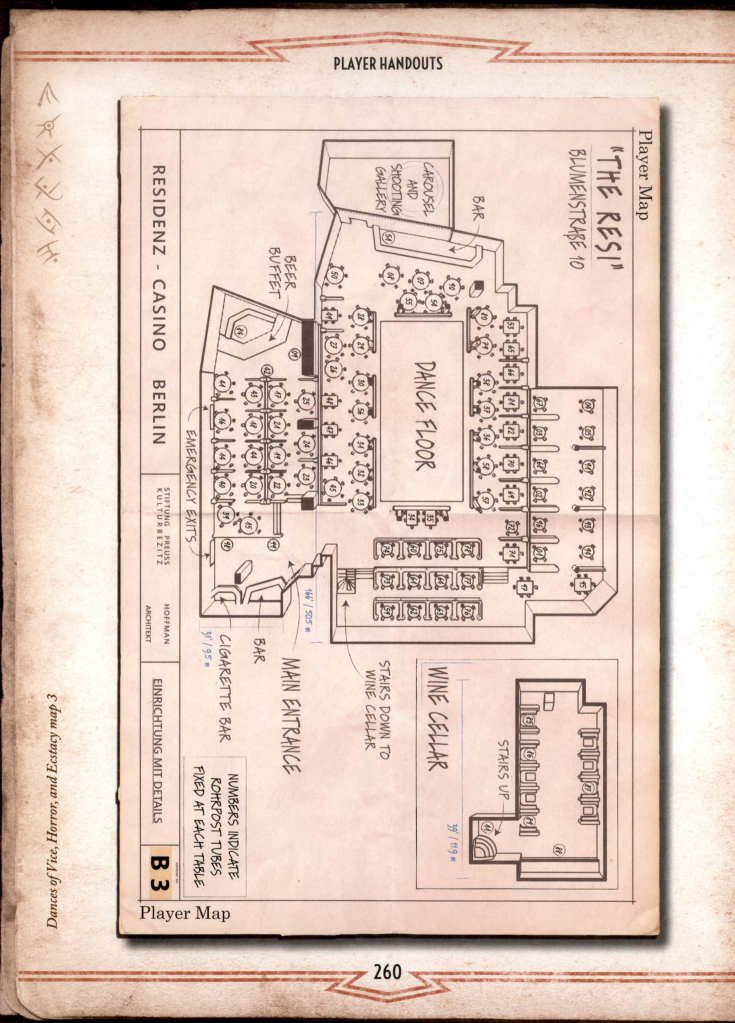

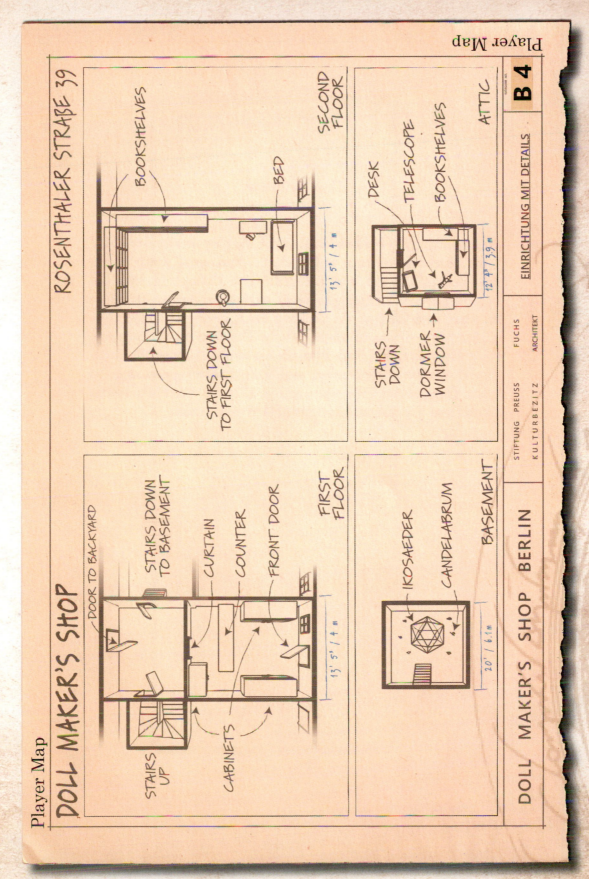

Player Map

DOLL MAKER'S SHOP

ROSENTHALER STRAßE 39

Player Map

B 4

SECOND FLOOR
BOOKSHELVES
BED
STAIRS DOWN TO FIRST FLOOR
13' 5" / 4 m

ATTIC
DESK
TELESCOPE
BOOKSHELVES
STAIRS DOWN
DORMER WINDOW
12' 4" / 3.9 m

EINRICHTUNG MIT DETAILS

FIRST FLOOR
DOOR TO BACKYARD
STAIRS DOWN TO BASEMENT
CURTAIN
COUNTER
FRONT DOOR
STAIRS UP
CABINETS
13' 5" / 4 m

BASEMENT
IKOSAEDER
CANDELABRUM
20' / 6.1 m

STIFTUNG PREUSS
KULTURBEZITZ
FUCHS
ARCHITEKT

DOLL MAKER'S SHOP   BERLIN

Dances of Vice, Horror, and Ecstacy map 4

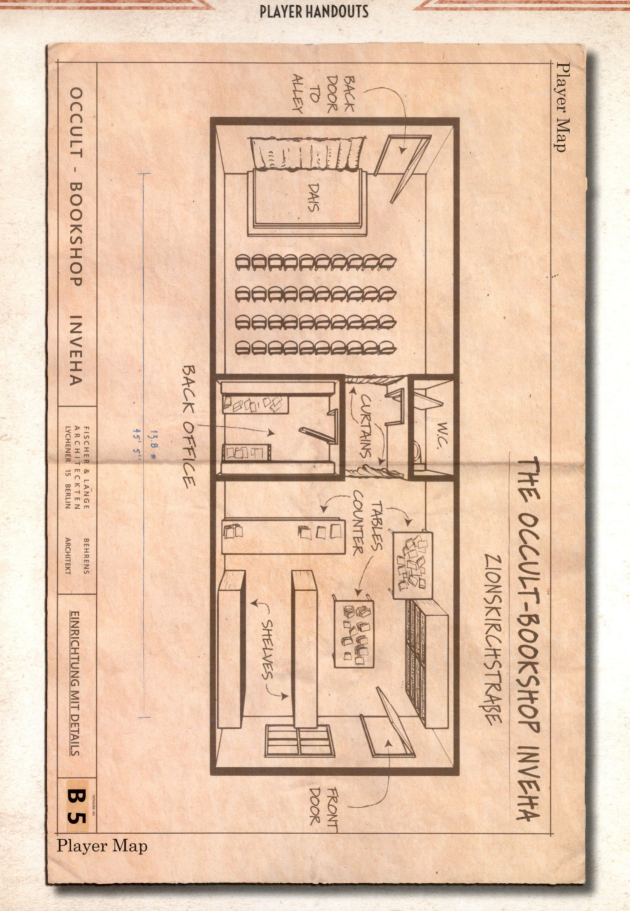

THE OCCULT-BOOKSHOP INVEHA

ZIONSKIRCHSTRAßE

OCCULT - BOOKSHOP INVEHA

FISCHER & LANGE ARCHITECKTEN LYCHENER 15 BERLIN	BEHRENS ARCHITEKT	EINRICHTUNG MIT DETAILS	**B 5**

BACK DOOR TO ALLEY

DAIS

BACK OFFICE

CURTAINS

W.C.

TABLES COUNTER

SHELVES

FRONT DOOR

13,8 m

45' 5''

Player Map

Player Map

GROßES SCHAUSPIELHAUS

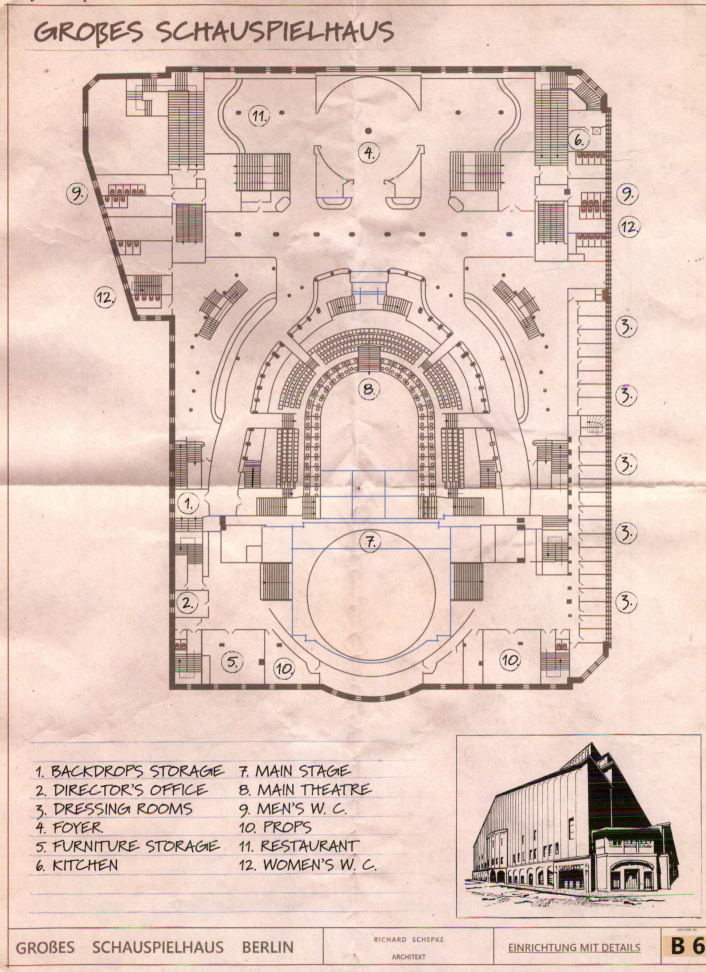

1. BACKDROPS STORAGE
2. DIRECTOR'S OFFICE
3. DRESSING ROOMS
4. FOYER
5. FURNITURE STORAGE
6. KITCHEN
7. MAIN STAGE
8. MAIN THEATRE
9. MEN'S W. C.
10. PROPS
11. RESTAURANT
12. WOMEN'S W. C.

GROßES SCHAUSPIELHAUS BERLIN

RICHARD SCHEPKE

ARCHITEKT

EINRICHTUNG MIT DETAILS

B 6

Player Map

Significant Locations
1. Auguste-Viktoria Platz
2. Zoological Gardens
3. Luna Park

Scale (in meters) 1: 2500
0
2500

Kurfürsten Damm

Geisbergstraße

Budapester Straße

Player Map

Schreckfilm map 1

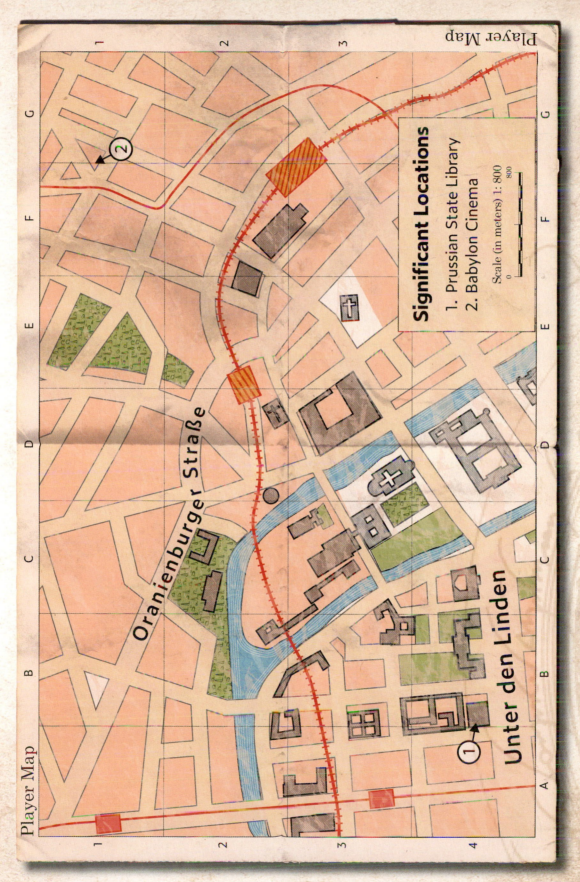

Player Map

Player Map

Significant Locations

1. Prussian State Library
2. Babylon Cinema

Scale (in meters) 1 : 800

0   800

Oranienburger Straße

Unter den Linden

Schreckfilm map 2

Player Map

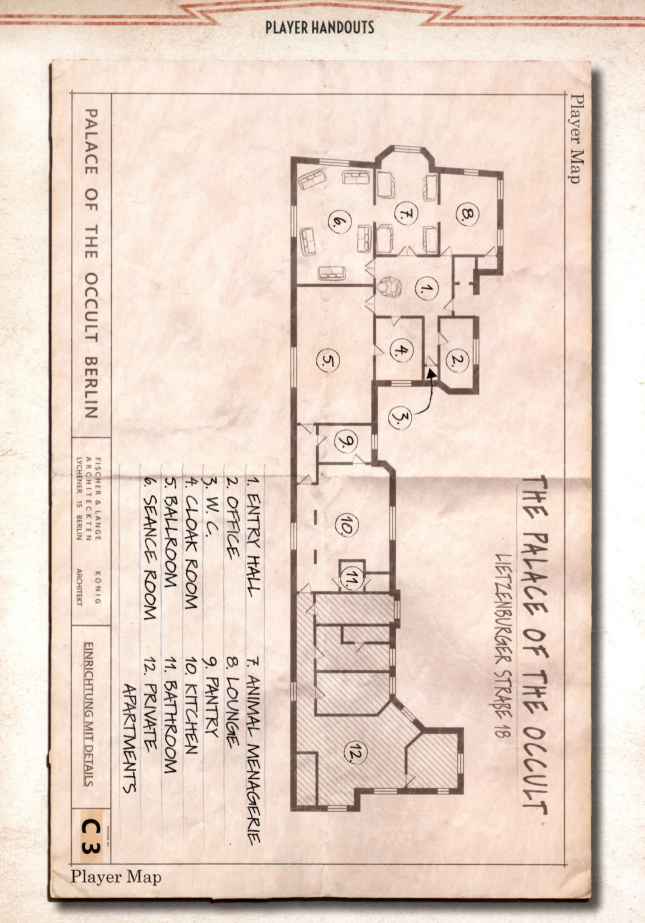

THE PALACE OF THE OCCULT

LIETZENBURGER STRAßE 18

PALACE OF THE OCCULT · BERLIN

FISCHER & LANGE
ARCHITECKTEN
LYCHENER 15 BERLIN

KÖNIG
ARCHITEKT

EINRICHTUNG MIT DETAILS

1. ENTRY HALL
2. OFFICE
3. W.C.
4. CLOAK ROOM
5. BALLROOM
6. SEANCE ROOM
7. ANIMAL MENAGERIE
8. LOUNGE
9. PANTRY
10. KITCHEN
11. BATHROOM
12. PRIVATE APARTMENTS

C3

Player Map

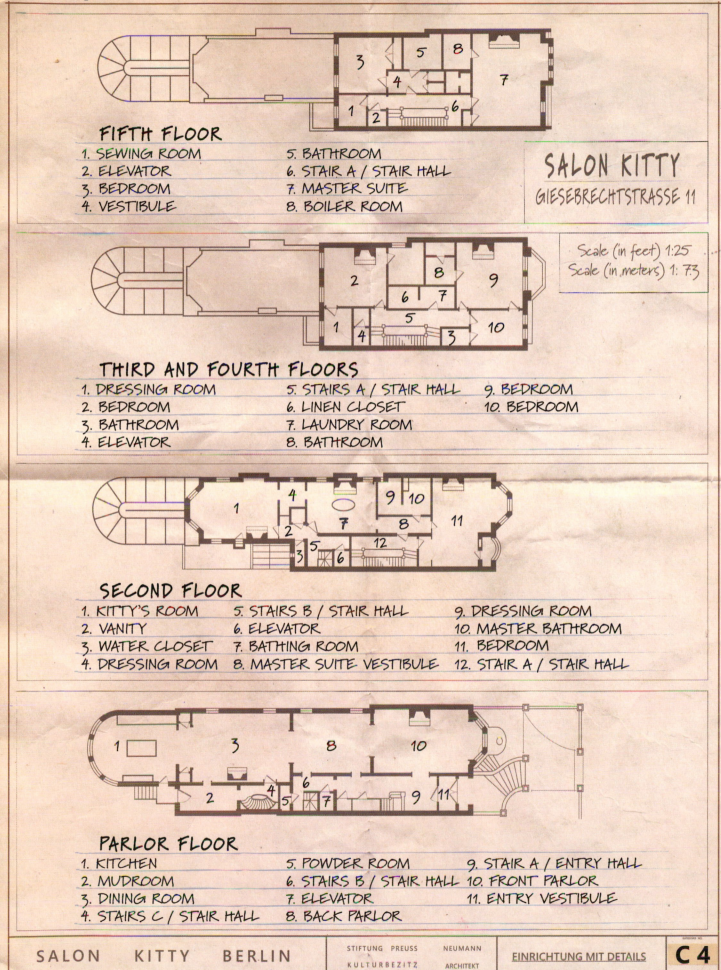

FIFTH FLOOR

1. SEWING ROOM
2. ELEVATOR
3. BEDROOM
4. VESTIBULE
5. BATHROOM
6. STAIR A / STAIR HALL
7. MASTER SUITE
8. BOILER ROOM

SALON KITTY
GIESEBRECHTSTRASSE 11

Scale (in feet) 1:25
Scale (in meters) 1:7.3

THIRD AND FOURTH FLOORS

1. DRESSING ROOM
2. BEDROOM
3. BATHROOM
4. ELEVATOR
5. STAIRS A / STAIR HALL
6. LINEN CLOSET
7. LAUNDRY ROOM
8. BATHROOM
9. BEDROOM
10. BEDROOM

SECOND FLOOR

1. KITTY'S ROOM
2. VANITY
3. WATER CLOSET
4. DRESSING ROOM
5. STAIRS B / STAIR HALL
6. ELEVATOR
7. BATHING ROOM
8. MASTER SUITE VESTIBULE
9. DRESSING ROOM
10. MASTER BATHROOM
11. BEDROOM
12. STAIR A / STAIR HALL

PARLOR FLOOR

1. KITCHEN
2. MUDROOM
3. DINING ROOM
4. STAIRS C / STAIR HALL
5. POWDER ROOM
6. STAIRS B / STAIR HALL
7. ELEVATOR
8. BACK PARLOR
9. STAIR A / ENTRY HALL
10. FRONT PARLOR
11. ENTRY VESTIBULE

SALON KITTY BERLIN

STIFTUNG PREUSS NEUMANN
KULTURBEZITZ ARCHITEKT

EINRICHTUNG MIT DETAILS

C 4

C 5

SPANDAU

KAISER WILHELM TOWER

HAVEL RIVER

ZEHLENDORF

TELTOW

OBSERVATION PLATFORM

180' / 55 m

KAISER WILHELM TOWER

GRUNEWALD FOREST

5   10   20 m

KAISER WILHELM TURM GRUNEWALD

TELTOW
GEMEINDEAMT
BRANDENBURG

PFEIFFER
ARCHITEKT

EINRICHTUNG MIT DETAILS

INDEX

Opposite: Schreckfilm map 5